"A Gleam of Shining Hope":

The Story of Theological Education and Christian Witness at Ashland Theological Seminary (1906–2006) and Ashland College/University (1878–2006)

by

Dale R. Stoffer

Dale R. Stoffer

Copyright © 2007 Ashland Theological Seminary

ISBN 978-0-9793775-0-1

LCCN 2007922266

Printed in the United States of America

Contents

Acknowledgments

The writing of history is a social, interpersonal enterprise. The historian must be able to locate himself/herself in the social context of the people, events, and worldview that shaped the story about which he/she is writing. Though absolute objectivity is impossible, the historian must make every effort to allow every member of the cast who plays upon the stage of history to speak with her/his own voice. There are plentiful scripts for understanding the cast members who played the leading roles in the early history of Ashland College, Ashland Theological Seminary, and the Brethren Church in such resources as church periodicals, local newspapers, minutes of the Ashland College/University Board, and student publications.

The social nature of historical writing is especially reinforced when the researcher tells the story of the recent past. Historical proximity impels the historian to move beyond reliance solely on the documentary evidence to listening to the stories of those who lived the events of that period. Gathering the stories of numerous people through interviews was a most enjoyable aspect of this project. I wish to thank all those who shared their memories with me: Frederick Finks, Jerry Flora, Lucille Ford, Malcolm Miller, Charles Munson, Donald Rinehart, Milton Robinson, Dorman and Joan Ronk, Ray and Ellen Sluss, Kenneth Solomon, and Kenneth Walther. I also made use of interviews that I recorded during the latter 1970s for my dissertation. Such firsthand experiences and insights help to create a record that is both personal and animated. Though names, dates, and places are necessary for the writing of good history, it is the personalizing of events and of their impact that makes history come alive. In this history numerous sidebars, i.e., personal interest stories, provide color, depth, and richness to the composition.

A book of this nature could not have been written within the encouragement, support, and assistance of many people. Numerous records of Ashland Theological Seminary, Ashland College/University, and the Brethren Church are found in documents housed in the archives of the university and the Brethren Church and in the office of the President of Ashland University. I wish to thank the archivist of the university and the Brethren Church, David Roepke, for his gracious lending of countless documents, many one-of-a-kind. Similarly, I am grateful to Presidents G. William Benz and Frederick J. Finks for their willingness to make the minutes of the Board of Trustees available to me. Thanks also to Lori Glick, the Administrative Assistant for the President's Office, for her patience in allowing me to keep the Board of Trustee minutes for a sufficient length of time to research them in detail. Fred Finks also deserves thanks for inviting me to take on this venture and for providing a study leave during which I completed much of the initial research.

Special recognition also needs to be given to Jim Hollinger for his vision and investment of resources that made possible an archives for materials relating to the history of The Brethren Church. This repository of all things Brethren will greatly benefit future generations of Brethren researchers. Brad Weidenhamer's innumerable hours of combing Brethren materials to document details relating to the people and churches of the Brethren Church is a priceless gift to all studying the Brethren. Many other people graciously answered my unending questions and/or gave valuable assistance: Lori Lower, Amy Burns, Dawn West, Keith Marlett, David Cooksey, John Shultz, Leroy Solomon, Vickie Taylor, and others at the seminary; Fred Finks, John Brandon, Karen Little, Jim Kirtland, Stephanie Radebaugh, Rick Thompson, Sherry Bowling, Steven Hannan, and others at the university; and Jerry Flora, Richard Allison, and Mary Ellen Drushal, all of whom I rousted out of retirement. I also want to express appreciation to graduate assistants Jason Barnhart and Benjamin Pippen for their help with the index and photographs respectively.

I would be remiss if I didn't thank my wife, Marcia, for her patient spirit in allowing several rooms of our house to be engulfed by the avalanche of materials that I used in the writing of this work. Her willingness to turn a "blind eye" to my clutter is a testimony to her gracious support of my work.

Aerial view of the Ashland Theological Seminary campus

Introduction

In 1906 J. Allen Miller resigned the presidency of Ashland College in order to devote himself fully to what had always been his first love in education: the training of pastors. This landmark in the life of Ashland University and The Brethren Church merits special recognition, for Ashland Theological Seminary has played a major role in the development of both college and church. In addition, the impact that the seminary has had and continues to have upon the wider Christian community through its education of men and women currently from over seventy denominations and parachurch organizations has been significant. This work seeks to tell the story of the people and events that have contributed to the various chapters of the seminary's life. The centennial of the school is an appropriate occasion to recognize those whose devotion and sacrifice have made the seminary what it is today.

By necessity the story of Ashland Theological Seminary must be told in relationship with other stories: those of the German Baptist Brethren Church of the last half of the nineteenth century; The Brethren Church; Ashland College, later named Ashland University; and the larger North American educational, religious, and cultural setting. Developments in these other arenas constantly left their impact upon the seminary. This observation is especially true of events in the life of The Brethren Church and Ashland College. The fortunes of the seminary have been inseparably linked to both entities throughout its existence.

As a matter of historical accuracy, I will refer to various organizations by the names that were current at the time. Thus, I will refer to the main body of the Brethren movement during the last half of the nineteenth century as the German Baptist Brethren or, more informally, the Conservatives (this term is appropriate for this group in the latter 1870s and the 1880s). This branch of the Brethren family would eventually adopt the name the Church of the Brethren in 1908. The Brethren Church, with which Ashland University is affiliated, arose from the Progressive movement in the German Baptist Brethren Church. When I use the term Progressive Brethren during the historical period from the late 1860s to 1883, I have reference to that portion of the German Baptist Brethren movement that would coalesce into The Brethren Church. In addition, I will refer to Ashland University by the designation Ashland College for developments up through 1989. The institution was generally called Ashland College throughout its history, even after it was reincorporated in 1888 with the title Ashland University. In fact, the Board of Trustees officially changed the name back to Ashland College in 1923. However, as the scope of programs, especially at the graduate level, increased during the 1970s and 80s, the Board of Trustees officially adopted the name Ashland University for the institution in 1989.

To have been asked to write this history of Ashland Theological Seminary by the former president of the seminary, Frederick Finks, has been an honor for me. This request has allowed me to become better acquainted with many people with whom I have been somewhat familiar through previous research. I have been struck by the debt that I and the rest of the university and seminary community owe to these pioneers of education, both liberal arts and theological, in The Brethren Church. The only reason there is a university and seminary in Ashland today is because of the tremendous sacrifice made by numerous men and women for the sake of future generations of leaders in the church and the world.

Chapter 1

Background to the Establishment of Ashland College and Its Early Years (to 1882)

Introduction

The story of Ashland Theological Seminary, for most of its existence, has been intertwined with the stories of The Brethren Church and Ashland College. Yet the genesis of all three entities is found in the German Baptist Brethren Church, a body that traces its roots to the early 1700s in Germany.

The primary leader of the early Brethren movement was Alexander Mack, who, under the influence of Radical Pietism, had separated from the established church in his hometown of Schriesheim in the Palatinate in Germany. Suppression of Radical Pietism by the authorities in the Palatinate led Mack to seek sanctuary for his family in the territory of Wittgenstein, Germany, ruled by the tolerant Count Henrich Albrecht. Mack, in the company of other separatists, settled near the village of Schwarzenau. These religious refugees began an earnest study of Scripture to discern God's leading. They became convinced that the New Testament mandated the practice of believer baptism, communion, including feetwashing and a love feast, and discipline, acts which would necessitate the formation of a new movement. After much prayer and counsel with other separatists, Mack and seven others gathered on the banks of the Eder River in Schwarzenau in early August 1708. They took the decisive and illegal step of believer baptism and thereby launched the Brethren movement. Though their spiritual pilgrimage reflects the impact of the Radical Pietist movement, their act of baptism and the pattern of their church life evidence the strong influence of Anabaptism as well.

The Brethren faith spread to several other locations in Germany, but continued pressure from state and church authorities as well as economic hardship

A view of Schwarzenau, Germany, in the 1950s

caused most of the adherents of the young movement to migrate to the colony of Pennsylvania between 1719 and 1735. The Brethren actively evangelized their German-speaking neighbors and spread rapidly in their new homeland. By the time of the Revolutionary War, Brethren were located from Pennsylvania to Georgia, including the Shenandoah Valley and western Pennsylvania. Estimates are that there were some 1500 adult members and as many as 5000 people with Brethren connections by the end of the colonial period.

The Brethren continued their expansion during the 1800s, moving primarily westward through Ohio, Indiana, Illinois, and the plains states, and eventually to the West coast. By the 1880s they numbered around 60,000 members. In 1836 they adopted the formal designation, Fraternity of German Baptists, which was modified in 1871 to the German Baptist Brethren. They were also popularly called the Dunkers or Dunkards because of their distinctive form of baptism by trine immersion.

Throughout the first third of the nineteenth century the Brethren were able to maintain their German subculture in the United States. Their cultural stability occurred for several reasons: they held onto German as their dominant language into the 1830s; many Brethren shared the American penchant for life on the frontier with its more isolated lifestyle; and the Brethren frequently settled in proximity to other culturally conservative groups, particularly the German-speaking Mennonites. This cultural isolation began to break down by the 1830s and 40s and would lead to significant changes and controversy later in the century.

A significant role in navigating the shifting cultural scene was played by the Annual Meeting of the Brethren. This yearly gathering of elders and members from throughout the United States sought to maintain unity within the church by handing down and, later in the nineteenth century, enforcing decisions that governed most aspects of the life of the church and its members. These decisions not only mandated proper patterns for church life but also dictated matters of individual dress and behavior. The Brethren prized highly the "gospel principles" of nonconformity, separation from the world, and unity in the faith, and Annual Meeting served to check departures from the norm. It must be noted, however, that Annual Meeting was willing to make changes to the "order of the Brethren" when an innovation had lost its novelty (it would no longer be a source of pride) and when the effects of a new practice were generally well known and considered safe for the fellowship.

By the 1860s and especially the 1870s the Brethren were adopting differing viewpoints toward the dominant American culture, both secular and religious. Some Brethren wanted to preserve the "old order" of the church by enforcing the earlier decisions of Annual Meeting. These "Old Order Brethren" rejected all "popular innovations" as expressions of a corrupted Christendom and sought security by remaining faithful to the old landmarks of the church's past.

On the opposite side of the issue of acculturation were the Progressive Brethren. Dubbed the "fast element" by those with more conservative leanings, they felt that the church needed to keep pace with the times. The church should make use of any and all practices and innovations that would help the church fulfill its mission in the world. Led by the outspoken and aggressive Henry R. Holsinger, the Progressives advocated a number of significant reforms and new practices: home and foreign missions, a paid ministry, higher education, Sunday Schools, and revival meetings. Holsinger gave voice to this progressive agenda through his papers, the *Christian Family Companion*, which he published from 1865 to 1873, and *The Progressive Christian*, which he published from 1878 until it became *The Brethren's Evangelist* in 1883 (in 1885 the spelling was modified to *The Brethren Evangelist*).

The main body of the German Baptist Brethren Church adopted a cautiously progressive position in the 1870s. In somewhat of a misnomer, they were called the Conservatives at the time. They were willing to see change, but it could not occur at the expense of the unity of the church. Even though they generally agreed with the Progressive reforms, they viewed Holsinger's behavior as brash and disrespectful and as creating dissension within the church.

Henry R. Holsinger as a younger man

Growing tensions within the church led to a three-way division in the early 1880s. The Old Older Brethren withdrew from the church and formed the Old German Baptist Brethren Church. Holsinger and his Progressive followers were disfellowshipped by Annual Meeting in 1882 and organized The Brethren Church in 1883. The largest group, which retained the designation German Baptist Brethren, would adopt the name Church of the Brethren at its bicentennial in 1908. As already intimated, one of the controversial issues that contributed to the division was higher education.

Brethren Attitudes toward Education

Sentiment for higher education was slow in developing among the German Baptist Brethren. Educated Brethren at the end of the nineteenth and beginning of the twentieth centuries, in order to legitimate their educational enterprises, often made sweeping claims about the advanced education of the early Brethren. But the historical sources paint a very different picture. The Brethren, based on their Anabaptist and Pietist heritage, avoided any practices that were deemed worldly or that were felt to promote a prideful spirit.

Title page of the 1743 Sauer Bible, the first
European language Bible printed in America

The gifted colonial printer and separatist, Christopher Sauer I, though he never joined the Brethren, unlike his son, certainly shared many of their views, including their perspective on education. In his usual pointed style, he observed, "Many are offered a whole manure wagon full of arts and sciences, for which many a rich father pays a lot of money, not a small amount of which goes to prevent him [the student] from receiving the proper discipline, to the detriment of his soul; . . . the true understanding of Christ is eternal life. This knowledge is lacking in the schools and cannot be found there."[1]

Most early Brethren did, however, acquire an elementary education, sufficient to be able to read and write. Likewise, the Brethren of the nineteenth century were advocates of a common school education, the basic elementary education provided by most states. Support of such education was entirely understandable; it made accessible the two books owned by nearly every Brethren family—the Bible and the hymnbook. The Brethren faith has always been dependent upon each member knowing and living the truth of Scripture. That the Brethren valued highly the basic educational skills necessary to navigate Scripture and the hymnbook is evidenced by the number of prominent Brethren elders during the nineteenth century who served as teachers in the common schools.[2]

Until the mid-1800s, the Brethren, through their Annual Meetings, consistently cautioned the fellowship about the dangers of higher education. The Annual Meetings of 1831, 1852, 1853, and 1857 expressed a common litany of objections to higher education, both high school and college. Such education led to a worldly spirit of pride and can "lead us astray from the faith and obedience to the gospel."[3] One of the greatest concerns raised by the opponents of higher education, however, was the fear that the founding of Brethren schools would lead to pressure for an educated ministry and, eventually, a salaried and professional ministry.[4] Given the longstanding commitment of the church to a free (unsalaried) ministry and its antipathy to a sharp clergy-lay distinction, this possibility indeed was a grave concern.

The first indications of a shift in the thinking of the church about higher education come from the pages of *The Gospel Visitor*, a monthly paper published by Henry Kurtz in the interests of the Brethren. Kurtz was a highly respected elder from Poland, Ohio. He had begun *The Gospel Visitor* in April 1851 as a means of fostering unity among the widely scattered Brethren and of promoting the distinctive beliefs and practices of the church. As editor of the paper, he had shown great sensitivity to the consensus of the church, but he was willing, when further light was made available on an issue, to reconsider traditional positions of the church. Such was the case with regard to education.

Initially, Kurtz supported the Annual Meeting position regarding higher education. In 1854, however, he felt that discussion of this topic in the pages of *The Gospel Visitor* was warranted, especially since more Brethren young people were attending academies and colleges.[5] It was his assistant editor, James Quinter, who joined Kurtz in 1856, who promoted the cause of higher education in the church. Quinter was more progressive than Kurtz about reforms needed by the church, but, like Kurtz, he was respectful and tactful in his attempts to develop support for the changes he advocated.

First page of the July 1854
Monthly Gospel-Visiter [sic]

In several articles that appeared in 1856, Quinter set forth his arguments in support of higher education. (1) Because states were adopting stricter qualifications for school teachers, if the Brethren wanted to continue to have their people serve as teachers in the common schools, they should support a Brethren sponsored school to ensure that moral and religious training would continue to be present in public education. (2) The continuation of Annual Meeting objections to higher education placed parents in a dilemma: either parents would have to disobey Annual Meeting if they desired higher education for their children or they could enforce Annual Meeting decisions and run the risk of having their children go their own way when free of parental authority. (3) If Brethren children did go to academies or colleges, these institutions often lacked a commitment to the

James Quinter

Christian influence desired by parents. (4) If the church did not modify its position, it could end up losing many of its most promising youth.[6]

The advocacy of Kurtz and especially Quinter in support of higher education was influencing church sentiment. In 1858, just one year after Annual Meeting had reiterated its opposition to such education, Annual Meeting reversed itself with the counsel: "Concerning the proposed school in the 'Gospel Visitor,' we think we have no right to interfere with an individual enterprise so long as there is no departure from gospel principles."[7] In 1853, when questions arose about the propriety of Kurtz's publication of *The Gospel Visitor*, Annual Meeting had established the precedent of not interfering with individual initiatives so long as they did not violate the traditional principles of the church.

Progressives within the church championed the cause of higher education, including the education of ministers. In 1856 Henry Holsinger began a one year apprenticeship with Henry Kurtz that launched a long-term interest in publication. In 1865 he began the *Christian Family Companion* as an "open forum" to provide a medium for Brethren to share their

First page of the 12 January 1869
Christian Family Companion

views on a wide range of controversial topics with little editorial comment. One of the topics that received considerable attention and generated significant controversy was education. In the late 1860s education, including the issue of an educated ministry, was thoroughly discussed. An article by J. L. Forney expressed the view of many Progressives:

> But I would ask the Brethren with all candor if it is not a solemn fact, true to a great extent, that many of our ministers, although ardent and zealous, are so unfavorable circumstanced and so deficient in knowledge as to be unable to promote in the most effectual manner the best interests of the holy cause of religion. If it is a matter of fact, then it behooves us to consider whether the Church is doing her duty if she exhibits so much indifference, in regard to the proper education of her ministers.[8]

In 1901 Holsinger, in his usual acerbic style, put the matter quite bluntly as he reflected back on this period of time.

> . . . the church was in great need of reformation. One unfortunate feature in the state of the church at this time was that the congregations were in the care of incompetent bishops. By incompetence insufficiency is meant in literary attainments, and all such shortcomings as may result from such condition. . . .
>
> I can even now close my eyes and name a dozen churches with whose elders I was personally acquainted who could not read intelligently a chapter from the Bible or a hymn from a hymnbook, nor write an intelligent notice or announcement of a communion meeting for a paper.[9]

For Progressive Brethren the solution for such lack of ministerial competence was education. Though the church was changing its mind about education in general, it was not yet ready, however, to reconsider its stance on the education of ministers.

With Annual Meeting's about-face on the founding of Brethren-related schools, the stage was set for enterprising Brethren to launch educational ventures. All of the attempts to begin advanced schools (mostly academies, the precursors of modern high schools) in the 1860s and early 1870s eventually ended in failure. The first successful Brethren educational venture was Huntingdon Normal School, founded in 1876 in Huntingdon, Pennsylvania, which later became Juniata College. The second successful school followed closely on its heels: Ashland College.

The Founding of Ashland College

A key figure in moving the concept of a Brethren-related college in northeastern Ohio from mere consideration to reality was Ezra Coburn Packer. Packer was a young, successful salesman and a member of the German Baptist Brethren from Canton, Ohio. He was known to be an advocate of Brethren schools and had been asked by Lewis Kimmel to help raise support for one of the Brethren-related schools, the Plum Creek Normal School, near Elderton, Pennsylvania. Packer found that Brethren in Ohio would not support a school in Pennsylvania, so he decided to explore the possibility of a college in northern Ohio. During 1876 Packer and others sought to arouse interest and support among Brethren congregations, especially in Ashland and Wayne counties, for such a venture. These congregations were blessed with outstanding leadership and with financial and numerical resources.[10]

A series of significant meetings advanced the cause of a college in northern Ohio. The first such meeting was held in March 1877 at the Maple Grove meetinghouse north of Ashland. Numerous Brethren from throughout the Northeastern District of Ohio attended the meeting and agreed to appoint a committee to gauge and gather support for the venture. The chairman of this committee was Henry K. Myers, a member of the Maple Grove church and an influential and successful businessman in Ashland. Myers was highly respected in the church and community for his integrity and business acumen.[11]

The committee contacted Solomon Z. Sharp to come and solicit support for the college. Sharp was one of the better-educated Brethren of the period, having earned both bachelor's and master's degrees.[12] At the time of the committee's inquiry, he was a professor in Maryville College in Tennessee, a Presbyterian school. Sharp played a leading role in many of the Brethren educational ventures between 1861 and 1900.[13] In company with Ezra Packer, Sharp visited numerous Brethren congregations during the summer of 1877 to explain the purpose of the college and ascertain financial support.

Sharp also examined the various locations proposed for the college: Canton, Akron, Louisville, Danville, Smithville, and Ashland. He came to the conclusion that Ashland afforded the best setting for the college. Before proceeding further, however, Henry K. Myers called a town meeting, which

Maple Grove German Baptist Brethren meetinghouse, outside Ashland, Ohio

Solomon Z. Sharp

gathered in the Ashland Opera House, on 28 June 1877, to determine the support that the city of Ashland would give to the work. Sharp served as the primary spokesman for the project. He explained that the purpose of the college would be "(1) to train teachers for the public schools, (2) to establish a department of science of the highest character, (3) to establish a classical course of like high character, (4) to offer the advantages of a higher education to the young people of the church . . ."[14] He pledged that if the city of Ashland would raise $10,000, the college would locate in the town. The meeting appointed a committee composed of several prominent Ashland citizens, including Myers, to solicit subscriptions for the college in the community.[15]

A follow-up meeting occurred in Ashland on 6 July 1877. By this time $4300 had been pledged. A letter from Ezra Packer was read in which he stated, "if Ashland will do what is asked of her she will get the college." Such was the enthusiasm that was generated during this meeting that the next day the solicitation committee had secured pledges for the full $10,000.

The next important meeting occurred on 27 July 1877, at the Beech Grove church in Wayne County where George Irwin (Irvin) was the presiding elder. At this gathering of Brethren supportive of the educational venture, it was decided that Ashland would indeed be the best location. This selection was based on "the inducement offered by the citizens of the place, together with the many advantages the vicinity affords for such an

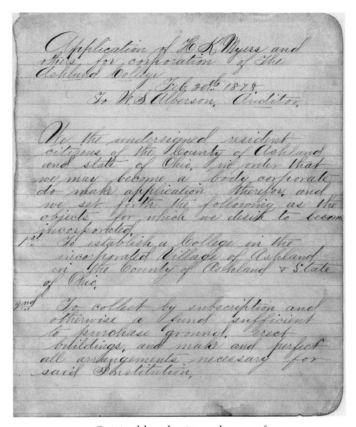

Original handwritten charter of
Ashland College, dated 20 February 1878

Institution."[16] The meeting appointed five temporary trustees, authorized the solicitation of funds in the church, and approved the construction of an initial building once sufficient funds were secured.[17]

Over the next year Sharp solicited pledges from Brethren in Ohio, Indiana, Illinois, and Michigan. He was joined in this work by Packer and, by 1879, Landon West, A. J. Hixson, J. H. Worst, and John Wise.[18] On 19 February 1878, a meeting was again held at the Maple Grove church to move ahead with plans to establish the college at Ashland. A board of incorporators was selected and authorized to proceed with incorporation.[19] The charter recognizing Ashland College as an Ohio corporation bears the date 20 February 1878. The charter lists the responsibilities of the trustees as:

> (1) To establish a college in the incorporated village of Ashland, in the county of Ashland and state of Ohio. (2) To collect by subscription and otherwise, a fund sufficient to purchase ground, erect buildings, and make

and perfect all arrangements necessary for said institution. (3) To provide for the education of the youths of both sexes. (4) To provide for the following courses of education, namely: Collegiate, or Classical Course, a Scientific Course, a Preparatory Course, and a course of Normal Instruction. (5) To raise all endowment funds for the support of teachers and professors, and (6) The name of said Institution shall be Ashland College.[20]

The charter also specified that all of the officers of the corporation were to be members of the Dunker Church.[21]

Several explanations and observations need to be made about the charter, especially the courses of study. By designating the institution a college, with a collegiate or classical course, Ashland's founders were following the classical model established in North America by Harvard College and adopted by most other American institutions referred to as colleges. Designed originally to train ministers, this course of study gave prominence to such disciplines as Latin, Greek, philosophy, rhetoric, and logic. Oddly, however, the charter and Sharp's earlier summary of the purpose of the proposed college say nothing about the training of ministers.[22] A Bible department is mentioned in the college's first catalogue in 1879–80, but the first theology course does not appear in a catalogue until the 1886–87 academic year. Church of the Brethren historian Donald Durnbaugh provided a very plausible explanation for this puzzle when he observed that the earliest Brethren schools omitted mention of ministerial education in order to allay fears that the schools would become training grounds for ministers and lead to a paid and professional ministry.[23] This explanation is reinforced by an Annual Meeting minute from 1882:

> We also declare distinctly that our loyal and faithful Brotherhood should neither fellowship, countenance nor tolerate those who would undertake to establish, under any pretense or color whatever, theological schools, or theological departments of schools or colleges, having in contemplation or purpose the training or graduation of any youth specially for the ministry of the Brotherhood or elsewhere, but we should faithfully adhere to our long-established practice in calling brethren to the ministry.[24]

As we have already seen, the fear of the loss of the traditional form of ministry was a major stumbling block for many Brethren regarding the issue of education. Brethren were qualified for the ministry not by their education but by the call to ministry by their local congregation. For anyone to suggest that he should be called to the ministry was considered an expression of pride, a vice that the Brethren particularly abhorred.

The other courses of study need some explanation as well. Ashland was following in the wake of other more recent "liberal arts" colleges, which were adding, beyond the classical course, newer curricular options reflecting advancements in the natural and social sciences.[25] For example, the first Ashland College catalogue, for the 1879–80 academic year, lists the following departments: the College Department, with Classical, Philosophical, and Scientific courses of study; Preparatory; Normal; Commercial; and Biblical Departments. The scientific course replaced the study of the ancient languages with additional coursework in the natural sciences, mathematics, modern languages, history, and philosophy. The philosophical course was a hybrid between the classical and scientific courses; it kept some Latin, omitted Greek, and offered advanced studies in history, the natural sciences, mathematics, and modern languages.[26] "Normal Instruction" in the charter is the customary term used to refer to teacher training. Throughout the history of Ashland College/University teacher training has been one of the principal commitments and strengths of the institution. The "Preparatory Course" was designed to prepare students for college level work. It essentially functioned as an academy; such schools were the precursors of today's high schools. This preparatory course at Ashland College was phased out as high schools became more prevalent during the early decades of the twentieth century.

The charter's restriction that officers of the trustees be Brethren leads to several observations. The earliest Brethren schools were not owned by the denomination. From its initial allowance of Brethren-related schools in 1858, the church clearly voiced its intention through Annual Meeting that it desired to stay out of the education business and insisted that these institutions be run as private ventures.[27] However, Ashland College may have been unique among the first schools begun by the Brethren because it was not funded and governed by stockholders or begun as a private enterprise. Rather, it was created as a chartered institution with funding being solicited from private individuals. Sharp offers the rationale for this approach.

> . . . the College not being gotten up on the basis of *stock* which may be taxed or assessed and bring the stockholders into trouble, or be sold and taken away from the brethren under certain circumstances neither owned by private individuals as private property, which they can dispose of at any time, but a chartered institution, whose charter gives it to the "Members of the church of the Brethren or German Baptists forever."[28]

The means by which the church would retain control over Ashland College would be through affirmations in the college's founding documents and through the requirements that the Board of Trustees be composed of

Henry K. Myers

Brethren and that the Board's officers be restricted to those with membership in the German Baptist Brethren Church. It would not be until 1888
that a new Ashland College constitution would explicitly allow non-
Brethren to serve on the Board of Trustees. This change allotted three positions on the board to people from the city and/or county of Ashland.

The incorporators selected the initial Board of Trustees, which met on
7 March 1878, and elected as officers William Sadler, president; Henry K.
Myers, secretary; and Austin Moherman, treasurer.[29] The trustees were all
members of the German Baptist Brethren Church and were predominantly
from the Maple Grove and Dickey churches outside of Ashland. The majority of the trustees were also prominent elders or ministers in the church, reflecting the priority that church leaders in Ashland County and northeast
Ohio in general gave to education.[30] At the meeting the trustees authorized
the selection of a site for the college and the erection of an initial building.

Developments now moved ahead quickly. In April 1878 the Board decided
to purchase a very desirable plot of twenty-eight acres on the hill overlooking
Ashland on the south side of town.[31] Construction of the building that came to
be known as Founders Hall (so named in 1922) began shortly thereafter. The architect for this building was a native Ashlander, George Washington Kramer,
who donated his $100 fee to the college; he later became a noted church archi-

tect in New York City. S. Z. Sharp, who had been appointed as president of the college on 12 April 1878, urged the construction of a boarding hall as well. This second building, which eventually was named Allen Hall after J. Allen Miller, was begun during the summer of 1879.[32] The brick for both buildings was made on site. Henry K. Myers, who served as foreman of the construction, supplied pre-sized lumber at a reduced cost from a sawmill that he owned.

The Ashland College-Presbyterian Church Connection

The stories of Ashland College and the First Presbyterian Church in Ashland have been intertwined in some fascinating ways over the years. At the same time that the original Founders Hall and Allen Hall were under construction, the First Presbyterian Church was also building its facility on West Third Street. All three buildings were the work of the architect George Washington Kramer. They shared bricks that came from the same source—the brick kiln on the college campus.

The 31 July 1879 edition of *The Ashland Times* reveals another interesting tie. "On Tuesday the bricklayers at the Presbyterian Church became slack of work, and were sent to the boarding house at the college to assist the force there, which 'made things lively' and the building is rising rapidly." When the new church building was dedicated on 1 August 1879, S. Z. Sharp, the President of Ashland College, read the Scripture text.

In 1933 the First Presbyterian Church building was destroyed by fire. The cornerstone was opened and found to contain copies of *The Ashland Times* that shared the history of the First Presbyterian Church but also shed light on the progress at the college. One of the items of interest from the 15 May 1879 edition of *The Ashland Times* was the report of the first meeting in Founders Hall mentioned elsewhere in the sidebar on the founding of the Ashland City Church. A final intriguing intersection of the histories of these two institutions was the use in 1933 of many of the bricks from the destroyed church building for constructing more walks at the college. These bricks returned full circle to the place of their origin.

May Pyle Andrews, "Excerpts from *The Ashland Times*," TMs [photocopy], Ronk Files, Brethren Church Archives, Brethren Church National Office, Ashland, OH and "Laying of Corner Stone," *The Ashland Times*, 7 August 1879, 5. The latter source reveals the contents of the original cornerstone.

A special challenge facing Sharp was the securing of a competent faculty. He desired to hire faculty who were members of the German Baptist Brethren, but there were very few Brethren with college degrees. His efforts were commendable. The first faculty was composed of Sharp, professor of mental and moral science; Leonard Huber, professor of Latin, German, and French; Joseph E. Stubbs, professor of Greek; Jacob Keim, professor of natural sciences; David Bailey, professor of mathematics; F. P. Foster, instructor in the Business Department; John C. Ewing, instructor of music; and H. F. Hixson, instructor in common branches. The educational background of the faculty is noteworthy. Sharp had received a bachelor's and a master's degree from the Pennsylvania State Normal School and a second master's degree from Jefferson College. Huber was

*Earliest known photograph of Ashland College from a glass slide, showing
Old Founders Hall on the left and Allen Hall (the dormitory) on the right in 1881*

a graduate of the University of Munich, Germany, and had taught at Vermil-
lion Institute and Wooster College. He had joined the German Baptist
Brethren Church during his association with Ashland College, being baptized
by Sharp. Stubbs was a graduate of Ohio Wesleyan University and held a master's degree. He was a Methodist pastor in Ashland and a former editor of *The
Ashland Times*; he was the only non-Brethren faculty member. He would later
serve as acting president of Ashland College and as president of both Baldwin-
Wallace College and the University of Nevada. Keim was a graduate of Mount
Union College while Bailey was a graduate of Southwestern Normal School
and Iowa State University and taught at a normal school in Lebanon, Ohio.[33]
Note that none of these men was designated as teaching Bible or theology.

Ashland College opened on 17 September 1879, with about 60 students and closed the academic year with 102 students.[34] Though the buildings were not yet completed at the beginning of the school year, their
completion and the general feeling of a successful first year seemed to portend well for the future. Indeed, college enrollment remained fairly consistent in the low 100s during the early 1880s.[35] But developments both inside
and outside the college belied such prospects.

The Beginnings of the Ashland City Church

The origins of Ashland College and the Ashland City Church, which became Park Street Brethren Church, are intimately linked. For many years the president or head of the college also served as the pastor of the church, which met in the chapel of old Founders Hall. During the first decades of the college's existence, Brethren college students were required to attend the city church. An article in *The Ashland Times* indicates that the first service in the new college building as well as the first Sunday service of the Brethren in the city of Ashland occurred on 11 May 1879. S. H. Bashor inaugurated both college and church with a message on the authenticity of the Bible. The first entry in the Ashland City Church's minute book records the circumstances behind the official founding of the Ashland City congregation on 22 May 1879.

"When it was fully settled more than a year ago that Ashland College was a fixed fact, a number of Brethren began to move into town and some living here before having no conveyance to attend church in the country [either the Maple Grove or Dickey churches], it seemed desirable to have meeting in town regularly. Furthermore being assured that quite a number of young brethren and sisters contemplated attending school here who would swell the number still more and make it inconvenient for them to present their church letters [of transfer] to the nearest church in the country, the matter of forming an organization in town was considerably discussed and in view of the district meeting being held close by, the members in town signed a petition to have a separate organization and presented it to the two churches from whose territory the new organization was to be taken.

After laying the matter before the churches adjoining [the new congregation] and getting the consent of all present in both, the absent members were visited as far as could be done and the consent so far as we know was unanimous.

"At the district meeting a number of Elders were invited to remain the next day and see whether an organization could be effected. Elder George Irwin of the Chippewa church, Elder Cyrus Hoover of the Wooster church, and Elder Henry Killhefner [sic] of the Ashland [Dickey] church, Israel Roop, P. J. Brown, George Worst, D. N. Workman, Wm. Sadler, A. M. Dickey, and I. D. Parker and perhaps other ministers from the surrounding churches with a goodly number of members in the churches adjoining, met in the College Chapel with the brethren and sisters in Ashland to organize this new body. The manner in which the movement was set on foot was stated to all present and the vote taken whether they were still all willing to go on with the organization and the vote being unanimous in favor, the limits of the territory were fixed to be the present limits of the City Corporation to which members living in town outside of the corporation were to be added.

"There being already a church in the country by the name of Ashland it was agreed to call this the Ashland City Church. The church had at its organization one Elder (S. Z. Sharp) and one Minister of the Second degree (S. H. Bashor). The members then chose Brother J. H. Worst to the ministry and J. N. Roop and E. J. Worst to the office of deacon. The officers were at once installed and the meeting closed in the usual manner with good feeling and general satisfaction to all. The Meetings are intended to be conducted regularly in the College at present at 3 O' Clock P. M."

Minute Book of the Ashland City Church [Park Street Brethren Church], 22 May 1879, 1–2, Brethren Church Archives, Brethren Church National Office, Ashland, OH. See also S. Z. S. [Sharp], "The Church in Ashland," *The Gospel Preacher* 1 (28 May 1879): 3 and *The Ashland Times*, 15 May 1879, 5.

Developments at Ashland College until 1883

Two serious problems plagued the college for its first twenty years: inconsistent leadership and financial crises. In truth, they are interrelated, for the lack of strong, responsible leadership meant that the financial woes of the college were left unaddressed. It certainly did not help, however, that the German Baptist Brethren Church was itself in turmoil. Events at Ashland College in the early 1880s were a kind of microcosm of the unrest that was enveloping the entire denomination.

Both the financial and leadership issues surfaced by the end of the first year. The Board of Trustees had borrowed between $15,000 and $20,000 to erect the boarding hall. Unfortunately, the three primary solicitors for the college turned their attention to other important responsibilities during the college's inaugural year. Sharp gave his time to the running of the school; Packer and his wife were placed in charge of the boarding hall; and J. H. Worst, who had been soliciting only a brief time, became office manager of a Brethren periodical, *The Gospel Preacher*.[36] Without any concerted effort to pay off this loan, interest began to add to the indebtedness of the college.

Sharp resigned as president on 22 June 1880 ostensibly to devote himself to the publishing of Sunday School literature for the German Baptist Brethren. In truth, there was friction between the Board of Trustees and Sharp. He continued, however, to serve on the faculty of the college until ongoing tension with the Board led to his dismissal on 29 December 1880.[37] In the summer of 1881 Sharp moved to Illinois to become acting president of another new Brethren school, Mount Morris College. At the same Board meeting that dismissed Sharp, Ezra Packer, who had borne the original vision for the college, was also released. Sharp testifies to the personal cost of Packer's dedication to the fledgling institution: he "not only gave all his time for four years, but sacrificed his home and worked at a salary which barely kept his family alive, and with dogged perseverance kept on under the most trying circumstances."[38]

On 22 June 1880 the Board of Trustees replaced Sharp as president with a staunch Conservative, R. H. Miller. Progressives felt that this selection was the "last bid to keep the college conservative."[39] At this time, those with Conservative leanings still held a majority on the Board of Trustees. Miller turned out to be an ineffectual president. Sharp, who, like Miller, stayed with the Conservatives, shares a revealing criticism of Miller. "He [Miller] was considered the most influential elder in the Church of the Brethren and was chosen, not for any work he could do in the College and never did any, but exclusively for his personal influence. . . . Miller spent

Robert H. Miller

most of his time among the churches in evangelistic work."[40] In his absence
Joseph E. Stubbs, a Methodist pastor who served as a professor of Greek and
English literature at the college, was elected as vice president and essentially
ran the college. This pattern of brief, ineffectual leadership plagued the college until 1898.

Sharp shares an intriguing episode in the life of the college and
church in 1881. The Board of Trustees, with Miller's full support, developed the idea of hosting the 1881 Annual Meeting at Ashland College.
With the mounting debt the trustees hoped that the beautiful location and
magnificent new buildings would move the fellowship to contribute liber-
ally to the new institution. The entire scheme backfired. When the visitors learned that a Methodist was running the college, they refused to have
anything to do with the institution.[41] Not even the weather cooperated.
Rain during much of the week turned the grounds into a quagmire and the
huge meeting tent even blew down during one of the storms and had to
be repaired.

Ironically, the Annual Meeting held on the grounds of Ashland College in June 1881 revealed the widening rifts within the German Baptist
Brethren Church. Annual Meeting for the second straight year refused to

View of the 1881 Annual Meeting of the German
Baptist Brethren on the grounds of Ashland College

deal with a petition representing Old Order concerns about the direction of the church. The Old Order Brethren began their withdrawal from the church following this Annual Meeting. Annual Meeting also dealt with the Progressive faction of the church. Annual Meeting approved sending a committee to Henry Holsinger's home congregation in Berlin, Pennsylvania, that was to "wait on him in his church and deal with him according to his transgressions."[42] This action would precipitate a series of events that culminated in the disfellowshipping of Holsinger and his Progressive supporters at the 1882 Annual Meeting.

The drama unfolding in the denomination had a significant impact on Ashland College. Only five of the original sixteen trustees would eventually side with the Progressive Brethren in the division, but there had been some changes in the composition of the original Board.[43] At one point in November 1881, Progressives despaired of keeping Ashland College, believing that the Conservatives were in firm control of all the Brethren-related institutions. There were even suggestions that a Progressive college should be started in a new location, possibly Bryan or Dayton, Ohio; Washington, DC; or Huntington, Indiana.[44] However, a month later on 13 December 1881, R. H. Miller resigned as president, feeling that "Progressive minds have gotten control of things at Ashland."[45] Apparently, there had been sufficient turnover on the Board to create a Progressive majority by this time.[46]

All the rest of the Conservative trustees resigned during 1882 and certainly by early 1883.[47] Clara Worst Miller observes, however, that these Conservative trustees were not forced out. The Progressives made no attempt to change the college's charter or constitution in order to manipulate their hold on the college.[48] In fact, following the momentous 1882 Annual Meeting, the Board adopted the following resolution, offered by E. L. Yoder:

> Resolved that no resolution or article in the By-laws shall be construed as to deprive any member in good standing of any division of the German Baptist church that now exists or that may hereafter exist, from voting or holding office on the Board of Trustees of Ashland College, provided he is entitled to a vote by virtue of having paid fifty dollars toward the building and maintaining of the institution.[49]

This action helped the Progressives to strengthen their control of the Board because over two-thirds of the legally constituted voters, that is, those who paid the fifty dollars, were Progressives.[50] The division that was rending the German Baptist Brethren Church did bring Ashland College into the hands of the Progressives, but it also exacerbated the leadership and financial problems facing the institution.

Theological Education during the Early Years

The written histories of Ashland College are consistent in the statement that the training of ministers and the development of a theological department did not occur until the rechartering of the college in 1888. This observation needs to be modified by evidence from the college catalogues from 1879 to 1882. The first catalogue, for the 1879–80 academic year, mentions a Biblical Department. It is advertised as a two-year course of study that included coursework in Bible history, Mental and Moral Philosophy, and New Testament Greek, in contrast to classical Greek. In a lengthy description of the department, there are several striking features, both stated and unstated. Noteworthy is the specific declaration that the course was open to "young men and *young women* who desire to enjoy the advantages of a short yet systematic course of Bible study [italics mine]."[51] From the very start, women were encouraged to study in the Biblical and, later, Theological Departments of the college. Striking because of its omission is any mention of the training of ministers. No doubt, this omission was meant to keep the college safe from the censure of Annual Meeting. A general approach to the

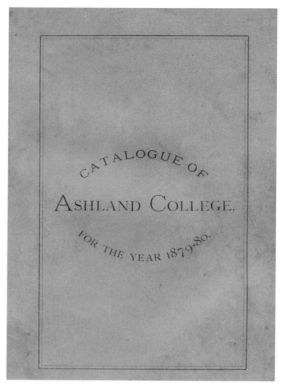

*Cover of the first catalogue of Ashland
College, for the 1879-80 academic year*

study of the Bible could meet with Annual Meeting approval but not a curriculum explicitly designed to train ministers.

The catalogue for 1881–82 contains a similar description of the Biblical Department. But there is one significant change. The Biblical Department is now described as meeting "the needs of many young men, especially
young ministers, who feel the need of some special preparation for the responsible work in which they are engaged . . ."[52] The administration at the
college had to know that the inclusion of such a clear statement about the
training of ministers would meet with strong words from Annual Meeting.
The previously cited minute from the 1882 Annual Meeting may have been
aimed at Ashland College. What is especially remarkable about this change
is that Conservatives still held a clear majority on the Board at this time.
Apparently some of the Conservatives held a sufficiently progressive perspective to be willing to transgress a line that had been firmly established as
the order of the church.

One other statement in the 1881–82 catalogue deserves comment. The tuition for the Biblical Department was the same as in the Collegiate Department. The exception was that "ministers and sons of ministers in the Brethren Church" would be charged only half tuition.[53] The underwriting of the education of ministers for the Brethren Church has been a long-standing practice in the college and seminary. A symbiotic relationship existed between the church and the college that both entities sought to nurture.

Concluding Observations

The German Baptist Brethren Church was the matrix of Ashland College. Many of the unique features of its early years reflect this origin. The college, in spite of receiving substantial financial support from the city of Ashland at its inception, had an overwhelmingly Brethren ethos. All of its first trustees were Brethren; in fact, most of them were Brethren elders. Nearly all of the first faculty were Brethren, as were most of the students. Brethren attitudes toward education were reflected in the curriculum. Though Brethren of both Conservative and Progressive persuasion were supportive of the typical classical and liberal arts curriculum and even the study of the Bible, Conservative Brethren did not approve of a course of study that would prepare ministers for the church. Theological education had to await reforms to the curriculum adopted by the Progressive Brethren.

The early development of Ashland College likewise reflected the upheaval that was occurring within the church. The escalating controversy that would lead to a three-way division within the German Baptist Brethren Church affected the college as well. It was an open question whether the future of the college would lie with the Conservatives or Progressives.

In addition, the financial and leadership challenges that plagued the young college for several decades were present from the beginning. The most trying years for the college were just ahead.

Chapter 2

Years of Crisis and the Beginning of Theological Education (1882–1898)

The Adoption of Ashland College by The Brethren Church

A lingering uncertainty about their claim on Ashland College would haunt the Progressive Brethren for some time following the division within the German Baptist Brethren Church.[1] Because, however, the title was made to the trustees of Ashland College and their successors and assigns forever, most of the Progressive leadership felt secure in their possession of the college. Thus, in spite of such doubts, the Progressives moved ahead with a commitment to Ashland College as their institution of higher education.

Shortly after the ouster of Holsinger and like-minded Progressives by the 1882 Annual Meeting, supporters of the Progressive cause met in convention at Ashland, Ohio, 29–30 June 1882. Significantly, the convention met at Ashland College. One of the resolutions adopted at the conference stated: "that we regard higher education as in harmony with the letter and spirit of the Gospel; that we regard Ashland College as in the hands of a prudent and careful Board of Progressive Brethren, and hence would advise all of our brethren to give it their hearty support."[2] J. H. Worst, the uncle of Clara Worst Miller, eloquently, if idealistically, expressed the priority that the Progressives placed upon education and the importance of the college to the future of the movement:

> Let the sentiment go forth from this meeting, that Ashland College is now in the hands of its friends—in the hands of a body of Christians who

27

can use a college to their advantage, and will no longer withhold their support because the knowledge it produces is detrimental to their weak cause. Education makes progressives, and we are glad that in starting out in this—one of the grandest crusades of the ages—we have a college for its head, and that all down through her future work, her efforts will be characterized by honorable intelligent and consistent action.[3]

The Progressive Brethren delayed the act of formal organization in order to see if the German Baptist Brethren Annual Meeting of 1883 would offer any hope of reconciliation. When the door to reunion was firmly shut by the German Baptist Brethren at the 1883 Annual Meeting,[4] the Progressives moved ahead with establishing a new denomination. At an organizing convention held in Dayton, Ohio, on 6–7 June 1883, the Progressives adopted the official name The Brethren Church and also gave considerable attention to the situation of Ashland College. The convention apparently urged each congregation to secure an agent to solicit funds and students for the college. Several leaders, including J. H. Worst, P. J. Brown, and the noted evangelist, S. H. Bashor, sought to highlight the church's responsibility to assume more of the financial burden of the college. Worst, declaring that "we have a college located at Ashland," spoke forcefully about reliev-

Early leaders in the Brethren Church; from left to right:
(back row) Jonathan Swihart, Henry Holsinger, Edward Mason,
and Eli Yoder; (front row) P. J. Brown and Stephen Bashor

ing the burden that rested "upon the shoulders of a few brave men."[5] Though the convention pledged itself to raise the funds to lift the college debt and appointed H. R. Holsinger and E. L. Yoder as solicitors for this purpose, Albert Ronk observes that the noble purposes of the church did not translate into a general willingness to provide financial relief for the college.[6] The church's hesitation to fully back the college was due to several factors: the financial strain local churches felt in beginning anew after the division, the lingering fears about the denomination's claim to the college, and the concern about the lack of sound management at the college.[7] Not until J. Allen Miller assumed leadership of the college in 1898 would the church develop growing emotional ties to Ashland as its alma mater. Until that time the college would face an ongoing cycle of financial and leadership crises.

Financial and Leadership Challenges at Ashland College

Clara Worst Miller, wife of J. Allen Miller, in her history of the college, has stated quite frankly: "the major part of all Ashland College's difficulties has been financial."[8] This statement is especially true of the college's first twenty years. The causes of this financial hardship are numerous: the indebtedness assumed with the construction of the boarding hall; poor fiscal management beginning with Sharp and continuing under subsequent heads of the institution; notes secured before the division from Conservative patrons which were not paid; members of the Brethren Church who did not fulfill their pledges; low student enrollment in the years immediately after the division; interest on the debt continuing to accumulate.[9] There were attempts to address the mounting indebtedness, notably the discontinuation of the philosophy degree, which had never been popular and required significant teaching resources; a renewed commitment to the normal school (both of these curricular changes occurred in 1883); and the fielding of a number of very capable solicitors on behalf of the college.[10] But these efforts were unable to stem the tide of increasing indebtedness.

The stories of the personal sacrifices made on behalf of the college during these years are overwhelming. An individual who deserves significant credit for saving the college was Henry Holsinger. Though both he and E. L. Yoder had been selected as solicitors for the college in 1883, Holsinger was the one who shouldered the burden of lifting the indebtedness. What he had expected to be a three-month job to canvass the Brethren churches turned into a twenty-month labor of love between 1884 and 1886 that took him from the Atlantic to the Pacific. During this period he received no

Stephen H. Bashor

remuneration for his time, nor did he ask for any. He covered his travel expenses through collections and special donations from churches and individuals, as well as by making liberal use of editorial passes for travel (though he sold his interest in *The Brethren Evangelist* to A. L. Garber and E. L. Yoder in 1885, he apparently continued to use his editorial perquisites).[11] In spite of his heroic efforts, the accumulating interest, unpaid pledges, and poor fiscal management created indebtedness that stood at over $40,000 in 1888 (ironically, when Holsinger began his canvass in July 1884, the indebtedness was said to be $40,000).[12]

At the 1887 Convention of the Brethren Church held at Ashland College, 21–23 September 1887, the situation of the college again was a major topic of discussion. Holsinger put forth the stark reality of the situation: the fate of the college "is *the* question of the church."[13] Holsinger sought to make the church directly responsible for the college by authorizing a deed conveying its assets to the trustees of the National Association of Brethren churches. Understandably, the convention balked at this idea and instead approved a rousing motion by S. H. Bashor that "earnestly" urged every member, every pastor, and the church at large to pay off the debt of the college.[14] As in 1883 "out of sight, out of mind" best describes the response of the church once the convention closed its meetings at the college.[15]

A Banner of Hope

The students at Ashland College in the fall of 1887 were very much aware of the financial crisis facing the college. Their hopes were pinned on deliberations concerning the college's future that were occurring at the General Convention of the Brethren Church, 21–23 September 1887. Meeting in the college chapel, the convention devoted much time to the plight of the college. S. H. Bashor, in what was depicted as "one of the grandest appeals of his life," moved the convention to action. Edward Mason described the moment in his official report of the convention:

" . . . The earnestness and eloquence with which he [Bashor] reasoned reached into every soul, and, as the sequel proved, into every pocket book. The fire took hold of the speaker and spread through the convention until every one was warmed up. The words seemed to burn as they entered the heart, and every one felt that the decisive moment had come as they had never felt it before.

"The speaker said he wanted the convention to vote on this question so that it would be felt: that the plan that was to rescue Ashland College must be commenced here tonight. He requested all the delegates to come and deposit their vote on the table in the shape of a dollar. The convention was ready for the vote. No sooner was the vote called for than there was a general uprising. The audience came forward and the chink of the silver was plainly heard. Bro. Ewing, with a peculiar inspiration, went to the organ, and hundreds of voices pealed forth the joyful song 'Rejoice and be glad, the Redeemer has come.' The dollars poured in, and Bro. Bashor mounted a chair and still continued to encourage the audience. It was a grand time. Tears and smiles could be seen on the same faces, and every one felt that the day of emancipation for the College was not far distant. When order was in part restored, it was found that ninety-four dollars votes had been cast . . .

" . . . the students had anxiously awaited the result [of the convention's deliberations]. They had draped a large flag in case of failure. But when the church so emphatically and enthusiastically voted to sustain it, the previous evening, the crape was torn off, and early [in the] morning the flag was hoisted to the tower [of Founders Hall], proclaiming the glad tidings to the world that the day of emancipation had dawned at last."

Proceedings of the General Convention of the Brethren Church Held at Ashland, Ohio, on September 21, 22 and 23, 1887, by Edward Mason, reporter (Ashland, OH: The Brethren Publishing House, 1887), 44–45.

The financial crisis came to a head in 1888. With the indebtedness standing at $41,000 in June 1888 and creditors pressing the college for payment, both the original and current trustees, all of whom were held to be liable for the debt, were anxious to settle the college's financial situation. The motivating factor for Conservative ex-trustees was to be relieved of continuing financial liability for the college; the motivation for trustees from the Brethren Church was to save the college for the church and to gain clear title to the institution. *The Brethren Evangelist* dated 2 May 1888 reported that both Conservative ex-trustees and Brethren Church trustees agreed to put the college through the process of a court-ordered sale in order to settle the finances and establish clear title. Henry K. Myers, one of the creditors of the college, petitioned for a receiver and the Common Pleas

Court of Ashland County appointed Cloyd Mansfield to this position on 12 March 1888.[16]

While the plans for the sale of the college were moving forward, a group of Brethren committed to keeping the college in Brethren hands met on 18 June 1888. Six men, Silas E. Shook, Samuel Brumbaugh, J. Allen Miller, Charles E. Deffenbaugh, Isaac Kilhefner, and Vernon E. Wampler, were appointed as incorporators to establish a "university to be located at Ashland." They agreed to pursue the purchase of the campus for a price not to exceed $20,000, to secure articles of incorporation, and to prepare a constitution and by-laws.[17]

In June 1888 the various parties agreed to the following settlement. The part of the college property that was bounded (today) by Grant Street, College Avenue (called Bank Street[18] at the time), Chestnut Street, and the north property lines of the homes on the north side of Samaritan Avenue, consisting of nine acres, was deeded to George Irvin, Austin Moherman, Reuben Buckwalter, I. D. Parker, and Simon Garver, all of whom were Conservatives, for the purchase price of $4,000. The part of the property on which the college buildings stood, today bounded by Grant Street, the north property lines of the homes formerly on the north side of Samaritan Avenue, King Road, and College Avenue, consisting of eighteen acres, was deeded to Josiah Keim, Vernon Wampler, J. Allen Miller, Isaac Kilhefner, Silas E. Shook, and Charles E. Deffenbaugh, all members of the Brethren Church, for $18,500. They also secured "personal property" for an additional $842. Mansfield oversaw the private sale of the property on 14 July 1888. The early trustees, both Conservative and Progressive, covered the remainder of the indebtedness.[19]

This settlement did not, however, end the financial difficulties of the college. The purchasers still needed to raise the $18,500 sale price for the college property and buildings. One-third of the purchase price was to be paid by 17 September 1888, one-third in one year, and one-third in two years.[20] Solicitors continued to raise funds within the Brethren Church both before and after the sale. Indebtedness and the threat of foreclosure would continue to plague Ashland College throughout the 1890s and would even cause the school to be closed from 1892 to 1894 and again from 1896 to 1898.[21] This situation was exacerbated by a string of short-term presidents and principals of the college, some of whom were non-resident, others of whom were non-Brethren and did not have the trust of the church, and many of whom were ineffective.[22] These issues led to a period of tension between the church and college between 1891 and 1894 that is reflected in the minutes of Brethren General Conferences and of the Ashland College Board of Trustees as well as in other documents.[23] The church had become frustrated by the ongoing financial crisis and especially the ineffective leadership of the college that contributed to the problem.[24] The 1892 General Conference's Committee on Ashland University had, in fact, made a recommendation, which was adopted by the conference, that "no one, trustees or others, shall be authorized to contract any further debt on said college property."[25] J. Allen Miller, reflecting on the anguish of the college and church during this period, poignantly stated in 1903: " . . . these were years of unremitted toil and sacrifice and sore disappointment; years that cost money and friendships and life; years that have been said to have been fruitless."[26]

The church also bore part of the responsibility for the financial difficulties faced by the college. Albert Ronk, upon reviewing this part of the college's history, commented: "When one reads the items of the *Evangelist* and the Convention Minutes of 1883 and 1887, he is impressed with the indecisions, pussyfooting, suspicions and general lack of business acumen all through the early transactions of the Church especially as relates to the College."[27] For the most part the rank and file in the German Baptist Brethren and the Brethren churches stood aloof from the gravity of the financial hardships faced by Ashland College during these early years. Were it not for the significant sacrifices of a few people, mainly trustees, there would not be an Ashland University today. These people were mainly farmers or ministers in the church and, for the most part, not wealthy. Some of them became bankrupt and lost their farms. What is most remarkable is that among the Brethren Church trustees, at least, who were financially ruined in the struggle to save the college, there is rarely a note of bitterness. One especially moving testimony comes from Annie Arnold, the daughter of Richard Arnold, one of the original trustees of the college who joined with the Progressives. In 1929 she wrote to Louis S. Bauman, a Brethren pastor:

> Ashland College . . . caused the financial ruin of the Arnold family, nevertheless I have a warm feeling for the institution. I saw the very beginning of it and was one of the first students to enroll, and enter the class rooms. . . . As long as one brick remains of the Old College building, I shall hold the place most sacred. It was there, within those walls that I was really born, an intellectual and spiritual being. I shall never cease to thank and bless my parents for all they sacrificed, suffered and endured, to help make possible the existence of such a school for the children of Dunkard Brethren. It was the answer to the questions that young people of that faith were asking in great seriousness.[28]

Though the financial struggles were not yet over, the college was now in the hands of those who were firmly committed to the Brethren Church.

The New Charter and Constitution and the Beginning of Theological Education

Even though Ashland College had been secured for the Brethren Church, trustees of the college seem to have had differing philosophies about the control of the college and the type of education offered at the college. One group of trustees and leaders from the Dayton area appear to have desired that the college property be deeded to the Brethren Church and directed by trustees selected by the church. A. L. Garber and other leaders in Ashland insisted that the college property be deeded to an individual to reduce the liability that might be incurred by the Brethren Church.[29] The Dayton group also was content with the original liberal arts emphasis of the college. Their perspective was reflected in a new charter for the college immediately after the sale of the property in July. This charter, dated 20 July 1888, bore the names of leaders from the Dayton area as well as those from Ashland. At this time, the legal name of the institution became Ashland University in order to bring the institution into compliance with certain legal requirements; it continued to be popularly called Ashland College, however (the name was legally changed back to Ashland College in 1923).[30] The charter indicated: "The object of said corporation is not for profit, but to establish and maintain a college or university for promoting education, religion, morality and the fine arts, and to secure to its members and patrons the advantages of education in all departments of learning and knowledge."[31] Significantly, there was no reference to the training of ministers or to a course of theological education.

Just over a month later, on 29 August 1888, Ashland College was rechartered. Though there was little change in the charter, the order of signatures of the new Board of Trustees reflects a shift of leadership from the Dayton to the Ashland group, among whom were Isaac Kilhefner, Silas Shook, and J. Allen Miller. In a new constitution that appeared in *The Brethren Evangelist* on 15 August 1888, some of the philosophical differences between the two leadership groups are evident. Control of the college was vested in trustees elected by the several district conferences of the Brethren Church, though the Ohio district was given nine positions on the Board, while other districts could have only three each. This arrangement reflects a trend that continues to the present in giving the districts of the Brethren Church preference over the national church in many areas of church polity and oversight. For the first time, three trustees were to be elected from Ashland City and County. Recognition was thereby given to the important role that the city and county of Ashland had in the founding and continued existence of the college.

Note that the church had a degree of control over the college through the direct selection of trustees, though the college property was not deeded to the church. During the 1890s, however, the Brethren Church, through its National Conference, did exercise various forms of control over the college by prohibiting the incurring of any further debt, by approving the Board's recommendations for faculty, and by auditing the finances of the college.[32] But these expressions of direct control are not found after the 1890s, probably indicating satisfaction with the college's improving financial and leadership picture and a willingness to allow a more trusted Board to oversee the affairs of the college.

The Pocket Deed

When the trustees of Ashland College reached a settlement with the receiver and the Conservative ex-trustees of the college in 1888, they were afraid to accept the financial liability for the property. The financial hardship that was faced by all present and former trustees was all too fresh in their minds. Therefore, for the next ten years the deed of the college was held in the name first of Silas Shook, a professor at the college who was in charge of the Commercial School, and then of Isaac D. Bowman, a Brethren pastor.

Silas E. Shook held the deed from 1888 until 1891. In 1891 Shook had a falling out with the Board of Trustees. He was charged with usurping his authority as a professor by maintaining an "absolute and unlimited control of the finances [of the college] and . . . withholding [sic] all knowledge and records pertaining to the same from the Pres. and Sec'y of the Faculty and through them from the Board of Trustees . . . " He had been asked to turn over the deed, but he refused until he had been given his back pay. The relationship between Shook and the Board became acrimonious; indeed, the Board secretary comments in the minutes that the whole affair was "peculiar and embarrassing [sic]." Finally, in February 1892 the Board secretary reported that "the University property was deeded by S. E. Shook to I. D. Bowman, to be held by him in trust for the Brethren Church."

Bowman, in some reminiscences, reported that he had held the deed for six years, from 1891 (apparently the deed was transferred late in December 1891) until 1897. In fact, he indi-

I. D. Bowman

cated that he carried the deed "in his pocket" during this period until in 1897 he deeded the property back to the trustees in the name of the college. In 1916 the Ashland College student newspaper gave Bowman the following tribute: "To him belongs the credit of helping redeem the whole college property to the ownership of the church. He assumed obligations which few men would now care to take upon themselves. He made many sacrifices for this cause."

Minute Book of the Board of Trustees of Ashland College, 36–37, 39, 42–43, 46, 48–49, 50, 54–55, Ashland University Archives, Ashland University, Ashland, OH; Glenn L. Clayton, "Whispering Pines and Purple Eagles," 1979, TMs [photocopy], 337, Ashland University Archives, Ashland University, Ashland, OH; J. Allen Miller, "The National Conference," *BE* 17 (11 September 1895): 3; D. C. Christner and the Board of Trustees, *The Legal and Historical Records and Official Report of Ashland University* (Ashland, OH: Johnson Bros., Print, n.d. [1892]), 35, 37, 39, 55; A. L. Garber, "A Brief Review of 'The Legal and Historical Records and Official Report of Ashland University,'" *Supplement to The Prophetic Age* (September 1892): 2; and "Personal Notes," *Purple and Gold* 16 (May 1916): 31.

1888 constitution of Ashland University, in J. Allen Miller's handwriting

The most important explicit change from the July charter is revealed in the opening sections of the constitution that set forth the object of the corporation. Here it is stated:

> Section 1. The object of this corporation shall be to establish and maintain a College or University for promoting education, morality, religion and the fine arts, and to secure to its members and patrons, the advantages of education in all departments of learning and knowledge, especially the education of men of approved piety and talents for the ministry of the Brethren church.

> Section 2. The training of suitable men for the ministry of the Gospel, shall always be sacredly regarded as one of the main objects of the Institution.

> Section 3. Religious instructions and exercises shall be connected as far as possible with all the relations of the Institution.[33]

In the first section of Article II, entitled "Course of Study," the constitution declares: "In order to accomplish the object of this Institution, such instructions shall be given as are usually embraced in the course of Colleges or Universities and Theological Seminaries of this and other countries."[34]

For the first time and in unambiguous language, theological education was set forth as one of the essential purposes of the college. It is quite clear that the incorporators continued to be committed to a liberal arts education, but the desire of leaders such as J. Allen Miller to provide theological education to ministers of the Brethren Church is highlighted. J. Allen Miller's influence seems to be behind these declarations. The original 1888 constitution housed in the Ashland University archives is in Miller's handwriting and his signature appears at the end of the document. Note also that the door is opened to the establishment of a seminary at Ashland College.

Another observation that arises from a perusal of the constitution is the close ties that existed between the Brethren Church and Ashland College. Though faculty had to be people of "approved piety" who were members of some "Evangelical Church," the constitution also specified that "So far as practicable Professors and Tutors shall be selected from members of the Brethren Church." One of the justifications for the dismissal of a faculty member was if a person was found "guilty of teaching doctrines detrimental to the success of the Brethren Church." As previously noted all members of the Board of Trustees were to be Brethren except for the three trustees selected from the city and county of Ashland.[35]

A review of the *Minute Book of the Ashland College Board of Trustees*, Ashland College catalogues, and minutes of Brethren Church General Conferences reveals an increasing commitment in both the college and church to the training of Brethren ministers between 1883 and 1898. Between 1883 and 1888 there is no mention of a Bible or Theological Department. Clara Worst Miller does indicate that the catalogue for the 1886–87 academic year for the first time offered a course in theology. Though at this time the college made no provision for an independent Theology Department, a student could add a reading course for ministerial preparation to studies in other departments of the college.[36]

In 1888 a "Ministerial Course" for the first time appears in an Ashland College catalogue. The one year course was "designed for mature young men" who might have just a common school education, but who also, through practical experience, had gained business and social skills. Completion of the coursework resulted in a diploma with the Bachelor of Literature degree.[37] Though ministerial students were encouraged to take the full Classical course in the next year's catalogue, this ministerial course remained the sole preparatory education for Brethren ministers until 1894.

An Example of Sacrifice

S. S. Garst had been appointed by the Board of Trustees in 1893 to secure a faculty for the 1894–95 academic year. However, when conflict arose between Garst and the Board of Trustees, the Board dismissed Garst just before the start of school in 1894. With the new college term beginning almost immediately, the Board faced a distressing quandary. George W. Rench relates the "rest of the story":

"Dr. Miller and I had just begun our first pastorates; he at Elkhart, Ind., and I at Milford, Ind., and only sixteen or twenty miles apart, when the General conference came on at Ashland, Ohio. This was in 1894. We both attended that Conference. The trustees of the College came to us, and with tears in their eyes placed before us a serious situation, and asked us to leave our pastorates at once and assist in opening the school. Students were already on the ground, but no faculty. We remained up most of the night trying to find a way out. Leave our pastorates, and that without notice to our people? Dr. Miller said to me, 'The interest of the College is above the interest of any one congregation.' His largeness of soul surmounted every other consideration, and we both said 'yes' to the trustees. At the close of the year he remained; I went back to my pastorate.

"No one will ever know the heart-aches of a faithful-few to put on the map a church school for Brethren young people. Some of God's heroes were discovered in that tremendous task. Some of these men with their families lived on half rations while they poured out their lives raising money to build, equip and endow a college free from the blighting influence of human creeds. Dr. Miller was just such a leader. Whether in some ministers' meeting, district, or general gathering of church-people, his voice in those early years rang out in no uncertain terms—to avoid the tragedies which befell the mother-church in the 80s.

"After he and his gifted wife returned from the graduating exercises at Hiram, Ohio, one of the first incidents related to me was how a few friends who had accompanied them to the old campus at Ashland, parted the weeds and kneeling before the God of all grace, implored the eternal Throne to open up a way by which religious life might once more possess those fine buildings, and the glee of youth might vibrate within those walls."

J. Allen Miller in the 1890s

G.W. Rench, "As a Church Leader," *Brethren Evangelist* 57 (April 27, 1935): 5–6.

In 1892 the General Conference of The Brethren Church had requested that the college establish a Theological Department for the training of Brethren ministers.[38] The Board of Trustees followed up this recommendation on 24 August 1893, with the motion that "the National Conference [of the Brethren Church] then in session at Eagle Lake [later renamed Winona

Lake] . . . appoint the following persons as a Com[mittee]. to draft a course of study for a Theological Department in Ashland University, viz.: D. C. Christner, J. M. Tombaugh, A. D. Gnagey, S. J. Harrison and W. C. Perry."[39] Planning for this department bore fruit, as reflected in several significant developments in the 1894–95 academic year. The Board of Trustees designated J. Allen Miller as Dean of the Theological Department at its August 1894 meeting.[40] With this appointment, Miller's long association with theological education at Ashland College began. The college also inaugurated a Theological Department in the 1894–95 academic year. The catalogue outlined a comprehensive curriculum for ministerial training. Students could choose between two courses of study, both of which lasted three years. The Bachelor of Divinity degree program included the study of Hebrew and Greek, while the Bachelor of Theology degree substituted an equal number of courses in English Bible for the number of Biblical language courses. The catalogue is unclear how these degree programs fit within the existing normal and collegiate programs in the college.[41]

Both the college and church sought to do their part in underwriting the costs of the Theological Department. As early as 1891 the Board of Trustees had committed itself to creating a Ministerial Aid Society. At the 1894 General Conference, the women's organization in the Brethren Church, the Sisters' Society of Christian Endeavor (SSCE), donated $150 toward the support of the theological chair at the college (the Board of Trustees had set the salary at $600). Following the lead of a recommendation adopted at the 1892 General Conference, the Board of Trustees, at its 1894 meeting, unanimously agreed that theological students should attend the college tuition free. Should they discontinue this course of studies, however, they were to repay the college the amount of tuition accruing during their time of attendance.[42] A report to the Board during its meeting at the end of the spring session in 1895 indicated that there were ten theological students at the college.

In the 1895–96 college catalogue the rationale for the Theological Department is spelled out more fully. The theological curriculum sought

> to meet the growing demand for a better prepared ministry. We not only need a better prepared ministry but *more* ministers. Many Brethren churches are without pastors. The management of this institution hopes *to train* consecrated young men for these vacant places and for other responsible positions.
>
> This Department is intended for the special advantage of those preparing to become either ministers or teachers, evangelists or missionaries of the Brethren church. And while the instruction of this Department

will be conducted in harmony with the distinctive doctrines of the
Brethren church, students of other Christian denominations, wishing to
avail themselves of its advantages, will be welcomed.[43]

Note that the main impetus for the creation of the department was the need
for providing quality theological education to a hoped-for growing number
of Brethren Church leaders. The curriculum was clearly slanted toward a
Brethren clientele, though students from other traditions were welcomed.
At this point, however, the training was aimed at the needs of the Brethren
Church. J. Allen Miller revealed in 1907 how critical, though still insufficient, these developments in 1895 were for the future of the Brethren
Church: "The dearth of pastors to-day, and the large number of fields we
have lost is due chiefly to the fact that we were not training men for min-
istry from 1881 to 1895."[44]

In some ways the theological curriculum for 1895–96 was similar to the
program of the previous academic year. There was still a three year course of
study designated an "English Divinity Course." Entrance into the English
course required no previous college work, nor even, apparently, the completion of a preparatory course. It offered practical training to both younger men,
who would enter the ministry if they were better prepared, and experienced
ministers, who recognized their need for theological education. Fulfillment
of the requirements of this course of study resulted in a diploma of graduation.

Quite surprising are the requirements for the "Classical Divinity
Course." It was designed as a graduate level program; those desiring entrance to this course were strongly advised to have an A.B. or B.S. degree.
Students who completed this program were awarded the Bachelor of
Divinity degree. Previous histories of the seminary have indicated that
"conscious theological training" did not begin until 1898 or 1906.[45] Addi-
tionally, the first graduate theological degree program at Ashland is generally acknowledged to have begun in 1930. But the expected educational
background of applicants to this course and the high standards for the degree itself call for a modification of these assumptions.

> *The Classical Divinity Course* . . . requires a thorough preparatory train-
> ing for admission. The foundation of general scholarship must be laid in
> college: the *preparation* necessary for the successful prosecution of special
> studies in any professional school must there be acquired. In this Depart-
> ment we can only assume to build upon the knowledge and culture acquired
> in college, and turn all to the highest use in preparing the student for the
> Christian ministry. It would therefore be our earnest advice to all to acquire
> first a Collegiate education then to pursue the studies in this Course.[46]

How do we reconcile this evidence with the historical claims about the beginning of theological education and of a graduate theological degree at the college? Additional data gleaned from later college catalogues may shed some light on this question. The catalogue for 1898–99 continued the theological curriculum found in the 1895–96 catalogue. But the catalogue for the next academic year folded the Classical Divinity Course into a four-year A.B. degree at the collegiate level. There is currently no extant rationale for any of these changes, though we may surmise that J. Allen Miller, strongly desiring a truly graduate level theological program at the college, realized that his dreams were a bit too ambitious at this point in time. There were few Brethren students with the requisite educational background to support a graduate theological program and the college was still struggling for its financial life. It is also true that students admitted to the Classical Divinity Course were not *required* to have a bachelor's degree. This two-year experiment (the college was closed from 1896 to 1898 due to the ongoing financial difficulties) with a quasi-graduate program was quietly discontinued until a more propitious time.

The Philosophy and Christian Character of Ashland College

Throughout the first twenty years of Ashland College's existence, the catalogues are replete with succinct statements about the character and philosophy of the college. These statements provide a window into the heart of those who so significantly invested their lives into the college. A brief section called "Distinguishing Features" appeared in catalogues through 1899–90. It summarized very well the philosophy that guided the college during its early years. Though it went through minor revisions, the statement as it appears in the 1884–85 catalogue is representative:

Distinguishing Features

1. It is thoroughly Christian, but not sectarian.
2. It aims to adorn the mind rather than the body.
3. It teaches self-government on the principles of love and respect.
4. It affords a liberal course of instruction at the least cost.
5. It aims to develop the student into true, noble manhood.[47]

This statement reflects an emphasis at the college on character development informed by Christian values. The same catalogue indicated that those who founded the college realized "the need of an institution for the promotion of higher education under Christian influences that would develop its students intellectually but not at the expense of the heart . . ."[48] The 1889–90 catalogue similarly emphasized the importance of the formation of inward character: "Character . . . is always kept in view and the student's attention is continually directed to the Bible as containing records of the noblest characters of history and the matchless life of mankind. What we are gives the value to what we do."[49] Attendance at chapel and Sunday worship were considered essential for the formation of Christian character. Students were required to attend weekday chapel and, in addition, Brethren students were required to attend the Sunday services held in the college chapel (students of other faiths were encouraged to attend this or another church service in the area). Reflecting the close ties between the college and the church was the motto that graced the 1895–96 catalogue and continued in subsequent catalogues into the first decade of the twentieth century: *Christo et Ecclesiae* (later it became *Pro Christo et Ecclesia*). (This motto had actually made a one year appearance in the 1881–82 catalogue prior to the division in the German Baptist Brethren Church.)

Several statements in the early catalogues reflect an affirmation of diversity at the college as well as the valuing of a simple, altruistic lifestyle. A well-crafted statement that appeared for about ten years in the college catalogues declared: "One of the distinctive features of Ashland College . . . is, that rich and poor meet upon the grounds of equality; that worth, not dress, is valued and respected; that economy, not extravagance, is fostered; and that a desire for usefulness, not show, is promoted."[50]

From the very beginning women as well as men were welcomed at Ashland College. The 1886–87 catalogue indicated that "Ashland College is not a respecter of persons, and the rich and poor, male and female, can enter it on an equal footing, and be impartially served."[51] Reflecting trends that were occurring concurrently in the Brethren Church in opening the ministry to women, the 1890–91 catalogue stated: "All departments and courses of study are open to ladies." Ironically, however, this statement is replaced in the 1894–95 catalogue with the declaration that both men and women would be trained for their chosen profession. This is the first year that the Theological Department appeared in the catalogue. There is a certain ambiguity for many years in the college catalogues about the training of women for pastoral ministry. Such ambiguity reflects J. Allen Miller's own position on the issue. Writing in 1910, Miller quite forthrightly rejected the idea of ordaining women as elders, but he was also convinced that women should be affirmed in the teaching and preaching of Scripture. In fact, he indicated that such women should be ordained as ministers (he distinguished the positions of minister and elder).[52]

Concluding Observations

The survival of Ashland College during its first twenty years is a tribute to the sacrifice and dedication of a few leaders in the Brethren Church who were convinced that the future of the church required a quality liberal arts college. Some of these leaders were financially ruined by this commitment, though they expressed the satisfaction that the college had been saved in the end. It is clear that the college had been begun as a liberal arts institution. But there were some influential Brethren, notably J. Allen Miller, who saw the college as the means for providing theological education for Brethren ministers and missionaries. With the rechartering of the college in 1888, this sacred calling was written into the official purpose of the corporation.

Statements about the philosophy of the institution make it clear that the formation of character was fundamental to the college's mission. It was not enough to train students intellectually; the moral and spiritual development of students' hearts through the Christian faith was vital if they were to make a positive impact in the church and the world. The 1890–91 catalogue puts it succinctly:

> Well knowing that colleges, generally, foster pride and extravagance, and realizing the need of an institution for the promotion of higher education under Christian influence that would develop its students morally as well as intellectually they determined to found a college, and offer a liberal [arts] course of study to all who would educate either themselves or their children for usefulness and not for ostentation.[53]

For the Progressive Brethren true education had to go beyond the training of the mind to the transformation of the heart both morally and spiritually.

Chapter 3

The Stabilization and Growth of Ashland College and the Beginning and Early Years of Ashland Theological Seminary (1898–1919)

Emergence from the Years of Financial Crisis

In his history of Ashland College, Edwin E. Jacobs observes that it is with the coming of J. Allen Miller, who had been asked to reopen the college in 1898, "that we reckon the modern history of the college for, from this time on it has been in continuous operation."[1] (J. C. Mackey served as the nominal head of the college until Miller was selected as president in 1899.) In an especially poignant memory from their early days of marriage, Clara Worst Miller describes the opening scene of this new chapter in the college's history: "The college grounds were covered with weeds, blackberry bushes, and Baldwin apple trees. Amid these discouraging and unlovely surroundings, two persons knelt in prayer, pledging their lives to the enrichment of youth and asking God's blessing upon their efforts."[2]

Biographical Background of John Allen Miller

Perhaps no one in the history of Ashland College and Seminary deserves more honor than J. Allen Miller. Glenn Clayton gives due praise to Miller and his wife: they "possessed a rare combination of faith and vision that changed an impossible situation into a gleam of shining hope."[3] It is only fitting that some attention should be given to the life of this remarkable leader.

J. Allen Miller was born 2 August 1866, near Rossville, Indiana. His father, William Miller, was a schoolteacher while his mother was the daughter of a German Baptist Brethren minister. John, at the age of seventeen, followed his father into school teaching. He studied at Hillsdale College and then matriculated at

Ashland College in 1887 and earned a B.S. degree in 1890; in 1895 Ashland College granted Miller the B.A. degree based upon his studies at Ashland and other institutions. He did graduate work at Hiram College, earning a B.D. and, in 1898, an M.A. He also pursued graduate studies at the University of Chicago. He received the honorary D.D. degree from Ashland College in 1904.

Miller joined the Edna Mills, Indiana, Brethren Church at the age of eighteen during the pastorate of J. H. Swihart. Recognizing the giftedness of this young man, the congregation called him to the ministry a few months after his baptism, and he preached his first sermon the following week. He pastored Brethren congregations at Glenford, Ohio (1887–92), and Elkhart, Indiana (1892–94). During his long service to Ashland College and Seminary, he also, for many years, was the pastor of the Ashland City Church, which met in the Ashland College chapel.

Miller married Clara Worst on 23 December 1896. She was the daughter of E. J. Worst, an Ashland area businessman and major benefactor of Ashland College. He also served on the Ashland College Board of Trustees from 1894 until his death in 1927; he was the treasurer of the Board this entire time. Clara was a gifted teacher in her own right, serving as a professor of Greek and Latin at Ashland College for fifty-four years. She and J. Allen had a daughter and two sons.

Clara Worst Miller in the 1890s

Miller's distinguished service to Ashland College and Seminary began even while he was a student at the college. In the college catalogue for 1887–88, he was listed as teaching history and English literature. The following year the catalogue indicates that he was teaching history and arithmetic. He was listed as one of the incorporators and members of the Board of Trustees when the college was rechartered in 1888 (he was only twenty-two at the time!).

In spite of his youth, Miller was viewed as *the* person who might be able to rescue the college from its financial and leadership crisis in the 1890s. In 1893 he was asked by the Board of Trustees to "take charge of the educational interests" of the college.[4] He must have declined this invitation, for he continued as a pastor in Indiana until 1894. In the fall of 1894 he was back at Ashland College, however; the catalogue lists him as teaching natural sciences and mathematics. Interestingly, the General Conference of the Brethren Church in 1894 endorsed him as the Dean of the Theological Department, the first time he bore this title. The new president of the college, S.S. Garst, was dismissed by the Board of Trustees shortly before the beginning of classes in the fall of 1894 apparently for failure to secure a faculty. Miller was asked to head the college; this time he accepted and guided the institution for the next two years. His first year as head of the college was heralded as a "decided success" because of the enrollment of 72 students and, even more importantly, the conclusion of the academic year with a deficit of only a few dollars![5] The crucial role that Miller played in the college is underscored by the fact that, during the two years he spent pursuing further studies at Hiram College (1896–98), the college was closed.

When Miller reopened the college in 1898, he taught in the areas of philosophy and theology. J. C. Mackey served as the nominal head of the college, but Miller again was appointed president in 1899, a position he held until 1906. In 1906 Miller resigned the presidency in order to become Dean of the Theological Department. He was named vice president for the 1907–08 academic year (E. E. Jacobs assumed this role beginning in the 1908–09 academic year) while President J. L. Gillin was on a leave of absence. Miller continued to serve as the Dean of the Theological Department (in 1913 the name became the Theological Seminary) until 1933, when he requested to be relieved of this office. He continued to teach in the seminary, however, until three weeks before his death on 27 March 1935.

Miller was undoubtedly the most influential leader in the Brethren Church during the first third of the twentieth century. He played key roles on every significant denominational committee after 1895. He served as the moderator of General Conference in 1907 and 1924 and held this same office on numerous occasions in the Ohio District Conferences. He was a charter member and from 1903 to 1935 president of the Foreign Missionary Society of the Brethren Church. He frequently served on the Board of the Brethren Publishing Company and was the first president of the Board of Directors of the Brethren Home, serving from 1901 to 1934.

Miller distinguished himself as a Christian scholar. Though he epitomized the classical, liberal arts education of the early twentieth century, his first love was theology and especially the biblical languages. He was equally at home in the big-picture, broad categories of philosophical theology and the close-to-the-text, exegetical discipline of biblical theology. He was a noted linguist, proficient in Latin, Greek, Hebrew, and Aramaic. He even excelled at deciphering Egyptian hieroglyphs.

Miller refused to be delimited by a particular theological system. In the day of the strident battles between liberalism and fundamentalism, he read and expected his students to read the works of both camps. He sought a reasoned faith that could face the challenges of critical scholarship and a confident faith that rested on the revealed truth of Scripture, not a creedal litmus test. He was irenic in spirit and sought to find a conciliatory path through the polarized religious setting inside and outside the Brethren Church.[6]

The testimony of his peers and students offers further insight into the character of this remarkable leader. Miller's students held him in high esteem as an outstanding mentor and model of faith. A brief biography of Miller in the student paper, *Purple and Gold*, declared that "Ministers all over the brotherhood who have come under his influence look back to him as the one who helped them find themselves, and they continue to seek his wise counsel."[7] One of his students, A. H. Lichty, wrote that "few if any, men will exert as wide an influence in Biblical teachings and doctrinal positions over the Brethren Church as Dean J. Allen Miller. Here [at Ashland College], you are privileged not only to be in his classes for four years, but you have an opportunity to come to know him as a personal friend and to be inspired by his Christian life."[8]

While an acknowledged scholar, Miller was also remarkably approachable as a person and manifested a humble, unassuming spirit. In eulogizing Miller, William H. Beachler highlighted these traits:

> As a teacher, Dr. Miller was human. By which I mean that his fine and broad learning never isolated him from the common run of us. Dr. Miller's life and bearing lent convincing proof that the highest educated can be simple, and at home, among the simple and common people. I shall remember Dr. Miller as a man who lived on earth among folks, and who kept his feet securely on the earth. . . .

*Sketch of J. Allen Miller as
he looked in his later years*

He was not a "know it all" teacher. His fine modesty was always out-standing in his life and work as a teacher. I cannot recall that Dr. Miller ever impressed me as a man who had complete control and possession of all truth. Dr. Miller could concede to those who even differed with him, some things, and it seemed possible for him to conceive of others being sincere even if they differed with him much. I like to remember just this about him. It was a proof of his broadmindedness, fairness, and courtesy, just as it was proof that in the presence of the endless fields to be explored he con-sidered that not one of us is more than a child. He was a humble, modest, unassuming teacher.[9]

Brethren minister Charles A. Bame revealed the qualities that en-deared Miller to the college and the church:

Learned without pomposity; keen without being cutting; good with-out being sanctimonious; strong despite weakness; strict without being se-vere; different without being queer, he could love without palaver, disagree without bombast, oppose without quarreling. All this begat in him the great qualities of leadership we know he had.[10]

One of the most noteworthy characteristics of Miller was his willingness to make significant sacrifices on behalf of the college and church. Not only did the tenuous financial situation of the college mean that he faced unpredictable personal finances, but the call of the college also caused him to put off many of his personal dreams as a scholar. In a most revealing reflection that he recorded in the travelogue that he kept when he visited Europe, the Middle East, and Egypt in 1926, Miller observed:

> From my student days Egypt has had a pull on my mind's strings. I read much in . . . [my] twenties on Egyptology which then from 1885 to 1900 always thrilled me. . . .
>
> But Ashland College and deep conviction of duty to my church cut all else off and away from me until at last I awoke to the stern reality that nothing else remained. My interests in Semitics, the O.T. and O.T. lands was evidenced by my choice of courses in my graduate work. I worked four years in Semitics, Hebrew, Arabic, Aramaic, Syriac, comparative grammar, etc. then gave it all up.[11]

Miller's personal sacrifice became untold blessing to the college and church as he guided the fortunes of both institutions for over forty years. As one surveys the occasionally turbulent history of both the college and church during these years, the unique role played by J. Allen Miller becomes abundantly apparent. Were it not for the gentle persuasion and patient perseverance of Miller, the centrifugal forces of powerful and competing personalities could have resulted in irreparable damage to the college and the denomination. It is indeed ironic that the college and denomination navigated the dangerous shoals of theological liberalism with only minimal loss while Miller was in his prime, but both experienced significant turmoil due to the impact of fundamentalism shortly after his death in 1935. In truth, the years both immediately before and after Miller became involved in the life of the college and denomination were some of the most devastating in the life of both institutions.[12]

The Rebirth of the College: Financial Stability and Sound Leadership

Prior to the reopening of the college in the fall of 1898, the Board of Trustees again sought to restructure the indebtedness of the institution. New notes were issued and eighteen property lots on the west side of the college's property were to be sold to raise money to pay off the creditors.[13]

This settlement allowed the college to move ahead with the opening of the school under J. Allen Miller.

Miller and the nominal head of the college, J. C. Mackey, were faced with the daunting task of drawing together a faculty, recruiting students, and attending to the continued indebtedness. Miller, who was named president in 1899, was primarily responsible for these concerns. He hired some very capable faculty members who gave sacrificial service to the college during some very lean financial years. Notable were L. Leedy Garber, brother of A. L. Garber, in English and history; C. Orville Witter, who resigned in 1904, followed by Edwin E. Jacobs, in the natural sciences; William D. Furry in philosophy; and Clara Worst Miller in Latin.

With Miller's capable hand guiding the college, a newfound optimism began to improve the image of the college. This optimism translated into more students and greater financial backing from both the church and the Ashland area. An article in *The Ashland Times* dated 15 January 1902 reflects this new attitude:

> . . . wisely, quietly, and persistently President Miller and his co-workers at Ashland College have applied themselves to the task of building up an institution of learning worthy not only of the patronage of their entire church, but of the community of Ashland as well. Victory has at last crowned their efforts. The tide has turned and . . . Ashland College, a subject which at one time was denied a hearing in their conferences, is now not only backed by the solid support of the Progressive Brethren church but is the moving spirit and central force in that church.[14]

The article went on to hail the fact that the college was debt free and even had an endowment of $25,000. Student enrollment had also surpassed the one hundred mark. All of these milestones led to a celebratory banquet in the college chapel; the gala event, which honored the dedicated leadership of J. Allen Miller and the sacrificial giving of men like Josiah Keim and E. J. Worst, signaled that a brighter future lay ahead.[15]

Class Warfare

A tradition that was already time-honored at Ashland College by the first decade of the twentieth century was the battle between the junior and senior classes over the senior class colors. Many today have played the game of "capture the flag," but in the late 1800s and the first decades of the 1900s, the attempt by the junior class to remove or destroy the flag of the senior

(continued)

class that was flying from the college flagpole was a spring-time tradition in colleges across the nation. The rivalry between these classes was taken seriously, and there were occasional injuries and even fatalities recorded at colleges as a result of these vernal skirmishes.

During their junior year a class would select its class colors. At commencement the pennant of the new senior class would begin its flight from the campus flagpole. In the spring of the following year, on a designated day, the junior class would engage in battle to bring down, by whatever means possible, the pennant of the senior class. A typical encounter occurred on 27 April 1906. The blue and white pennant of the senior class was proudly flying from the college pole. The senior class positioned themselves around the pole, waiting the onslaught of the juniors. Several forays of the junior class failed to achieve the goal. As the time approached noon, when the factory whistles would sound the end of the struggle, the battle became more intense. Finally the juniors resorted to the strategy that had been used by the current senior class in bringing down the banner of the seniors the previous year. They hurled gasoline fire-balls at the flag but did not possess the accuracy of their elder classmates. This year the seniors prevailed when the whistles from downtown factories announced the end of hostilities.

One other honorable mention from the class warfare occurred in 1922. About four years before, the rope for the flagpole at the front of the campus had disappeared. It was rumored that it had been cut and removed by a student who wished to foil the attempt of a rival class to

hoist their colors. For these four years no flag, including the United States flag, had flown from the pole. A number of attempts over the years to solve the problem of attaching a new pulley and rope had failed. Finally the resourceful duo of Herman Koontz and Charles Mayes, both new students to the campus, though not freshmen, provided a solution on 20 April 1922. As told in the *Purple and Gold* student paper:

"The device which Koontz and Mayes invented and constructed to carry and fasten a new pulley, with a rope through it to the top of the pole was a sort of mechanical monkey. It had two sets of climbers, comparable to hands and feet. While one set of climbers was hoisted up to secure a higher grip, the other held the device to the place it had already climbed. After it had reached the top, and the pulley fastened by means of pulling some strings, the device was so constructed that pulling other strings completely unjoined it, and it fell to the ground." The paper expressed appropriate appreciation to the ingenious duo: " . . . since the success of the effort is a genuine service to the College, considerable credit should be given to the two men who put the job across." It is not known whether the tradition of capturing the colors of another class was renewed after the extended hiatus. It is noteworthy, however, that Charles Mayes was a theological student who organized and directed the first college band. He was a 1924 graduate of Ashland College and served pastorates in Illinois, Iowa, and California before assuming the role of editor for *The Brethren Evangelist* (1936–39). He went with the Grace Brethren at the time of the division in 1939.

Junior Editor, "The Juniors," *Purple and Gold* 5 (Commencement Number 1905): 31; "Senior Notes," *Purple and Gold* 6 (May 1906): 7; "Rope again Attached to Flagpole," *Purple and Gold* 22 (May 1922): 12; and Donald F. Durnbaugh, ed. *The Brethren Encyclopedia* (Philadelphia, PA: The Brethren Encyclopedia, Inc, 1983), s.v. "Mayes, Charles W.," by John W. Mayes.

The college assumed new indebtedness to construct a gymnasium in 1903. The college's indebtedness once again became a matter of concern, having grown to $11,452 in 1907; concerted fundraising in the Brethren Church liquidated the debt, however, in 1908.[16] The college would not face such severe financial challenges again until the depression years of the mid-1930s.

*A view of the Ashland College campus in 1910; the
building on the right was the first gymnasium, constructed in 1903*

The prolonged history of financial heartbreak and struggle gradually became a memory that was replaced by a new spirit of optimism and progress.

Contributing to the progress of the college during the first two decades of the twentieth century were several men who followed in Miller's wake and provided stable leadership for the institution: John L. Gillin, Edwin E. Jacobs, and William D. Furry. Gillin (1871–1958) came to the college in the fall of 1905 as a professor of economics and sociology. He had received a B.Litt. degree from Upper Iowa University in 1894, an A.B. from Grinnell College in 1895, an A.M. from Columbia University in 1903, a B.D. from Union Theological Seminary in 1904, and a Ph.D. from Columbia University in 1906. He served as president

John L. Gillin

of the Ashland College from 1907 to 1911, though he was non-resident in Ashland for nearly the entire time, traveling in Europe and then taking a position as a professor of sociology at the University of Iowa. From 1912 to 1942 he was a professor of sociology at the University of Wisconsin. Gillin performed valuable service for Ashland College in raising the funds that liquidated the indebtedness incurred in the construction of the gymnasium.[17] Theologically, Gillin adopted a liberal, social gospel perspective that influenced some within the Brethren Church during the first two decades of the twentieth century.[18]

Pastoral Pranks

Pranks are an expected part of college life. Theological students were not above their share of mischief. Albert Ronk shares one such episode from his student days at the college. He had agreed to teach a Wednesday evening Bible class for young people at the Evangelical Church in Ashland. Unfortunately the class was not concluded before the dormitory was locked for the night. Ronk secured permission from President Gillin for the first night, but Gillin was unwilling to give Ronk a blanket consent for the entire length of the course. Ronk continues:

" . . . The first time I came to the Dorm to a locked door, I found a loose window in the laundry and crawled in. Other weeks when I found all other entrances secure, I remembered that Professor and Mrs. Price occupied the two room suite in front of which the outside steps of the boy's entrance ran [the dorm had a divider between the male and female boarders]. The Prices used the front room as a living room, sleeping in the rear one. I could reach the window, raise it carefully, climb into their sitting room and thus to the hall. All went well a couple of times, then I made some noise and wakened the Professor. The next week when I was ready to raise the window, it being a full-moonlit night, I saw something glistening on the window sill. It was white paint lavishly applied to trap me and smear on my clothes. I backed away, and since I was Gym janitor and had a key, I went into a dressing room, lighted the gas heater and slept on a bench all night. When morning came and the door unlocked, I went to my room. Within minutes I heard Dr. Gillin unlock the door separating the girl's and boy's quarters and go down to Price's room. Shortly a loud knock on my door admitted the president where I was busy with my Greek lesson. Gillin said, 'Ronk, do you want to have trouble with me?' At my negative reply, he informed me he knew how I had been getting into the Dorm and it had to stop. Maybe I was insubordinate, but I came back at him with, 'Dr. Gillin, I came from out west where there is a lot of space and open sky, and they do not lock anyone up at night except convicts. You are locking a Dorm full of students into a building without fire escapes which is unlawful. One more threat from you and I will write a letter to the state fire marshall.' That was it. Livid with anger he retreated to his quarters. The next week I pulled the hinge pins from the locked door and threw it over the balustrade. The next week when I noticed before going out that the hinge pins were headless, I removed the lock and hid it. That was the last of the locked door that year. That summer, fire escapes were installed."

Albert T. Ronk, *A Search for Truth* (Ashland, OH: Brethren Publishing Company, 1973), 77–78.

Due to Gillin's non-resident status, J. Allen Miller filled in as acting president during the 1907–08 academic year. Edwin E. Jacobs (1877–1953), the professor of natural sciences, assumed the role of acting president from 1908 to 1911. Jacobs had Brethren roots in his hometown of Congress, Ohio. He was

William D. Furry

educated at Wooster College (B.A. 1901), Mount Union College (M.Sc. 1906), the University of Chicago, Harvard University, and Clark University (Ph.D. 1917). He joined the faculty of Ashland College in 1904 and remained with the college until his retirement in 1947. He served as president of the college from 1919 to 1935. He provided capable and visionary leadership during some of the most crucial and turbulent years of the college's history.

William D. Furry (1874–1959) served as a Brethren pastor before joining the faculty of the college as a professor of philosophy in 1900. He received his education at the University of Notre Dame (B.A. and M.A.), the University of Chicago, and Johns Hopkins University (Ph.D. 1907). He taught philosophy at Ashland College from 1900 to 1904 and again from 1943 to 1957. He served as president of the college from 1911 to 1919 and dean from 1919 to 1933. Between his stints at Ashland College, he was a professor of philosophy and psychology and eventually president (1933–43) of Shorter College. Furry brought a scholarly perspective to his tenure as president and sought to upgrade the academic programs of the college.

Years of Progress and Change at the College (1898–1919)

The new spirit of optimism coming to the fore at Ashland College was a microcosm of the progressive spirit that pervaded the opening decades of the twentieth century in the United States. Technological advances that would transform American culture during the new century were coming to the college as well. Ashland College acquired the first phone for Founders Hall in 1904 for use by college and Brethren Publishing Company personnel. During the first decade of the twentieth century natural gas was made available in the boarding hall; gas stoves now replaced the coal stoves and gas mantle lights displaced oil lamps in each of the rooms. Students must have felt that they were living in luxury when inside toilets replaced the outside latrines. In 1912–13 a steam-heating system was installed in all the college buildings to replace "the dangerous and expensive gas stoves."[19]

Until the construction of Miller Hall in 1922 all the administrative and academic functions of the college were housed in the three floors of Founders Hall. Classrooms for English and mathematics occupied the east side of the first floor. The classrooms and laboratories for the sciences, notably, chemistry, physics, and biology, were on the first and second floors on the west side of the building. The remainder of the second floor as well as the third floor saw only limited use for such activities as music, business classes, oratory, and the literary societies. The third floor also provided ample room for storage.

Pigskin Pastors and other Gleanings from the Gridiron

Ashland College entered the twentieth century with a desire to participate in many of the student movements and activities that were common to other colleges and schools. This included not only such organizations as the YMCA, YWCA, and Student Volunteer Movement, but also such sports as baseball, basketball, tennis, and the rather controversial game of football. The student paper, *Purple and Gold*, ran an article in 1902 by Woodrow Wilson, president of Princeton University at the time, in which he acknowledged the frequent criticism of football as being little better than prize-fighting. However, he praised the virtues of football: it required intelligence and self-restraint; it promoted "hearty social relationships"; it forced the individual to "sink his personal ambitions for the glory of the whole"; it taught "a man to take hard knocks good naturedly."

In the very same issue of the *Purple and Gold* as Wilson's article, a summary appears of Ashland College's first football game, a contest between Ashland College and Ashland High School. Though there was no score, the high school team left the field before time had expired and forfeited the game. A post-game analysis by the *Ashland Daily Gazette* declared: "The College has the making of the best football team in the state of Ohio. Their line was superb and there was not a vulnerable spirit in it. They held like a stone wall against all line plunges." It was common during the early years of football at the college for Ashland to play squads representing various high schools, colleges, and other organizations.

The football team of 1905 had the distinction of being the first undefeated sports team in the history of the college. The original schedule included Ashland High School, Shelby High School, Hiram, Mt. Union, Heidelberg, Buchtel, and Wooster. However, as was probably common at this time, most of these games never

(continued)

materialized due either to financial reasons (lack of equipment) or to teams simply being "dissolved." The college team did play three contests, beating Wellington 6 to 0, Marion 6 to 5, and Wooster 11 to 2 (at least the first two contests were probably against high school teams). The glorious winning streak of three games was brought to a sudden end, however, around Thanksgiving when the Board of Trustees voted to prohibit the playing of football. In anticipation of this vote some of the students who were loyal fans of the sport had "draped the goal posts in black, thinking at least to give the best game of the kind a decent burial with the hope of a glorious resurrection." The team also had the distinction of having a number of men who would became prominent pastors in the Brethren Church: B. T. Burnworth, H. L. Goughnour, W. C. Benshoff, and George S. Baer. It also included future seminary professor, J. A. Garber; future Ashland College President E. Glenn Mason; and was coached by the new professor of natural sciences and also a future Ashland College president, Edwin E. Jacobs.

Football was played intermittently, however, over the next several years, though it may have been more of an intramural sport than intercollegiate. In 1907 football was abolished as an intercollegiate sport and it ended altogether in 1911. This latter prohibition was the result of a condition that had been placed in the will of Lydia Fox of Miamisburg, Ohio. A fascinating sidelight is that a relatively unknown sport made its debut at Ashland in 1914 as a substitute for football—soccer!

In 1919 football was resurrected at Ashland College by the Board of Trustees, initially as an intramural sport. Then on 29 January 1920 the Board went on record as favoring "all forms of recognized inter-collegiate athletics." (The condition in the will of Lydia Fox was lifted.) The renewal of football at the college started with an ignominious defeat, however. Heidelberg University demolished Ashland 74 to 0. However, the team must have learned a lot from this shellacking, because they beat Kent State Normal 6 to 0 in the very next game. One other note of interest is that Ashland defeated Juniata College, a Church of the Brethren school, 20 to 8 in 1928. Miles Taber quipped in a letter to Louis Bauman that Ashland had thus won "the Brethren championship of the world."

"Ashland College 0–High School 0," *Purple and Gold* 3 (December 1902): 6–7; "President Wilson on Foot-Ball," *Purple and Gold* 3 (December 1902): 7–8; "Personal and Local," *Purple and Gold* 3 (December 1902): 8; "Athletic Notes," *Purple and Gold* 8 (October 1907): 2; "Athletics," *Purple and Gold* 11 (October 1911): 13; "Athletics," *Purple and Gold* 15 (November 1914): 14–15; *Minute Book of the Board of Trustees of Ashland College*, 4 September 1919, 224; and 29 January 1920, 228; Clara Worst Miller and E. Glenn Mason, *A Short History of Ashland College to 1953* (n.p. [Ashland, OH]: Ashland College Diamond Jubilee Committee, 1953), 78; "Athletics," *Purple and Gold* 21 (October 1920): 12; "Football," *Purple and Gold* 21 (November 1920): 12; "The Undefeated Team," *Purple and Gold* 21 (March 1921): 16d; and Miles H. Taber, Ashland, OH, to L. S. Bauman, 21 October 1928, L. S. Bauman Papers, Grace College Library, Grace College, Winona Lake, IN, microfiche, 314:21.

Because Allen Hall was the sole dormitory for the college, it housed both men and women. Originally, women occupied the first floor while men were on the second and third floors. Eventually, wooden partitions were installed in the halls, which separated the women in the front half of the building from the men in the rear half.[20]

Total enrollment in all departments in the college throughout most of this period had grown to around two hundred students, though the college did suffer a drop in the student population in 1917 and 1918 due to the United States' involvement in World War I. Representative of the curricular offerings during this period are the departments listed in the college catalogue for the 1908–09 academic year: the College, offering distinct courses of study in the classics, classical divinity, science, philosophy, and literature; the Preparatory Department; the Normal Department; and Special Departments, listed as Music, Art, Business (Bookkeeping), Shorthand and Typewriting, Penmanship, Elocution and Oratory.

Some important curricular changes occurred during these years, especially under William D. Furry. In 1913, two years after his selection as president of the college, Furry not only thoroughly revised the catalogue but also introduced a number of significant modifications. The college adopted semesters for the first time in 1913. Furry restructured the former departments of the college into schools: the College, the Seminary, the School of Education (the former Normal Department), the Academy (the former Preparatory Department), the School of Business, the School of Music, and the School of Art. The curricular programs of several of these schools, notably the college, seminary, academy, and education, were all upgraded. The College curriculum was reorganized into six groupings of courses (referred to as the "Group Plan") that allowed students greater flexibility in choosing a focus (what today would be called a major) for their collegiate education. A further refinement of the curriculum occurred in 1915 when the former courses of study in the bachelor's degree (e.g., scientific, classical, philosophical) were discontinued. The faculty approved the conferral of the Bachelor of Arts degree on all candidates who completed the requisite hours for the degree. There are also indications that the college was more attuned to the recommendations of the North Central Association of Colleges and Secondary Schools, specifically in the admission requirements for the college.[21] In an intriguing action, the Board in 1916 approved the recommendation that the college become a Junior College of The Ohio State University. Presumably, this action was taken because of the accreditation of Ohio State, which would be critical for those seeking specialized degrees and advanced degrees.[22]

Due to the importance of the teacher education program at the college,[23] Furry sought and in 1915 obtained recognition from the Ohio State Board of Education for graduates of Ashland's education program to be granted provisional certification in the state without passing a state examination. This allowance had been made possible by the passage of the Morris Act in 1914 by Congress and was highly coveted by colleges in the United States. The 1915–16 catalogue also announced for the first time the offering of a summer school program for teacher education. The college had gained approval from the Superintendent of Public Instruction for the State of Ohio to begin offering courses in this format.[24] L. L. Garber is credited with obtaining state recognition of the college's normal school program and its continuing advancement.[25]

A Nostalgic Reflection on Gospel Team Trips

Current Ashland University and Seminary students may have little or no knowledge of gospel team trips. But from the late teens through the early 1980s they were a vital part of the Christian ministry at Ashland College. The teams would go out to churches, usually Brethren, over weekends and during vacations at the college.

The first gospel team at Ashland College was organized in 1916 and spent its Christmas vacation ministering to the Brethren congregation at Ankenytown, Ohio. The team was composed of Harvey Becknell, E. A. Rowsey, Bryan Stoffer, and L. V. King. Originally, the work of gospel teams was associated with the Y.M.C.A. organization on the campus.

The 1920 *Pine Whispers* describes the mission of these teams:

"The young men who go out from the college seek to hold constantly and consistently before the people of the community to which they go, the uncompromising ideals of Jesus Christ as demonstrated through loving service. They not only seek to reflect the real life of Jesus Christ but endeavor to reveal the real Christ spirit that characterizes Christian college life. In this way the enthusiastic, optimistic, consecrated young people who are willing to enlist for real service are helped. Often young people who are anxious to enter college and prepare for larger and more useful service are fired to action. The purpose of the team might be called two-fold: first. To help men and women to know Christ as their personal Savior, and secondly, to help them in preparation that they may help others to know and appreciate the beauty and value of the Christian life."

As indicated in the quotation, gospel teams served a number of significant functions. They provided a Christian witness to the congregation to which they were invited. They served as a recruitment tool for the college, evidencing the caliber of students who made up the student body. In a similar way gospel teams spread good will for the college among Brethren churches. For Brethren churches to have a positive image of the college paid benefits financially for the college. The teams also built camaraderie among the young people of the denomination.

The students who served on gospel teams also benefited greatly from these trips. They gained valuable experience in leading worship and in public speaking. For many, these teams offered the first opportunity to preach a sermon. Some young people for the first time began to consider seriously the call to Christian ministry; others had their call affirmed. At least one romance sprang from a gospel team trip; Jerry and Julie Flora began to take an interest in each other as a result of a gospel team trip they took together to Waterloo, Iowa.

Initially, the number of trips taken by the gospel teams was limited. In 1916–17 there was only one trip; in 1917–18 and 1919–20 there were only two trips each of these academic years. The infrequency of these trips was probably due to the need to arrange transportation to rather distant locations, often without benefit of an automobile. As the number of student vehicles at Ashland College began to slowly grow in the 1920s, more teams took to the roads on weekends, not just vacations.

Gospel teams remained very active at the college up through the end of the 1970s. Alpha Theta, the primary Christian organization on the campus in the latter part of the 1960s and throughout the 1970s, placed a priority on gospel team trips. HOPE Fellowship, however, which replaced Alpha Theta as the main Christian organization by 1980, tended to deemphasize gospel teams in favor of Christian witness to the college campus.

Many people are in Christian ministry and other forms of Christian service today because of the opportunity they had to be a part of these teams. A large percentage of the leadership of the Brethren Church today had its first exposure to Christian service through gospel teams. The legacy of the gospel team remains in the lives of countless people who were impacted both as participants in and recipients of the ministry of these teams.

"Gospel Team," in *Pine Whispers 1917* (Ashland, OH: Garber Publishing Co., 1917), 52; "Gospel Team," in *Pine Whispers 1918* (Ashland, OH: n.p., 1918), 37; "Gospel Team," in *Pine Whispers 1920* (Ashland, OH: The Brethren Publishing Co., 1920), [51]; Jerry Flora, interview by author, 7 July 2005, Ashland, OH.

During the first decade of the new century Ashland College reflected a significant trend in American Christianity at this time by initiating numerous interdenominational Christian organizations. These organizations highlighted the broad commitment within the American church to foreign missions, men's and women's work, and social and moral issues. Among the groups formed at the college during this period were a Student Volunteer Band, a Christian Endeavor Society, a chapter of the Young Men's Christian Association, a chapter of the Young Women's Christian Association, and a chapter of the Young Women's Christian Temperance Union.[26] As one student observed in 1902, "Ashland College is affiliating herself with every movement that looks toward the deepening of Christian character and activity."[27] This spirit of openness in both the college and the Brethren Church to the wider religious currents of the day had both beneficial and detrimental effects. The college and church were discovering the larger world outside their parochial Dunker worldview; however, both would come under the influence of liberalism, while the church would be impacted by fundamentalism.

The Impact of Liberalism and World War I on the College

During the last quarter of the nineteenth century a quiet revolution occurred in the higher education institutions of the United States. Not only had the educational community generally accepted the theory of evolution, but it had also adopted an accompanying developmental, progressive worldview that was being applied to such disciplines as science, economics, sociology, and religion. The spirit of the times was thoroughly optimistic, believing the future held unlimited potential for the further progress of humanity through discoveries in science and medicine and the eradication of social ills such as poverty, economic exploitation, and political corruption.

Ashland College was no stranger to these convictions. William D. Furry, writing in 1903, exuded the characteristic optimism of the period. He observed that evolution and the Bible both spoke of a process that was moving toward a future golden age. Progress was already occurring in overcoming humanity's brutish side. There was advancement in overthrowing individualism and competition within society and there were even signs pointing to the possibility of peace among the nations. In a creative interpretation of the Apostle Paul's thought, Furry looked forward to humanity's mastery even over the forces of nature:

The race is eventually to reach the fullness of stature in Jesus; then it will be able to do what he did [have sovereignty over nature]. There are already hints of the coming of such a time. More and more we are bringing the powers of nature to do our work. Medical science has made progress almost incredible. Our messages are carried as quick as lightning *by lightning*. . . . Distance has been annihilated. Conveniences have multiplied. This is not the same world our fathers lived in. And each day the marvels increase. Science speaks of a day, not very far away, when man's mastery over nature and physical force will attain the fullness of Christ. What then will be realized it is difficult to imagine; but it will certainly be a great and glorious thing to be no longer hampered by matter, space and force.[28]

Men like Furry, Gillin, and Charles F. Yoder imbibed evolutionary, developmental perspectives in their education at such institutions as Columbia University, the University of Chicago, and Johns Hopkins University. They were also exposed to theological liberalism, which they brought with them to their teaching at Ashland College, especially during the first decade of the twentieth century. Eventually, some of these men, notably Furry and Yoder, would reject or modify their liberal perspectives. Gillin, however, was a leading spokesman for theological liberalism in the church and, during the two years he was resident in Ashland (1905–07), in the college. Albert Ronk, in his autobiography, notes the difference in the theological perspective between J. Allen Miller and Gillin.

The first year [that Ronk was] at Ashland [1906–07] developed nothing that disturbed my conservative theology of Brethrenism. The Bible teaching under Dean Miller was true to the historic form. . . .

However, during my second year a new teacher [Gillin] with liberal theological leanings taught in the seminary department. We were gradually introduced to higher criticism, especially of the destructive sort. . . . Books were suggested that rationalized much of Scripture.[29]

Gillin remained active in the Brethren Church through the mid-1920s, even though he had taken a faculty position at the University of Iowa and then at the University of Wisconsin. During the teens he and others with liberal perspectives, Herbert L. Goughnour and Charles E. Weidner in particular (both were Ashland College graduates), became outspoken in their advocacy of liberal views both in the pages of *The Brethren Evangelist* and on the floor of General Conference. Representative of their views was support of the social gospel, Gillin's rejection of the infallibility of Scripture in favor of the infallibility of personal experience, and the adoption of postmillennialism and corresponding opposition to premillennialism.[30]

Louis S. Bauman

The open advocacy of these views created a firestorm of opposition in the Brethren Church between 1913 and 1916, especially among those who had been influenced by the developing Fundamentalist movement. Significant spokesmen for this perspective were Louis S. Bauman, Alva J. McClain, and George Ronk. Bauman (1875–1950) was the very successful pastor of the Long Beach, California, church, which he founded in 1913. He had a pugnacious spirit, especially when he felt that the fundamental truths of the gospel were at stake. Bauman always maintained a deep commitment to the Brethren Church, but he was also an early advocate in the church of both foreign missions and eschatology, specifically dispensational premillennialism.[31] Bauman had close personal ties with many of the outstanding leaders of the Fundamentalist and dispensationalist movements. He also invested his life in mentoring young men from the Long Beach church for pastoral ministry. Dozens of "Bauman's boys" took up his mantle of ministry, including his fundamentalist, dispensational perspective.

One of the more prominent among those mentored by Bauman was Alva J. McClain (1888–1968). Converted at a revival service held by Bauman at Sunnyside, Washington, McClain was an outstanding scholar who would provide a cohesive theological system for those Brethren adopting a Fundamentalist posi-

Alva J. McClain   *George T. Ronk*

tion. He taught at Ashland Seminary (1925–27; 1930–37; dean 1933–37) and served as professor and president at Grace Theological Seminary (1937–62).

George Ronk (1881–1964) was one of three Ronk brothers who provided outstanding leadership in both the college and the church during some of the most turbulent periods in the history of both institutions. George had fallen under the influence of liberalism while a student at Stanford University. His disavowal of liberalism was a slow process, aided by his education at Ashland College (B.A. 1911) and the realization that theological liberalism was incompatible with the Brethren faith at several crucial points. He served the Brethren Church as a pastor and evangelist between 1909 and 1924, after which he made use of his considerable entrepreneurial gifts as an industrialist. He was a member of the Ashland College Board of Trustees from 1924 until 1963, serving a number of these years as its president. Two of his brothers, Albert T. (1886–1972) and Willis E. (1891–1956), likewise shared their pastoral, educational, and leadership gifts with the church, college, and seminary.[32]

The course of the liberal/fundamentalist controversy played out initially in the Brethren Church, rather than the college. Those who were the most vocal and vehement in their opposition to theological liberalism were Bauman, McClain, and George Ronk. In answer to the positions of the liberals in the church, these men felt that the social gospel was something less than the whole gospel of Jesus Christ, that the Bible is God's infallible Word, and that Scripture supports a dispensational premillennial view of the end times. McClain, reflecting his training at Xenia Theological Seminary, also argued that the "original words" of Scripture were verbally inspired and therefore inerrant. In addition to these voices, reflecting the influence of Fundamentalism, a number of traditional Brethren, who generally deplored controversy, also spoke out due to their conviction that some of the foundational truths of the Brethren faith were being challenged.[33]

Two actions that occurred at the 1916 General Conference had a calming effect upon the controversy. Bauman proposed adoption of a resolution that set forth an essentially fundamentalist view of Scripture.[34] After considerable debate a committee of eleven, with equal representation of those from the two more extreme positions, drafted a statement that was unanimously adopted by the conference. The pertinent section stated:

> Resolved, That this conference of Brethren churches, without attempting to establish a creed, desires to bear testimony to the belief that God's supreme revelation has been made through Jesus Christ, a complete and authentic record of which revelation is the New Testament; and to the belief that the Holy Scriptures of the Old and New Testaments, as originally given of God, are the infallible record of the perfect, final and authoritative revelation of God's will, altogether sufficient in themselves as a rule of faith and practice.[35]

Several important differences can be discerned between Bauman's resolution and the one finally adopted. (1) In keeping with historic Brethren convictions, the adopted resolution made it clear that the statement was not to be considered a creed. (2) The wording of Bauman's resolution revealed indebtedness to Fundamentalism in anchoring the authority of Scripture in an inerrant *autographa* (the conviction that the inspiration of the Holy Spirit rendered the Scriptures errorless in the original writings). The compromise resolution reflected a more traditional Brethren approach in rooting the authority of Scripture in Jesus Christ as God's supreme revelation and the New Testament as the complete record of this revelation. (3) The negative description of this revelation as "free from error" in Bauman's resolution is replaced by the affirmation "perfect, final and authoritative." This latter wording reflects the thought of J. Allen Miller. (4) The compromise resolution sets forth more clearly the purpose and aim of Scripture: a sufficient rule of faith and practice.

The second action at the 1916 General Conference that helped to bring some measure of calm to the church was the launching of a bold denominational "Four Year Program." Proposed by the Moderator, William

William H. Beachler

Beachler, the program established goals at the local, district, and national level for the various departments of the church. A significant goal relating to Ashland College was the raising of $100,000 for the permanent endowment of the college. Beachler became the lead figure in canvassing the denomination for this endowment campaign.

The above actions, combined with the focus of attention on the events of World War I, seemed to quell the liberal/fundamentalist controversy in the church during the latter part of the teens. However, developments at Ashland College related to the war effort would draw the college into the fray. Furry, the president of Ashland College during the war years, was a strong advocate of the country's participation in the war. This advocacy seems to have been linked with postmillennial optimism, a linkage Furry shared with leading figures of the interdenominational missions movement and liberalism: John R. Mott, Robert E. Speer, and William Adams Brown (Furry had more in common with the missions views of Mott and Speer at this point in his life than the liberal perspective of Brown).[36] Such leaders felt that America bore a special responsibility to preserve the world for democracy and for the advance of God's kingdom.

Furry was active both on a personal level and as the college president in supporting the military effort. He served on the County Exemption (draft) Board and the Committee for National Defense and was the county chairman of the Food Conservation Committee. He actively sought and secured a Students' Army Training Corps (SATC) unit on the college campus, though none of the members of the unit went into combat.[37]

Patriotic Fervor at the College

Once the United States entered World War I, editorials in the student paper, *Purple and Gold*, took a decidedly nationalistic turn in support of the crucial role that America could play in the war. The war was portrayed as a clash between the principles of democracy and Prussian militarism, freedom and autocratic domination, a vision for universal peace and the lust for power.

As an expression of the commitment to the war and especially to the current and former students who were in the armed services, the college created a "Service Flag." The flag had forty-six blue stars, representing all the Ashland College servicemen. Two of the stars became gold, signifying the two men who died during the war, Frank Lambert and Dwight Strayer, and two became silver, signifying the two men who were seriously wounded, Howard Leslie and Hugo P. Wise.

"Editorial," *Purple and Gold* 18 (February 1918): 4 and "Our Service Flag," *Purple and Gold* 19 (January 1919): 20.

Furry's support of the war effort and especially his sponsoring of a SATC unit at the college rankled those Brethren who still held firmly to the traditional Brethren nonresistant position against participation in war. Notable in his criticism was Louis Bauman. He had sought Furry's permission to appear before the Board of Trustees in 1918 to protest the militarism in the college; Bauman revealed in correspondence that Furry's reply was that Bauman "had no business before the Board."[38] An interesting side note is that Bauman's own strong nonresistant position had earned him a warning from the United States Department of Justice in 1918 that his nonresistant stance in his booklet, *The Faith once for all Delivered unto the Saints*, could be in violation of the Espionage Act.[39]

Furry's pro-war stance seems to have brought to the surface latent suspicions about the college's commitment to Brethren ideals and to a conservative (for some, a fundamentalist) Christian perspective. Such suspicions had been present at least since 1915. Herbert L. Goughnour, a Brethren pastor who advocated a more liberal theological perspective, had given passing reference in December 1915 to unnamed people having doubts about the college because its leaders "would not become advocates of this interloping doctrine of 'the blessed hope' [dispensational premillennialism]."[40] He further noted that students and financial support were being turned away from the college. No doubt the reference applies at least to Louis Bauman and the Southern California District of the Brethren Church.

Bauman was at the forefront not only of the battle to keep the church from straying from "the faith once for all delivered unto the saints" (Jude 3), as his popular booklet on Brethren doctrine was entitled, but he also was the point man in making sure that the college did not waver from this same faith.[41] In his Moderator's address at the 1918 General Conference (the same year he registered his displeasure with the militarism at the college), he fired warning shots across the bow of the college. He emphasized that there were two things that were essential for the success of the college. First was Beachler's ongoing effort to raise funds for the endowment campaign.

> Secondly, absolute faithfulness on her part to the Word of God, and the cause for which the church stands. There must be no whispers of disloyalty to God's Word among the teachers in that institution. . . . To be disloyal here [to the authority of Scripture] is treason; and treason can never be tolerated in Ashland College. So far as we know, Ashland College is loyal today. But in these times when all Christendom is being permeated with the leaven of the destructive higher criticism, it is well for us to bear some things continually in mind. We shall never allow the "tag" to be "chawed up" there. Now, you professors and trustees say Amen![42]

Bauman and his Long Beach church took direct aim at the college the next year. In July 1919 the Long Beach church adopted a resolution asking that the Board of Trustees give assurance that the college would remain true to Scripture and the basic doctrines of the Brethren Church. This assurance was expected before the Long Beach church could give "her loyal and unwavering support." (Beachler had not yet come to California to raise endowment funds for the college.) As an outline of the basic beliefs of the Brethren Church, the resolution set forth nine articles:

1. The Deity and virgin birth of Jesus Christ, the Son of God.
2. The fall of man, his subsequent depravity, and the necessity of his new birth.
3. The substitutional [sic] atonement of Jesus Christ through the shedding of His blood.
4. The resurrection of the body of Jesus Christ from the dead, the earnest of the bodily resurrection of all men.
5. Justification by faith in our Lord Jesus Christ, of which obedience to the will of God and works of righteousness are the evidence and result.
6. The Personality of the Holy Ghost as the Comforter and Guide of the members of the body of Christ.

7. The personal and visible return of Jesus Christ, the King of Kings, to this earth.
8. Non-resistance and the forbidding to take an oath.
9. The duty of believers to observe the ordinances of God as set forth in the Scripture, among which are, (a) Baptism by trine immersion; (b) the Lord's supper; (c) The Holy Communion; and, (d) the washing of the saint's [sic] feet.[43]

Understandably, the Board of Trustees felt themselves "under the gun" regarding this resolution. With the endowment campaign poised to move to the West Coast, the new president, E. E. Jacobs, must have felt an overture of good faith was in the best interests of the college. At the Board of Trustees meeting in September 1919, a committee was assigned the task of formulating a doctrinal statement. The committee was composed of Jacobs, J. Allen Miller, Henry V. Wall, a close associate of Bauman from Long Beach, William Kolb Jr., A. D. Gnagey, and William Beachler. Significantly, the doctrinal statement was to apply to the seminary; the Board minutes are silent about any discussion of applying the statement to the college. (The statement appeared in issues of the *Ashland College Quarterly* and *Ashland College Bulletin* devoted to the seminary during the 1920s; it infrequently appeared in the college catalogue and always in the seminary section.)

The resulting doctrinal statement combines two important documents: an excerpt from the 1916 declaration adopted by the General Conference (the Long Beach resolution had also included this declaration immediately before its nine points) and a slightly edited version of the Long Beach nine-point statement.[44] Most of the points of difference between the Long Beach statement and that adopted by the Board were minor. The one major difference was the omission of the word "visible" from the article about Christ's return. This change particularly upset Bauman, who viewed the omission as a dismissal of premillennialism. In a letter to Jacobs, Bauman reveals how important this change was to him: "To US [sic], it [the word 'visible'] is immensely important, because it is the program of the eternal God; and, to work apart from His program is folly."[45]

Bauman followed up this challenge with another in September 1919, the same month as the above Board of Trustees meeting. The previous month he had preached a sermon at his Long Beach church entitled "The Problem of the Christian College." He was able to have the sermon published in the 24 September and 1 October issues of *The Brethren Evangelist*. In the article he listed what he considered the serious dangers posed by the higher criticism that had swept most educational institutions: the acceptance of evolution, the "leaven" of unbelief, the rejection of the inspiration of Scripture, the assured superiority of science over "Sunday School religion," and the precedence of personal interpretations of Scripture over literal ones. Bauman emphasized that the "college is the servant of the church." As such a Brethren college ought to be maintaining the distinctive ordinances of the church, its distinctive teachings, notably nonswearing and nonresistance, and its historic commitment to the final authority of Scripture. He forcefully concluded:

> They [denominational schools] must tell us exactly what the teaching is that we are being called upon to support with the Lord's money. They must tell us exactly what they are going to teach our children when we send them off to college. WE HAVE AN ABSOLUTE RIGHT TO KNOW, AND TO KNOW EXACTLY.[46]

This impassioned demand is all the more intriguing when it is compared with resolutions passed at the World's Conference on Christian Fundamentals held in Philadelphia in May 1919. This conference, heavily attended by dispensationalists and leaders of the Bible institutes, was a watershed in the Fundamentalist movement. The conference took a far more strident and aggressive tone in its opposition to liberalism and modernism than had been true up to this point in Fundamentalism. McClain had attended the conference, though Bauman probably was not able to attend.[47] In the report of the Committee on Correlation of Colleges, Seminaries, and Academies at the conference, two resolutions stand out in light of Bauman's statements and of later developments regarding the college.

> Resolved, That in this day, when infidelity, atheism, anti-Christianity are making such inroads on the higher and professional education of our time, it is the duty of all Christian preachers and parents and young people to know definitely what the teaching of the schools in which they are interested is. Unfortunately, most schools of these classes profess to be Christian, but they teach doctrines respecting the Word of God, the person and work of Christ and the origin of the human race which are contrary to the teaching of the Bible and destructive to Christian faith and morals.

> Resolved, That Christian people should positively refuse to support with money or send their children to institutions which teach the anti-Christian, atheistic and irrational doctrines to which reference is made above.[48]

Bauman seems to have taken seriously the counsel set forth in these resolutions.

The more aggressive stance being taken by those with fundamentalist perspectives in the church was impacting the college faculty. In June 1919 Gillin revealed that the college and its faculty were being "threatened unless they stultify themselves and deny themselves liberty of thought and teaching . . . and teach only one interpretation of certain Biblical statements, and a science which has been exploded for fifty years."[49]

A new phase of the controversy, which engulfed both the church and the college, was associated with the short-lived Interchurch World Movement (IWM). This grandiose interdenominational program was launched on the heels of World War I. It was fueled by the optimistic belief that just as America had rallied militarily to "make the world safe for democracy," so also the churches in America could join forces to advance the kingdom of God throughout the world through large-scale, concerted activity. American church leaders such as John R. Mott and Robert E. Speer designed the IWM to unite every phase of Protestant church work, domestic and foreign. The IWM proposed an extravagant budget, eventually set at a billion dollars, to be raised by the participating denominations.

Those Brethren with a more social gospel or postmillennial perspective were very enthusiastic about joining the movement. At a meeting 1 January 1920, representatives of the various boards of the General Conference of the Brethren Church met in Ashland to decide on a denominational policy toward the IWM. Though not unanimous, the agreement reached was that each board would be free to decide its own involvement. The Board of Trustees of Ashland College decided to commit the college to cooperate with the program. Support for the college's involvement also came from the new president of the college, E. E. Jacobs, and J. A. Garber, a professor in the seminary.

Opposition to the movement was not long in coming. Bauman led the attack, fitting the IWM into his dispensational schema, questioning the doctrinal position of the movement (little had been said in official IWM documents about doctrine), and portraying the IWM as a program reflecting the agenda of postmillennialism, modernism, and the social gospel. The renewed controversy sparked by the IWM ended abruptly when the financial support from the denominations that was needed to fund the elaborate scheme did not materialize.[50]

The final act in the liberal controversy occurred in 1921. The previous year the National Ministerial Association of the Brethren Church had appointed a Committee of Twenty-five to draft a statement of faith that could be supported by the ministry of the church. The committee was composed of men who represented the entire theological spectrum from liberal to fundamentalist. The product of the committee's work, "The Message of the Brethren Ministry," was actually the work of Alva McClain, J. Allen Miller, and a third member of the committee. The only entirely new section in the doctrinal statement was a preamble that reinforced the statement's continuity with previous declarations of the church: "the essential and constituent elements of our message shall continue to be the following declarations . . ." The body of the doctrinal statement was a compilation and expansion of two statements that had been adopted earlier by either the church or college: the motto of the Brethren Church, "The Bible, the whole Bible and nothing but the Bible," adopted at the 1883 Dayton Convention, and the doctrinal statement adopted by the college trustees in 1919 that included the 1916 General Conference declaration on Scripture and the nine-point statement formulated by Bauman's Long Beach church.

The primary differences between the 1919 statement adopted by the college trustees and the 1921 "Message" are more of a Reformed slant in the statements on humanity and the appropriation of salvation, a shifting of focus of the Holy Spirit's work from the church to the individual believer, the inclusion of anointing in the section on Brethren ordinances, and some concessions to dispensational premillennialism. Significantly, the word "visible" reappears in the section on Christ's second coming.[51] These changes reflect the influence primarily of Alva McClain. J. Allen Miller contributed the preamble and part of the statement concerning biblical inspiration.[52] This doctrinal statement appeared in seminary catalogues beginning in the early 1930s until 1942 and then again from 1960 until 2000.

"The Message of the Brethren Ministry" received the support of the Ministerial Association in 1921. Albert Ronk indicates that, as a result of the passage of this conservative statement of faith, "practically all" of the young liberals in the denomination left during the next five years. Many of these men joined the Presbyterian or Methodist Churches.[53] Gillin took a less active role in the church, though retaining his membership in the Brethren church in Waterloo, Iowa, and the Ministerial Association. Significantly, he reversed his theological position during the 1940s, not only upholding the authority of the Bible in a General Conference lecture in 1945, but also publicly asking for forgiveness from conference for his former position.[54]

The Beginning and Development of Ashland Theological Seminary

After the short-lived experiment with a quasi-graduate level theological program at Ashland College in the 1895–96 and 1898–99 academic years, J. Allen Miller returned the ministerial training degree program to the bachelor's level in the 1899–1900 academic year. Throughout the period from 1899

The earliest known photograph of the theological students at Ashland College, taken in 1902; the seven students in the back from left to right: Clarence I. Shock, Edward E. Byers, George E. Drushal, William S. Baker, Harvey L. Holsinger, Dyoll Belote, and Marcus A. Witter; the nine students in the middle from left to right: William C. Benshoff, George C. Carpenter, Herbert L. Goughnour, Albert H. Lichty, Charles E. Weidner, William H. Beachler, Lorin A. Hazlett, L. A. Myers, and unidentified; the six people in the front from left to right: Roy S. Long, Edward D. Burnworth, Professor John C. Beal, unidentified, Harvey M. Harley, and Charles E. Beekley

to 1919 the college's theological courses of study remained relatively unchanged. There were three training programs for ministers and church workers. The Classical Divinity Course was a four-year collegiate degree that resulted in the A.B. degree. Students in this course of study could take at least half their courses in the theological department and the remainder from courses in the classical studies of the college. The 1913–14 catalogue indicated that the completion of coursework would result in the Bachelor of Arts in Theology degree. This degree was especially designed for those preparing for pastoral or missionary service. The English Divinity Course was, in the 1899–1900 catalogue, described as a three-year program but was expanded in the 1913–14 catalogue to a four-year program. This program was designed for those without the requisite education for admission to a collegiate program. Though preparing the student for pastoral ministry, this course of study was also considered "helpful and practical for ladies who wish to do special religious or missionary work in our cities and towns."[55] Graduates from this program received a "Diploma of Graduation." In 1907 the college began to offer a one-year training course that was tailored for lay people who desired additional preparation through biblical and practical coursework. The course was extended to two years in the 1913–14 catalogue.[56]

The most significant change in the theological curriculum of the college was the addition of a graduate level theological degree in 1915. Students with a Bachelor of Arts degree could enroll in a three-year graduate level program that resulted in the Bachelor of Divinity degree.[57]

Organizationally, the period of 1898 to 1919 witnessed some significant changes in the theological department of Ashland College. One of the most important changes was J. Allen Miller's transition from the presidency of the college to the position of Dean of the Theological Department in 1906. At the Board of Trustee meeting on 14 June 1906, the motion was unanimously passed, "That for the Theological Department which has been implied in the catalog and heretofore recognized in business relations by the acceptance of gifts and endowments, a Dean now be appointed."[58] This action by the Board realized a dream for Miller that he had carried since the late 1880s. As Brethren student E. D. Burnworth observed in 1908, Miller had until recently "never had the chance to give to the church his best work. Heretofore he has been burdened with the management of the school and consequently was unable to plan largely for this department."[59] As Dean of the Theological Department, Miller was given full control over the curriculum and faculty of the department as well as the advisement of students. He also was designated as the pastor and preacher of the college church (the Ashland City church), a role that had generally been assigned to the president of the college.[60]

As previously noted, William D. Furry made some noteworthy changes in the curriculum and organization of the college shortly after his selection as the new president of the college in 1911. One of these changes was the designation, for the first time in 1913, of the theological department as a seminary. In the 1913–14 college catalogue, the declaration is made: "The Divinity courses, both disciplinary and professional, will hereafter be offered in a distinct school to be known as the Seminary of Ashland College." Designating the theological department of the college a seminary brought to fruition a dream that had been imbedded in the 1888 revised constitution of the college and had been harbored for many years by J. Allen Miller. This action also would begin a lengthy process in which the seminary would develop an identity increasingly independent of the College of Arts and Sciences.

The 1913–14 catalogue contains some other intriguing statements concerning the seminary. It sets forth the purpose of the seminary as "the education and training of men for the Christian ministry." Previous to this purpose statement, however, the catalogue offered the more inclusive declaration that the "teaching of the Word of God and the training of men and women for Christian service" had been a prominent commitment of the college from the beginning. The ambivalence toward women, which has been previously noted, continues, with training for pastoral ministry being reserved for men while training for more generalized Christian service being open to both men and women.[61] Interestingly, the same catalogue indicates that in the graduating class women outnumbered men seven to one in the Classical Divinity Course and were evenly divided (two each) in the English Divinity Course.

Other noteworthy affirmations are made about the governance and affiliation of the seminary: "The Seminary is under the direction and care of the Trustees of Ashland College. The administration of its affairs is vested in the President of the College and the Dean of the Seminary. . . . The Seminary is affiliated with Ashland College." Several observations can be made about these statements. First, the seminary is afforded a degree of independence from the rest of the college, especially the faculty and most administrators in the collegiate program. Second, the statement on affiliation links the seminary to the college, but, curiously, not the Brethren Church. Though nothing necessarily needs to be read into this observation, it is, nonetheless, noteworthy. Any questions about the connection of the college to the Brethren Church are clarified by statements at the beginning of the catalogue that indicate that the college is committed to remaining faithful "to the spirit and teachings of the Church" (clearly the Brethren Church is to be inferred).[62]

A question that does need to be considered, however, concerns the date for the beginning of Ashland Theological Seminary. Over the years a number of dates have been proposed for the beginning of the seminary: 1878, 1898, and 1906. Seminary catalogues throughout the 1930s and again in the late 1940s and early 1950s state that the seminary was founded in 1878. As evidence, the catalogues cite the declaration that first appeared in the 1888 revised constitution: "The training of suitable men for the ministry of the Gospel shall always be sacredly regarded as one of the main objects of this Institution."[63] As observed in previous chapters, theological education did not begin at Ashland College until the late 1880s. The year 1878 is clearly an inaccurate date for the inception of the seminary.

The two dates that could, with justification, vie for the actual date for the beginning of the seminary are 1898 and 1906. Seminary catalogues from the first half of the 1940s identified either 1878 or 1898 as the origin of the seminary.[64] The year 1898 is selected presumably because this is the date for the reopening of the college under J. Allen Miller and the resumption of the theological department that actually had existed since 1894. The date of 1906 is first cited as the beginning of the seminary in the mid-1920s but not again until the mid-1950s, after which 1906 becomes the accepted date.[65] This date seems preferable to 1898 for several reasons. First, the theological courses of study found in the 1898 catalogue were no different from those found in the catalogue for 1895–96; nothing really changed in 1898. Second, in 1906 Miller was finally able to turn his full attention to theological education. He did not carry the title Dean of the Theological Department throughout his years as president of the college. Prior to 1906 there were very few resources, either financial or personnel, that were dedicated to theological training and there were relatively few students in the theological department.[66] Miller's transition to the dean's role in 1906 made possible significant expansion of the theological program at the college. As evidence of this renewed commitment to resourcing the theological program, note the following reflections that accompany the report of the 12 June 1906 Board of Trustee meeting that appointed Miller as the dean of the theological school.

> The institution [Ashland College] bears the name of a university in the [1888] charter but has heretofore been conducted as a college. The trustees decided to make it now more truly a university[!] by selecting a dean of the theological school apart from the head of the college so that this most important department in the school may be pushed to the utmost. . . . we believe that he [Miller] will throw himself into the building up of a strong theological school. He can now do this unencumbered by the cares of finance and discipline and executive work, which work Professor Gillin has been asked to undertake.[67]

Of all the suggested dates for the founding of the seminary, 1906 has the greatest weight of evidence.

Some corrections need to be made to claims about what occurred in 1906, however. First, a separate "Department of Theology" did not make its initial appearance in 1906. As noted in the previous chapter, a theological department had been created at the college in 1894. Second, this theological department was not for the first time designated a seminary in 1906.[68] That landmark occurred in 1913 (the theological program at the college was informally called a seminary as early as 1905,[69] but the formal designation did not occur until 1913). What changed in 1906 was neither the curriculum nor nomenclature but the investment of the personnel and resources that were necessary to move theological education to a prominent place in the work of the college.

Miller began to share his dream for the future of theological education at the college in 1907. At the General Conference of the Brethren Church that year, he expressed the need for two full-time professors in the theological

J. C. Mackey's 1910 Homiletics class

department. In 1910 he expanded his vision to three full-time Brethren professors in the department and a separate building to consolidate the program of the theological department.[70] Though the last item in his wish list would not occur until 1922, with the completion of the library/seminary building, steps began to be taken in expanding the faculty in the theological department. During the first fifteen years of the twentieth century, several college faculty supplemented the teaching in the theological department, notably Gillin, Furry, and J. C. Mackey, a Brethren pastor who taught at the college from 1909 to 1912. There were also some adjunct or part-time faculty: Charles F. Yoder, who taught some courses from 1902 until 1907, when he left to begin preparing for missionary work in Argentina, and Roy E. Bowers, pastor of the Congregational Church in Ashland, who taught in 1908.[71]

College Professors Attend Séance

One of the most bizarre stories related to the college occurred in November 1906 when college personnel J. Allen Miller, Charles F. Yoder, J. C. Beal, and Edwin Jacobs joined about fifteen other guests at a séance on Main Street in Ashland. Paying a dollar apiece, the guests assembled at the home of Mr. and Mrs. D. F. Brubaker to participate in a séance led by

Mr. H. E. Chase and his sister, Mrs. Alice McCoy, of Cleveland. The college representatives were in for a most unusual evening.

After the lights had been considerably dimmed, Mr. Chase gave instructions for the séance. If a spirit approached a guest, the guest was to rise, greet the spirit, and follow it. In this way the spirit would feel welcome and "free and

(continued)

easy" in the guest's presence. But under no circumstances was the guest to touch the spirit.
During the séance six "manifestations" appeared,
several taking a definite shining to Yoder.

The sixth "manifestation" was a tall Indian.
This spirit became quite at ease with Yoder, so
much so that when he bowed one of the long
feathers in his headgear touched Yoder's cheek.
Yoder, by this time, had noticed a striking resem-
blance in the voice of the different spirits and was
also aware of the floor creaking when the spirit
approached him. His "incredulity became down-
right skepticism when he asked the spirit: 'Are
you my dead sister?' and the answer came back
a plaintive 'yes.' Prof. Yoder never had a sister."

"All these things prompted Prof. Yoder to investigate a little on his own account, and when he
arose for the third time to follow the big Indian
spirit he sent his hand ahead on a reconnoitering
expedition with the result it got mixed up in the
Indian's feathered headgear. No sooner had this
happened than things were doing and the spirit
and flesh became hopelessly mixed. There was a
sound like the muffled report of a revolver shot.
Prof. Yoder was seen to stagger for an instant,
then dash forward and seize the spirit which, true
to its Indian instincts, proved very much of an
athlete, wrenched away from his grasp, and disappeared just as Mr. C. G. Phillips struck a match
in order to throw a little more light on the rapidly

shifting scenes. When the light was turned up
Prof. Yoder looked as though he had just
emerged from a football scrimmage. Blood was
trickling from two wounds on his forehead and
one on his nose, and he had been slightly dazed
for an instant, which is his explanation why the
spirit got away. He says when he seized the supposed spirit it felt very much as though he had a
woman by the arm and shoulder."

In the aftermath of the encounter, Mr. Chase
indicated that he had been following closely behind each spirit and that it was he who had struck
Yoder. Though Chase apologized, a policeman
was summoned and Chase was taken to the police station where he spent the night. In Chase's
possession was a pair of handcuffs with which,
he admitted, he had struck Yoder.

The next afternoon Chase was arraigned
on the charge of assault and battery. The de-
fendant pled "not guilty," but the evidence was
so clear that the verdict was obvious. Chase was
fined $25 and court costs, which amounted to
$31.35 in all. Fortunately for Chase his friends
bailed him out, or he would have had to go to
the workhouse until the fine was paid.

This was one spirit with whom Yoder wished
he had not become quite so familiar. Yet Yoder got
the last word when he preached a sermon on the
following Sunday evening denouncing spiritualism as a "fraud and a deception."

"Séance" and "Spiritualism," *The Ashland Press*, 7 November 1906, 1, 2.

In 1915 the college took the first significant step in realizing Miller's
dream of additional full-time faculty. In the fall of 1915 John Adam Garber
became head of the Department of Religious Education in the seminary.
After completing the English Divinity Course at the college in 1907, he pastored Brethren congregations in Elkhart, Indiana; Johnstown, Pennsylvania; and West Alexandria, Ohio. He graduated from Bonebrake Theological
Seminary in 1915 with the Bachelor of Divinity degree. With Garber's hiring, the seminary was able to offer better training, especially of laity, in the
field of religious education.

As previously noted, part of Miller's hopes for theological education at
the college was space dedicated exclusively to the theological department. A

John Adam Garber

small step in this direction occurred in 1907 when the largest recitation room on the first floor of Founders Hall was renovated as a theology room. Continued acquisition of books for the theological library contributed to what was described in 1909 as a "comparatively large theological library."[72]

All of these positive developments led to significant growth in the theological department and, in 1913, the seminary. In 1898 there were only about 6 theological students. In 1907 this number had grown to 24 and had reached over 40 in 1910. The number of students in the theological department/seminary from 1910 to 1919 generally remained between 30 and 40.[73]

The growing numbers of theological students at the college contributed to the beginning of a Theological Association on 20 January 1912. The association met monthly "to develop a sense of comradeship among the students of this department and to discuss or have discussed before them the vital and fundamental problems of the Christian ministry." The association also maintained a record of all those students who had received their theological education at the college and sought to serve as a contact point for pastors in the field and churches desiring to get in touch with current theological students.[74]

Members of the Theological Association in 1911

The Brethren Church continued to support the work of the theological department/seminary financially during the first decades of the twentieth century. A significant role was played by the women's organization in the Brethren Church, the Sisters' Society of Christian Endeavor (SSCE). Throughout this period the SSCE raised scholarship funds to provide free tuition for Brethren students preparing for pastoral ministry and missionary work. Though at times students abused this blessing by failing to enter the ministry, it nonetheless allowed countless students to receive the education they needed to become more effective ministers in the church. The 1913–14 catalogue also indicated that the SSCE had made a substantial gift to the college for the purchase of theological books. The Department of Religious Education, begun when J. A. Garber was hired in 1915, was made possible by generous annual donations from the Brethren Sunday School Association and the denomination's Christian Endeavor Society ($500 and $200 respectively in 1915). By 1919 the SSCE was also funding the work of this department.[75]

An endowment fund for the theological department that never materialized was announced in the 1906 Brethren Annual. Henry R. Holsinger had died in 1905. As a tribute to the impact that he had upon the Brethren Church and the Brethren movement at large, the 1905 General Conference adopted a resolution authorizing the Board of Trustees to raise an endowment of $15,000 to fund the theological chair. The so-called Holsinger Memorial Fund does not seem to be mentioned in any records after this conference action, however.[76]

There were special expectations placed upon theological students that were not necessarily true of students in other college programs. Those theological students receiving free tuition were expected to engage in some form of Christian work under Dean Miller's direction. This stipulation applied even to those students living and working outside Ashland. All unmarried theological students who received free tuition, except those who had to support their family, had to live in the dormitory. Presumably, this requirement was for two reasons: to provide greater supervision over their behavior and to bring some income to the college while they were students. Interestingly, this ruling by the Board of Trustees in 1908 met with the first documented protest from California Brethren churches concerning the college. They issued an objection through their Scholarship League to this policy, though there is nothing in the trustee minutes that reveals the reasons for the protest.[77] Seminary students were also to form no "matrimonial engagements" with a member of the opposite sex during their course of study; failure to follow this counsel could result in discipline and the withholding of financial aid.[78] Theological students were expected to hold themselves to the highest standards of conduct, befitting the high calling for which they were preparing.

The Philosophy and Christian Character of Ashland College

During the first decades of the twentieth century several statements revealing the philosophy of education at Ashland College appeared in the catalogues. These statements are an excellent gauge of the unique sense of calling that guided the college during these years. In the 1900–01 catalogue the "Distinguishing Features" affirmation, which had consistently appeared in catalogues until this catalogue (see the previous chapter), was dropped. A statement that cited the third article of the Articles of Incorporation of 1888 replaced it. This new purpose statement continued to appear, with minor revision, through the 1913–14 catalogue. As presented in the 1910–11 catalogue, it declared:

> "The object of said corporation is not for profit, but to establish and maintain a College or University for promoting education, morality, religion and the fine arts and to secure to its members and patrons the advantages of education in all departments of learning and knowledge." It is the purpose of the Board of Trustees to thoroughly and efficiently equip every department of collegiate instruction.[79]

A short-lived statement of philosophy, set against the concerns being raised in the Brethren Church about liberalism, appeared in the 1913–14 catalogue: "The actuating motive of the College is fidelity to the whole of revealed truth, to the spirit and teachings of the [Brethren] Church to which it support [sic], and to all its benefactors through whose generosity the College has been established and its work continued."[80]

A long-running statement that appeared from the 1915–16 catalogue through the 1928–29 catalogue very well captured the distinctive character of the college during these years.

> Ashland College was established to provide liberal education under Christian influence and under teachers of genuine piety as well as profound scholarship. It has always regarded as its greatest work the preparation of young men for the Christian ministry and young persons of both sexes for all forms of Christian service.[81]

Taken together, these declarations about the identity of Ashland College during the early twentieth century yield several observations. (1) The college was committed to a liberal arts philosophy of education that sought to provide a diverse educational experience. Though at times in the late 1800s the college saw itself primarily as a normal (teacher education) school, the college had recaptured the original liberal arts vision of its founders. (2) The college had an undeniably strong Christian character. Not only is this seen in the priority given to training people for Christian ministry and service, but it also comes out forcefully in the expectation that professors exhibit a "genuine piety." (3) There is a commitment to balancing the emphases of scholarship and piety, head and heart. Neither ought to be sacrificed for the sake of the other. (4) The college had a deep sense of indebtedness to its spiritual heritage and to those who had made significant financial sacrifices on its behalf.

Articles and advertisements that appeared in the *Purple and Gold* student paper reinforce these observations. An advertisement that appeared in February 1906 identified "three factors that ought to determine the choice of a school: Personnel [sic] of its Faculty, Educational Ideal, Moral and Spiritual Environment." The case for choosing Ashland College was then set forth:

> **Ashland College** will not disappoint you in the first factor. The Faculty is strong: in point of Scholarship, efficient; in method, practical and up-to-date; in ideal of life, conscientious and sympathetically Christian.
>
> **Ashland College** seeks to realize the correct **Educational Ideals.** Knowledge should be linked with Culture and both should be devoted to

Service. Education prepares one to live the best life and to help others to the better life.

> **Ashland College** lays stress upon the best expression of the **Religious Life.** The Moral and Spiritual influences here are of the highest order. Both Faculty and Student-body take a deep and sincere interest in the various religious activities of the College. . . . [82]

The emphasis upon development of Christian character that was observed in the previous chapter continued in this period. In 1905 J. Allen Miller declared: "The end to be aimed at in all education ought always to be character. Character at its best must be Christian."[83] As suggested in the above advertisement, one of the important aspects of character development and of true education was the commitment to service. In 1904 Miller shared the philosophy of education he brought to the college:

> Ashland College seeks to promote education in its truest sense. It is our constant aim to point men and women to the most excellent ways of life. We believe in an education that empowers for service; an education that not only makes a man, a woman stronger and better and happier in his or her own life, but makes every life rise; an education that contributes to the world some element of lasting worth.[84]

Another distinguishing feature of Ashland College was the way in which faculty served as mentors to the students. In 1914 one student commented on the way in which spiritual growth occurred at the college:

> There are three main sources of spiritual growth accessible to every student of Ashland College; the actual character of the courses which are provided, the professors who are pre-eminently Christian, and the organizations which have as their object the spiritual growth of the student.
>
> . . . more than half of the teachers of Ashland College are allied with activities, outside their college work, in which they promote Christianity and be of active service to humanity. Surely a faculty composed of men of that type cannot but serve as a spiritual stimulus to a student body.[85]

The college took very seriously its responsibility not only to mold the thinking of its students but also to shape them morally, spiritually, and civically.

The Relationship of the College and the Brethren Church

Throughout the first two decades of the twentieth century, the college and Brethren Church maintained very close ties. The college still relied upon the church for the majority of its financial support and for a significant number of its students. As previously noted, the theological department/seminary was highly dependent on the denomination financially. In numerous other ways the two institutions were intertwined. The Brethren Publishing Company had occupied the west basement rooms plus one room and an office in Founders Hall from 1894 to 1909. The Brethren Publishing Company also published the student paper, *Purple and Gold*, and, while the company was housed at the college, the college catalogue. There was even an offer made in 1912 that provided both *Purple and Gold* and *The Brethren Evangelist* for the special price of $1.60 per year. The college president or the dean of the seminary served as the pastor of the Ashland City Church throughout most of this period. This church was housed in the chapel in Founders Hall. Brethren theology students served as student pastors in many of the smaller Brethren congregations in Ohio. By 1916 over sixty Brethren ministers trained at Ashland College were serving or had served Brethren congregations. College faculty and administrators held significant positions on Ohio district and denominational committees and boards. All but three of the members on the Board of Trustees of the college had to be Brethren. There was no doubt that Ashland College was *the* college of the Brethren Church.

Yet there were signs even at this time that the college sought to raise its sights beyond the limited horizon of the Brethren Church. In 1910 the Board of Trustees adopted a revised constitution for the college. Though most changes were minor, a few stand out. The Board modified the qualifications of a professor in Article III, Section 4 from "No person shall be elected as Professor in the institution, who is not a person of approved piety, and a communicant of some branch of the Evangelical Church" to "So far as practicable no person shall be elected as professor in the institution who is not a person of approved piety and a communicant of some branch of the evangelical church." The inclusion of the qualifier, "so far as practicable," could conceivably have allowed the hiring of faculty whose Christian faith was nominal or questionable. The 1910 constitution dropped Article IV, Section 12 of the 1888 constitution, which had listed as one of the grounds for dismissal of a faculty member "teaching doctrines detrimental to the success of the Brethren Church." In its place Article III, Section 4 indicated that faculty were responsible "to prevent any erroneous religious views and immoral practices in the College; to secure the proper observance of the Lord's Day, and to promote religious knowledge and piety among the members of the institution."[86] Gone was the expectation that all faculty support, or at least not undermine, Brethren doctrine; in its place was a more generic expectation that faculty uphold general Christian faith and practice.

Other indications of a movement away from strict ties to the Brethren Church were new attempts to raise financial support and recruit students for the college from the Ashland area (for example, the raising of endowment funds from the city and county of Ashland and the beginning of summer school in the 1915–16 academic year to offer more options for training area teachers[87]). From the catalogues of this period, one would have difficulty knowing that the college was affiliated with the Brethren Church. About the only reference to the church that appeared in most of the catalogues was the requirement that students who were members of the Brethren Church attend the college church on Sunday. Even this reference to the denomination was dropped in the 1913–14 catalogue, being replaced by the generic: "All students are expected to be present [at the Sunday service] except those who are permitted to worship elsewhere."[88] Of course, there would not have been any doubt concerning what church was meant by the non-specific reference to "the Church" in the same catalogue.[89] The college did seek to be true to the principle found in catalogues in the late 1800s that it was "thoroughly Christian, but not sectarian."

Concluding Observations

The score of years that began the twentieth century were of incalculable significance to the college and seminary. The years of financial and leadership crisis were behind. Stability and growth in all aspects of the college's life were evident. J. Allen Miller's leadership in both the college and theological department/seminary played a major role in this radical turnabout.

Yet the progress at the college would be placed in jeopardy at the end of this period by doubts about its faithfulness to conservative Christian principles. What had begun in the Brethren Church in 1913 as a conflict between a small group of leaders influenced by liberalism and another group influenced by Fundamentalism spilled over into the college as well by the late teens. Though these doubts would be laid to rest for a period in the 1920s and early 1930s, they would surface with even greater force in the mid-1930s with devastating results for the college, seminary, and church.

In spite of these ominous clouds on the horizon, the college still retained its firm commitment to a liberal arts educational philosophy, founded upon the Christian faith. A strong Christian commitment pervaded the college and seminary, even if it did not fit the litmus test of Fundamentalism. An editorial from *Purple and Gold* in 1916 is an apt summary of the outlook of the college and seminary at this time.

. . . most of the students of the College are also students of the Bible. Both Dean Miller and Professor Garber find great pleasure in teaching the Word of God to these young persons and it ought to be a source of great joy to the friends of the College and the parents of the students to know that there is at least one College in the land that is giving the Bible a vital place in its work of instruction. For the most part the study of the Bible has been eliminated from our public schools and colleges. In some States its reading is forbidden by statute. State Universities make no provision for the study of the Bible other than the handing over of the work of religious instruction to certain organizations of a more or less irresponsible character. . . . Ashland College is one of a very few institutions in the United States that makes liberal provision for the study of the Bible. . . . The ideal of the College is: EVERY STUDENT A STUDENT OF THE WORD OF GOD; EVERY GRADUATE A TRAINED TEACHER OF THE WORD OF GOD.[90]

In spite of the trends at other colleges, Ashland was committed to retaining its Christian and biblical foundations for the educational process.

Chapter 4

Years of Challenge: College Accreditation, Graduate Theological Education, Depression, and Division (1919–1939)

Introduction

During the 1920s and 30s two radically different visions of the preferred future for Ashland College and Seminary collided. Exacerbated by the affects of the depression and by the demands of accreditation, the conflict between these two visions would lead to a heart-wrenching division that enveloped the college, seminary, and denomination.

Challenges and Opportunities facing the College in the 1920s

Under the administration of William D. Furry (1911–19) Ashland College had made significant strides in upgrading the academic program of the institution. However, many other areas of the college's life were in desperate need of attention. Student enrollment, which had remained between one and two hundred for the first two decades of the twentieth century, had dropped well below one hundred in the latter teens as many young men entered the military or took industrial jobs during World War I (enrollment for the 1917–18 academic year was 72). No more than half of these students were of college rank; the others took advantage of the college's non-degree programs. Relatively few students came from the Ashland area. Creative, new academic programs were needed; the administrative structure needed an overhaul; greater expertise was called for in handling the finances; the

Edwin E. Jacobs

buildings and grounds showed the effect of deferred maintenance; the sci-entific equipment and library holdings were quite inadequate; the faculty, though dedicated, needed enlarged; the college suffered from lack of name recognition by outside agencies. Financially, the college was seeking to sur-vive on a budget of less than $7,000 a year. The endowment was still woe-fully inadequate.[1] This is the situation that Edwin E. Jacobs inherited when he assumed the presidency of the college in 1919.

Jacobs was a man who seemed to enjoy taking on difficult situations. He had the ability to see the big picture of what the college needed to do not only to survive but to thrive. He also brought to this long-range plan-ning the gifts of discerning and implementing the short-term steps neces-sary to realize the larger goals. Undoubtedly, he had the administrative gifts that the college needed at this point in its history.

Jacobs brought to his tenure as president two linked concerns: the more immediate desire to complete the endowment campaign among the Brethren churches being directed by William Beachler and the long-range commitment to attain membership in The Ohio Association of Colleges. The endowment campaign had been conceived as one of the thrusts of the denomination's Four Year Program begun in 1916. It had already surpassed its goal of $100,000 in May 1919, and by the time Beachler finished the canvass of churches in 1920, the total was around $200,000.

One of the greatest challenges of Jacobs' presidency was to meet the demands for membership in The Ohio Association of Colleges and, eventually, the North Central Association of Colleges. Shortly after assuming his new role, Jacobs wrote two articles in *The Brethren Evangelist* that set forth the challenges facing the college in order to meet the standards of the Ohio Association. In his first article Jacobs listed six conditions that had to be addressed: a productive endowment of at least $200,000; a teaching staff with at least eight faculty holding the minimum of a Master's degree; a faculty teaching load of no more than fifteen hours a week (at times some faculty taught thirty hours a week); standardized admission and graduation requirements; adequate library and science facilities; and properly equipped buildings. In his second article Jacobs made an impassioned plea to the church to supply two elements critical to the future of the college: students for the college and seminary and an endowment of $225,000, of which $200,000 should come from the church and the rest from Ashland city and county.[2] To a great extent, the goals shared in these articles formed the agenda for Jacobs' presidency.

During the 1920s Jacobs and the Board of Trustees launched two initiatives to achieve many of these goals. In 1920 the Board announced a Five-Year Forward Program that featured the building of a new library and seminary building and a ladies' dormitory. In 1925 the Board committed itself to a new set of institutional goals: attaining membership in recognized accrediting associations of standard colleges; increasing the endowment to at least $400,000; upgrading the scientific equipment; enlarging the library; making significant improvements to existing buildings; and hiring faculty in harmony with the spirit of Ashland College and of its founders.[3] In order to fulfill these goals, Jacobs aggressively pursued additional funding for the college during the 1920s from such sources as the Brethren Church, the city and county of Ashland, and the alumni.

The above-mentioned Beachler canvass of the Brethren Church during the church's Four Year Program (1916–20) was followed by a second canvass of the church by W. S. Bell between 1926 and 1933. In both cases funds raised in the church were designated for the college's endowment. The church also began an Educational Day offering in 1921 that was collected for a number of years on the first Sunday in June. Initiated as part of the denomination's three-year Brethren Bicentenary Movement (1920–23), the

Miller Hall, the home of the seminary from 1922 until 1958

Educational Day offering was designated for the college and its endowment.[4] By 1937 these fundraising efforts primarily in the church had netted an endowment of $412,893. Yearly giving, however, by the church, especially through the Educational Day offering, dropped during the 1930s due both to the effects of the depression and an increasing financial commitment by the church to its rapidly expanding home and foreign missions programs.[5]

During the 1920s the college twice solicited funds from the city and county of Ashland. The first solicitation, aided by a lead gift of $10,000 from Gilbert Hess, realized over $100,000. These funds made possible the building of the new library/seminary building in 1922, eventually named Miller Hall in 1955 in honor of J. Allen Miller, as well as the installation of a modern heating plant in Founders Hall. The second solicitation occurred in 1926. When the gymnasium burned in October 1926, funds from this canvass of the city were diverted to replace this building. This construction forced the deferment of plans to build other buildings.[6] The city and county also made possible the completion of an athletic field and stadium (Redwood) in 1923. In 1937 these gifts from Ashland city and county for buildings and other improvements to the college property had resulted in an accrued real estate value of $527,437.[7]

Students Petition Board for an Increase in Tuition

An entry in the minute book of the Board of Trustees deserves to be in Ripley's *Believe It or Not.* In the minutes for 30 January 1920 is a reference to a petition from the students at Ashland College requesting an increase in the tuition paid by students. The Board readily obliged and increased tuition $3.00, from $25.00 to $28.00. The entry indicates that the increased revenue was to be used to "meet expenses of athletics."

The details behind this improbable request are drawn from several other sources. Intercollegiate athletics had never been a high priority during the first decades of the college. Indeed, due to the drop in the number of men at Ashland College and the resulting financial pressure during World War I, intercollegiate sports had been completely dropped. The Board of Trustees had gone on record at its 29 January 1920 meeting as supporting "all forms of recognized inter-collegiate athletics." The next day the student petition was presented to the Board. The students were desirous of a "progressive and widening athletic program." They were well aware that significant funding would be necessary both to properly equip athletic teams, especially after a lengthy period of inactivity, and to train these teams to the point that they would be competitive with teams from colleges that had not discontinued their programs during the war years. The student body was willing to make the financial sacrifice to build an athletic program of which they could be proud.

Minute Book of the Board of Trustees of Ashland College, 29 January 1920, 228; *Minute Book of the Board of Trustees of Ashland College,* 30 January 1920, 232; "Athletics—Past, Present and Future," *Purple and Gold* 21 (March 1921): [17]; and "Editorial," *Purple and Gold* 22 (March 1922): 7.

The ties to the city and county of Ashland, which had generally languished since the late 1870s, were renewed in the 1920s as the college sought both new sources of funding and additional students. Teacher training had always been a significant part of the educational program at Ashland College. As national and state legislation was enacted to make education beyond elementary school compulsory and as the states developed stricter standards for teacher training, the need for more and better-trained teachers increased. Ashland College initiated and expanded several creative programs to meet this need, specifically summer and Saturday courses and a short normal course between the close of the county schools in May and the beginning of the college's summer session in June. These programs benefited teachers in Ashland and surrounding counties because they could gain additional college credit and thereby receive higher salaries and more rapid advancement in the public schools. But there was also great benefit to the college, as student enrollment exploded in the 1920s. By 1926–27 total student attendance was 778, which included 295 in the summer session and 72 in the Saturday session. Total student enrollment figures over the next twenty years would range from a low of 454 in the depression years of 1931–32 to a high of 820 in 1947–48 as veterans of

World War II flooded into the colleges of the United States.[8] Not only did these creative programs lead to rapid growth, but under Jacobs and his successor, Charles Anspach, Ashland College became one of the leading teacher training institutions in Ohio. The college further benefited from increased name-recognition and prestige.

Other curricular changes occurred during the 1920s. The 1922–23 catalogue introduced some significant modifications. The academy had been discontinued in 1921–22. All other programs of the college, including physical education, domestic science, and the normal school, were folded into the regular college program. Only three distinct departments were recognized: the College of Arts and Sciences, the Seminary, and the Department of Music (an Education department was first introduced in the 1927–28 catalogue). Students preparing for elementary school teaching could take a two-year Normal course, though those preparing for secondary education were required to take the four-year bachelor's program. Students needed 124 semester hours for graduation in the arts and sciences program. The former Group Plan was replaced with the requirement that students have one major and two minors.[9] These changes brought the curriculum into the format that, with only minor modifications, would become the norm throughout the rest of the twentieth century.

During the 1920s and 30s some changes occurred in the degrees offered by the college. The four-year Bachelor of Science in Education degree first appeared in the 1925–26 catalogue. Education courses were frequently offered in the summer school; in fact the 1928 Summer School bulletin indicated that all the courses necessary for the B.S. in Education degree were offered in the summer session, though four years of resident work was required (presumably the non-education courses had to be taken during the fall and spring semesters). The Bachelor of Science degree debuted in the 1930–31 catalogue. Students had the option of receiving the B.S. degree rather than the B.A. degree if they had completed the requirements for the B.A. degree and had taken at least 50 of the requisite 124 hours in mathematics and the physical and biological sciences. The B.S. degree was discontinued after the 1935–36 catalogue (the B.S. in Education was still offered).[10]

The growth that the college was experiencing and the standards for faculty mandated by the accrediting agencies led to a significant increase in the number of faculty and greater expectation that faculty hold advanced degrees. In 1920 there were thirteen faculty in the college; the faculty had grown to twenty-nine in 1930 and thirty-two in 1938. The first faculty member with a Ph.D. was J. L. Gillin in 1906. From 1906 to 1929 the number of faculty with Ph.D.s generally was from one to three. The North Central Association put pressure on the college to increase the number of faculty with a Ph.D. to four in the 1929–30 academic year. By 1938 the number of faculty with a Ph.D. or equivalent had reached fifteen; it would range between eleven and fifteen through the early 1950s. The number of faculty with M.A.s varied between three and five until 1920 and it increased rapidly during the 1920s and 30s. In 1938 twelve of the thirty-two faculty members held an M.A.; only five had less than an M.A.[11]

During the 1920s Ashland College was not only adjusting to meet the challenges of a growing student body, but it was also striving to make the necessary changes to become a standard college, based on the guidelines of the Ohio Association of Colleges and the North Central Association of Colleges. Prior to 1920 the college generally felt little pressure to seek accreditation, but such recognition was becoming more crucial for the future of the college. Accreditation had direct bearing on recruitment of students and on recognition of its graduates by other educational institutions and by state agencies that certified public school teachers. By 1926 the college was focusing on complying with the North Central Association's standards, because recognition by the North Central Association was broader and because the Ohio standards were based on those of the North Central Association.[12]

In 1930 the push for accreditation bore fruit, when Ashland College gained membership in North Central Association and, shortly thereafter, the Ohio Association. The college experienced a major setback, however, in 1933 when it lost accreditation with the North Central Association (this action became effective in 1934). This blow was partially the result of a major revision in the standards by the North Central Association. During the 1920s the standards were basically quantitative in nature; in the 1930s the North Central Association adopted standards that were far more qualitative. Ashland College served as a guinea pig to test the new standards and was found to be deficient in several areas. Though the college felt that the evaluative process was unfair, given the radical shift in standards, the administration made a concerted effort to address its weaknesses and regained membership in 1938.[13]

Developments in the Seminary and in the College-Denomination Relationship during the 1920s

Just as significant changes marked the 1920s for the college, the same was also true of the seminary. Though there were still very close ties between the college and seminary in 1920, the seminary was taking steps through-out the decade that would give it an identity less dependent on the arts col-lege. These developments were not without tension within either the college or the denomination.

The 1920s began with continuing suspicion about the college's ortho-doxy on the part of Brethren influenced by Fundamentalism. The gravity of knowing what the college was actually teaching became weightier during the course of Beachler's endowment campaign in the denomination. In 1920 the Southern California District churches sent a resolution to the Brethren General Conference indicating that they were withholding sup-port from the college and asking conference to form a board to examine all current and prospective faculty concerning their positions on various theo-logical and moral issues.[14] There is nothing in the 1920 conference minutes to indicate what happened to this resolution. Another tactic used by the Southern California churches was the proposal to send in their pledges for the endowment campaign with conditions attached, possibly relating to their concerns about the alleged teaching of postmillennialism and evolu-tion. E. E. Jacobs made it clear in correspondence with Southern California leaders in mid-1922 that as college president he would accept no gifts with conditions attached. He insisted that collegiate policies would be estab-lished by the Board of Trustees alone; that the only theological statement that he would accept was that adopted by the Board in 1919; and that this statement would apply only to the seminary, not the college.[15] Indeed, the statement of faith either was omitted from the college catalogues during the 1920s and early 30s or was placed in the section devoted to the seminary. It also appeared in special issues of the *Ashland College Quarterly* and *Ashland College Bulletin* devoted to the seminary.

In 1923 the issue of sending conditional gifts to the college had be-come public knowledge. It led to a lively debate in the pages of *The Brethren Evangelist*. J. L. Gillin opened the discussion with an article that dealt only with the concept of conditional gifts; he gave no hint of the behind-the-scenes maneuvering. He indicated that acceptance of such gifts restricted a college's freedom and would eventually lead "to the decay of intellectual life." E. Glenn Mason expressed his concern about the factionalism in the denomination, taking direct aim at an unspecified faction that he felt wanted to force its views on the college. The target of his complaint became abundantly clear when he opined that the laity of the church considered the issue of pre- versus postmillennialism a nonessential and when he in-sisted that materialistic evolution had never been taught at the college. George T. Ronk, who would become a staunch supporter of the college in the 1930s, insisted that those who sent their funds and children to the college ought to have a say in its policies. L. S. Bauman maintained that millennial views did make a difference to his laity and attacked the haughty attitude with which "education" advocated evolution.[16] This exchange reveals that by the early 1920s there were already two divergent viewpoints in the church related to both theological perspective and educational philosophy. On one hand were those Brethren influenced by Fundamentalism who tended to be far more dogmatic about their beliefs and who felt that the college, similar to the Bible institute model, should be overtly Christian in its expectations of faculty and students alike. On the other hand were those more traditional Brethren who emphasized a more relational form of Christian faith that avoided the use of creeds to enforce belief and who generally favored a liberal arts approach at the college, though with unmistakable Christian influence.

The tension between these two perspectives in the church eased considerably between 1925 and 1933. Bauman had been elected as one of the members of the Board of Trustees from the Southern California District in 1923. In 1925 he and another trustee from the Long Beach church, Henry V. Wall, were instrumental in getting the Board to add a third faculty member to the seminary, Alva J. McClain. By 1926 Bauman's view of the college had so moderated that he was even willing to have his son, Paul, enroll at the college that year.

McClain's hiring at Ashland as professor of Old Testament History and Theology greatly encouraged those with more fundamentalist leanings. During his first term of service at the college, between 1925 and 1927, there were no overt indications of conflict between him and the college administration, though he had let Jacobs and Miller know in 1925 that the college was "still on trial" with him.[17] McClain struggled with his health during this period and felt it necessary to resign and head for California in June 1927. He reassured Jacobs and the readers of *The Brethren Evangelist* that his departure was entirely for health reasons.[18] Writing twenty-five years later, however, McClain indicated that he was frustrated by the situation at the college. He was disillusioned by the lack of interest that the college had for a graduate seminary program, by the tendency of students planning on graduate theological studies to take the basic liberal arts A.B. degree rather than a Bible major in order to fulfill entrance requirements for graduate study, and by a "liberal" bent in the life and faith of the college.[19]

In 1927 the seminary needed to find a replacement for not only McClain but also J. A. Garber. The latter had resigned to assume a position at Lane Theological Seminary. Kenneth Monroe was hired in place of

Kenneth Monroe

McClain as professor of Old Testament History and Literature and Melvin A. Stuckey became the professor of Christian Education, Church History, and Homiletics, filling the vacancy left by Garber. Monroe had received his education at the University of Southern California (A.B.), and Xenia Theological Seminary (Th.B., Th.M.). Stuckey was raised in Louisville, Ohio, and had been educated at Ashland College (A.B. 1924; B.D. 1927), Geneva Training School, Princeton Theological Seminary (Th.M. 1927), and (Case) Western Reserve University.

Throughout the first half of the 1920s the seminary curriculum remained generally the same as that found in the 1915–16 catalogue. Important changes, however, occurred in the 1925–26 academic year and especially in 1926–27. The changes adopted for the 1926–27 academic year were designated the "New Plan." Though these years coincide with McClain's first two years at the college, the impetus for these changes is primarily credited to revisions in the Arts Course that necessitated modifications to the seminary courses as well.[20] The "New Plan" offered three courses of study: the Arts-Seminary Course (it was called the Arts-Divinity Course in 1925–26), the

Melvin A. Stuckey

Classical Divinity Course, and the English Bible Course. The Arts-Seminary Course represented the most significant change to the curriculum. Theological students were to take three years of study in the arts college. They could then enroll in the seminary. Upon completing their first year in the seminary, they were awarded the A.B. degree. Two additional years in the seminary resulted in the Th.B. degree (in 1925–26 the degree was still the B.D. degree). The Classical Divinity Course was designed for those who did not wish to pursue a six-year program. It involved two years' study in the college, including two years of Greek and one year of Bible history and literature, followed by two years in the seminary. According to the 1926–27 catalogue, this course of study resulted in the A.B. in Theology degree (in 1925–26 and again in 1929–30 the degree was listed as the A.B. in Divinity). The English Bible Course (English Divinity Course in the 1925–26 catalogue) was designed for those students who did not have the requisite high school preparation for admission to the college. It was a very practical four-year course utilizing the English Bible and resulting in a diploma only. The former two-year Christian Workers' Course was dropped in 1925.[21]

The seminary experienced other significant changes during the 1920s. In 1922 the completion of the library/seminary building provided a home for the seminary program, though no space was dedicated exclusively for seminary use.[22] Seminary men continued to be housed in Allen Hall, but in 1926 J. Allen Miller proposed that an off-campus house be purchased as a dormitory for the seminary men. McClain also supported such an arrangement because it would afford them a setting separated from the "high-jinks" of the college dorm and it was more conducive to serious study and to the holding of devotional meetings. The Board of Trustees adopted the proposal in 1926, though a similar recommendation, approved in 1931, suggests no action was taken until 1931. Eventually a house was purchased at 109 West Walnut Street as a boarding hall for seminary men.[23] Enrollment in the seminary remained consistently in the 30s and 40s during the 1920s.

Ashland Student-Pastor Draws Attention of *Cleveland Plain Dealer*

Though many seminary and preseminary students have served pastorates during their years at Ashland, few have done so with the drive and dedication exhibited by J. Ray Klingensmith. Klingensmith grew up in southern California, and attended Louis Bauman's Long Beach, California, congregation. He attended Ashland College (1927–31; B.A. 1931) and Ashland Theological Seminary (1931–34; B.Th. 1934) and pastored Brethren congregations at Ankenytown, Ohio; Oakville, Indiana; and Washington, DC. He served as the general secretary of the Missionary Board of The Brethren Church (1940–45) and as professor of English Bible at Ashland College (1956–77). He also taught as an adjunct at Ashland Theological Seminary following his retirement from the college. The following article from the *Cleveland Plain Dealer* captures the qualities that made Klingensmith an outstanding pastor and teacher.

SHINES IN CLASS AND PULPIT, TOO

Smiling Student-Preacher Is Idol of Ashland
College and Mission District
(Plain Dealer Special)

ASHLAND, O., March 15–"Preacher" Ray Klingensmith isn't exactly sure whether he is a college student with preaching as a sideline or a minister with college as an avocation, but he's positive that the two are a great combination and, furthermore, that preaching is a good way to earn one's way though college. Klingensmith, who is 22, hails from Long Beach, Cal. His curly hair won't stay down. Neither will the corners of his mouth. Nor will he. He doesn't have time.

Attending Ashland College Theological Seminary as a junior and pastoring a full-sized congregation at Union Mission [this congregation eventually became the Ashland Grace Brethren Church], near here, form a pretty stiff schedule.

Authorities of the college commend him for his high scholarship, his activities in the Y.M.C.A., glee club, varsity quartet and other organizations, and city law and health officials say that in three years he has greatly reduced their work in the Union Mission district.

Law-breaking and unhealthy conditions were taken for granted there until the mission chapel began to flourish, they say.

In the college, Ray carries a full schedule, makes nearly all A's, sings bass in the glee club, varsity quartet, leads music at the college "Y," lustily sells peanuts at football games and never wears a hat.

(continued)

In Northwest Ashland, where $18 a week is "good money," he conducts a Sunday school, preaches every Sunday night, teaches four Bible classes a week, attends all mission social events, visits the sick and discouraged, conducts funerals, welds together wrecked home [sic], cleans up dirty homes, finds jobs for the jobless, clothes for those that need them and advises mothers, fathers, boys and girls on their problems, and smiles and smiles and smiles.

"Fellows at school declare they don't see how I stay serious long enough to preach, but when I realize how these folks are groping for help and comfort, its [sic] mighty serious business with me," says the young preacher. "Many of them, who used to come to the meetings to disturb and sneer, are now my greatest aids and they are wonderful friends." They pay their pastor a salary which takes care of his school expenses.

"I nose around into their personal affairs a lot," the student-pastor explained. "If I'm preaching and see a man enter who I know is bootlegging, the sermon switches to the evils of liquor."

"I learned about a couple that had been living together without being married, so I called on them, and after a talk waltzed them down for a license and a wedding before they could change their minds. I don't beat around the bush with those folks. I tell 'em exactly what I mean in plain words."

"Sometimes I've received threats, but nothing has come of them. One man threatened to beat his wife for attending the mission, but she came anyway and took the beating."

"He was so curious to find out what the attraction was that he dropped in one night, too. Now they attend together all the time."

L. S. Bauman Papers, Grace College Library, Grace College, Winona Lake, IN, microfiche, 348:22.

Free tuition continued to be offered to seminary students up to the mid-20s. They were expected to pay the usual college fees, however, amounting to $25 for the 1925–26 academic year. When the seminary curriculum was revised in 1925–26 and 1926–27, seminary students in the Arts-Seminary Course were expected to pay full tuition for their three years in the college, but their three years in the seminary would be tuition free (this policy began in 1926).[24] This generous financial aid did pose a challenge to the college. The following statement appeared in all college catalogues between 1915–16 and 1928–29: "In the case of theological students whose tuition is remitted the cost to the college is even greater. To provide for the deficit thus made from year to year endowments are asked for and liberally granted."[25] The women's organization of the Brethren Church, the Sisters' Society of Christian Endeavor, renamed the Woman's Missionary Society in 1919, continued to supply most of the support for this scholarship aid.

The status of women in the seminary continued to be ambiguous. The 1922–23 catalogue states that the mission of the seminary "is to train men for the Christian Ministry. Besides this definite aim it affords laymen and women the education and training so essential for the Christian leadership of the day and for the work of Missions, Religious Education and the many varied activities of Church life."[26] Yet on the very next page the catalogue observed:

> The highest Calling of Man is that to the Christian Ministry. The
> Ministry is not a profession which a man may or may not choose to follow.
> It is distinctively a Holy and Divine Vocation. The man or woman who re-
> sponds to the Call does so through a profound sense of duty and privilege.[27]

The sentiment at the seminary at this time seems to have been that the professional ministry was to be reserved for men but that women should not be
excluded from ministry if they felt so called. But the more appropriate role
of women in Christian service was in missions and religious education.

During the 1920s the seminary continued the process begun in the
teens to define itself as a program separate from that of the College of Arts
and Sciences. Several exclusively seminary catalogues appeared during the
period while a few college catalogues (1920–21, 1921–22, and 1926–27) either omitted the seminary or gave it only brief consideration. The housing
of the seminary program in Miller Hall and the purchase of a separate boarding house for male seminary students provided additional identity for the
seminary and separation from the collegiate program. While the college had
adopted a non-sectarian, liberal arts perspective, the seminary was un-
apologetically Brethren. The 1922–23 college catalogue stated: "While the
Seminary is open to students of any religious body it constantly stresses the
teachings of the Holy Scriptures as believed and practiced by the Brethren
Church."[28] These developments were clearly supported by the Board of
Trustees and also by President Jacobs and Dean Miller. The 1920s became
a significant time for both the college and seminary as they defined their
mission and purpose on their own terms. This redefinition process for both
programs tended to move them in directions that were increasingly distinct
from each other. Yet it is also clear that this defining process was necessary
for the success, if not also the survival, of both. Jacobs and Miller seemed to
have understood this reality clearly. But the increasing disparity in the direction of the two educational programs would lead to conflict both in the
college and the denomination.

Philosophical Differences regarding Education that Distinguished the Fundamentalist Brethren and the Supporters of Ashland College

During the 1920s and 30s Ashland College and the Brethren Church were
faced with a number of critical issues that would begin to polarize constituencies in the college and church. The first was linked to the very survival

of the college. If graduates of the college were to be credentialed for teaching in the public schools and if those desiring advanced education were to have the opportunity of entering the best universities and graduate programs, the college had to be accredited. By this time both students and financial support were going to colleges and universities that were accredited. Numerous small colleges would not survive this transition process in the 1920s and 30s. At the same time, the growth in faculty, programs, physical plant, and endowment that accreditation required meant that the college no longer could rely primarily on the Brethren denomination for underwriting its financial needs. The denomination could not even supply sufficient numbers of qualified faculty and staff to meet its personnel needs. These realities would force the college during this period to look increasingly beyond the Brethren Church for financial support, students, and personnel. But to ask non-Brethren to shoulder greater responsibilities at the college and to have a student body that was increasingly non-Brethren put pressure on the Board of Trustees to further expand the Board beyond the confines of the Brethren Church.[29]

A second issue, related to the developments above, was a difference within the Brethren Church over the very notion of what Christian education meant. McClain, in a 1925 address at the Brethren General Conference, set forth the platform of those Brethren impacted by Fundamentalism. For him Christian education had three distinctive features: it must "yield to Jesus Christ complete lordship over the educative process," "teach Christian truth as well as Christian ethics," and "be carried on by Christian men and women." He shared further his deep reservations about what was occurring at many Christian colleges.

> In order to build any kind of college he [the Christian college president] must have three things: money, teachers and students. If the church supplied all these, his task would be much easier. But the church seldom does this. As a result, the administration turns to the general public. And the moment this is done, certain dangers are incurred. The general public like to patronize educational institutions which maintain a fair degree of moral and ethical respectability, but it is not greatly interested in education that is definitely Christian. Therefore, there is constant pressure brought to bear upon the managements to soften the Christian emphasis, and to strengthen the emphasis upon the interests of the non-Christian public. I have no sympathy with this tendency. I would rather fail than compromise.[30]

This either-or perspective on the eve of McClain's arrival at Ashland College would, in time, clash with the direction that Jacobs and his successor, Charles Anspach, were pursuing at the college.

A third issue was the difference in the philosophy of education between J. Allen Miller and those who emulated him and McClain and those who followed his example.

> Miller used an "open" method of teaching and gave the impression to his students that his search for God's truth was an ongoing task. He was eclectic and Biblical, committed to no one theological system. His desire for his students was that they develop a mature faith based upon the full consideration of all facets of a given issue, using whatever interpretative (linguistic, exegetical) tools were available.

> McClain was a skilled systematician and utilized a propositional approach to theology (Delbert Flora has termed Miller's approach "behavioral," i.e., dealing with life). In his teaching he was more dogmatic than Miller and projected a far more confident, self-assured aura with respect to his theological conclusions than his colleague. He was far less committed to traditional Brethren thought than Miller. The basic ingredients of McClain's system were Calvinism, dispensationalism, and Fundamentalism, though within these parameters he demonstrated much creativity.[31]

These two perspectives looked at points of disagreement through vastly different lenses. McClain's uncompromising fundamentalist spirit, with its heightened concern for truth, could be very divisive. Miller was far more conciliatory in the midst of conflict and would seek to build bridges between divergent viewpoints. The Fundamentalist Brethren saw this quality as a significant weakness.[32]

A fourth issue that tended to divide the Fundamentalist Brethren and those Brethren who supported Jacobs was the relative importance of the college versus the seminary. The primary concern of the Fundamentalist Brethren was the training of men for Christian ministry. Louis Bauman, for example, realized that the college, in spite of its perceived failings, provided the institutional structure and resources that made possible the existence of the seminary. But it was the seminary that was the true future of the Brethren Church. In a letter to a fellow Brethren pastor, Charles Mayes, Bauman stated: "if there is any future for the Brethren Church, we must educate our ministry in Brethren schools, and it is for us to work for the interests of Ashland College and to control it for the Lord."[33] Jacobs, for his part, though supporting the upgrading of the seminary, understood that the advancement and accreditation of the College of Arts and Sciences was foundational for any other programs in the college. Jacobs' first priority was placing the liberal arts program on the firmest possible footing to ensure the future viability and progress of the college.[34]

A fifth issue, related to the previous one, concerned the very nature of Ashland College itself. McClain, during his stay in Southern California in the late 1920s, contemplated the creation of a graduate level theological seminary in the friendly confines of Bauman's Long Beach First Brethren Church. His goal was the creation of a "school where the competent scholarship of a seminary might function within the warm spiritual and practical atmosphere of a Bible institute."[35] McClain's ideal for a collegiate level program was the Bible institute that could provide the biblical and spiritual matrix for graduate theological education. Obviously, such a vision for collegiate studies was radically counter to the liberal arts philosophy that was deeply-rooted at Ashland.

These two visions for Ashland College, each of which had strong proponents in the denomination, coexisted with an uneasy truce during the later 1920s and early 1930s. In fact, Louis Bauman in 1929 both publicly and privately supported the college, in spite of his reservations. That year in a Long Beach church calendar he vouched for Ashland College as being "free from the taint of modernism." He even went so far as to downplay the necessity of being a premillennialist in order to be in the Lord's (and his own) good graces. Though he believed postmillennialism was a misinterpretation of Scripture, the acceptance of this theological position did not make one a modernist. "I can conceive of men being Post-millennial and not Modernists, and I believe that this is true of the Post-millennialists that are at Ashland."[36] There was a willingness on the part of both parties to work together for the common cause of the college and seminary, even though they harbored divergent views on a number of critical issues.

The Creation of a Graduate Level Theological Seminary

In 1930 the college seemed to be on the verge of a very promising future. On 20 May 1930 Alva McClain, the current moderator of the General Conference of the Brethren Church, sent out an announcement to Brethren pastors on behalf of E. E. Jacobs and Ashland College of two momentous events: the recognition of the arts college by the North Central Association of Colleges and the advancement of the Seminary Department to the rank of a "Standard [graduate] Theological Seminary."[37]

After leaving Ashland for health reasons in 1927, McClain had spent three years in Southern California, two years as the Professor of Bible Doctrine and Church History at the Bible Institute of Los Angeles (1927–29) and one year as the Minister of Education at Bauman's Long Beach congregation

(1929–30). Ever since the late teens Bauman and others in his circle had entertained the notion of starting a Bible college and/or seminary in Southern California.[38] McClain's presence in Long Beach and the completion of a significant building project at the Long Beach church that included a large educational wing brought the subject of the creation of a seminary on the West coast to the fore once again in 1929. The administration and the Board of Trustees of Ashland College were quite alarmed when they became aware of these plans. They feared that significant financial support from the denomination would be diverted away from Ashland College, bringing into question its very survival.

The Board of Trustees, of which Bauman was a member, invited McClain to its spring meeting in 1930 to find a satisfactory compromise. At this meeting McClain presented his proposals for a graduate level seminary in a paper entitled "Work of a Theological Seminary." The Board appointed a seven-member committee to consider McClain's proposals. The committee brought back the recommendation, which was adopted, that "the Seminary Department of the Arts College should be made a Theological Seminary for college graduates; continuing, however, the admission of a limited number of undergraduates by special arrangement and for special courses; . . ."[39] The Board also adopted the committee's recommendation that a fourth faculty member be added to the seminary. This agreement meant that the seminary faculty would consist of Miller, Monroe, Stuckey, and McClain.[40] Though the Board persuaded McClain to locate the graduate seminary at Ashland, McClain won several concessions from the Board. Among the most significant were: (1) "the dean of the seminary should have complete jurisdiction in all seminary matters similar to the jurisdiction of the president in the arts college"; (2) "the continuance of the seminary on the college grounds should be regarded as an experiment" only; and (3) a plan was to be developed to ensure the financial autonomy of the seminary. The Board also agreed, with J. Allen Miller's assent, that Miller would retain the title of dean, but that McClain, as the associate dean, was to assume "complete responsibility and authority in the reorganization and direction of the seminary."[41] The Board further demonstrated its commitment to advancing the seminary program by including a recommendation to construct a building housing a chapel and the seminary as part of its newly unveiled "Ten Year Forward Program for Ashland College."[42]

The graduate level seminary program opened at the college in the fall of 1930 with four students. It was a three-year course of study, culminating in the Bachelor of Theology degree, which moved students through a prescribed curriculum during Junior, Middler, and Senior years. Each year was divided into two semesters. The curriculum was composed of the following general areas:

> (1) *Exegetical* courses, dealing with the Revelation of Christianity in the Scriptures. (2) *Doctrinal* courses, dealing with the Interpretation of Christianity as a system of Truth. (3) *Historical* courses, dealing with the History of Christianity as apprehended and realized in the Church and its various relations. (4) *Practical* courses, dealing with the Propagation of Christianity through the preaching, teaching and pastoral functions.[43]

This statement, which appeared intermittently in seminary catalogues until 1963–64, clearly reveals the influence of McClain, with its emphasis on a more propositional, systematic approach to truth. Revelation is primarily centered in Scripture; missing is Miller's characteristic emphasis on Jesus Christ as God's supreme revelation.

The seminary also admitted a limited number of "special students" to an "English course." These students, who were either women (no women appear in the graduate program during the 1930s) or who did not have a bachelor's degree, could take the regular course of study, minus certain technical studies, and be granted a certificate upon the completion of their studies. Though the curriculum was based on the assumption that students were residential, there was also provision made for part-time students, either pastors already in active service or college upperclassmen who wanted advanced Christian training but did not intend to go into the ordained ministry.[44]

The seminary program continued to be housed in the library building (Miller Hall). Enrollment averaged in the upper teens and twenties through 1937, with an equal or greater number of preseminary students in the undergraduate program. The first graduate of the revised graduate program was Delbert Flora, who graduated in 1931. He would later become a professor and dean at the seminary.

Generous financial aid still was available to seminary students in the restructured seminary. They were expected to pay full tuition ($165 for the academic year 1931–32) as preseminary students in the college, but no tuition was charged during their seminary years. In addition, for each year of study in the college, preseminary students accrued a credit of $100 toward their seminary expenses. They could thus accumulate a maximum of $400 that would be equally distributed over students' three years in the seminary. This financial aid was made available not only to Brethren students who attended both the college and seminary but also to students of other evangelical denominations.[45] In

1937 some restrictions were placed on this generous aid, including the discontinuation of support for non-Brethren students.[46]

Expanded seminary catalogues, distinct from the college catalogue, date from the beginning of the graduate program (the first catalogue of which copies exist was the 1931–32 catalogue). Very few changes occur to the catalogue between 1931 and 1937. The material in these catalogues, for the most part written by Alva McClain,[47] is very revealing about the unique theological perspective that characterized Ashland Theological Seminary at this time. The catalogues also reflect the historical setting of the college and denomination. The seminary catalogue, far more than the college catalogue, reinforces the connection of the school to the Brethren denomination: "The Brethren Church . . . maintains and controls both the Seminary and College . . ."[48] In fact the catalogues from this period are entitled: *The Ashland Theological Seminary of The Brethren Church* . . . In a statement that evidences the wariness of the Fundamentalist Brethren in particular about liberalism and modernism, the catalogue indicates that the Brethren Church "is conservative, holding firmly to all the great fundamental truths of biblical and historical Christianity. It has no 'modernistic' controversy."[49] Given charges that would be made in the ensuing controversy in the college and church, this statement is noteworthy. It is also interesting that this statement, framed against the events in the denomination in the 1920s and early 1930s, continued to appear in seminary catalogues through the 1998–2000 catalogue.

Several statements in the catalogues retain the historic Progressive Brethren balance of scholarship and spiritual vitality. The Brethren Church is described as "progressive in methods and education, believing there is no necessary opposition between higher education and Christian spirituality; that if such an opposition arises, either the educative process is not Christian or else the spirituality is spurious . . ."[50] The catalogue is very clear, however, that the end of this educative process is preparation for Christian service, not academic expertise.

> The important technical disciplines of a standard theological curriculum are taught, but always with a practical purpose. Each course is brought to the test of this question: How can this be used in the practical work of the Christian ministry? High academic scholarship is inculcated, but not as an end in itself. The function of the Seminary, as conceived by this Institution, is to produce able preachers and pastors, not merely scholars.[51]

This statement continued to appear in seminary catalogues through the 1963–64 academic year.

Another statement that expresses a commendable balance among orthodox faith, competent scholarship, spiritual vitality, and practical ministry first appeared in the 1937–38 seminary catalogue and probably was written by McClain before his dismissal (there is a correction page pasted over the list of faculty in the catalogue that identifies the new faculty appointed by the Board in 1937; the text underneath still had the names of McClain and Hoyt).

> The main emphases of the Seminary are complete and uncompromising loyalty to the biblical and historical *Christian Faith*, the inculcation of competent *Christian Scholarship*, the nurture of a deeper spirituality in the *Christian Life*—all directed toward the goal of a practical *Christian Ministry*.[52]

This statement remained in seminary catalogues until 2000–01.

The catalogue exemplifies the Brethren concern for a balanced understanding of the nature of the Christian faith and life. Critiquing the "inadequate conceptions and one-sided emphases" found in the moral and religious landscape of the time, the following statement exhibits a most commendable symmetry regarding the Christian faith.

> Considered objectively, Christianity is held to be distinctively a SUPERNATURAL REVELATION exhibiting a threefold content: a *Person*, the eternal and incarnate Son, our only Savior, in whom the invisible God is perfectly and finally disclosed; a *Doctrine*, the medium of divinely inspired Truth by which the revelation of the Son is brought intelligibly to men; and an *Ethic*, in which there is embodied the Will of God for moral beings.
>
> On the subjective side, Christianity is presented as a PERSONAL EXPERIENCE having three distinct aspects: a *Relationship* with the Living God mediated through the Person and redeeming work of Christ; a *Faith* which lays hold upon Christ through the Truths which reveal Him in the record of the Written Word; and a *Life* in which the believer progressively realizes the revealed Will of God.
>
> Thus in Christianity, both on its objective and subjective sides, there appear correlating elements which are *mystical, doctrinal*, and *ethical*; answering to the deepest needs of men—spiritual, intellectual and moral. The neglect of any one of these constituent elements in the interest of a "simplified religion" is a tendency with which this school has no sympathy.[53]

This statement, written by McClain[54] and retained through the 1938–39 seminary catalogue, expresses very well a number of the traditional emphases of the Brethren: the balance between the head and heart; the truth that revelation is first of all personal in Jesus Christ; the nature of Christianity as relationship, faith, and life. In spite of McClain's bias toward a more propositional form of Christianity, he still evidences an understanding of the Christian faith that is Brethren at the core. He likewise captures a number of those essential qualities that have epitomized the core identity of Ashland Theological Seminary throughout its history. This is why several statements penned by McClain continue to appear in the seminary catalogue even today.

The Polarizing of the Parties

The year 1930 seemed to hold great promise for the future of Ashland College and Seminary. However, before the end of the decade two devastating experiences led to one of the college's most challenging periods: the Great Depression during the first half of the 1930s and the heart-wrenching dissension within the college and seminary that would engulf the denomination as well in the last half of the 1930s.

The Great Depression placed severe financial constraints on the college due to a decrease in both students and financial support. Enrollment in the collegiate program peaked in 1930–31 at 340 students but had dropped to a low of 252 students in 1934–35. Both the depression and especially the loss of accreditation (1933) shrunk the summer enrollment (teacher training courses predominated in the summer session) to about half of what it had been earlier in the decade. The resulting drop in tuition revenues caused the Board of Trustees to authorize the college to borrow funds on several occasions between 1933 and 1935. The financial situation even forced the Board to adopt the motion that in the case of a financial deficit, faculty salaries would be paid on a prorated basis from the available funds.[55] The college never missed a payroll for its non-Brethren faculty; however, this was the case only because Brethren faculty willingly turned down six of their nine payments during one academic year.[56]

The controversy that would engulf the seminary, college, and eventually the denomination had its origins in a volatile situation that exploded in the hollows of Kentucky. For over twenty years the Brethren, through the Home Mission Board of the denomination, had supported an educational outreach to the Appalachian community of Lost Creek, Kentucky. A significant portion of the Home Mission Board's funding (46% in 1927) went to sustaining the Riverside Training Institute and mission work in Lost Creek directed by George Drushal, a 1902 graduate of Ashland College. For a variety of reasons the Board voted in 1931 to close the institute, but Drushal, in defiance of the Board, reopened the school a short distance away. The situation was finally resolved by dividing the property between Drushal, who operated a school, and the Home Mission Board, which supported the evangelistic and pastoral work.

What made this affair so explosive was that some very vocal Brethren pastors, with radical Fundamentalist leanings, were deeply committed to Drushal's work. Most notable was H. C. Marlin of the Pleasant Hill, Ohio, congregation. In 1931 and 1932 Marlin railed against Ashland College and Seminary, the Home Mission Board, and the General Conference leadership in his fortnightly publication *The Postscript*. He charged these groups with all kinds of unfounded moral and theological errors and with using arbitrary, dictatorial power. The accusations were broadcast before an interdenominational, Fundamentalist audience of about one thousand subscribers.

Marlin was roundly denounced by both the traditional Brethren, or Brethrenist, leaders and the Fundamentalist Brethren, who were also implicated in his sweeping denunciations. (R. Paul Miller, the field secretary of the Home Mission Board, was aligned with Bauman and the Fundamentalist Brethren.) Marlin was summoned to appear before the National Ministerial Association at the 1932 General Conference. When asked to produce evidence for his charges, he admitted that he relied upon the unsubstantiated report of one student. Though he made an apology to the Ministerial Association for the damage he had caused to the college, seminary, and denomination, he did not refrain from his invective against these institutions following General Conference.[57] Prior to the 1933 General Conference Marlin resigned his pastorate. However, at this conference the National Ministerial Association still formally excommunicated him from its membership and recommended the withdrawal of fellowship from Marlin by the conference.[58] The most damaging result of Marlin's flagrant allegations was the spreading of seeds of doubt about the college within the denomination. As Albert Ronk observed: "Suspicions were aroused, not only by the published charges in 'The Postscript' but by the whispering gallery as 'The Postscript' revealed."[59]

The attacks of the "whispering gallery" were behind E. E. Jacob's carefully worded statement in *The Brethren Evangelist* in February 1933 concerning the teaching of evolution at the college. Jacobs emphatically denied that evolution, either in the sense of more advanced species developing from lower forms or in the sense of man evolving from primates, had ever been taught during his presidency. He did make quite clear, however, that "there is a world of difference between TEACHING evolution and TEACHING ABOUT evolution."[60] Yet the revelation of the fact that there was teaching about evolution was sufficient in some people's minds to create further suspicion about the orthodoxy of the college.

The 1932 meeting of the National Ministerial Association had also called upon the college and seminary to appoint a committee to investigate the charges made against both by Marlin. At its 1933 meeting the Board of Trustees appointed an investigation committee composed of Board members W. I. Duker, W. C. Benshoff, and George F. Kem. This committee gave its report to the 1933 meeting of the National Ministerial Association at General Conference. It made special reference to the faculty's unanimous adoption of a statement of faith earlier in 1933 (see below). It also exonerated the college of Marlin's specific charges related to the teaching of evolution. This whole process kept the issue of the beliefs and teaching of the college on the "front page" for the Brethren.[61]

Doubts were harbored about the teaching of the college not only in the denomination but also within the college itself. Ever since his return to the college in 1930, McClain had been questioning students about the teaching in the arts college.[62] He felt that some college faculty were critical of the Christian convictions of preseminary students. The presentation of conflicting religious perspectives by the college faculty on one hand and seminary faculty on the other in the general chapel services did not help the matter. McClain sought to address these concerns with President Jacobs and Dean E. Glenn Mason, but he felt that no satisfactory action was ever taken. He then appealed directly to the Board of Trustees in 1933, recommending the adoption of a statement of faith that could be used as a standard for determining the orthodoxy of faculty members. This recommendation, strongly opposed by the college administration, which must have seen this action as a subversion of its authority, won the support of the Board.[63] The Board appointed a committee composed of McClain, Frank Coleman, George Ronk, Charles Ashman, and W. C. Benshoff to prepare a statement of faith for the college.[64] McClain penned the initial draft of the statement. It covered the basic doctrines of belief held by evangelical Christians but omitted distinctive Brethren doctrines since over half of the college faculty were members of other denominations.[65]

The statement of faith won the approval of the Board in spite of the strong objections by the college administration about imposing the statement on the faculty. The administration finally dropped its objections when the Board added the provision that it would not require individual faculty members to sign the statement. The seminary quickly adopted the document and featured it in its catalogues beginning with the 1933–34 catalogue. The college faculty, however, "in an atmosphere of restrained hostility," adopted the statement by a voice vote, with only a few "ayes," while the vast majority of faculty withheld their vote. The statement was mailed out to all

Brethren ministers, undoubtedly to give the impression that the college faculty had taken a strong Christian stance. Though both McClain and Bauman greeted the statement with enthusiasm, McClain, looking back on the event, felt that its adoption was a hollow victory. The statement did not appear in the college catalogue during the remainder of Jacobs' presidency and Jacobs failed to enforce the doctrinal standards with the stringency McClain desired.[66]

Several observations should be made concerning the statement of faith. In the midst of the controversy over the Interchurch World Movement in 1920, McClain had indicated that he favored the development of written creeds no doubt to test the faith of those whom he felt were moving away from orthodox Christianity. He recognized that this position put him at odds with the non-credal stance of the Brethren, but he felt that the adoption of statements of faith was an excellent means of reining in those whose appeal to freedom of thought was used as a license for disseminating unorthodox views.[67] Ironically, McClain and Bauman respectfully disagreed on this issue. At the 1938 Brethren General Conference McClain moved the adoption of the "Message of the Brethren Ministry" as the church's creed. He undoubtedly sought the apologetic value of having the non-credal Brethrenist group vote down this time-honored statement. The motion indeed was rejected, but McClain's plan was foiled when even Bauman voted against it![68]

The Brethren criticism of creeds has focused on several issues. First, creeds all too often shift the emphasis away from Scripture to a humanly constructed summary of faith. This reality introduces the very real danger of adding to or subtracting from Scripture. The Brethren, who often declared that their only creed was Scripture, have taken this danger seriously. Second, the Brethren have always maintained the conviction that faith must be a free-willing response to God's grace; faith must not be coerced. The use of a creed to guarantee or force a person's compliance to a doctrinal position has always grated against the Brethren psyche. Third, the Brethren have historically held that a person's word is his/her bond, based on Jesus' teaching in the Sermon on the Mount that one should not swear oaths. To force a person to sign a statement of faith violates the good-faith approach to dealing with people that has typified the Brethren throughout their history. Liberalism did, however, take license with the non-credal stance when it used the position to legitimize its right to recast the traditional faith in more modern forms. The non-credal position never was meant to be an allowance for deviation from Scripture as the arbiter of truth.

In one of the intriguing ironies of the history of the seminary, the statement of faith composed by McClain has continued to appear as the doctrinal standard in Ashland Theological Seminary's catalogue to the present. Though it was omitted from the streamlined catalogues between 1942 and 1946, the statement has appeared, with only minor revisions, in every other catalogue. In 1941 the disclaimer was added that "The Brethren Church sponsors no creed and the above statement is not to be considered as such." Though faculty at the seminary after the division with the Grace (Fundamentalist) Brethren in 1939 would certainly have known its origins, the continued use of the statement may have been a means of countering Grace Brethren charges of modernism and liberalism at the college and seminary.[69]

At the 1933 meeting of the Board of Trustees, J. Allen Miller was named dean emeritus and McClain was given the designation dean of the seminary. Miller, who was well aware of the developing tensions between the college and seminary, was deeply troubled by them.[70] His death in 1935 would remove one of the gifted leaders in the college and church whose moderating influence had so capably guided both institutions through very troubled waters for over four decades. Herman A. Hoyt was hired in Miller's place as professor of New Testament and Greek. Hoyt was raised in a Brethren family in Dallas Center, Iowa, and received his B.A. from Ashland College in 1932 and his B.D. from Ashland Theological Seminary in 1935.

Herman A. Hoyt

Events during the rest of 1933 and throughout 1934 continued a downward spiral in the college and seminary. The loss of accreditation in 1933, combined with the effects of the depression, led to a deteriorating financial situation in the college. Relations between the college and seminary worsened. McClain's attempt to force the statement of faith on the faculty was deeply resented. The college students were pushing for more open policies concerning fraternities, dancing, and theater attendance. The seminary faculty felt that the "worldly" perspective of the college students was a detrimental influence on the preseminary students. Many college students resented the free tuition granted seminary students while they struggled to meet their financial obligations in a depressed economy. The combination of these factors led Jacobs to resign, under some pressure, as president in 1935.[71]

The Battle between Sinners and Saints

At times there was tension between the arts college students and the theological students on the Ashland College campus. Theological students were resented because they received free tuition and were perceived at times as "holier than thou." Theological students sometimes complained about the unruly behavior of their fellow students and the lackadaisical attitude brought by the arts students to their studies.

But these two groups of students had a most appropriate venue for venting their irritation with each other: an annual classic aptly called the "Saint and Sinner Game." The 1922 rendition of the classic was touted as "the thirty-second annual baseball battle for the supremacy of the college campus." The rivalry was taken seriously, but the saints were invariably no match for the sinners. Though one should be careful about reading too much philosophically or theologically into the usually lopsided score, the editors of the *Purple and Gold* student paper had fun with announcing the final scores in 1921 and 1922. In 1921 the official score was printed as: Sinners 8; Saints (?????????) 2. The following year the paper announced: "Annual Saint-Sinner Game Easy for Sinners; Bad Men Cop Annual Fiasco by 10–1 Score." Fortunately the destiny of the saints was not determined by their play on the diamond.

"Annual Title Tilt," *Purple and Gold* 21 (May 1921): 16, 32 and "Annual Saint-Sinner Game Easy for Sinners," *Purple and Gold* 22 (June 1922): 13.

McClain and Bauman welcomed the appointment of the new president, Charles L. Anspach.[72] Anspach (1895–1977) was raised in a Brethren family from Fremont, Ohio. His grandfather was Brethren elder Samuel M. Loose of the Fremont congregation. He received his education at Ashland College (B.A. 1919, M.A. 1920) and the University of Michigan (Ph.D. 1930). He had a long and distinguished career in higher education, beginning at Ashland College as a professor of education, registrar, and eventually dean and head of the education department (1923–30) and then as

Charles L. Anspach

president (1935–39). At Eastern Michigan University he was head of the department of education and dean of administration (1930–35). His longest service was as president of Central Michigan University (1939–59). He was a very able administrator and served in a wide range of educational, religious, civic, and professional organizations.[73]

What especially pleased McClain was Anspach's commitment, in a letter to McClain in February 1935, to reorganize the college "with the Wheaton [College] viewpoint," to "contact conservative men in all denominations," and to steer clear of liberalism.[74] Anspach also went on public record in *The Brethren Evangelist* that he would maintain a conservative perspective at the college, emphasizing pure and righteous living and offering both liberal arts and theological training in a distinctly Christian setting.[75]

The clash between McClain's more fundamentalist, separatist view of Christian education and the college's, particularly Anspach's, conservative, yet open, Christian liberal arts perspective surfaced during the first year of Anspach's presidency.[76] Anspach was rankled when the seminary professors protested the inclusion of certain local clergy deemed "modernist" as speakers at his inauguration. But McClain was incensed, as were the Fundamentalist Brethren, over decisions made at the 1936 meeting of the Board of

Trustees. In his later reflections on the controversy that wracked the college and denomination, McClain lays considerable blame on Anspach for precipitating the crisis by his "almost cynical violation of his solemn promises."[77]

In fairness to Anspach, he inherited the college when it was struggling with the loss of accreditation, severe financial constraints, and a divided campus and faculty. He sought to address these issues at the 1936 Board meeting. Four developments at the Board meeting would reveal the deep divide within the college and ultimately the denomination. (1) One of the realities that Anspach undoubtedly realized was the limited support that a small denomination could provide the college and the significant financial support coming from the Ashland community. At the 1936 meeting of the Board of Trustees, Anspach proposed two significant changes to the Board structure, one of which dealt with this reality. Anspach proposed a change to the Ashland College constitution that would alter the composition of the Board. The amendment, which awaited final action in 1937, would enlarge the Board from 36 to 42 members. Of the 6 new positions, 3 were allotted to the Ashland community, 1 to the alumni, and 2 to members-at-large appointed by the Board.

(2) The second change relative to the Board that was discussed at the 1936 meeting dealt with a modification in the process for the selection of trustees. From 1910 until 1927, the district conferences of the Brethren Church presented nominees to the Board of Trustees; the Board then made its selection from each district's nominees. In 1927 the procedure was changed to permit direct election by the districts. (Louis Bauman was instrumental in bringing about this change.)[78] The Board discovered, however, that this new procedure was in violation of the constitution that governed the college and that a return to the pre-1927 selection process was necessary. Under the 1936 proposal each district would nominate twice its allotted number of trustees and the Board would make its selection from these nominees. This change would make the Board essentially self-perpetuating and thereby reduce the denomination's direct influence over the college.[79] Another proposed change also served to negate the influence of dissident districts upon the college: "Any conference that withdraws or withholds its support, previously pledged, shall forthwith forfeit its right to membership on the Board of Trustees."[80]

(3) The third significant development at the Board meeting was Anspach's sharp criticism of a group of preseminary students for distributing tracts on the college campus. (4) Finally, Anspach proposed a "double standard" of conduct for the student body. A "restricted" standard would be

applied to those preparing for pastoral or missionary service while a more lenient standard would be expected of those preparing for secular professions. Anspach argued that it was not reasonable to require the large percentage of local students living at home to live a completely separated life.[81] Though all four of these developments raised the ire of the Fundamentalist Brethren, the Board's adoption of the last point led to the resignation of Louis Bauman and Charles H. Ashman from the Board.

These events served to widen the chasm between the supporters of Ashland College and the Fundamentalist Brethren and would have momentous ramifications for both the college and denomination. In response to the 1936 Board of Trustee meeting,

> the Southern California District Ministerial Examining Board sent a letter to Anspach demanding a response to nine specific protests: (1) the alleged use of a "gag rule" on the minority of the members of the Board; (2) the "dominant place" on the Board given to "wealthy men of Ashland" who "are not in sympathy either with Brethren doctrines or standards of life"; (3) what was deemed as a transfer of control of the college and seminary to men who are not only non-Brethren but not even "numbered among the *Fundamentalist* [italics mine] forces outside the Church";[82] (4) the "double standard" passed by the Board; (5) Anspach's alleged personal favor for the lower standard (he maintained his family's right to attend movies); (6) his attack on tract passing; (7) the very existence of conflict between the college and seminary; (8) the reduction of the seminary staff from four to three (the position left vacant by Monroe's resignation in 1935 was not filled);[83] (9) the alleged effort "to wrest the College from the control of the Church" and turn it over "to a group of Ashland people."[84]

The letter had been sent to Anspach on 16 June and called for a response by 27 June. Anspach had been away from Ashland on church-related work and, upon his return, hurriedly sent a cable on 25 June and follow-up letter on 26 June to Paul R. Bauman, the son of Louis Bauman. Anspach proposed in his letter that a committee of leaders from Southern California discuss the issues with representatives from the college Board and faculty prior to the Brethren National Conference.[85] The Southern California leaders felt that Anspach was trying to buy some time with his proposal and decided to broadcast the contents of their letter on 31 July as an "Open Letter" to the entire denomination.

The timing of the distribution of the letter was meant to have maximum impact on the 1936 General Conference, 24–30 August. The problem of Ashland College became a focal point of discussion at the conference, which appointed a committee to investigate the matter. The

conference disapproved the proposed amendment to change the composition of the college Board and tabled a vote of confidence in Anspach and
the "entire administration" of the college.[86] The conference's rejection of
the proposed amendment was not binding on the Board, however, since the
church had only an indirect authority over the college through the trustees
who were selected to serve on the Board.

Tension at Ashland College escalated during the 1936–37 academic
year between the seminary faculty, especially McClain and Hoyt, on one
side, and the administration and arts faculty on the other. Early in 1937 the
faculty considered a proposed "Rules and Regulations" to govern their
body. When the issue of grounds for dismissal was under discussion, Mc-
Clain moved that one additional ground be added: "teaching anything contrary to the college Statement of Faith." When Hoyt asked for a roll call
vote, only five affirmative votes were cast, three from the seminary professors. Anspach, early in the roll call, gave an angry denunciation of the use
of the statement in this way and punctuated his comments with an em-
phatic "No."[87]

The Board meeting in 1937 brought the college controversy to a head.
Bauman and Ashman, the two trustees from Southern California who had
resigned in protest in 1936, were reappointed by their district for reelection
to fill the two district slots on the Board in 1937. However, the Board made
use of the yet-to-be adopted change that there had to be twice the number
of nominees for each district position. (The election of new Board members
preceded the adoption of the controversial amendments to the constitution.) The Board nominated two additional men from Southern California
and proceeded to elect them to the two vacant positions.[88]

McClain, who could sense the direction that the institutional "winds"
were blowing, presented a lengthy annual report that laid out in very clear
terms his proposals for the seminary and his frustrations with the current
situation. He recommended, among other points, that the seminary be separated from Ashland College and moved to another location; that the seminary be given possession of the theological library; and that an equitable
proportion of the income from the endowment funds be given to the seminary. McClain's report gave detailed justification for the separation of the
seminary and college. In his rationale McClain revealed an awareness of the
deep philosophical divide between him and the college administration. For
example, he opposed the push for accreditation because of the perception
that the North Central Association was not interested in theological education; he advocated that the priority of the college should be the training
of men for the pastorate and that "if we should limit the ministerial training

of our men to four years, those years should be spent in a theological seminary instead of an arts college"; he recognized the need to broaden the recruitment of college students beyond the church to the greater Ashland area, but saw this development as leading to "further concessions in the direction of liberalization."[89] Although McClain, in his later reflections on these events, framed the issue solely as a "problem of Christian faith,"[90] the radically divergent views about the purpose and identity of the college were at the heart of the controversy. At the conclusion of McClain's report a motion was made to approve the report and the separation of the seminary; instead, a substitute motion was adopted that accepted the report but tabled his recommendation to remove the seminary from the college.

The Board realized that decisive action needed to be taken to quell the unrest on the campus. The President of the Board of Trustees, W. I. Duker, had received a petition from twenty faculty members related to the tensions among the faculty and, as a result, appointed a Committee of Investigation to consider the issues. This committee, after interviewing the Arts and Seminary faculties, recommended:

> That the President of the College be instructed to secure by resignation or dismissal the elimination of Professors Alva J. McClain and Herman Hoyt from the Seminary Faculty, because of continued lack of harmony and co-operation between the Arts College and Seminary, which are essential to the success of the institution.[91]

When McClain and Hoyt refused to resign, they were dismissed on 4 June 1937.

The Board immediately acted to reorganize the seminary with Willis E. Ronk, serving as dean, Melvin A. Stuckey, and Leslie E. Lindower. Ronk had been a student at both Ashland College and the University of Chicago and eventually received his B.A. from Juniata College. He furthered his education at Bonebrake Seminary (B.D.) and Pittsburgh-Xenia Seminary (Th.M.). He pastored congregations in the Brethren Church at Roann, Indiana; West Alexandria, Ohio; Meyersdale, Pennsylvania; Ashland, Ohio; and Goshen, Indiana. He served as the dean and professor of New Testament and Greek at the seminary from 1937 until 1943 and taught briefly again in the 1955–56 academic year.[92]

Stuckey (1899–1986) had served on the seminary faculty since 1927. After the reorganization of the seminary, he taught homiletics and practical theology and became dean (1943–51) following Willis Ronk. He pastored the South Bend, Indiana, Brethren Church (1951–53) before serving as a

Willis E. Ronk

Leslie E. Lindower

professor of religion at Trinity University in San Antonio, Texas (1953–67).[93] Lindower (1903–93) grew up in the Brethren congregation in Canton, Ohio. He received his education at Ashland College (B.A. 1926), Ashland Theological Seminary (B.D. 1928), and Dallas Theological Seminary (Th.D. 1932). He served several student pastorates before pastoring at Warsaw, Indiana (1932–37). He taught Old Testament, Hebrew, theology, and archeology at the seminary from 1937 until 1949. After additional education at Ohio State University, he served in various positions at Ashland College from 1950 until 1974, the longest as academic dean (1952–72).[94]

At its 1937 meeting the Board of Trustees also reaffirmed its fidelity to the statement of faith adopted in 1933. Anspach, at his first Board meeting in 1935, had recommended that the statement be published in the college catalogue to underscore the college's commitment to the orthodox Christian faith.[95] He broke with Jacobs' precedent of omitting the statement from the college catalogue by publishing it in the college catalogues for the 1936–37 and 1937–38 academic years. McClain was highly critical of this use of the statement (remember that McClain was the primary author of the statement of faith). In his historical reflections on this period, McClain commented:

the college belatedly attempted to shroud itself with a cloak of orthodoxy by publishing the troublesome Statement of Faith both in its current catalog [1937–38] and a special bulletin sent out to the churches. But later, when the futility of this gesture became apparent, the Statement of Faith was dropped from the next catalog (1938–39) and in its place was substituted a watered-down version of religion which left room for "liberal" and Unitarian variations.[96]

It is noteworthy that the "watered-down version of religion" represented by the statement of faith in the 1938–39 catalogue was the Apostles' Creed![97]

McClain and Hoyt quickly joined with other supporters[98] and established a new seminary, Grace Theological Seminary, which opened its doors in the fall of 1937 in the Akron (Ellet), Ohio, Brethren Church. The seminary moved to its present location, Winona Lake, Indiana, in 1939. The faculty was composed of McClain, Hoyt, and Homer A. Kent, and all but two of the current Ashland Seminary students relocated to the new seminary (the two students who remained were Kenneth Hulit and Chester Zimmerman).

A subplot that was overshadowed by the other events at the 1937 Board of Trustees meeting was the investigation of the college by the committee authorized by the 1936 Brethren General Conference. Because the Board of Trustees had notified the committee that its investigation had to await the invitation of the Board, the committee did not actually function until it received this invitation at the 1937 Board meeting. By this time, however, the committee had only one active member, William Schaffer; two members had resigned, one was considered ineligible because he was a member of the Board, and three others failed to participate. The final report was extremely critical of the college for

(1) the adoption of the new constitution with the controversial amendment, (2) the antagonism between the college and seminary, (3) unorthodox teaching at the college, (4) the printing of highly objectionable matter in the college paper, and (5) the friction between the administration of the college and the faculty of the seminary.[99]

Ashland supporters as well as the college itself strongly criticized the report as grossly biased. The college faulted Shaffer for his

(1) failure to interview any professors or administrators, though this courtesy was extended by the Board, (2) prejudiced selection of student witnesses without corroborating their testimony or examining their character, and (3) blanket indictment of professors without giving any opportunity for defense.[100]

The rejection of the report by a nearly evenly divided vote (a two-thirds vote had been called for) gave dramatic evidence to the significant rift that was occurring in the Brethren Church.

This work will not consider the rancorous developments in the Brethren Church that eventually led to a split in 1939 between the so-called Ashland Brethren and Grace Brethren, designations derived from allegiance to one or the other educational institutions.[101] But it is significant that this division had its genesis, to a major degree, in two radically different views of the college. Other issues would be drawn into the fray and strong personalities would polarize the conflict, but philosophical differences about the identity of the college and its relationship to the church were the original point of departure. McClain's fundamentalist perspective informed his view of education. He desired an educational institution that had uncompromising safeguards against liberalism and modernism. To this end he pushed for the enforcement of a conservative statement of faith that could be used to maintain the fidelity of faculty and the proper Christian conduct of students. The administration and Board of Trustees of the college, however, were committed to an open liberal arts education and sought to do all they could to preserve and advance this view of college.

> These developments were read by McClain and the Fundamentalist
> Brethren as an attempt to protect liberal sentiments. The record indicates,
> however, that continuing pressure from the Fundamentalist Brethren
> forced the college to do exactly what the Fundamentalists feared—seek
> greater support from non-Brethren sources due to decreasing financial
> backing from the church.[102]

These divergent positions and the realities connected with each created an ever widening chasm that eventually divided the Brethren Church.

The Philosophy and Christian Character of Ashland College

Throughout the presidencies of Jacobs and Anspach, the college remained avowedly Christian. Attendance at chapel services continued to be required throughout this period and students were urged to attend either the Brethren Church or their own denominational church in Ashland. Yet under both presidents this Christian emphasis was wed to the commitment to offer a quality liberal arts education.

Reflective of this dual emphasis are comments that Jacobs included in the brochure for the golden jubilee of the college in 1928. In a section entitled "Outlook and Ideals," Jacobs wrote:

> . . . in this day of religious uncertainty, Ashland means to represent the best in historic Christianity. It is our desire to hold to all that is sound in Christian idealism and at the same time to be progressive in intellectual fields. There is no good reason why a small denominational college should in any way be in the back-wash of educational interests and by proper control, such a college may be devotedly Christian and at the same time rigorously intellectual.

> . . . [No college can] discharge its most profound obligation to [its students] unless the teachers are motivated in both overt act and in philosophy of life, by ideals which mark close accord with Christianity. Nothing can take the place of sound scholarship on the one hand, nor of genuine piety of life on the other.[103]

In the 1934–35 college catalogue a statement appeared that reinforced this same dual focus. The first of three "Institutional Objectives" began: "To offer the opportunities to both men and women to gain a liberal [arts] education under influences which are frankly and avowedly Christian but not sectarian."[104]

In spite of Anspach's brief and turbulent presidency, he was the architect of a philosophy of education that would guide Ashland College through the remainder of the twentieth century. His "Ashland Plan," which first appeared in the 1936–37 catalogue, was built upon four basic principles. (1) **Growth and Development.** "We believe . . . that education can not be measured in terms of time nor the accumulation of units of credit, but must be evaluated in terms of individual development and growth. We are not so interested in subjects, as such, as we are in the stimulation to growth which the studying of certain subjects brings to the individual." (2) **Varying Rates of Growth.** Colleges must realize that individual students grow at varying rates based on unique personal differences. (3) **Experiences and Backgrounds.** Differences among students in their ability to deal with instructional materials derive from both inherited ability and differing experiences. "These differences need to be considered in planning a student's program." (4) **Supplementary Educational Agencies.** "The experiences obtained outside of the classroom are just as vital as those obtained within the classroom. Colleges have too long ignored the educational value of experiences obtained in industrial, religious, social, and professional groups."[105] These statements were buttressed with strategies that created an individualized approach to education. Components of this educational model were: personalized counseling; laying a broad educational foundation in the first two years of study and then adapting the remaining program to a student's progress; and enriching what took place in the classroom with exposure to the broader world of business, professional, and social life.

Revealing also is a list of five institutional objectives that further illuminate the emphases of Anspach's tenure. These objectives continued to appear nearly unchanged in college catalogues until the 1975–77 catalogue and in a revised form until the 1994–95 catalogue:

1. To assist students in the development of Christian character, refinement, sound scholarship, and Christian experience under influences which are frankly and avowedly Christian;
2. To aid men and women in organizing and unifying their experiences into a workable and satisfying philosophy of life;
3. To furnish ministers, missionaries, and religious workers, especially for the Brethren Church;
4. To provide a broad liberal education, for future specialization with a sufficient trend to the technical to acquaint the student with the practical pursuits of life.
5. To develop the whole personality of the individual student by coordinating and integrating the instructional process with the physical education, health service, extra-curricular, student guidance and religious programs.[106]

These statements of philosophy and purpose contain emphases that look both backward and forward, for they reflect qualities that drew upon the rich legacy of the college but they also portend new initiatives that would define the college from the 1950s on, especially the emphasis on the individual's holistic development.[107] Collectively, these and statements from Jacob's presidency reveal a strong commitment to maintaining the highest quality liberal arts education possible. Yet this education was intentionally imbued with Christian principles and with a concern for the multi-dimensional development of each student.

The Relationship of the College and the Brethren Church

Throughout the 1920s and 30s the college continued to maintain its close ties to the Brethren Church. Ashland College was the college of choice for

Brethren students; even Louis S. Bauman by the later 1920s supported the attendance of his son and other students from his Long Beach church at Ashland College. The Board of Trustees was predominantly composed of members of the Brethren Church. The church supported the college and seminary with its finances and with church members called to serve the college as administrators, faculty, and staff.

Yet changes were also occurring that were moving the college in directions more independent of the church. The drive for accreditation and additional financial support meant that the college increasingly sought resources outside the Brethren Church. Not only did the college look outside the church to a greater degree for funding, but it also did so for students, faculty, and staff. These trends would cause the Board of Trustees to expand representation of non-Brethren members. Alva McClain could justifiably comment in 1937 that the arts college had pushed denominational ties into the background.[108] This point is underscored by college catalogues from the 20s and 30s which rarely mention the Brethren Church. During Jacobs' presidency the only exceptions were in the discussions of church attendance (after the construction of Park Street Brethren Church, the former college church, in 1926) and of the college's history. In the latter case, the official

Park Street Brethren Church

name of the church does not appear; rather, mention is made of the Progressive branch of the German Baptist Brethren. Under Anspach, however, there are more explicit references to the Brethren Church in the catalogues, suggesting a desire to make people more aware of the denominational affiliation.[109] The overall impression is that the college, though continuing to recognize its historic and political ties to the church, was portraying itself as having an identity that was larger than the Brethren Church. This was especially true of the arts college. The seminary continued to understand itself, however, as primarily serving the Brethren Church.

Concluding Observations

During the 1920s and 30s subtle changes were occurring in the self-identity of the college. Perhaps no greater evidence of these shifts can be found than when the catalogue for 1929–30 is compared to preceding catalogues. Subtle, yet substantial, changes can be identified. (1) J. Allen Miller's title of Dean of the Seminary is omitted; he also is no longer Professor of Greek and New Testament but Professor of Philosophy (the former two titles are retained in the seminary bulletin for 1929). (2) The long-running statement that the college "is frankly Christian but not sectarian" now becomes the college "is thus, by its history, frankly Christian but its control is not purely sectarian." The relegation of this conviction to an aspect of its history may suggest that its continuation owes more to the college's heritage than to any sense of inward conviction. (3) The four departments of the college are listed as: Arts and Sciences, Theological (not Seminary, as in previous catalogues!), Education, and Music. (4) The section of the catalogue containing course descriptions categorized these courses alphabetically by discipline. In previous catalogues beginning in the 1922–23 academic year, Bible appeared as the first category and contained the following strong rationale for the centrality of the Bible in the college curriculum:

> The Bible is a recognized text-book in the college. Bible study is required of all students, for no one can be truly educated without a knowledge of the Book of books. While the courses are conducted in a scholarly way, the approach is reverent and practical. Faith is strengthened and devotion deepened.[110]

In the 1929–30 catalogue not only is the category of Bible dropped, to be replaced by such categories as Christian Education and Old Testament History and Theology (there is no listing for New Testament), but also the above statement about the place of the Bible in the curriculum is entirely omitted.

(5) Unlike previous catalogues there is not even a brief section devoted to the seminary in the college catalogue. It is true, however, that a supplement to the *Ashland College Bulletin* does focus entirely on the seminary for the 1928–29 and 1929–30 academic years. (6) Prior to the 1929–30 catalogue, in the section designated "The Needs of the College," which had been found in every catalogue beginning in the 1915–16 academic year, appeared this statement: "It has always regarded as its greatest work the preparation of young men for the Christian ministry . . ."[111] This statement is conspicuously missing in the 1929–30 catalogue.[112]

Taken together, these changes reflect a significant refocusing of the identity of the college. Whereas the college still thought of itself through much of the 1920s as a Christian liberal arts college,[113] one of whose central purposes was theological education, by the end of the decade the college recast itself as a liberal arts college with Christian influence, with theological training relegated to a distinct school, the seminary. These shifts mirror a growing distance between the arts college and seminary. Though hints of these developments can be seen in the teens and 20s, events in the later 1920s accelerated this redefinition of the mission and propose of the college. The college relied heavily on its reputation for teacher training for its financial survival; over half of its students were in this program. The tighter federal and state requirements in this field forced Jacobs to give more attention to the education of teachers. Even more importantly, the push for accreditation with the North Central Association, whose primary concern lay with the liberal arts and sciences, not theological training, caused Jacobs and the Board to focus attention on the arts college. This shift in emphasis occurred at the expense of the previous highlighting of theological education.

Events in the 1930s did not help the relationship between the arts college and the seminary. The expansion and upgrading of the seminary were, in reality, forced on Jacobs and the Board of Trustees by developments in Long Beach, California, in 1930. There was some resentment that the seminary program placed a financial drain on the college at a time of financial crisis due to the depression. Certainly the perceived spiritual haughtiness of some seminary professors exacerbated the situation.

In spite of this tension between the arts college and seminary that would set off a cascade of events that ultimately led to the division in the Brethren Church in 1939, there is reason to believe that a separate identity for both the college and seminary were necessary for the success of each. The college could not have survived if it had sought to exist supported only by the resources of the Brethren Church. In order to be a college that was positioned for the new era of state and federal regulation of teacher education and regional accreditation agencies, the college had no other recourse than to develop a vision beyond the Brethren Church. The liberal arts curriculum as well as the teacher education program of the college needed to be strengthened to compete in this new era. E. E. Jacobs and Charles Anspach understood this; Alva J. McClain did not.

If Ashland Theological Seminary were to become a graduate theological program that provided quality education for men and women preparing for varied forms of ministry, it was necessary that the seminary be upgraded. There was wisdom in McClain's recommendations that the seminary have a greater degree of autonomy from the college in matters of administration, budget, and location. A different location was especially important, though more recent developments have shown that the location did not have to be outside Ashland. Even J. Allen Miller had suggested in 1910 a separate building for the seminary in order to establish the seminary's own identity.[114] The differences in outlook between college and seminary students as well as between faculty in the arts college and those in the seminary were strong arguments for some measure of physical separation of the campuses. Likewise, faculty in the seminary differed significantly from their counterparts in the college in their degree of attachment to the Brethren Church. The necessity of preparing people for ministry in the Brethren Church was not a priority shared by many in the arts college. The need to nourish the spiritual life that is fundamental to seminary education can be at odds with the goal of a liberal arts education: providing exposure to the full range of the arts and sciences, developing reflective, self-critical thinkers, and fostering an objective, dispassionate perspective towards objects of study. McClain understood this; Jacobs did not, though Anspach was sympathetic to some of the seminary concerns.

Ironically, these somewhat divergent visions of Ashland College both find support in the college's foundational documents of the nineteenth century. The liberal arts perspective championed by Jacobs carries on the spirit and vision of the original charter of 1878. The seminary is fulfilling the sacred calling of the college set forth in the 1888 charter of the college. It is intriguing that Jacobs, in reflecting on these two charters, gives subtle emphasis to the original charter:

> If the constitution of 1888 and the incorporation papers of that date are compared with those of the original founders of the institution, 1878, it will become clear that Ashland College was founded as a college of liberal

arts and so continued up till after its control had passed into the hands of the Brethren Church, when it was decided that it should also serve as a place for the training of Christian ministers.[115]

Clara Worst Miller quotes the above statement word-for-word. But she changes the whole thrust of the statement by adding one more sentence: "And this has since been regarded as one of Ashland College's major functions."[116] Jacobs and Miller clearly reveal where their primary, though differing, allegiance lies.

Another irony of this historical period is that the Brethren Church and Ashland Theological Seminary are indebted to the Fundamentalist Brethren in several areas. First, the Brethren Church may have had an ongoing liberal presence and controversy had not the Fundamentalist Brethren pushed for "The Message of the Brethren Ministry." Bauman makes the fascinating comment in 1928 that "people in the east [those who would later be called the Ashland Brethren] are now admitting that in the past it [Bauman's 'fighting blood'] saved our Church from Modernism."[117] Second, the proposed creation of a seminary in the facilities of Bauman's Long Beach church in 1930 spurred Ashland College to develop a graduate level program at Ashland Theological Seminary sooner than otherwise would have occurred. Given Jacob's priorities, it is doubtful whether a graduate level seminary would have been developed during his presidency. Third, the primary statement of faith used by the Brethren Church until 1983, "The Message of the Brethren Ministry," and the statement of faith still used by Ashland Theological Seminary both owe their genesis to the Fundamentalist Brethren. Though relations between the Ashland and Grace Brethren groups remained strained for some sixty years, open dialogue has begun during the new millennium that betokens a more healthy relationship between these two branches of the Brethren movement.

Chapter 5

Rising from the Ashes: Renewed Vision for the Future (1940–1963)

Introduction

The devastating division with the Grace Brethren in 1939, followed immediately by World War II, created a lingering malaise in the Brethren Church that also affected the college and especially the seminary. With student numbers already significantly depleted with the beginning of Grace Theological Seminary, Ashland Theological Seminary's enrollment continued to suffer from the drain of young men created by the war. The war years affected the college's enrollment figures as well. Just as the college began to realize a new sense of direction in the early 1950s, the fire that destroyed Founders Hall cast a pall of disillusionment in many quarters of the college and church. Yet from the ashes of the building that had been the centerpiece of the college rose a new building whose very existence symbolized a new sense of vision for the college. This renewed optimism born of adversity set the stage for remarkable growth at the college during the later 1950s and throughout the 1960s. The success of Ashland College, to a significant degree, served as the catalyst for a new vision for the seminary in the 1960s and even contributed to the emergence of a new sense of purpose in the Brethren Church.

Overcoming a Spirit of Apathy and Defeatism in the College and Church

The experiences of the college and the church remarkably parallel one another during the 1940s and early 50s. This is to be expected because of the close ties that the two entities continued to have during this period. The deep emotional scars left by the division with the Grace Brethren especially affected the Brethren Church. The potential for healing in the church was interrupted by the outbreak of World War II, when many young men, who otherwise could have stepped into leadership positions at all levels of the church, served in the military. A shortage of ministerial recruits, a lack of visionary leadership, and general discouragement at the local, district, and national levels of the Brethren Church led to a lingering period of "defeatism, lethargy, gloom"[1] in the church. It would not be until the later 1950s and especially the early 1960s that a renewed spirit of hope and vision would begin to oust the malaise of twenty years. Several of the leaders responsible for this changed perspective were connected to the college and seminary.

Ashland College was facing its own challenges during the 1940s and early 50s. Any progress during the first half of the 1940s was severely

E. Glenn Mason

stymied by the effects of World War II. The president during this period was E. Glenn Mason, who followed Anspach as president in 1939. Mason (1882–1956) came from Brethren roots in Wayne County, Ohio. He attended Ashland College, Defiance College (B.A. 1911), and Ohio State University (M.A. 1925). After working as a teacher and administrator in public schools, he began a long career of service to Ashland College as a professor of history (1925–30), dean (1930–39), president (1939–45), and professor of education and history (1945–52).

The war affected every aspect of college life. Total enrollment shrunk from 725 students in the 1938–39 academic year (Anspach's last year) to a low of 344 students in 1944–45 (actual enrollment in the collegiate day program had shrunk to 112 students in 1943–44). The decrease resulted not only from men serving in the military but also from the allure of high wages in industry (these factors also affected the retention of faculty). At one point as many as 90% of the students were women during the war years. In fact, in 1943 the college made a special effort to recruit women to help stabilize enrollment.[2] Though these factors placed severe strains on the college's finances, the institution weathered the challenge without significantly increasing its indebtedness or tapping the endowment funds. Obviously, student life was disrupted by the realities of the war. Football was discontinued after the 1941 season; it resumed in 1945. Homecoming was replaced by an event dubbed "Hilltop Holiday." May Day continued to be observed, though sometimes with an all-women court.[3] Though there was lengthy discussion by the Board about authorizing a military unit on the campus, no unit was established. Apparently the adverse reaction that occurred within the church over Furry's support of such a unit in World War I was too fresh in the minds of the Board.[4]

Pastoral Pranks II

Over the years the college buildings have had some unusual visitors. Before the days of lawnmowers, goats played the important role of keeping the grass on the campus down to an acceptable height. However, every so often a goat would find his or her way into Founders Hall, where the animal would be found tethered to a faculty member's desk.

Two of the most unusual guests, however, were ushered into college buildings by future Brethren pastors. J. Ray Klingensmith (B.A. 1931; B.Th. 1934) was the mastermind behind one of these pranks. Klingensmith was one of six or seven men from Louis Bauman's Long Beach Brethren Church who attended Ashland College at about the same time in the late 1920s and early 1930s. Bauman's boys, as they were called, were a very close-knit group, comprising many of the gospel teams that ministered to Brethren churches during this time. They also

(continued)

had a knack for getting into all kinds of adventures and mis-adventures. On one occasion they went outside of Ashland late one night and "borrowed" a cow from a farmer. They transported the bovine to the Library (Miller Hall). Some of them were in front of the cow, pulling on a halter, while others took up the rear. They somehow got her up on the third floor of Miller Hall that night. The next morning it was difficult to know who was doing more bellowing—the cow or the librarian who encountered not only the cow but quite a few "piles" as well.

The president, Edwin E. Jacobs, called four or five of the California crew into his office. Though he was well known for his own mischievous nature, he was no-nonsense on this occasion. He gave them half-an-hour to get the cow back to her home. The pranksters protested vociferously that they had nothing to do with it, but Jacobs knew he had the right culprits, in spite of their claims to the contrary. They obliged in taking the cow back, but they found it far more difficult getting the cow down the stairs than up.

Another unusual visitor found its way into Founders Hall. The instigator of this prank was Milton Robinson (B.A. 1942). A classmate of his, Archie Martin, had a Bantam auto, a small car with only a brief production run. One night Milt and some others got together and took it up the steps of Old Founders and put it in front of the auditorium. Milt then went back to the house where he was living and went to sleep. The next day he was in the library and Archie came up to him and said, "Hey, someone stole my car! You wouldn't know anything about it, would you?" Milt responded, "Why are you asking me?" Milt, who quipped in the interview that he didn't believe in lying, told Archie that the car was where it was supposed to be when he came home for the night at 11:00. Of course Milt didn't tell Archie that he was up at 1:00 in the morning pulling off the caper. Archie querried: "Do you think someone stole it or is just playing a joke on me?" Milt assured him that he was sure someone was just playing a joke and that he would find it somewhere. Later that morning Milt saw Archie driving his Bantam down the walk from Founders Hall. Preseminary students could enjoy a prank just as much as their fellow students and were at times at the center of these less serious moments of college life.

Donald Rinehart, interview by author, 1 November 2006, Ashland, OH and Milton Robinson, interview by author, 22 July 2004, Ashland, OH.

Even the curriculum was affected. In order to help students accelerate their college program prior to entering military service, the college made summer sessions an integral part of the college program. The content of traditional courses was altered and new courses were added in order to be responsive to the national and international crisis. Graduation was even moved forward to accommodate the departure of seniors for the military. All of these modifications occurred, however, without lowering the academic standards of the college.[5] Other curricular changes that took place during Mason's tenure were the introduction in 1939 of evening classes for those seeking coursework in education and business and the phasing out of Saturday classes by the 1941–42 academic year.[6] Mason also received Board approval in 1943 for the beginning of extension work. The first extension site, Mansfield, was a harbinger of things to come at the college in the latter half of the century when the development of extensions helped to spur significant growth.[7]

The college acquired a fifth building in 1940. Mrs. T. W. Miller, Sr., donated a stately mansion on Center Street to the college to honor Mr. and Mrs. F. E. Myers. Mrs. Miller and the Myers family desired that the home might encourage youth to greater enjoyment of music and of life. Very appropriately the home was called the Mr. and Mrs. F. E. Myers Memorial Music Building and housed the college's exceptional music program until the completion of the Arts and Humanities building in 1969. It was eventually sold in 1972 to the Good Shepherd Home and razed in 1975.

When Mason returned to the faculty, another faculty member, Raymond W. Bixler, became acting president in 1945 and then president from 1946 until 1948. Bixler (1897–1990) had studied at Mt. Union College (B.A. 1921), Harvard University, Columbia University (M.A. 1924), the University of Chicago, and Ohio State University (Ph.D. 1929). He began his lengthy service to Ashland College in 1929 as a professor of history; he served as the dean of the college (1943–45) and, after stepping down from the presidency, returned to the faculty as a professor of history until his retirement in 1972. Bixler was faced with another challenge created by World War II: the problems associated with the influx of significant numbers of

F. E. Myers Memorial Music Building

Raymond W. Bixler

veterans into college life after the war. The following enrollments for the first semester of the 1946–47 academic year are quite revealing both in regard to the drop in enrollment during the war years and the burgeoning enrollment in the aftermath of the war:

Class of 1947	29
Class of 1948	51
Class of 1949	77
Class of 1950	364[8]

The return of veterans to the college ranks also radically shifted the male-female ratio at the college. While the student body was disproportionately composed of women during the war years, just the opposite was true in the years immediately following the end of the war. In the 1949–50 academic year, for example, men composed about 73% of the student body.[9]

The flood of veterans taking advantage of the G. I. Bill in the years immediately following 1945 was a financial boon to colleges, especially after the exceptionally lean years of 1942–45. But there were also unique chal-

Glenn Haller Court

lenges. Veterans brought with them a lifestyle often punctuated by coarse language and openness to smoking and drinking, behaviors that in the late 1940s and 50s were generally frowned upon. Housing also was a major problem. The federal government eased some of the housing pressure by making available eleven housing units (Quonset huts) that were placed on property owned by the college on the west side of King Road. This small complex was named Glenn Haller Court, in honor of the son of Glenn Haller, Sr., the mayor of Ashland, who was killed in action during World War II. It provided housing for 24 single men and 18 families, with priority given to veterans. Rather appropriately it was popularly dubbed Vetsville.

In 1946 Bixler expressed a desire to step down from the presidency. The Search Committee was highly impressed by a young man from the New Lebanon, Ohio, Brethren Church who was currently working on his Ph.D. Glenn L. Clayton (1910–2006) had received his education at Miami University (B.S. 1932) and Ohio State University (M.A. 1937; Ph.D. 1948). He was encouraged to apply for the presidency and received a call to this office in December 1947. He began his duties on 1 September 1948 after completing his Ph.D. in March.[10]

The Story of the Eagle's Nest

Not until the 1940s did Ashland College have a student center for both men and women. The men had been privileged to have a lounge set aside for their exclusive use in 1937 when Frederick L. and Mary Estelle Parker donated funds for the creation of the Parker Men's Lounge in the southwest corner of the basement of Founders Hall. There is a bit of a story behind the Parkers, who lived in Westfield, Massachusetts. Mary Estelle was the daughter of F. E. Myers, the outstanding industrialist and philanthropist, who, with his brothers, had founded the F. E. Myers and Brothers Company in Ashland. Frederick Parker was a member of the Parker family which owned Parker Brothers, the company that had made a significant fortune by the late 1930s with such board games as Pit, Flinch, Rook, and Monopoly (Parker Brothers had also created the very first jigsaw puzzle).

During World War II, with so few men on campus, the students appealed for a place where all students could socialize. In the *Ashland Collegian* dated 24 March 1944, the origins of the first student union are recounted:

"At a cry from A. C. students for an all-student recreation room (personal hang-out), the Student Council conceived the idea of a Student Union. This union would be, literally, a big room adorned with comfortable chairs, ping-pong tables, gay decorations, a classy bar where soft drinks, sandwiches, and other knick-knacks are sold, a radio, and STUDENTS. It would be a place where all fun-loving students of A. C. could gather to visit, or eat, or get in on the latest gossip, or simply loaf. Through the efforts of the faculty and the push of a group of students themselves, the A. C. Eds and Co-eds will now own and manage such a room. It was originally planned to convert the social room into a student union, but the idea was conceived to take over the boys' lounge instead, since it was much more conveniently located and there were so few boys on campus."

The commandeered Parker Lounge was transformed into the Eagle's Nest and had its grand opening 24 March 1944. The concession was stated, however, that when the men returned to the campus at the conclusion of the war, the room would revert back to a men's lounge and another suitable location for the student union would need to be found. There is one further bit of information that sheds light on the naming of the student union. The article cited above notes: "No contest [for naming the room] has been opened because a name has already been suggested and accepted as official—'The Eaglets' Nest.'" Of course, the official name actually became the "Eagle's Nest," but this statement leaves out some important details. Consideration was given at first to locating the student union on the third floor of Founders Hall. Ellen Stoffer, the sophomore class president at the time and aunt of the author, suggested that if that were to be the location, the student union should be called the "Aerie," since that was the name of an eagle's nest. This location was felt to be impractical, however, both for safety reasons and because of the numerous flights of stairs to the third floor. When the Parker Lounge became the leading contender for the location, Stoffer suggested that the student union should simply be called the "Eagle's Nest." The name immediately stuck.

The first Eagle's Nest had a short life. It was closed in December 1944. The causes of its demise, according to the *Collegian*, were "the lack of workers, dishonesty, and the use of it by a few as a 'memorial to romance.'" Eventually, it was reopened under the watchful and efficient care of the Y.W.C.A. and remained under its supervision into the 1950s. A second "grand opening" of the Eagle's Nest was announced 6 January 1949, after some renovations were made to the room. Likewise, an additional room that apparently was adjacent to the Eagle's Nest was cleaned and remodeled between 1950 and 1951 largely with student labor and with funds raised by the students themselves. This is the room that Joseph Shultz may have referred to as the "old coal bin"

(continued)

in his memoirs that students of his era cleaned for use as the student union.

There have been three buildings that have served as the home of the Eagle's Nest since the early 1950s. The first building set aside for student use was the Student Union, now designated the Kates Center for Family and Consumer Sciences, which was dedicated 20 August 1954. With the completion of the present library in 1970, the former library was renovated into the Patterson Student Center; it was ready for its new use in January 1975. This building is now the Patterson Instructional Technology Center. The newest location of the Eagle's Nest is the Hawkins-Conard Student Center, completed in 1995. The Eagle's Nest is still a congregating place for students, though its roomy and high-tech setting is in stark contrast to its humble beginnings as an appropriated room in the basement of Old Founders.

"They Park, In Parker Lounge," *Ashland Collegian* 16 (18 November 1937), 1; "Grand Opening of Student Union Tonight," *Ashland Collegian* 22 (24 March 1944), 1; "Student Union Opened on College Campus," *Ashland Collegian* 22 (14 April 1944), 1; "'Elbow-Grease,' Paint and Wax Brighten 'Nest,'" *Ashland Collegian* 27 (12 January 1949), 1; "'Eagles Nest' Has Gone Far in Past Seven Years," *Ashland Collegian* 29 (19 January 1951), 1; Ray and Ellen Sluss, interview by author, 8 October 2005, Ashland, OH; and Joseph R. Shultz, *Ashland: From College to University* ([Ashland, OH]: Landoll, Inc., n.d.), 69–70.

Clayton inherited a college that was facing a number of challenges. The most significant were overcoming a spirit of apathy, addressing a lack of unified purpose created by competing interests, fostering greater acceptance for the college in the community, and dealing with the discouragement of running an educational institution with limited financial resources.[11] Clayton brought exceptional administrative abilities to his work. Most important, he maintained a bold spirit of optimism, even in the midst of adversity, that was contagious. He saw possibilities where others saw only reason for despair. His visionary leadership over the next twenty-nine years would lead the college from a small, church related college, drawing students primarily from the Brethren Church and from Ashland and surrounding counties, to a medium-sized liberal arts college, whose students came from throughout the northeastern United States.[12] The college would also transition from primarily a commuter college to a residential college.

Probably the defining moment of Clayton's presidency occurred in the aftermath of the devastating fire that destroyed Founders Hall 19 October 1952. The conflagration consumed not only the facility that housed a significant proportion of the college's classrooms, offices, and meeting rooms (some were available in Miller Hall), but also the glimmer of hope held by a growing number that the college might not just survive but begin to thrive. Clayton had been able to make some important advances during his first few years: raising $60,000 in a brief amount of time to meet the State Fire Marshall's demand to remove the open stairways in Founders and Allen

Glenn L. Clayton

Halls or close the school;[13] developing better relations with the Ashland community; establishing greater name recognition for the college in state educational, business, and political circles and with the North Central Association.[14] Through the fundraising efforts of the Woman's Missionary Society of the Brethren Church, Clayton was also able to construct the Memorial Chapel at the corner of College Avenue and King Road. Dedicated at the Brethren Church's General Conference in August 1952, the chapel was symbolic of the continuing close ties that existed between the college and church.[15] But all this progress seemed to many to have been buried in the ashes of Founders Hall.

When Clayton first arrived at the scene, former president William D. Furry expressed to Clayton the feelings of many as they watched the losing battle of the firefighters: "It's all over now. This is the end."[16] Yet the Founders Hall fire gave birth to a new vision for the college that was first glimpsed the morning after the fire. Clayton called a campus meeting to update the situation and to gather suggestions of what could be done. Clayton shares what happened when he declared the meeting open.

> The response was electric and spontaneous. Nothing I might have done by planning could have been more encouraging to me and to all present that

Memorial Chapel (rededicated as the Jack and Deb Miller Chapel in January 2007)

morning. Students offered to stay on campus and to help with the cleanup, faculty volunteered their help, and townspeople offered machinery, pumps, electric motors and labor too.[17]

The day following this meeting an added morale booster was given by the surprise visit of the Governor of Ohio, Frank J. Lausche, who had been the college's commencement speaker in June 1951. He was especially impressed by the dedication of the students in the cleanup and salvage effort. Indeed the enthusiasm of the student body in the face of the daunting challenges caused by the fire served as an inspiration for the entire college community. One of the most propitious elements for the survival of the college, however, was the completion of Memorial Chapel just a few months before the fire. It would provide temporary classrooms to permit the continuation of classes with only minimal interruption.[18]

Clayton's leadership abilities were demonstrated in the aftermath of the fire. He faced competing agendas in the campus community and the Board of Trustees about what should be done with the Founders Hall site. He especially found frustrating the defeatist attitude of some on the Board. In the midst of these challenges, he developed deeper ties with some trusted members on the

Board, notably Harvey Amstutz, George Ronk, Myron Kem, and Julius Lutz, and with outstanding leaders with ties to the city and county of Ashland, particulary Charles F. Kettering, to forge a new vision for the college.

The Transformation of Ashland College

Clayton epitomized the leadership qualities of the "Builder" generation who came to the fore after World War II. He gathered around himself other quality administrators who became partners in fulfilling his vision. He developed an excellent working relationship with the Board of Trustees that, for the most part, shared his goals and dreams. His entrepreneurial gifts oversaw an aggressive construction and financial program that added nearly thirty buildings to the campus. He established creative, new programs that partnered with business, economic, and educational communities at the city, state, and national levels. He had the unique ability to marshal the resources necessary for realizing his vision for the college.

Clayton developed bold initiatives that guided the college during the 1950s and 60s. His "Facing the Fifties" plan was inaugurated at the Board of Trustees meeting on 12 April 1950. Integral to this plan was the "Ten-Year Program for the Development of Ashland College." This program had six major goals:

> (1) Strengthen and encourage the Christian objectives of the college; (2) Broaden the base of financial support and increase giving in all sectors; (3) Revise the curriculum to meet the needs of the individual student and improve course content to make it more responsive to present-day needs. Develop a two-year "general education" course and provide career interests in both two- and four-year programs. Work for greater emphasis upon summer courses, evening school and specialized areas like home management, business and radio; (4) Plan and provide for the construction of new buildings to include the new chapel, a men's dormitory, a women's dormitory, a science building and an industrial arts building. . . . (5) Encouragement of faculty by providing an incentive of $1000 for completion of the doctorate and an escalating salary schedule; and (6) Development of the seminary.[19]

The decade witnessed significant progress on all of these goals.

At the Board of Trustees meeting on 17 August 1961, Clayton unveiled his "Program for Quality" initiative that sought to give direction to the college for the next decade. Building on the success of the previous "Ten-Year Program," this initiative attempted to vitalize the liberal arts at Ashland College while at the same time strengthening certain areas of specialization. Mentioned among the latter fields were theology, teacher training, business and economics, human development, and the fine arts. Physical education and athletics would receive special attention, student recruitment would be refined with emphasis on the individual needs of students, faculty assistance and encouragement of advanced studies would be provided, and development of the Seminary would move ahead. Anticipating growth in number of students and quality of work offered, the announced "Program for Quality" called for financing and construction of at least six new buildings, both for housing and instruction.

It was an ambitious program designed to upgrade all departments. Its objective was to convert the relatively unknown regional school of 1961 into a nationally known and respected college by 1970.[20]

Clayton's visionary leadership turned most of these dreams into reality by the 1970s, though the college would still struggle for name recognition and respect outside of northern Ohio into the 1980s and even the 1990s.

The centerpiece of Clayton's educational philosophy was an emphasis on the individual student, for which he acknowledged indebtedness to Anspach's "Ashland Plan." In fact, specific reference to and the general outline of the "Ashland Plan" continued to appear in college catalogues through the 1962–63 catalogue.[21] Clayton sought to make Ashland a place where the worth of each individual student was emphasized. Unlike other educational institutions which almost reveled in their high "washout" rate, due to their extremely high academic expectations, or which lost students due to the hazards of their size and impersonal educational process, Ashland sought to "attract a type of student who was scholastically capable but whose personal interests would respond to a quieter and more sympathetic atmosphere."[22] This unique approach to education became epitomized in the slogan "Ac'cent on the Individual." The phrase was coined by Richard Topper, an Ashland College alumnus who volunteered his services as a public relations specialist to the college for a dollar a year. The "Ac'cent Program," launched in 1964, gave new focus to the "Program for Quality" initiative and became the guiding philosophy throughout the rest of Clayton's presidency. The graphic that symbolized this philosophy was a hexagon with the words "Ac'cent on the Individual" cutting through its sides. Each of the six sides signified a unique thrust of the program: continued strengthening of the liberal arts environment; development of a capable teaching faculty; cultivation of target locations for student recruitment and provision for individualized student counseling (Ashland called itself "the

The "Ac'cent on the Individual" logo

college that cares"); commitment to being a respected unit of society in relation to the church, business, family, and government; development of an
adequate physical plant and equipment; and cultivation of adequate financial resources.[23] This individualized approach to education, originally
crafted by Anspach and honed by Clayton, continues to be a foundational
commitment of Ashland's educational program to the present.

The appeal of Clayton's educational philosophy to prospective students and their parents was a significant reason for the rapid growth of the
college until the early 1970s. Equally important, however, was his aggressive expansion of the physical plant, which positioned the college well for
riding the cresting waves of both the burgeoning population of Baby
Boomers and the commitment of their parents' generation to provide a college education for their children. The remarkable growth of the college
through the end of Clayton's presidency in 1977 can be seen by the following fall enrollment figures:

1950	615
1955	811
1960	1238
1965	2036
1970	2987
1976	2135

The faculty grew apace with this growing enrollment. In 1950 there were 57 faculty members; of these two were retired and only 19 were full-time teachers or administrators. In 1960 there were 72 with faculty status; 56 were teaching faculty and one was retired. In 1970 there were 257 total faculty; the teaching faculty numbered 200 and administrative faculty numbered 48. Throughout this period the percentage of faculty with a doctoral degree continued to increase.

The Clayton years saw a radical transformation of Ashland College. He had inherited a small liberal arts college with very close ties to the Brethren Church. The college drew the majority of its students from the counties surrounding Ashland County. It was essentially a commuter college. By the end of his presidency Ashland College was a medium size college with the beginning of graduate programs that would, in time, change the college into a university. The aggressive building program included numerous dormitories that made possible the shift in the college from a commuter to a residential campus. Though Clayton maintained a personal commitment to strong ties to the Brethren Church and to a Christian foundation for college life, changes occurring in the student body and faculty would gradually erode both of these historic foundations.

The Christian Character of Ashland College and College-Brethren Church Ties

In the years between 1940 and 1963 college documents continue to reflect the commitment to a Christian foundation for the college. Particularly during the first half of Clayton's presidency, the college is regularly referred to as a Christian college.[24] Chapel was still compulsory throughout these years. Chapel was held daily at least through the 1955–56 academic year. During the post-war years with the swelling student population and before the Memorial Chapel was built in 1952, student classes alternated attendance at chapel, with all students attending the Wednesday chapel held at Park Street Brethren Church. Attendance at three chapels per week was required of all students during this period.

Clayton in his presidential reports regularly underscored his commitment to maintaining a strong Christian emphasis at the college. Note the following statements from 1952, 1954, and 1961 respectively:

> As a Christian College of Liberal Arts we have a definite responsibility to keep Jesus Christ as the center of our total effort. Believing that all moral

worth as well as any effective educative process develops richly and freely in a Christian atmosphere and philosophy, we must strive to incorporate it into all classroom teaching as well as the extra-curricular activities sponsored by the College.[25]

. . . the seventy-five years of distinguished and loyal Christian higher education have been most worth while. The liberal arts have been taught at Ashland College with dignity, authority and within a framework of conservative Christianity. This, we are convinced has been good.

This quality, backed and endorsed by the Brethren Church, must remain at the core of whatever development Ashland College undertakes, for it is the essence of the college. Alteration of it would remove the character and real historic reason for an Ashland College and leave the school without a purpose.[26]

The need to encourage this interest [the interest of the Brethren Church in Ashland College] in every possible way remains as great today as ever before. Education without the steadying influence of the church or without the positive conviction of the centrality of Jesus Christ in all knowledge lacks purpose and meaning which make it vital.[27]

Clayton embedded these convictions in his initiative for the 1950s: "The Ten-Year Program." The first major objective of the "Ten-Year Program" was "to assist students in the development of sound scholarship, character, and refinement under influences which are frankly and avowedly Christian and to provide opportunities for Christian experience."[28] Clayton had already initiated in 1949 regular Christian Emphasis Programs that brought leading Christian figures to the campus. The purpose of these programs was to enrich the spiritual lives of both students and faculty. Faculty were also encouraged to bring a Christian emphasis and perspective to interaction with students in and out of the classroom.[29]

Significantly, Clayton's bold initiative for the 1960s, "Building Together for Quality," which he unveiled in 1961, originally omitted any mention of enhancing the spiritual life of the college. It did, however, single out the theology program as one of three areas for special attention.[30] Interestingly, two years later Clayton indicated that one of the seven major objectives of this initiative was the "fostering of an honest, personal spiritual experience integrated with a good liberal arts education."[31] But what took center stage was now "a determined effort to vitalize the liberal arts as the basic program of Ashland College."[32] Though subtle, this shift to the academic side of the life of the college was reinforced by Clayton in comments he made in his 1960 presidential report: "Ashland College should continue to cherish her role as a college—a Christian college—but, above all, a quality institution where the quest for learning is looked upon with honor at all times. Only in this way can she continue to justify her existence as a liberal arts institution . . ."[33] This elevation of the quest for learning and the liberal arts identity of the college would, over time, marginalize the spiritual side of the college's character.

The relationship of the college and the Brethren Church during the presidencies of Mason and Bixler had remained cordial, but gauged by both giving and the number of Brethren students attending the college, there was definitely room for improvement. The Educational Day offering raised in Brethren churches for support of the college continued to be lackluster throughout the 1940s. Brethren enrollment rode the same war-related rollercoaster as the general enrollment of the college. From a low of 34 Brethren students in 1943–44, the ranks of Brethren students swelled to a high of 99 in 1946–47. Mason especially complained about the failure of the church to take seriously its obligations to the college. All this was to change during the first part of Clayton's presidency as the relationship between the college and church experienced a renaissance.

Clayton made a concerted effort to court the favor of the Brethren Church. As an active layman in the church, he was aware of the workings of the church and the potential for financial support and students within the church. The construction of Memorial Chapel, sparked by the Woman's Missionary Society, helped to rekindle the interest of the church in the college. The church also responded to the challenge faced by the college in the aftermath of the fire that destroyed Founders Hall. Between 1950 and 1955 $475,000 was raised in the church in cash and pledges on behalf of the college. The increasing commitment to the college also translated into record numbers of Brethren attending the college. Though Brethren enrollment in the college was around 50 in the mid-1950s, significant growth was achieved by the end of the decade. There were 63 Brethren students in the college during the 1957–58 academic year, 82 in 1958–59, and 96 in 1959–60. In 1961–62 there were 123 Brethren students enrolled in the various divisions of the college.

This remarkable turnaround in college-church relations was the result of closer cooperation between both institutions. National Youth Directors of the Brethren Church, notably Charles Munson and Phil Lersch, were active on the Ashland College campus, counseling and encouraging both Brethren and non-Brethren students. Virgil Meyer, the Director of Church Relations (retitled Director of Religious Affairs) for the college from 1956 to 1972, played an especially significant role in improving relations. He publicized the work of the college in local Brethren churches and district conferences and camps. He began sponsoring Brethren College Days for prospective Brethren students in the late 1950s. This program helped contribute to a record freshman class enrollment of 43 Brethren students in 1960. In addition to these links, the Board in 1951 approved offering children of Brethren pastors a 40% reduction in tuition. The Brethren Ministerial Association held its annual Pastors Conference in the new chapel twice during the 1950s. Clayton also served on the Central Planning and Coordinating Committee of the Brethren Church as the representative from the Board of Trustees. In this role Clayton was able to keep the denominational leadership apprized of the status of the college. All these efforts, especially those of Meyer, caused Clayton in 1960 to speak of the "closer understanding and mutual service between the college and the Brethren Church."[34]

The optimistic spirit that pervaded the college in the late 1950s and throughout the 1960s had an important impact on the church as well. Clayton was well aware of the significant role that the college should play in training young people for lay and pastoral service in the Brethren Church.[35]

Virgil E. Meyer

But education was only one of the roles that the college could play in the life of the denomination. A host of other benefits resulted from Ashland College serving as *the* college for Brethren youth: life-long friendships between Brethren students who did not know each other prior to attending the college were forged; many Brethren found their spouses at the college; the opportunity to serve on gospel teams gave Brethren students experience in leading worship, acquainted them with laity and pastors in local Brethren congregations, and helped them to develop deeper commitments to involvement in and service to the Brethren Church. These gospel team trips to Brethren congregations throughout the United States also helped to publicize the work of the college and to recruit Brethren young people for the college.

The college played a significant role in helping the church rebound from the trauma of the 1939 division and the hardships posed by the dearth of visionary leadership in the 1940s and 50s. The college, through such faculty and administrators as Glenn Clayton, Leslie Lindower, Delbert Flora, Charles Munson, J. Ray Klingensmith, and Virgil Meyer, sought to serve the church in a host of ways: providing educational opportunities for pastors; filling pulpits whenever possible; serving as mentors for Brethren youth; challenging young people to consider full-time Christian service; serving as speakers at local, district, and national church functions; modeling by word and example a spirit of optimism for the future of the church. Clayton commented in 1955 that the college had become "a constant and influential force for unity and Christian growth within the church."[36] Certainly the remarkable growth of the seminary beginning in the 1960s under the leadership of Joseph Shultz would accelerate the new spirit of hope that was taking root in the church.

In spite of all of these advances in the relationship of the college and church, important, often subtle, changes were occurring. The Brethren complexion of the college was diminishing due to a number of factors. Despite increasing numbers of Brethren students, the percentage of Brethren in the student body was dropping. Brethren enrollment had consistently run between 20% and 33% of the student body in the 1930s and up to 1945. The post-war flood of veterans in the second half of the 1940s and the more aggressive recruitment program that began in the 1950s swelled the non-Brethren student population. Between 1945 and 1955 Brethren enrollment was generally between 14% and 20% of the student body; until 1962 Brethren enrollment was generally between 10% and 15% of the student body but dropped below 10% in 1963. This percentage would continue to decrease until Brethren formed only 2.6% of the undergraduate student body in fall 2006. The difficulty of finding qualified Brethren faculty members also led to a diminishing percentage of faculty from the Brethren Church. Whereas about 35% of the college faculty (not including the seminary faculty) were Brethren in 1950, by 1960, this number had dropped to about 21%; in 1980 Brethren faculty were only 4.2% of the total faculty.

Even the Board of Trustees had a lower percentage of Brethren members in 1959 than it did in 1937. Several changes to the composition of the Board had occurred between these years to reflect the broader constituencies of the college. A significant majority of the Board of Trustees continued to be Brethren in 1959 (a minimum of 34 of the 48 seats on the Board), but the percentage of Brethren on the Board dropped from 79% after the restructuring of the Board in 1937 to 71% in 1959.[37]

One of the most noteworthy changes that occurred in the relationship of the college and the church was how the official relationship between the two institutions was described in college catalogues. Throughout all of the 1940s and 50s and until the 1961–62 catalogue, the statement appears that "the institution is controlled and owned by the Brethren Church." Intriguingly, the Prudential Committee of the Board of Trustees had used this understanding in 1951 to avoid dealing with a call by students to allow square dancing on the campus. The committee cited a provision in the *Administrative Handbook* of the college that indicated that "the college is under the direction of the Brethren Church." In the 1962–63 catalogue the long-standing statement is significantly changed: "The institution is governed by a board of trustees composed of representatives of the seven conferences of the Brethren Church, of the city of Ashland, of the Alumni Association and of the territory at large. . . . The college is affiliated with the Brethren Church . . ." This change also coincides with what may have been the last reference, in 1961, to Ashland College as a Christian college in the official documents of the college in the Board minutes.[38] Thereafter Ashland College is generally referred to as a church-affiliated or church-related college in college documents. For example, a revised history and purpose section in the 1963–64 catalogue states that the college is affiliated with the Brethren Church, but there is no mention of the governance of the school.[39] Though the new statements are truer to the legal reality, there were undoubtedly those in the Brethren Church who still felt that the church controlled and owned the college. The legal fiction of the church owning the college was added to the catalogue in 1938 in the aftermath of the division with the Grace Brethren to counter criticism that the church was losing control of the college, especially when the composition of the Board was changed in 1937.[40]

Taken together, these shifts in the college and church relationship point to a diminishing influence by the church on the college. Though relationships between the two were still harmonious through 1963, there would be escalating criticism of the college's direction during the remainder of the 1960s and throughout most of the 1970s. Clayton himself acknowledged the difficulty of upholding commitments to the Christian faith and the ideals of the Brethren Church while at the same time strengthening the liberal arts perspective at the college.[41] Several developments in the college in the 1960s heightened the tension between the commitment to the liberal arts on one hand and strengthening the Christian life of the campus and the relationship with the Brethren Church on the other. Notable was Clayton's commitment to focus on the liberal arts as the basic program of Ashland College in his "Building Together for Quality" initiative in the 1960s. Also contributing to this tension was the diminishing percentages of Brethren students, faculty, and Board members. It can also be argued that as long as the seminary remained on the college campus there was a physical and psychological reminder of the importance of the Christian and Brethren identity of the institution. With the removal of the seminary to its own campus in 1958, this reminder of the historic foundations of the college was less influential.

These developments may indeed be symptomatic of the "split personality" that has been inherent in the identity of the college. The foundational documents of the college reinforce commitment to both the liberal arts and training people for service in the Brethren Church. At best, maintaining balance between these two identities is difficult. But when factors such as rapid non-Brethren growth in all constituencies in the college, a resulting lessening of the Brethren presence in the college, increasing non-Brethren financial support for the college, reinforcement of the college's liberal arts program, and removal of the seminary from the college campus are entered into the equation, the direction taken by the college since the 1960s is understandable. In the latter part of the twentieth century the commitment to the Christian heritage of the college and the role of the Brethren Church in the college continued to diminish while emphasis on the liberal arts identity became foremost at the college.

Quandary over the Future of Ashland Theological Seminary

Challenges during the 1940s

The same challenges that faced the Brethren Church and the undergraduate program of Ashland College also faced the seminary during the 1940s. In certain ways, however, the division with the Grace Brethren and the effects of World War II hit the seminary harder than the college. The college could continue to rely upon its strong appeal in Ashland County and sur-rounding counties to maintain its enrollment following the division with the Grace Brethren and it could also seek to attract women to alleviate somewhat the significant downturn in enrollment created by World War II. However, the seminary relied almost exclusively on the Brethren Church for its students; with half of the denomination going with the Grace Brethren in the 1939 division, including most of the ministerial recruits, the seminary was fortunate to have enrollments in the 20s in the first years of the 1940s. The war years were especially difficult for the seminary. With the ministry in the Brethren Church almost exclusively male, women generally did not attend the seminary, except those who might take advantage of coursework in Christian Education. Most Brethren men considering the pastorate en-listed or were drafted into military service. The historic nonresistant stance of the Brethren was overshadowed in World War II by a stronger impulse to serve one's country in the struggle against the Axis powers. For these reasons enrollments stayed around ten between 1941 and 1948.

The 1940s opened with the faculty of the seminary being Willis E. Ronk, serving as dean, Melvin A. Stuckey, and Leslie E. Lindower. No changes in the faculty had occurred since 1937. This same faculty continued until 1943 when apparent friction between Willis Ronk and President

Delbert B. Flora

Mason led to Ronk's leaving the seminary during the summer of 1943.[42] Stuckey had planned on spending one or two years on study leave for graduate work at Western Reserve Graduate School, but was recalled to serve as the new dean in August 1943. To help with the additional teaching load left by Ronk's departure, William D. Furry returned to the college in 1943 after serving at Shorter College for ten years; he split his time between the college, where he taught philosophy, and the seminary, where he taught some Church history and philosophical theology. In 1946 Delbert B. Flora (1901–95) joined the seminary faculty. He was the grandson of Benjamin H. Flora, a leader in the early Brethren Church. He received his education at Ashland College (B.A. 1929), Ashland Theological Seminary (Th.B. 1931), Winona Lake School of Theology (S.T.M. 1950), and did post-graduate studies at the American School of Oriental Research in Jerusalem. He pastored Brethren congregations in Illinois and Indiana.[43]

In spite of regular requests from Willis Ronk that the seminary faculty be increased to four,[44] there were at most three faculty members throughout most of the 1940s; between 1943 and 1946 there were only two full-time seminary faculty. With the coming of Glenn L. Clayton in 1948, who shared the vision for expanding the seminary program, the seminary again had its fourth faculty member in 1949, Edwin E. Boardman Jr. (1892–1968). Boardman had

Edwin E. Boardman Jr.

attended Ashland College (B.A. 1919) and served as a missionary in the Brethren mission field in Argentina (1922–24). He pastored Brethren and non-Brethren congregations in West Virginia, Maryland, Iowa, Pennsylvania, and Ohio. He completed additional education at Iowa State Teachers College (B.A. 1929), Princeton University (M.A. 1931), and Princeton Theological Seminary (Th.B. 1931; Th.M. 1932) as well as taking coursework at The Ohio State University toward a doctorate.[45] During his years at the seminary (1949–68), Boardman taught in the areas of homiletics, philosophy, and Church history.

Several college faculty helped to supplement the coursework offered in the seminary during the 1940s and early 50s: Allen R. Thompson in sacred music (1941–45), Alice Catherine Ferguson in Greek (1944–49), Wilbert H. Miley in public speaking and radio preaching (1946–56), Eunice Lea Kettering in sacred music (1947–56), and Paul H. Saleste in the psychology of religion (1949–56). In addition, Brethren pastors and church leaders served as special lecturers in various fields: John F. Locke in preaching (1943–52), J. Ray Klingensmith in evangelism (1943–46), and J. G. Dodds in great Christian leaders (1943–44).

Besides the drop in enrollment, the war years placed other challenges on the seminary. The Selective Service System had ruled that all pre-professional students, including preseminary students, had to attend school year-round in order to retain their pre-professional deferment. This guideline was followed by another that required students in graduate theological programs to attend school year-round as well. In order to comply, the seminary held its first "Summer School of Theology" in 1944.[46] This summer session continued to be offered through 1948, though, presumably, there was no longer a governmental requirement for its continuation. These war-time guidelines placed financial hardships on some theological students because they were not able to pursue summer employment to cover their educational expenses.

Until the seminary achieved accreditation with the American Association of Theological Schools in 1969, most seminary students came from the Brethren Church and were graduates of Ashland College. In addition, the seminary faculty taught all the Bible courses in the undergraduate program at the college until 1961. For these reasons the seminary was able to set forth a well coordinated course of study for theological students through their four years of college and three years of seminary. In 1937 the seminary established minimum curricular requirements for preseminary students during their undergraduate training. This "pre-theological curriculum" was built upon a solid liberal arts foundation and followed recommendations adopted by the American Association of Theological Schools. It also included elements that were consistent with the special educational objectives of the seminary. The required curriculum, as set forth in the 1940–41 college catalogue, was composed of:

English and Speech	8–12 semester hours
Composition	6 semester hours
Literature	3–6 semester hours
Public Speaking	2–4 semester hours
Classical and Modern Languages	12–16 semester hours
Greek	12–16 semester hours
Science and Mathematics	6–8 semester hours
Social Sciences	27–39 semester hours
History	6–9 semester hours
Sociology, Economics	4–6 semester hours
Psychology	3 semester hours
Philosophy	6–9 semester hours
Religion or Bible	8–12 semester hours[47]

These requirements remained fairly consistent through the 1974–75 catalogue.[48]

In 1943 the Religion Department of the college was renamed the Bible Department. This same year the requirements for admission to the seminary were revised to include a Bible and theology major of 32 semester hours. This major was designed "to give the preseminary student as much immediate preparation as possible for Christian service during his college experience."[49] Another significant modification to the relationship between the undergraduate and graduate theological programs, which first appeared in the 1941–42 college catalogue, was the allowance that preseminary students who had completed the Bible and theology major could apply 24 semester hours of credit from their undergraduate Bible courses to their seminary work.[50] Further background on this exchange of courses between the college and seminary is revealed in the Board minutes. Many preseminary students were already preaching, due, no doubt, to the pastoral shortage after the 1939 division in the church. It was considered wise to offer these students better Bible and theology training during their undergraduate program. But there were not sufficient courses offered in the college curriculum to provide adequate training for this need. Therefore, preseminary students were allowed to take seminary level courses and receive dual credit for them in both their college and seminary programs.[51]

In 1947 another variation of this same practice was initiated. Students entering seminary without the Bible and theology major could elect to take undergraduate courses to complete their seminary degree.[52] The assumption is that this integrating of the college and seminary theological programs was necessary because of the insufficient number of faculty to service both programs. The seminary faculty simply could not offer all the courses necessary to meet all the degree requirements exclusive to each program. Interchange of credits was necessary. This dual recognition of credits was eventually discontinued in 1952.

Other curricular changes occurred during the 1940s. In 1944 the seminary began offering the Master of Religious Education (M.R.E.) degree. This new degree was occasioned by the demand in the state of Ohio for teachers of the Bible in the public schools. Religious classes could be offered either on school property or students could have release time to attend classes at another location. The degree required two years of special seminary training, with at least one year in residence. It was discontinued in 1952 when the seminary reorganized its curricula and the college began to offer a two year course leading to a certificate in Christian Education.[53] Following the recommendation of the American Association of Theological Schools, the seminary changed the Th.B. degree, offered since 1926, to the Bachelor of Divinity (B.D.) degree in 1945. Interestingly, the seminary had called this degree the B.D. degree prior to the adoption of the Th.B. nomenclature. In 1946 the seminary began offering the Master of Theology (Th.M.) degree. It involved an additional year of advanced theological studies beyond the B.D. degree. This degree was last offered in the 1951–52 catalogue.

The seminary was very cognizant of its responsibility to serve the needs of the Brethren Church. The seminary offered various degree and non-degree programs to those desiring additional Bible training. The English Course, introduced in a new format in 1937, was designed for those preparing for Christian service other than the ordained ministry. It required fifty-one semester hours of credit, about one and one-half years of study, and led to the Bachelor of Christian Education degree. By 1946 sixty-eight semester hours or two years of study were required for this degree. In his report for the 1943–44 academic year, Dean Stuckey announced that Lindower had instituted a Home Study Bible Course for those who were unable to enter the resident theological program at Ashland. At the time the majority of the men enrolled (there were sixteen men and women total) were deferred by local draft boards for farm and defense service. Following the war the course appealed especially to people in two situations: those who intended eventually to enroll in the seminary and those who were unable to enter the normal resident program at Ashland. Those in the first case could receive a maximum of eight hours toward seminary credit. Those in the second case were issued a certificate of credit for the work completed. The course as designed used qualified people in the person's local congregation, usually the pastor, to supervise the study and examinations. Papers and grades were then sent to the seminary to keep record of the coursework.[54] The course is last listed in seminary catalogues in the 1951–52 academic year. In his 1948 annual report Dean Stuckey announced the seminary's sponsorship of a Leadership Training Institute for Brethren youth. It was to be held on a weekend each semester and guided by seminary faculty and other Brethren leaders. The purpose was to train youth to assist in Brethren congregations in Sunday School and general youth work primarily during the summer months.[55]

The 1940s witnessed some of the most trying years for the seminary. The faculty who served during these years kept a grueling schedule. The understaffed seminary faculty was responsible for teaching not only most of the seminary courses but also all the courses in the college Bible department. They needed to cover the summer session and assist in recruiting for pastors during very difficult years in the history of the Brethren Church. The low enrollment was an ongoing concern that led to questions about the viability of the seminary. Yet these servants of the Lord were dedicated to the work of supplying leaders for the Brethren Church and were determined to see the seminary survive these years of hardship.

A Renewed Sense of Vision for the Seminary

Unlike some of the previous college presidents, Glenn L. Clayton understood very well the critical importance of the seminary to the future of the Brethren Church. Though a layman, he played key roles in the life of the church at local, district, and national levels. He was an active member and adult Sunday School teacher in Park Street Brethren Church. He served as the moderator of the Brethren General Conference in 1949 and the president of the National Laymen's Organization from 1946 to 1948. He brought the same visionary gifts to bear on the future of the seminary that he did on the future of the college.

In 1949, shortly after beginning his tenure as the president of the college, Clayton hired Boardman, increasing the seminary faculty to four for the first time since 1937. In reality, however, the seminary still had the equivalent of only three full-time faculty, because Lindower took on the major responsibility of administering the new Veteran's Administration

Henry Bates

program for the college in 1946. His teaching load in the seminary was appropriately reduced. Lindower eventually moved into the education department in the college in 1950; in 1952 Clayton would appoint him to the position of academic dean, a position which had been discontinued during the war years due to financial reasons. To fill Lindower's position at the seminary, Henry Bates (1919–88) was hired in 1950 in the fields of Old Testament and Hebrew. He had been educated at Ashland College (B.A. 1944), Ashland Theological Seminary (B.D. 1946), and Gettysburg Theological Seminary (S.T.M. 1948).

As had occurred with the previous two seminary deans, friction arose between the president of the college and the seminary dean. Clayton observed that Stuckey, like McClain, "insisted upon virtual autonomy for himself and the seminary, and was free in his criticism of both college faculty and students."[56] Clayton was especially upset by Stuckey's patronizing attitude toward him and the disrespect exhibited in lecturing him on issues related to the college and seminary. Stuckey, for example, criticized the presence of the "war-hardened" and "worldly" veterans on the campus and the resulting negative influence they had on the younger students. Clayton, on his part, though recognizing the problems associated with the veterans, felt that they brought a mature focus and drive to their studies and that they could benefit from the Christian ethos of the campus. Obviously opening the doors of the college to veterans also brought significant financial benefits to the institution. Stuckey's continuing criticism caused Clayton to bring the matter to the Board at its August 1951 meeting. He called for Stuckey's immediate termination from the seminary. To Clayton's relief the Board and even the ministers of the Brethren Church backed his request; there was general dislike of Stuckey's arbitrary leadership style.[57]

Stuckey's departure allowed for the restructuring of the seminary. Clayton played an active role in this process. He asked Flora to serve as the "chairman" of the seminary faculty. There was to be no dean for the time being, ostensibly to allow for any repercussions from Stuckey's ouster to blow over. Certainly the past track record of the relationship between the college president and the seminary dean would have caused Clayton to be cautious about replacing this position too quickly. This arrangement lasted for two years; Clayton was so impressed with Flora's capable leadership that he appointed Flora dean of the seminary in 1953. Clayton and Flora maintained an excellent working relationship while Flora served as dean.[58]

Flora, Boardman, and Bates covered the seminary curriculum, assisted by college faculty in specialized fields as noted previously, until 1954. Charles R. Munson (b. 1919) joined the seminary faculty that year in the

Charles R. Munson

field of practical theology. Munson received his education at Ashland College (B.A. 1947), Ashland Theological Seminary (B.D. 1952), Western Theological Seminary (Th.M. 1954), and Case Reserve University (Ph.D. 1971). He had served very capably as the National Brethren Youth Director (1948–53) and had pastored in Ohio and Pennsylvania. Clarence S. Fairbanks, the pastor of Park Street Brethren Church, also served part-time as the Supervisor of Field Work for several years, beginning in the 1953–54 academic year. The seminary brought in two or three special lecturers every year who further supplemented the seminary curriculum.

Other faculty changes occurred during the 1950s and early 60s that kept the seminary faculty numbers at four or four and one-half. Henry Bates left the seminary for the pastorate in 1955. He was replaced by Conrad Ralph Verno, a graduate of the University of Pittsburgh (B.A.) and Westminster Theological Seminary (B.D.). Verno taught in the fields of Hebrew and Old Testament. He had the distinction of being the first non-Brethren faculty member in the seminary. He was also the first of several professors in Hebrew and Old Testament who brought a Reformed theological perspective to the seminary (Bruce Stark and Joseph Kickasola would be others). Willis Ronk returned to the seminary for the 1955–56 academic year, teaching in New Testament. Unfortunately, he died during the spring semester of 1956. In the fall of 1956, J. Ray Klingensmith joined the faculty of the college and seminary. Klingensmith (1907–96) served Brethren pastorates in Ohio, Indiana, and Washington, DC. He had served as general secretary of the Missionary Board of the Brethren Church from 1940 to

J. Ray Klingensmith

1945 and had been a regular guest lecturer at the seminary during the 1940s and early 1950s. He was educated at Ashland College (B.A. 1931) and Ashland Theological Seminary (Th.B. 1934). He taught English Bible, splitting his time between the Bible department in the college and the seminary. When Verno resigned in 1957, Richard L. Hash was hired in the fields of Hebrew and Old Testament. Hash received his education at Asbury College (B.A. 1955) and Asbury Theological Seminary (B.D. 1957). When Hash resigned in 1959, Bruce Stark was hired in the same fields of Hebrew and Old Testament. Stark, who maintained a strong Reformed theological commitment, received degrees from Wheaton College (B.A.) and Northern Baptist Theological Seminary (B.D., Th.M., and Th.D.).

The dismissal of Stuckey opened the door for a thorough analysis of the seminary curriculum. Significant reorganization of the curriculum occurred in the 1952–53 academic year in order to bring the seminary curriculum more in line with the guidelines of the American Association of Theological Schools. Following are the major changes that were implemented.

1. Both the Master of Religious Education (M.R.E.) and Master of Theology (Th.M). degrees were discontinued. The focus of the seminary curriculum would be the B.D. degree.
2. Every student in the B.D. degree program would be required to complete one year of supervised field work as a student pastor (as noted earlier, Clarence Fairbanks provided supervision for this part of the curriculum).
3. Every Brethren student would be required to take three semester hours of "Distinctive Doctrines of the Brethren Church."
4. Those students who could not complete the full three-year B.D. degree due to the inability to fulfill the language requirements would be awarded a two-year graduate certificate.
5. Admission to the seminary required a four-year baccalaureate degree. Students should have had a Bible minor of at least 16 hours and 8 hours of Speech within their undergraduate program.
6. The college offered a major in the Bible for those not contemplating graduate work. These English Bible courses were taught by the seminary faculty. Students could no longer receive dual recognition of courses by the college and seminary.
7. The seminary continued to cooperate with the college in offering a two-year course of studies leading to a certificate in Christian Education. This certificate program would be folded into the new two-year programs being developed in the college curriculum.[59]

The revised seminary curriculum was fully implemented in the 1954–55 academic year.

As can be inferred from the above list, the seminary faculty continued to carry a significant work load, beyond that recommended by the American Association of Theological Schools. They were responsible for teaching courses not only in the seminary program but also in the college's Bible department and Christian Education certificate program. They served on committees in the college as well as overseeing the work of the seminary. They regularly filled pulpits, some as pastors, and were involved in recruitment on behalf of the seminary.[60] Though these demands on their time were considerable, they understood that their labors were critical for the future of the Brethren Church; they took seriously their stewardship of the education and spiritual formation of young lives and minds for the service of the Lord and his church.

The faculty under Flora developed a strong sense of camaraderie; they enjoyed being with each other as well as with their students. An excellent example of this shared fellowship was Delbert Flora's "flying seminar," as it was called. He led a tour of twenty-four people in the summer of 1958 to Europe and the Near East. Joining Flora and his wife on the tour were professors Munson and Boardman. Most of the other participants were from the Brethren Church. The party was greatly disappointed that they were not allowed into Lebanon and the Holy Land because of the volatile political situation (U.S. Marines had been dispatched to Beirut, Lebanon); they were

Members of the 1958 "Flying Seminar" to Europe and the Near East

forced to leave Egypt and return to Europe. They were, however, able to join in celebrating the 250th anniversary of the beginning of the Brethren movement in Schwarzenau, Germany, on 6 August 1958.[61]

Student enrollment stayed fairly consistent in the mid to upper teens during the 1950s. The end of the influx of World War II veterans who went to college and then on for seminary training occurred in the 1953–54 academic year. However, a revitalized youth program and a renewed sense of direction in the Brethren Church kept enrollment numbers from declining after the wave of veterans had passed. There were generally a few women enrolled in the seminary during the 1940s through the early 1960s, but none were enrolled in the B.D. degree program.

The student body of the seminary played important roles in the life of the seminary and church. Monthly socials for theological students, their spouses, and friends were held in the Myers Memorial Music Building, donated to the college in 1940. These socials gave the seminary student community an alternative to the social life of students in the college. In 1947 the wives of seminary students began an organization called Sem Wives. Their monthly social gatherings featured devotional talks and discussions about the role of the minister's wife. The president of the Seminary Student organization published a newsletter, the *Sem News*, that was distributed monthly to Brethren pastors. Brethren seminary students were active in serving the Brethren Church as student pastors, through Gospel Teams, and through working with youth.[62]

Seminary Students and the Cased Eagles

In their book, *The Eagles of Ashland*, Duncan Jamieson and Kristine Kleptach document the clandestine history of the appearance and, occasionally, the disappearance of over two dozen cast iron eagles on the Ashland College campus. "Liberated" from regional dealerships of the J. I. Case Implement Company, these eagles have become a revered symbol of Ashland College/University. Casing the Midwest for the Case eagles became a favorite pastime of Ashland College students throughout the 1940s, 50s, and 60s. Seminary and preseminary students played leading roles in a number of these heists.

Henry Bates (A.B. 1945; B.D. 1946; taught at seminary 1950–55) was involved in the caper that brought the eagle named Louie to the campus in November 1944. Louie had previously resided at a Case dealership near Canton, Ohio. Bates brought specialized skills to the heist. As a former English gravedigger, he was put in charge of the hole that would cement Louie's place between the old Gym and Redwood Stadium.

Gene Hollinger (A.B. 1960; B.D. 1964) had done reconnaissance on an eagle at a Case dealership in Brookville, Ohio, near his hometown in New Lebanon. He and five other college students hatched the clever plan in May 1958 to drive to the dealership in two cars. The ruse involved one of the cars appearing to have engine problems with its hood being appropriately

(continued)

raised. The second car stopped to provide assistance. Within minutes, however, the eagle had flown from his nest and was on his way to his new home in front of the Student Union. Dubbed Roscoe, the eagle's residence at the college was short-lived; presumable Roscoe returned to his former nesting place.

The following year future seminarian Don Rinehart (B.S. in Ed. 1959, B.D. 1965, M.Div. 1972, D.Min. 1975) was involved with three other upperclassmen in the plot that brought Kate to the Ashland campus. The well planned caper occurred the night of 31 May 1959 from the Case dealership in Lebanon, Ohio. Named after Ashland College benefactor Kate Myers, who had been killed in an auto accident in 1957, Kate found her new roost in front of Myers Hall. Her appearance was timely, since abundant cement was on hand from the construction of Myers Hall to keep her well planted.

Two preseminary students were part of a heist that went awry on 20 October 1963. Bill Walk (A.B. 1965; M.Div. 1969) and Bill Winter (A.B. 1965) were part of a Gospel Team which sent some its members to minister at the Brethren congregation in Maurertown, Virginia, and others to serve the Brethren church at St. James, Maryland. On their return trip, they spotted an eagle in Stephens City, Virginia, in front of Clem's Garage. They decided on the spur-of-the-moment to complete their hallowed trek by adding the eagle to others that were rapidly congregating on the college campus. As they were loading the eagle into the trunk of the car, Richard Clem, the owner of the gas station and garage and a Case dealer, came out with a shotgun, removed the keys from the ignition, and detained them until Virginia State Police arrived. The four team members were brought before the Frederick County Justice of the Peace, charged with one count of grand larceny apiece, and were released after posting bail of $100 each (a fifth person who was on the trip was not charged). Upon their return to Ashland, Virgil Meyer, Director of Religious Affairs, drove to Stephens City and prevailed upon Clem to drop the charges against the students. They were relieved that the matter was laid to rest with the payment of only court costs and without having to spend time in the coop.

This was not the only Gospel Team that was diverted from its higher calling. A few months later Michael Drushal was on a team that was in the Johnstown, Pennsylvania, area where, according to official lists circulating at the college, a Case eagle was roosting. They were equipped with a chain for the caper which they had attached to the bird. However, the untimely appearance of a police car in the distance caused the team to make a quick exit, minus their chain.

There is a footnote that needs to be added to stories recorded in *The Eagles of Ashland*. Milton Robinson (B.A. 1942) in an interview in 2004, revealed that he, Archie Martin (B.A. 1943), and a third student appropriated an eagle, possibly from Medina. Robinson indicated that the eagle was loaded into the trunk of his 1934 Ford coupe and relocated to Ashland. Though he could not remember other details such as dates or what happened to the eagle, this episode does not appear in the official list of eagle heists.

It may seem out of character for preseminary and seminary students to have been involved in such capers. Yet they shared the same school spirit and youthful abandon that characterized the typical college student. In so doing, they contributed to a tradition that is part of the rich history of Ashland College/University.

Duncan R. Jamieson and Kristine M. Kleptach, *The Eagles of Ashland* (Ashland, OH: Ashland University Press, 1994), 19, 25–26, 28–29, 38–39, 69 and Milton Robinson, interview by author, 22 July 2004, Ashland, OH.

Students continued to receive considerable financial aid during the 1940s and 50s. There was no charge for tuition for students in the seminary, including non-Brethren students. There were various fees assessed, all

The seminary faculty and students in front of Memorial Chapel; the faculty (in front), from left to right, are Edwin Boardman, Ralph Verno, Charles Munson, and Delbert Flora

of which were quite minimal. In addition, the tuition reimbursement for those theological students who had studied at Ashland College continued through 1943. Though preseminary students were charged full tuition for their undergraduate education, they received a refund of $100 for each year they attended Ashland College (in 1940 college tuition was $100 a semester). A modification to this policy was instated on 1 September 1943, when collegiate students who intended to attend the seminary were no longer given the $100 per year as a refund during their seminary years but as a scholarship that was credited against their second semester tuition during their collegiate program. Theological students who enrolled in the college prior to 1943 were still covered by the previous policy. The Board approved another modification in 1944 when the Board established the policy that no seminary student could receive more than a 90% rebate of college tuition (seminary students who were children of ministers received additional financial aid). In 1947 the Board returned to the previous policy of granting partial refunds of college tuition to seminary students who had attended Ashland College. The refund was again paid during their seminary program. The amount of the refund, however, was changed; it was now to be one-half of the amount students had paid for their college tuition. Tuition per semester in the college had risen to $140 by this time, while the seminary reimbursement/scholarship had remained unchanged at $100 per year of attendance at the college (the reimbursement was originally begun in 1931). This modification made the policy more equitable as tuition costs continued to rise; the original refund had been $100 of the $165 per year tuition in 1931–32.[63] The National Sunday School Association of the Brethren Church provided another financial benefit to seminary students: purchasing books for students' libraries at significantly discounted prices.[64]

The Birth of a New Era for Ashland Theological Seminary

Accreditation of the seminary through the American Association of Theological Schools began to be taken seriously by 1941. Dean Willis Ronk, in his annual report to the President in 1941, had observed: "We should be awake to the fact that accrediting agencies for seminaries are now here and that sooner or later we will be forced to qualify. This will compel some vital changes."[65] The challenges of the war years forced the issue into the background, but Dean Stuckey regularly advocated the pursuit of accreditation with the American Association of Theological Schools during his tenure.[66] Very early in his presidency, Clayton gave his full support for the push toward accreditation. He recognized that accreditation was "very important in the growth and life of the Seminary" and that significant progress was very difficult for the seminary without such recognition.[67] With Stuckey's departure Clayton felt that the necessary changes to the seminary program to bring it more in line with accreditation standards could be addressed. The aforementioned curricular changes in 1952 were part of this initiative as were the strengthening of the seminary faculty in both numbers and educational qualifications (both Flora and Munson were given financial support by the college to pursue advanced degrees).

Clayton set the fiftieth anniversary of the seminary in 1956 as the goal for securing accreditation.[68] But this goal proved to be unrealistic. The seminary program was faced with a number of daunting challenges: insufficient faculty resources, low student enrollment, meager library holdings, and limited financial support. There were some in the church and college who questioned whether the continuation of the seminary was viable.

In the midst of this uncertainty surrounding the seminary, one of the most significant developments for the future of the seminary began to un-

John C. Myers home as it looked in 1958

fold. The issue of a suitable site dedicated exclusively for seminary use had been raised by both Miller in the 1910s and McClain in the 1930s. Though the Library (Miller) building had provided a temporary solution to this issue when it was completed in 1922, the subsequent growth of the college had necessitated that significant space be allotted for the collegiate program. There had been on-going conversations in the 1940s about including space for the seminary in the proposed chapel, but this recommendation was not realized in the final construction.[69] The issue of dedicated space for the seminary continued to be unresolved until the Myers family once again made a significant donation to the college. In the minutes of the Prudential Committee on 29 December 1955 there appears the first mention of the offer of the children of the late John C. Myers to donate his home at 910 Center Street to the college. The spacious home had been built in 1908 as the residence of John C. Myers (1878–1952) an industrialist, art collector, and philanthropist.[70] The Prudential Committee recommended that a decision on the offer be postponed until the August 1956 Board meeting to provide sufficient time to explore possible uses of the home and the costs associated with it.[72] The Board minutes suggest that discussions within the Board and with the Myers family were a drawn-out process. At its April 1956 meeting, the Board expressed interest in the home; the Board minutes for 16 August 1956 report that negotiations were continuing with the Myers family. In

April 1957 the Board "favorably received" the offer of the home by the Myers family, "pending completion of details by the administration and the Myers Building Committee."[72] Finally the following Board motion appeared in the minutes for 22 August 1957:

> Robert D. Ingmand read the minutes of the Myers Building Committee meeting of August 20, 1957. George T. Ronk moved, seconded by Virgil E. Meyer, that we accept the gift of the John C. Myers home and that the building be reserved for Seminary use as recommended by the Myers Building Committee. Motion carried.[73]

At the same meeting the Board approved the allocation of $3000 for moving expenses to the new seminary campus. The home was formally received by the college in January 1958. In June 1958 the college received an additional plot of land adjoining the Myers home at the corner of Center and High Streets; it also became part of the seminary campus.[74] In addition to the property, the Myers family donated part of John C. Myers' sizeable art collection that had decorated the home.

During the summer of 1958 alterations were made to transform the residence into the new home of the seminary. Existing rooms were easily converted into offices and classrooms. Other rooms were reserved for receptions

The garages of the Myers home that became the seminary library

and two of the bedroom suites and a bathroom were retained for guest housing. More challenging was the conversion of the four-car garage and service area into the seminary library.

The seminary moved into the Myers home in the late summer of 1958. This move to a location off the main Ashland College campus was one of the significant factors in creating a new identity for the seminary. It achieved more than just the physical separation of the seminary from the college. It allowed the seminary to develop its own ethos with its own academic and spiritual character. It was symbolic of the reality that Ashland College possessed a dual mission, the liberal arts and theological training, each of which needed the freedom to cultivate its own character and calling. The physical separation likewise became the first of a number of steps that separated other important elements of the seminary from the college: the library, the chapel, the student body, the faculty, the administration, the budget. Though the separation of some of these elements occurred at the same time as the occupation of the new facility, others took place over time as logical steps in fashioning a discrete identity for the seminary. The seminary has retained its formal identity as a graduate division of Ashland College/University, but the four blocks that separate the seminary and the college campuses provide the requisite distance for each to pursue its unique mission.

The Seminary's Naked Lady

The centerpiece of the gardens on the south side of the John C. Myers home was a reflecting pool in the middle of which was the statue of a naked lady, the handiwork of a French sculptor. She was made of bright white cement and struck a graceful pose amidst the gardens. The dean at the time that the seminary took possession of the home in 1958, Delbert Flora, decided that the lady was a bit too risqué for public display at the seminary. She was discreetly placed in storage. The next dean, however, Joseph Shultz, did not share Flora's reservations and restored the lady to her former place of honor in the middle of the reflecting pool.

During Shultz's tenure the lady had a habit of turning up in his office while he was away. At these times, however, she would be appropriately dressed in clothes for her stay in the dean's office. The next vice president of the seminary, Frederick Finks, who, with other students, had ushered the lady into Shultz's office on several occasions, found that she had the same affinity for taking up residence in his office while he was gone. Once or twice she made her appearance, again, well attired in clothes, hat, and scarf.

The naked lady met an untimely demise, however. The pool had not been working because there were insurance concerns about children falling into the pool. On one occasion a church group was using the seminary campus and a youth pushed her over and broke her ankle. Finks sought help from the Art Department at the university to repair her damaged ankle, but the repair did not hold. She was returned to storage once again.

(continued)

The final chapter of the naked lady's story occurred in 2004. The seminary was sponsoring a garage sale to raise funds for supporting a team of students and staff from the seminary to help with a construction project at the South American Theological Seminary in Colon, Argentina. The lady was a late addition to the sale items. A buyer took a fancy for her and she found a new home. An apocryphal sidelight to this story is that Finks had threatened to give her a home at his own house. Upon hearing of the lady's sale, Finks' wife, Holly, was said to have been quite relieved.

The reflecting pool in the south lawn of the Myers home with the statue of the naked lady

Frederick Finks, interview by author, 28 July 2005, Ashland, OH.

Though the issue of space dedicated exclusively to the seminary had been resolved, other issues regarding the seminary greatly concerned the Board of Trustees, notably accreditation and low student enrollment. On 27 January 1958 the Prudential Committee of the Board requested that the seminary faculty develop a timetable for achieving accreditation and propose a budget to support such a thrust. When apparently nothing had been done on this request, the Prudential Committee renewed its request for a timetable and budget at its 20 August 1958 meeting. In his annual report to the Board dated 21 August 1958, Clayton underscored the need to address these issues when he listed three major needs of the seminary: (1) more students preparing for full-time Christian service, (2) recognition by the American Association of Theological Schools, and (3) greater service to the church and community (Clayton cited, as a positive example, Flora's recent tour of Europe and the Near East).[75]

There is no indication that the seminary faculty acted upon the Prudential Committee's request during the 1958–59 academic year, though they were preoccupied with adjusting to their new facility. Without doubt one of the most significant developments in the history of the seminary occurred at the Board meeting on 20 August 1959. In his recommendations to the Board, Clayton presented a well-conceived six-year Seminary Development Program. It became a roadmap for guiding seminary development between 1959 and 1965. As originally proposed the program was as follows:

A. Objectives (by August 1965)
    1. Full accreditation of the Seminary by the American Association of Theological Schools by August 1965
    2. Enrollment of 50 Seminary students
    3. Setting up of new College Department of Bible and Philosophy
    4. Encouragement of Faculty Research and Study
    5. Enlarged Curricular offerings:
        a. Enriched B. D. Program
        b. Two-Year Associate in Theology
        c. Two-Year Associate in Religious Education
        d. Two-Year Pastoral Certificate
    6. Development of Seminary Library
    7. Alteration of Seminary Building

B. Phases of Program
    1. Phase I: August 1959–August 1960
        a. Development of Special Board Committee on Seminary Development
        b. Visitation of College and Churches by faculty and administration for recruitment
        c. Curricular study and reform
    2. Phase II: August 1960–August 1963
        a. Stepped up recruitment program
        b. Set up new College Department of Bible and Philosophy
        c. Begin program of assisting one faculty member each year in research and study
        d. Complete library development
        e. Apply for Associate accreditation
    3. Phase III: August 1963–August 1965
        a. Continued recruitment program
        b. Alter Chapel and [meet] other plant needs
        c. Add faculty for Religious Education
        d. Apply for full accreditation[76]

Based on Clayton's recommendation, the Board approved the general outline of the development program, with the goals to be attained by the beginning of the sixtieth year of the seminary in 1965. The Board specifically adopted phase I of the program; the other two phases were to be considered in August 1960, pending the recommendations of the special Seminary Development Committee. The chairman of the Board, Myron Kem, appointed three members of the Board to the new Seminary Development Committee: J. Garber Drushal, Spencer Gentle, and Joseph Shultz, who served as chairman. Clayton and Flora also served on the committee. Though not all the goals were met within the specified time frames, most of them were eventually realized. The development program steered the course of the seminary through much of the 1960s.

The Seminary Development Committee took its task very seriously. The Board members who served on the committee all had significant responsibilities for their "day jobs." Shultz was the pastor of the Washington, DC Brethren Church; Drushal was on the faculty of the College of Wooster; Gentle pastored the Goshen, Indiana, Brethren Church. Yet they devoted significant hours to a cause to which all were committed. Their duties on the committee involved not only attendance of the meetings but also visitation of other seminaries and consultation with officers of the American Association of Theological Schools.

In the time between the August 1959 and August 1960 Board meetings, the committee discussed a wide range of options concerning the seminary, such as dissolving the seminary and merging with a seminary of another denomination. The committee concluded that it was not in the best interests of the Brethren Church to pursue these alternate plans any further; they were committed to move ahead with "the assumption that the seminary would be developed further as a graduate school of Ashland College."[77] The committee members then focused their attention on specific issues: Shultz on administration and curriculum, Drushal on size and structure, and Gentle on recruitment policies. The committee recommended to the Board at its August 1960 meeting that a slightly revised phase II and III be adopted as the goals of the Seminary Development Program. The revised phases were as follows:

Phase II: August 1960 to August 1963

    a. Visitation by seminary faculty of churches for purpose of recruitment.

    b. Set up the new Department of Bible and Philosophy in the college undergraduate program.

  c. Begin program of assisting one faculty member each year in research and study.

  d. Additions to the library in this period as follows:

    1960–61 500 books at $2500
    1961–62 750 books at $3750
    1962–63 1000 books at $5000

  e. Apply for Associate membership in AATS.

Phase III: August 1963 to August 1965

  a. Continued recruitment program.

  b. Adapt building to needs (details to be worked out nearer the time.)

  c. Add faculty for Religious Education.

  d. Additions to the library in this period as follows:

    1963–64 1000 books at $5000
    1964–65 1250 books at $6250

  e. Apply for full accreditation.[78]

The Board approved these revised phases in the development plan.

  Meanwhile the seminary, in conjunction with the Brethren Ministerial Association, was addressing the issue of recruitment of pastors for the Brethren Church. Two steps were taken to obtain additional pastors more quickly. First, the Ministerial Association solicited funds for a student aid fund that allowed students to devote their time and attention to their schooling rather than employment. Second, the seminary sponsored a so-called Pastoral Orientation Program, an individualized reading program whereby men over the age of 32 who could not attend seminary could study under the direction of a seminary professor. The program provided approximately two years of non-credit instruction. It was implemented in 1960 but was eventually discontinued in 1963.[79]

  At its April 1961 meeting the Board of Trustees approved a set of significant recommendations from the Seminary Development Committee, all of which were related to the push toward accreditation. The recommendations were:

1. That the Seminary implement the quarter system, effective September 1961.

2. That the new curriculum be approved in principle.

3. That a seminary library fee of $10.00 per quarter become effective September 1961.
4. That beginning with the undergraduate freshmen class entering September 1962 a schedule of reduction in preseminary rebates be initiated so that the program could be concluded June 1966 with final rebates paid by June 1969.
5. That a Board Standing Committee called the Seminary Committee be created.
6. That the Seminary Committee, with the concurrence of the president of the college, could add an advisory group of non-Board members to augment the committee in order to consider seminary development and problems as the committee deemed advisable.[80]

By the August 1961 Board meeting all of these recommendations were either carried out or in process.

Some further comment is needed on several of these points. The rationale for adopting the quarter system was set forth in the annual report of the seminary dean. The seminary felt that there was a psychological advantage in not having the long drawn-out periods of concentration in one subject area that was true of semesters. There also was an advantage in concluding quarters before Christmas and spring breaks. Quarters further allowed the offering of more subjects. The B.D. degree would now consist of 144 quarter hours, divided among the four areas of biblical, historical, theological, and practical courses. This four-fold division had been followed since the 1930s and conformed to the curricular standards of the American Association of Theological Schools. In the redistribution of courses made possible by the move to quarters, more coursework was devoted to areas of practical theology.[81]

The financial aid program for seminary students who had attended Ashland College, which had been in place, with some modifications, since the early 1930s, was now phased out. It had provided a rebate or scholarship for each year theological students had attended the college. Seminary tuition continued to be free for all students. The Student Aid Fund, begun in 1960 as a cooperative venture of the seminary and the Brethren Ministerial Association, provided additional financial assistance to Brethren students. The seminary continued to depend upon the Brethren Church to fund a significant portion of the seminary program. The college's Church Relations Director, Virgil E. Meyer, was entrusted with the responsibility of keeping the work of the college before the Brethren Church. Especially important was highlighting the financial needs of the seminary.

The Seminary Development Committee had been so effective in providing the drive for the "revisioning" of the seminary that the Board, at the recommendation of the Seminary Development Committee, elevated the committee to a standing committee of the Board in 1961. The Board members of the committee continued to be Shultz, Drushal, and Gentle. The provision for supplementing this committee with an advisory group of non-Board members has been an excellent way of bringing additional expertise to the work of the committee and of gaining the perspective of various constituencies that are important to the life and work of the seminary. The initial members of the Seminary Advisory Committee were Vernon Grisso, Ted Hevel, Clarence Stogsdill, and Harold Bender. Bender, the Dean of the Mennonite seminary at Goshen College, had provided valuable guidance to the Seminary Development Committee during the previous few years.[82]

One is struck by the significant progress made between 1958 and 1963 in positioning the seminary for its rapid growth beginning in the mid-1960s. Much credit goes to Clayton, Flora, and the Seminary Development Committee. Clayton, more so than any previous president of the seminary since Miller, maintained a steady commitment to advance the mission of the seminary. Flora, though more of a scholar than an administrator, worked in concert with Clayton and the Seminary Development Committee to continue to upgrade all aspects of the seminary's life. The Seminary Development Committee provided the thrust for the progress of the seminary. Composed of very capable and highly motivated leaders, the committee was able to envision a future for the seminary that few others could even imagine. The transformation of the seminary from an extremely small, denominationally oriented school to one of the largest seminaries in the United States and Canada, serving over seventy denominations and parachurch organizations today, owes much to the vision and gifted leadership of these servants of the seminary and the church.

From the time that the seminary had transitioned to a graduate level school in 1930, the seminary professors had taught not only the seminary curriculum but also the courses in the Bible Department and some in the Philosophy Department of the college. The push toward accreditation as well as the physical and psychological break of the seminary from the college campus in 1958 led the college and seminary administration and the Board and Seminary Development Committee to advocate that the college develop a Bible Department in the college totally staffed by non-seminary faculty. First mentioned in a Prudential Committee recommendation on 2 April 1959, the recommendation became part of Clayton's Seminary Development Program presented at the August 1959 Board meeting. The rationale for the change was that the removal of the seminary faculty from undergraduate teaching would allow them to devote their time and energy to the development of the seminary. The change occurred during the 1961–62 academic year when J. Ray Klingensmith shifted most of his teaching load into the college's Bible Department. He was appointed the chairman of the upgraded Bible Department in 1962.[83]

The Seminary Committee continued to set its sights on accreditation for the seminary. In its April 1962 meeting the committee felt that Associate membership could be achieved when (1) the seminary teaching faculty increased from 4½ to 6, (2) the development of the seminary library was acceptable, and (3) full-time enrollment was at least 25 students (there were 27 students enrolled for the 1963–64 academic year). Recognizing the need to begin recruitment beyond Ashland College if enrollment was to increase, the seminary began to recruit at other college campuses, notably Malone College.[84]

Delbert Flora, who had guided the seminary since 1951, felt inadequate to lead the seminary in its continued push toward accreditation. In the spring of 1962 he expressed his desire to Clayton to leave the deanship of the seminary in order to pursue further studies in Biblical archaeology in the Holy Land. Clayton supported Flora's requests and Flora was given a special leave for 1963–64 to study in the Holy Land. It was understood that he would return to the seminary faculty in the fall of 1964 as professor of archaeology.[85]

As Clayton considered possible successors for Flora, one man came to the fore: Joseph R. Shultz. Shultz (1927–2003) was well qualified for the position. He had been raised in the Berlin, Pennsylvania, Brethren Church. He received his education at Ashland College (B.A. 1950), Ashland Theological Seminary (M.R.E. 1952), and Southwestern Baptist Theological Seminary (Ed.D. 1954; Ph.D. 1994). He had pastored the Williamstown, Ohio, Brethren Church and the First Brethren Church of Washington, DC. He had served as a member of the Board of Trustees of Ashland College since 1958 and had chaired the Seminary Development Committee and the new Seminary Committee. He was actively involved in the life of the Brethren Church at the local, district, and national levels. He served as the moderator of the General Conference of The Brethren Church in 1960. He was also a board member of numerous educational and religious organizations.

Clayton visited Shultz to ascertain his interest in the position of dean of the seminary. Shultz was quite favorable to the offer, and at its August 1962 meeting the Board approved his hiring, effective September 1963. Shultz brought a vigor and entrepreneurial quality to every position that he

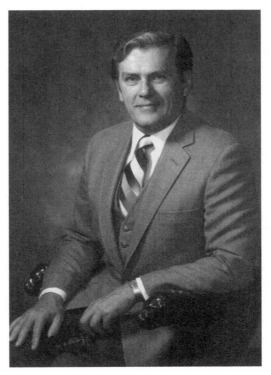

Joseph R. Shultz

held. Knowing the needs of the seminary from his work on both the Seminary Development Committee and the Seminary Committee, Shultz plunged ahead with a host of initiatives: curricular, financial, physical plant, library, recruiting, faculty, church relations.

At the same August 1962 Board meeting that hired Shultz, Clayton set forth plans, supported by the Seminary Committee, for improvements to the physical plant of the seminary. They included enlarging the seminary chapel, adding a library wing (the initial library space was nearly full), planning and construction of student housing, and, as a long range goal, the construction of a chapel building. Clayton also addressed the financial needs of the seminary: initiating a publicity campaign in the church, planning for an operating budget of $50,000 per year by 1963–64, developing a capital fund campaign for the above projects, and creating an endowment fund specifically designated for the seminary. Finally, Clayton recommended that an architect be employed to develop tentative plans and an estimate for the proposed improvements to the seminary building.[86]

In the spring of 1963 Clayton had sent the Seminary Committee a list of seven basic assumptions that would further define the seminary's relationship to the college and church and provide a clear direction for the seminary's ongoing development. The Seminary Committee affirmed the entire list. The assumptions were:

1. "The Seminary is essential to the survival and growth of the Brethren Church. . . ."
2. The Seminary's stability is dependent on accreditation by the American Association of Theological Schools. This goal necessitates continued promotion of enrollment, faculty, and library resources.
3. "The Seminary will continue to operate as a division of Ashland College but with a separate budget. . . .
4. Financial support of the Seminary will derive from independent church and community sources, separated from college support. An allocation from College income commensurate with income from endowment and other gifts designated for the Seminary will be made annually."

Shultz presented a detailed response to point #4 in Clayton's "assumptions," focusing on the administration and finances of the seminary.

Administration

    a. The Board delegated "the responsibility of the trusteeship of the Seminary to the Seminary Committee. This trusteeship shall be exercised within the Board of Trustees, and shall be responsible for the general policy making, development, and financial and budget planning of the Seminary.

    (1) The membership of the Seminary Committee shall consist of the President, the Dean, three members of the Board of Trustees, and three members of General Conference of The Brethren Church, electing one per year for a three year term.

    (2) The Seminary Committee shall meet regularly twice a year, and otherwise at the call of the officers.

    (3) The Dean shall be the standing Chairman of the Seminary Committee.

Financial

  a. The Seminary is a specialized institution and by this very nature shall always have a limited constituency. Any Seminary has little persuasion in the general community, industry, and financial world. Seminaries generally do not charge substantial tuition. The Seminary shall never desire, or be eligible, for government loans. For these, and others, it is essential that a Seminary Foundation be established. This endowment shall be established in the following way:

    (1) The Board of Trustees designate a just amount of the present endowment to the Seminary Foundation.

    (2) Twenty-five percent of all Seminary development funds be set aside for the Foundation.

    (3) A continuous effort be made for the establishment of 'Chairs' in the Seminary: Old Testament, New Testament, Christian Education, etc.

The General Conference be asked to give a yearly appropriation to the Seminary. Be it understood that this basic endowment, and yearly financial responsibility of the Denomination is necessary to become accredited by the AATS [American Association of Theological Schools]. . . .

  5. The present property occupied by the Seminary is to be considered its permanent location. . . .

  6. An effort will be made to secure additional and adjacent land for expansion purposes. . . .

  7. Plans for such expansion will be drawn and included in promotional releases for the Seminary. Such plans will be considered for implementation as funds become available. . . ."[87]

These assumptions have, for the most part, guided the seminary in its relationship to the church and the college/university since 1963. Though some points have been modified over the years, the general operating assumption has been that the seminary remains a graduate division of the college but with its own governance, subject to the Board of Trustees, its own budget, and its own endowment. Though the seminary is less dependent on the Brethren Church financially in recent years, at this time in its history the seminary's budget depended significantly on the support of the denomination. The seminary is deeply rooted in its present location and has sought to acquire strategically located properties as they have become available.

The seminary in the 1960s continued to service primarily those considering ministry in the Brethren Church. The leaders in the college, seminary, and denomination who were guiding the push toward accreditation were aware that this goal would allow the seminary to recruit more non-Brethren students. Though such recruitment could lead to Brethren students becoming a minority in the seminary, Brethren leaders accepted this reality, knowing that opening the seminary to a wider student body was necessary if the seminary was to exist and continue its service to the Brethren Church. The ties between the seminary and the Brethren Church were strong throughout the period of the 1940s, 50s, and 60s. The seminary drew a significant portion of its income from the Brethren Church. In 1963, for example, the college and seminary received the following support from entities in the church (though some gifts were listed for Ashland College, there is no doubt that some or most of this support was directed toward the seminary; there is no break-out of budget numbers in the college budget for the seminary as of 1963): $10,600 from the General Conference (college and seminary); $3,396.25 from the National Laymen's Organization (student aid); $2,000 from the Sunday School Board (seminary); $5,400 from the Woman's Missionary Society (seminary).[88] These numbers do not include other gifts from Brethren individuals and districts. To gain some perspective on these numbers, bear in mind that Clayton had projected a seminary budget of $50,000 for 1963–64. Recognition of the seminary's significance to the denomination is reflected in the approval by General Conference in 1963 of a recommendation that the dean of the seminary, or an alternative, be a regular member of the Central Planning and Co-ordinating Committee. This body coordinated the work of the denomination's boards and guided the work of the denomination between conferences.[89]

The remarkable progress that was occurring in the life of the seminary during the late 1950s and early 1960s was setting the stage for dramatic growth in the coming decades. Shultz would serve as the catalyst driving the advance for the following two decades.

Concluding Observations

The 1940s were a difficult decade for the college, the seminary, and the Brethren Church. The division with the Grace Brethren left its toll on the seminary and church, but all three institutions were also adversely affected by World War II. The dawn of a new era for the college and seminary in particular began with the presidency of Glenn L. Clayton. A man of profound energy and vision, his work in transforming the college from a small, commuter, denominationally-oriented school to a medium-sized, residential, regional college had begun in the aftermath of the Founders Hall fire in 1952. The college's rapid growth in every significant indicator—students, faculty, budget, buildings, name recognition—was well underway by the end of the 1950s. Clayton turned his attention to the significant issues facing the seminary during the 1950s as well. He provided the impetus and Delbert Flora and the Seminary Development Committee, especially its irrepressible chairman, Joseph Shultz, provided the energy for the transformation of the seminary that would occur beginning in the 1960s. The renaissance of the college and seminary and their work in turning out Brethren youth highly committed to the church helped to breathe new life into the Brethren Church during the 1960s as well. The seminary was well positioned for significant growth by 1963 when Joseph Shultz assumed leadership of the school.

Chapter 6

A Time of Crisis and Opportunity
(1963–1982)

Introduction

The period from the late 1950s to 1970 was marked by unprecedented growth at Ashland College. Records were set nearly every year in student enrollment, the number of faculty, and budget revenue and expenses. Land was continuously being bought for the new buildings that were perennially springing up. New academic programs and collegiate departments were added regularly. All of this changed by 1970 as a decade of significant challenges was inaugurated during which the college fought for its very survival. In sharp contrast the seminary began a period of unparalleled growth in 1963 that would continue unabated into the opening decade of the twenty-first century. The key elements of leadership and finances that have played such crucial roles in the history of the college and seminary again were center stage in these developments.

The Decade of Crises at Ashland College

Since the end of World War II, Ashland College had remained fairly insulated from the impact of significant national and international events. However, the college would become a microcosm of the major issues and trends that radically changed the American cultural landscape in the 1970s. As if a portent of this reality, the student unrest that swept American colleges and universities in protest of the Vietnam War in the spring of 1970 spilled over onto the conservative campus of Ashland College in May 1970. Bob Hope,

181

who was perceived as an icon of President Richard Nixon's Vietnam War policy, was scheduled to speak at the college on 10 and 11 May 1970. On 4 May 1970 four students were killed by Ohio National Guardsmen on the Kent State University campus. When Hope's appearance at Ashland College became known at other Ohio campuses, some of which had closed in the aftermath of the Kent State incident, flyers began to appear, urging students to migrate to Ashland College in protest. After a homemade bomb was found in the student center on 8 May, Clayton and the administration cancelled Hope's appearance and closed the campus for a week.[1]

While this situation had little lasting effect on the college, another set of developments that generally went undetected would have a major impact on the college throughout the 1970s. The administration and Board had continued to project increases in student enrollment throughout the 1970s. Plans in 1968 called for adding 150 students per year and for developing a campus capable of serving 3300 students in 1978.[2] However, in 1970 undergraduate student enrollment peaked at 2570 and began a steady decline to a low of 1196 full-time undergraduate students in 1982. This drop in student enrollment was due, at least initially, to a number of demographic and cultural developments in America. The bubble of baby boomer enrollment had burst by the early 1970s and all colleges and universities began to vie more fiercely for the diminishing student pool. The end of the Vietnam War led to the end of the draft. Young people whose principal reason to attend college was to be deferred from the draft for four years could now look at other options following high school graduation. The 1970s were years of increasing inflation, making college education less affordable for middle class families. Job opportunities were good for high school graduates, who could earn about the same wage as those fresh with a college diploma. Declining student enrollment contributed to a number of critical issues that faced the college in the 1970s.

The most immediate problem was financial. The declining enrollments during the 1970s were difficult enough, but the budget situation was exacerbated by the cost of financing the building programs of the 1960s. In 1968 Clayton explained the fiscal philosophy that undergirded the significant expansion of the physical plant in the 1960s: "Since the college constituency is very limited and contributed funds [gifts] remain inadequate, long-term indebtedness with amortization on a self-pay basis [dormitories and cafeterias would pay for themselves through room and board fees] is the answer."[3] This philosophy was workable only as long as student enrollment continued to increase, but, even with positive growth, financing the debt would have been a challenge. In 1975 the yearly cost for servicing the long term indebtedness, which stood at $16.3 million, was $1.4 million. Debt service accounted for over 16% of the $8.5 million budget![4] The pressure on the budget from these realities created an accumulated operating deficit of over $1.8 million by 1976. In 1976 the banks in Ashland that were carrying the college loans were reluctant to cover such a sizeable sum without security. The only unsecured assets still available to the college were its endowment. In June 1976 the college was forced to declare "an extraordinary financial emergency" in order to use unrestricted endowment funds as security for the bank loans.[5] The college's financial situation continued to be precarious through the early 1980s.

The downturn in student enrollment also precipitated another crisis that began in 1971. The administration and Board determined that the college needed to make serious staff cuts in order to balance the budget. In all forty-two people received non-renewal notices, which unfortunately arrived the same day as the campus Christmas party in 1971. The faculty, who were already pushing for a new faculty handbook that would give them greater authority in the areas of grievances, dismissals, and establishment of salary schedules, were especially upset by this action. Their proposed changes to the handbook were rebuffed by the Board, however, which resented the inherent limitations to Board and presidential authority represented by the changes. The incident that ignited the already volatile situation occurred in March 1972 when Clayton issued contracts that, on his own authority, included the condition that salary increases might need to be scaled back if there were another budget shortfall. This action, together with the Board's rejection of the proposed revisions to the faculty handbook, led the faculty to vote on 9 May 1972 in favor of naming the Ohio Conference of the American Association of University Professors (AAUP) as the official bargaining unit for the Ashland College faculty.

After tense negotiations between the Board and the AAUP, an agreement was reached 14 August 1972, thereby averting a threatened strike. The faculty won concessions in the areas of faculty dismissals and non-renewals, teaching load, and selection of new faculty members. Though at times the administration and Board were able to work in concert with the AAUP, particularly when another round of dismissals was necessitated by the financial crisis in 1977,[6] the administration felt that the agreement hampered its ability to respond to critical situations and represented a departure from the more collegial relationship between faculty and administration that had formerly been true of the college. In 1980, during the presidency of Joseph Shultz, the National Labor Relations Board (NLRB) issued a complaint against the college that it had failed to bargain with the

Ashland Chapter of the AAUP. The administration made use of a recent Supreme Court case, invoking the so-called Yeshiva Principle, that under a collegial system of governance faculty members are in fact "managerial employees." Because they carried administrative responsibilities, they were excluded from coverage by the National Labor Relations Act. Based on this court decision the administration petitioned the NLRB in 1982 to rescind the ruling that the AAUP was to be the bargaining unit for the college faculty. Under the supervision of the NLRB, the administration reached an agreement with the AAUP to discontinue its role in bargaining on behalf of the faculty. As part of the settlement with the Ashland Chapter of the AAUP, a "faculty forum" was established at the college that was given legislative responsibilities in the areas of admissions and graduation requirements; curriculum and subject matter; areas of student life relating to policy, research, and instruction; and matters related to faculty welfare, duties, and organization.[7]

Not only was there faculty unrest during the 1970s, but there was also increasing agitation among the student body for more liberal policies, especially regarding the use of alcohol on campus, dorm visitation, and representation on the Board of Trustees, Executive Committee, and other policy making bodies. In fact, a number of students, in order to push their demands and in what may have been a sympathy action in support of the faculty against the administration, boycotted classes on 4 May 1972 immediately before spring break.[8]

The Board and administration did make some significant concessions to students during the 1970s. In January 1972 the Board approved the creation of two new policy making organizations. The Student Activities Budget Committee, made up of students, faculty, and administrators, considered budgetary requests for special student activities such as concerts and lectures and even for the athletic and music programs. The Student Life Policy Board was composed of students, parents, trustees, faculty, and administrators and established policies relating to campus life. The decisions of both bodies could be vetoed by the president, but this rarely occurred. Beginning in 1972 students were also invited as guests to meetings of the Board and the Executive Committee.[9]

The most controversial concession to student demands related to the allowance of alcohol on the campus. Students had begun to agitate for the right to drink 3.2% beer on campus in the late 1960s. The Board and administration had consistently taken a strict stand against all alcoholic beverages, but this began to change in 1971. In the face of mounting student pressure in 1971, the Executive Committee of the Board ruled on 15 April

1971 that "the question of the legal use of alcohol on the Ashland College campus was not a matter of board policy" and it would fully support the administration in whatever decision it made on the matter.[10] During the 1971–72 academic year the administration endorsed limited use of 3.2% beer. At a heated meeting on 14 August 1972 the Board, by secret ballot, voted down a motion to allow only non-alcoholic beverages on campus. The vote was 12 for and 24 against.[11] The alcohol policy was further liberalized in 1976 when students were permitted to drink 3.2% beer in the privacy of their own rooms.[12] Alcohol would not be completely removed from the campus until August 1989.[13]

Another student issue arose in the mid and later 1970s that was related to both the alcohol policy and the critical financial situation at the college. The college was forced to defer maintenance on the dorms and other buildings in the 1970s. The poor condition of the dorms and the campus in general negatively impacted student spirit and their respect for college property. Student vandalism of college property increased significantly in the latter 1970s.[14] Student drinking no doubt contributed to the vandalism. A student who was asked during the 1979–1980 school year about the spirit of the student body stated succinctly, "It's the pits!"[15] During his presidency Joseph Shultz aggressively addressed the issues of deferred maintenance and campus beautification. These and other initiatives in such areas as student activities, campus governance, and judicial affairs contributed to a dramatic reversal in student attitudes by 1981. Student vandalism was reduced to only $3000 for the entire academic year in 1980–81, while judicial cases dropped 20% from the previous year.[16]

Even the weather seemed to conspire against the college in the latter 1970s. A critical shortage of natural gas, worsened by one of the most severe winters on record in 1976–77, led to severe cutbacks in natural gas. Columbia Gas required the college to reduce consumption by 85% from its 1972–74 usage. Though there was discussion about closing the campus for a period of time, students and faculty voted to continue classes in spite of the frigid conditions. Most of the classroom space as well as the library was heated by fuel oil or electricity; only the Physical Education Center needed the assistance of space heaters to cut the cold.[17]

In 1977, at the close of his twenty-ninth year as president of the college, Clayton retired after a distinguished career. Even today he is highly respected for the leadership that he provided the college in both good times and periods of crisis. In 1977 the Board selected as the next president Arthur Schultz, who had been serving as the president of Albright College. Schultz received his education at Otterbein College (B.A.), United Theological

Arthur Schultz

Seminary (M.Div.), and the University of Pittsburgh (M.Ed. and Ph.D.). During his tenure the Board sought to address the array of problems facing the college. The Board appointed a Joint Committee on Program and Priorities Assessment in July 1979 with a charge to bring a report to the 6 August 1979 Executive Committee. Using a number of previous studies as resources, the Joint Committee brought an interim report to the Executive Committee with thirteen recommendations. Most of the recommendations needed further examination, such as combining multiple sections of courses, requiring an enrollment of at least eight students in a course, and expansion of continuing education programs with a strong growth potential. However, the Executive Committee did approve the sale of all properties that were not essential to the operation of the college and the reduction of non-academic secretarial staff through non-replacement and reassignment.[18] Over the next few years the Board authorized the sale of a number of non-essential properties and even considered the sale or lease of college buildings between Claremont and Broad (Kem, Amstutz, and Andrews).

Schultz proved to be an ineffectual leader, generally failing to address the grave issues facing the college. He was released by the Board in August 1979. The Board was faced with a dire situation. The difficulties facing the college were serious and the beginning of school was just weeks away. Without someone to give capable leadership to the college, the school might not open. At this critical juncture the Board turned to a man who had proven his ability to lead an educational institution with vision, creativity, and decisive action—Joseph Shultz.[19] Though at times the latter of these qualities would rankle those with whom he worked, he possessed the gifts needed to weather the storm threatening the college at this time.

The Forging of a New Era for the College

Leaving a highly successful career at the seminary, Shultz threw his energies into restoring the fiscal soundness and reversing the demoralized outlook of the college. He worked with the local banks and scrounged the limited assets of the college to continue to pay the bills and meet the payroll. He launched an aggressive program to upgrade the campus buildings and beautify the campus. He worked with accrediting organizations to remove notations and avoid probation. He sought to bring better organization to the diverse academic programs at the college.[20] Appointed initially as the interim president in 1979, Shultz made such significant headway in reversing the direction of the college in one year that he was unanimously called by the Board as the next president of the college on 25 April 1980.

Shultz realized that if he were to successfully address the long-term financial challenges of the college, he needed to deal with the harsh realities created by a declining student pool among 18 to 24 year olds. His strategy included giving priority to recruitment and retention and adding at least one new program and/or extension per year. Shultz developed a variety of new programs such as a B.S. in Nursing degree, the Ashland Academy, and varied continuing education programs, and he aggressively expanded the M.Ed. and M.B.A. programs by opening new extensions.

Interestingly, Clayton had initially opposed graduate level education at the college, insisting that the institution first needed an exceptional undergraduate program. But by the mid-1970s he lent his support to this venture. After receiving approval from the Ohio Board of Regents for graduate education in 1975, the college opened the M.Ed. program in January 1976 on a limited basis, pending North Central Association accreditation, which was achieved later that year.[21] The M.B.A. degree began in 1978. Shultz's decision to invest the limited resources of the college into the graduate program has proven over the last twenty-five years to have been one of the most financially astute investments the college has even made. Not only did it help to underwrite the liberal arts program, renovate the campus, upgrade equipment, and pay off the college's short-term and long-term indebtedness,[22] but it would also establish Ashland College/University as one of the leading private graduate institutions in the entire region.

The growth of the college administratively and academically caused both Clayton and Shultz to address the organization of the institution. During his tenure Clayton streamlined the administrative structure of the college. In August 1972 the Executive Committee of the Board approved a recommendation by Clayton to create a new administrative structure which consolidated all the administrative functions of the college into four divisions, each with its own vice president. The four divisions were: Academic Affairs, Finance or Business Affairs, Seminary, and Public Relations and Development. Each of these divisions had a corresponding committee within the Board of Trustees. The vice presidents formed an administrative committee that advised the President on significant institutional matters. They also attended meetings of the Board but did not vote. The new structure was phased in during 1972 and 1973.[23]

In 1968 Clayton also sought a reorganization of the college curricula into seven divisions: science, which had already been designated a division; humanities; social science; communicative arts; economics and business administration; teacher education; and health, physical education and athletics. Each division had a director and the directors met together with the dean of the college to form an Academic Council. This council met regularly to address important academic matters. Under Arthur Schultz, this structure gave way to a more decentralized system of departments.[24]

When Joseph Shultz came to the college in 1979, the academic program of the college was organized into nineteen departments, each with its own chairperson. At the time the Philosophy Department consisted of only one person, who served as the chairperson; in other cases departments had only a few members. The continuing financial crisis might have warranted cutbacks in the academic program, but Shultz was determined not to take this course of action because it would jeopardize the liberal arts identity of the college. Relying on some of the recommendations of the Joint Committee on Program and Priorities Assessment, he sought to reorganize the academic program of the college and make cost-savings through consolidation rather than cuts.[25] He gained support to restructure the college into four schools: the School of Arts and Humanities; the School of Business Administration, Economics, and Radio/TV; the School of Education and Related Professions; and the School of Sciences. The restructuring, proposed in early 1980, was in place for the 1980–81 academic year. The School of Nursing was added later in 1980. As part of the restructuring, a dean was selected from each school and formed a Deans' Council. The Deans' Council worked with the administration to strengthen and expand the academic program of the college. The Council helped to deal with faculty concerns and played a role in bringing an end to the AAUP bargaining unit.[26] Shultz also created an Academic Affairs Council in 1979, which took a comprehensive look at the academic program in a follow-up to the work of the Joint Committee on Program and Priorities Assessment. The council made recommendations for trimming $250,000 from the 1980–81 budget and for covering various academic program expenses.[27] Completing its work in 1980, the Council's recommendations were forwarded to the Deans' Council.

This reorganization had a number of positive effects. Sufficient numbers of faculty in related fields were brought together to be able to develop a greater spirit of collegiality and mutual support and to create a synergy to address significant academic issues. The faculty was empowered to make decisions about their colleagues and the academic program. Above all, the faculty expressed a new confidence in the future of the college that was in stark contrast to the demoralized attitude that prevailed prior to Shultz's appointment as interim president in 1979.[28] The reorganization also prepared the way for the transition to a university structure in 1989.[29]

In August 1979 the Board of Trustees began a process that would further infuse a renewed sense of accomplishment within the college community. The Board expressed a desire to hire an outside professional fund raising organization to address the grim fiscal outlook. On 14 December 1979 the Executive Committee contracted with Goettler Associates, Inc. of Columbus, Ohio, to conduct a feasibility study for a capital campaign. Representatives of Goettler Associates brought their report to the Board on 25 April 1980 and were very supportive of launching a major fund drive. The capital campaign was designated "A Time of Opportunity" and chaired by John H. McConnell, a member of the Board of Trustees. It sought to raise $7.7 million, divided into five categories: Plant Endowment Program ($1 million), Energy Conservation and Campus Renewal Program ($300,000), Scholarship Endowment Program ($2.5 million), Faculty Endowment Program ($1.2 million), and Unrestricted Annual Giving ($2.7 million). The campaign, launched in 1980, continued to run through June 1985, beyond its initial termination date of June 1982. At the Victory Dinner and Reception for the campaign on 18 April 1985, it was announced that the campaign total had reached $8,792,333. The final accounting, which included deferred giving, attained $10.6 million. The campaign infused much needed capital into the college and, more importantly, helped to generate additional enthusiasm among the college's constituencies.[30]

After a decade of crisis and disillusionment throughout most of the 1970s, the college, soon-to-be university, was positioned for another period of remarkable progress and growth throughout the remainder of the twentieth and into the twenty-first century. Whatever weaknesses Shultz possessed, he does need to be credited with laying the foundation upon which much of the present success of the university rests.

The Institutional Philosophy of Ashland College

Between 1976 and 1980 three succinct statements concerning the identity and institutional philosophy of Ashland College appeared. Even in the midst of significant crisis and change, these statements reflect that much of the core identity of the college remained unchanged. The first statement appeared in Clayton's annual report to the Board in 1976 as he reprised the major developments of his tenure as president.

> The philosophy and policy of Ashland College have been determined by factors that are both historical and empirical. Among the former are: (1) a basic allegiance to the liberal arts at least as a core program; (2) a relationship with the Brethren Church; (3) a personal and friendly concern for students springing from a compact campus and a relatively small enrollment; (4) a sense of responsibility for the success of graduates through career orientation and (5) a commitment to private higher education as basic to a valuable concept of American tradition.

> Among the latter are: (1) a flexibility in programs to meet the changing needs of society; (2) an increasing awareness of vocationally-related courses of study both to attract students and to remain current with the needs of society; (3) an adaptation to budgetary restrictions while striving to improve quality of productive effort and (4) a policy of student recruitment aimed at breadth of economic, spiritual and social experience, within the limits of available students who can qualify for and afford Ashland College.[31]

There were several elements of Clayton's Ashland College that would undergo significant transformation in Joseph Shultz's Ashland University, notably the size of the campus and student body and the financial restraints of the 1970s. Nevertheless, there were also a number of points of continuity between the college of the 1970s and the university of the late 1980s and 1990s (see discussion below).

The second statement is probably the first college document to be called a "statement of mission." It was prepared at the request of the Board of Trustees by a special committee that included Arthur Schultz. It was formally adopted by the Board on 17 August 1978 and continued to be used in official college documents through the 1993–94 academic year.

Ashland College Statement of Mission

Ashland College in its undergraduate, graduate, and continuing education programs believes that its mission is to prepare students to be successful human beings—successful morally, spiritually, intellectually, culturally, physically, socially, and economically. Our goal is to develop the best possible scholars in all areas. We want our graduates to be leaders in society, and we want them to bring philosophically sound ideas into their professions and into our culture, and thus to combine the values of the liberal arts with a career in a professional area.

This philosophy requires that the student gain awareness of the universe around us, our culture, and the institutions that we use and shape as we live our lives. It requires a liberating of the mind through a development of critical appreciation of the different ways of knowledge and understanding known to man and through awareness of other cultures and times that lead to informed judgments relevant to the moral and ethical problems of man and his society. It also requires that the student achieve depth in some chosen area of study by developing the powers of reasoning and analysis in that field.

To achieve this, Ashland College provides for an integrated education, an education that infuses the best that has been thought and said in the world into all the disciplines pursued at the college. At the baccalaureate level the college requires a strong core curriculum of literature, history, science, the arts, philosophy, religion, physical education, and languages, including a sound understanding of our English language. Symbolically, the library stands as the center of learning where all areas of knowledge meet.

The liberal arts are not exclusive of one another but together form the basis for the understanding of the human experience. As a church-related college, we also believe that our students should be well grounded in the Judeo-Christian tradition through appropriate classroom situations and campus activities.[32]

Note that this statement contains the first reference to "Judeo-Christian tradition" in official Ashland College literature. The general impression given by this statement is that it could be applicable to just about any liberal arts college that was church-related. It contains less content that is uniquely characteristic of Ashland College than the other two statements in this section.

The third statement appeared as part of the institutional analysis prepared in 1980 by Goettler Associates, Inc. in preparation for the college's $7.7 million capital campaign.

> Ashland [College] looks forward with solid determination and conviction to this coming decade and the end of this century wherein the College can provide those basics of higher education so desperately needed for the continuance of the American scene. Ashland accepts its role in the personal total development of leaders for the implementation of the American dream. . . . Within this total commitment, Ashland College will continue to provide specifically the following:
>
> 1.   A combination of an excellent liberal arts program with an unusually wide range of career-oriented programs thereby offering its students many of the advantages of a large university within a small college setting.
>
> 2.   A moral and spiritual foundation within Ashland's philosophy and perspective, as influenced by its historic association with the Brethren Church—a strong asset in times that demand morality in personal as well as in professional decision-making.
>
> 3.   An emphasis on free enterprise which remains vital in a society where understanding and appreciation of the private enterprise system are often lacking. Ashland recognizes its responsibility to help build in its own way a global society which affirms the essential inter-relationship of democracy, private enterprise and ethical conduct.
>
> 4.   An emphasis on the human service professions and on direct service to the community and society to make it more attractive to today's young people.[33]

Goettler Associates did a commendable job in capturing a number of the unique features of Ashland College in the above four points.

Each of these statements contains elements that are peculiar to its own context. Yet, taken together, they also reinforce many of the historic emphases of the college: the liberal arts are the foundation for a well-rounded and grounded education; education properly conceived is a process impacting the total person; education ought to open our minds to the larger world around us and our responsibility to serve others; the liberal arts should be tied to career preparation in a professional area; a liberal arts education needs to expose students to the realities of faith, particularly, though not exclusively, the Christian faith; the ties to the Brethren Church are an asset to the moral and spiritual formation of college students.

Changing Perspectives concerning the Christian Faith and the Brethren Church

The decades of the 1960s and 70s witnessed some dramatic changes in both the college's attitude toward the Christian faith and its historic ties to the Brethren Church. With the percentage of Brethren students within the entire student body continuing to drop during the 1960s (less than 10% in 1963), the administration faced the reality that students came from a broad spectrum of denominational perspectives or even lacked any religious background. Roman Catholic and Jewish students were also coming in increasing numbers. By the early 1960s the administration had come to view

> the religious objective of the college not as one aiming at the "evangelizing" of the campus for any one spiritual position [though the college had previously declared itself as Christian, it had always committed itself to being non-sectarian], but as encouraging a respect for religion as a part of one's life style and of growing involvement in the church and faith professed by the student.[34]

Reflective of this new perspective, specific references to the Christian faith gradually diminish during the 1960s in the catalogue and official records, to be replaced by a more generic reference to "spiritual values" or, more frequently, "religion." It is revealing to see how Christianity and even religion are dealt with in the centerpiece of Clayton's educational philosophy, the Ac'cent Program. The fourth side of the hexagon that visually portrayed the college's commitment to "Ac'cent on the Individual" was originally "Strengthening of the Religious Atmosphere." In 1965 Clayton had declared: "Emphasis upon spiritual values, upon the importance and value of the church as a vital institution in our society, and upon Christian decision is an ever-present concern in the program of 'Accent on the Individual.'"[35] Yet just three years later the fourth side of the hexagon was delineated as "Emphasis on Society." In the explanation for the label, Clayton indicated religion was one of several aspects of society in which the college sought to educate and involve its students (others were economics, human resources development, and government). In 1969 Clayton explained that the "College views its role as one of encouraging religion as a vital part of society and seeks to create such as ecumenical atmosphere as should prevail in any community."[36] This new label on the hexagon represents a continuing shift away from the longstanding view that Christianity was foundational for the identity of the college to the new perspective that placed it within the context of religion and considered it as one of a number of sociological and anthropological phenomena that contributed to the welfare of society.

Several significant changes in the late 1960s and early 1970s underscore this shift. In 1969 the Bible Department was replaced by the Religion Department. It is striking to compare the descriptions or purpose statements for these departments. Regarding the Bible Department the catalogue prior to 1969 stated:

> Because of the profound influence of the Bible upon human thought and conduct, a general knowledge of its literature, history, and ideas should be regarded as an essential part of any liberal education. This is to say nothing of the vital and permanent interests of the Church in the literary documents which record the historic facts of the Christian faith.[37]

In contrast, note the statement in the catalogue for 1969–70:

> Because of the profound influence of Religion upon human thought and conduct, a general knowledge of its literature, history, and ideas should be regarded as an essential part of any liberal education. Religion centers in the human search for meaning and purpose and is presented as one of the important means to intellectual and emotional growth, and thus, individual and social maturity.[38]

Religion has replaced the Bible as a major cultural force. Likewise, attention is no longer on the church and the literary deposits of the Christian faith but on religion as a subject of sociological inquiry and a means to human betterment. It is true that these shifts were tempered by a list of objectives that retained the focus on the Bible and Christianity and that the Religion Department continued to have faculty who were deeply committed to the Christian faith.[39] But the above subtle changes reflect the impact of modernity's investigation of religion as a social and psychological science, with its accompanying commitment to a disengaged, objective analysis of its subject matter.

The administration had been struggling for a number of years over the issue of required chapels. Mandatory chapel became increasingly unpopular with a generation of students who rebelled against social conventions. There was also the feeling that to require chapel was counterproductive for evoking an inner desire in students for the deepening of their spiritual life. In 1971 required chapels ended; in their place the college offered a series of voluntary chapel programs. Weekly convocations were reestablished in 1977, though their focus was not solely religious in nature.[40] Even these weekly convocations seem to have been discontinued by the time Shultz became president in 1979.

The administration moved from a structured approach to religious life to a more informal approach during the 1970s. In 1972 the position of Director of Religious Affairs, held by Virgil Meyer since 1956, was discontinued, presumably for both philosophical and financial reasons. This action meant that there was no administrator on the campus whose title indicated responsibility for religious affairs. Technically, religious affairs became a function of the office of the President; more direct oversight, however, was to be given by the Office of Student Affairs.[41] The significant responsibilities of these offices, however, meant that there was only minimal attention given to spiritual matters. Religious life on the campus was supported through the Religion Department and the Religious Interests Faculty Committee and especially through various Christian student organizations such as Alpha Theta (begun in the mid-1960s and discontinued in 1980), the Coalition for Christian Outreach, and, in 1979, HOPE Fellowship (HOPE is an acronym for His Own People Eternally).

In his yearly *President's Report to the Trustees*, Clayton continued to make brief comments about the importance of the religious and even the Christian heritage of the college in the 1970s up to his retirement, but the priority given to the Christian life throughout the 1950s and the first half of the 1960s is lacking. Indeed, with the end of the position of the Director of Religious Life, the omission of any significant discussion of campus religious life in these reports is striking.[42] The position of Director of Religious Affairs was reinstated by Arthur Schultz in 1978 and continued by Joseph Shultz. Fred Burkey held this position from 1978 until 1980 and was followed by James Menninger in 1981. Jim Miller served as the Interim Director in the 1980–81 academic year.

In the mid-1970s the Brethren Church sought to be pro-active in addressing the lack of any structured campus ministry at the college. The 1973 General Conference lent its support to a Christian Campus Ministry being spearheaded by Park Street Brethren Church and guided by Jim Geaslen. The conference recommended that all Brethren districts back this effort with funding of fifty cents a member. In 1975 General Conference voted to move oversight of the Christian Campus Ministry position to an advisory council at the denominational level and called upon this council to work in concert with the college administration and the Religious Interests Committee. Donald Snell, a seminary student, was hired for this new position. Also in 1975 the National Laymen's Organization of the Brethren Church began to provide financial backing of $2500 a year for its own campus ministry. Michael Gleason and, later, Susan Canfield, were supported by the Laymen. To the credit of these two ministries, they worked in concert on the college campus, though Snell took the lead. In November 1976 the Central Council of the Brethren Church, in an effort to unify the work of Campus Ministry, recommended that the National Laymen's Organization forward "all designated monies, recommendations for personnel, and suggestions to the Committee charged with the responsibility of administering the program of campus ministry [the Campus Ministry Advisory Council], beginning with the school year 1977–78."[43] When the position of Director of Religious Affairs was restored in 1978 under Arthur Schultz, financial support continued to come for this position from the Laymen, districts in the Brethren Church, and some local Woman's Missionary Society groups.[44]

The shifting perspective of the administration concerning matters of faith is underscored by an examination of the college catalogues during the 1960s and 70s. In 1963 the catalogue was revised. The following strong affirmation of the importance of faith appeared in the section headed "History and Purpose."

> . . . all members of the college community are expected to accept sympathetically several basic premises: (a) orientation of life with God and the development of a religious philosophy is [sic] a definite part of education. To this end students are encouraged to grow in religious service through active support of the church of their choice . . . [45]

In the 1966–67 catalogue a revised "History and Purpose" section omits any mention of faith except for the concluding sentence which affirms that the student is allowed "freedom to develop responsibility along intellectual, social, and spiritual lines."[46] An equally strong declaration about the importance of Christian conviction and practice appears in the revised 1963 catalogue in the section on "Student Life."

> Since the College is proud of its church affiliation and believes firmly that no education can be complete without the spiritual and moral influence of Christian conviction and growth, all members of the community will be expected to practice their religious convictions, to attend religious services, and to seek to develop a positive Christian philosophy of life.[47]

This statement remained in the catalogue until the next major revision of the catalogue in 1971. In this catalogue there is no mention of religious services or Christian commitments in the student life section. As a sign of the times, the positive goal of developing a Christian philosophy of life found in catalogues through 1970–71 gives way in the 1972–73 catalogue to a discussion of student conduct that contains prohibitions of the use of alcohol and illegal drugs.

One of the most intriguing changes found in the catalogues from the 1960s through the 1970s is the rationale for the maintenance of proper standards of conduct by students. The 1963–64 catalogue declared that student behavior should be dictated by what befits proper Christian conduct. The 1972–73 catalogue changed the rationale, encouraging students "to observe standards of conduct conducive to the purposes of the College." The "overriding general regulation" was that "no student may interfere with the growth opportunities of another."[48] Institutional and altruistic considerations replaced Christian principles as a foundation for ethical behavior. Interestingly, there is no mention of standards for student conduct in the 1975–77 catalogue.

Changes also occurred to several features that had been present in catalogues since the 1930s. In 1965 the statement of faith (the Apostles' Creed) that had appeared in the catalogue since 1938 was moved to the back of the catalogue in the section dealing with the seminary. The statement was dropped altogether in 1975. In 1975 the five institutional objectives that had been developed by Anspach in 1936 and that had continued to guide the college for decades were substantially revised. The first objective, which framed students' collegiate program within "influences which are frankly and avowedly Christian" and which expressed the desire "to provide opportunities for Christian experience," was edited in a way that weakened the strong affirmation and promotion of a Christian ethos for the college. The new objective pledged the college to provide an academic environment that was "under influences that are based on sound Christian ideals and designed to make possible viable Christian experiences."[49] The difference in the two statements may be framed as a promotion versus a possibility of Christian experience. A substantial change to the objectives was the entire deletion of the third objective: "To prepare students for service as ministers, missionaries and religious workers, especially in the Brethren Church." However, a similar statement was added to the history section in the front of the catalogue. The removal of this objective, nevertheless, highlights where the emphasis is being placed with regard to the historic dual mission of Ashland College: the liberal arts are given priority over the training of people for service in the church at the collegiate level. It also is symptomatic of a weakening of the ties to the Brethren Church and of the transferal of any institutional mission for serving the broader church to the seminary.

With the changes occurring in the life of Ashland College during the 1960s and 70s, it is entirely understandable that a strain would develop between the college and the Brethren Church. Throughout this period catalogues continued to declare that the college was affiliated with the Brethren Church. Likewise, the catalogues through most of this period indicate that the college "has sought to serve the interests of the church educationally."[50] This statement was, however, dropped from the revised catalogue of 1979–80. In spite of these official pronouncements, there were a number of factors that served to weaken the historic ties. The church was not committing and simply could not commit the financial and human resources to a college that had grown so significantly in the latter 1960s. The enrollment of Brethren students in the college peaked at 150 in the 1965–66 academic year; this number represented 9.18% of the student body. By the 1971–72 academic year only 68 Brethren were enrolled in the college, representing a meager 2.66% of the student body. Between the 1970–71 and 1975–76 budget years, giving from the church ranged from a low of $22,791 in 1970–71 to a high of $86,123 in 1974–75. In a total budget that had grown to $8.5 million in the 1974–75 budget year, such amounts were a drop-in-the-bucket.[51] By the 1980–81 academic year only 4 Brethren were present in a college faculty numbering 95 (4.2%). Interestingly, the constitution of the college continued to declare, as it currently still does (though with minor edits), that "So far as practicable, the professors and assistants shall be elected from members of The Brethren Church in the United States of America."[52]

The church certainly was feeling that its influence over the college was slipping by the 1970s. The church had already begun to express some concern over the direction of Ashland College in the mid-1960s. In 1964 General Conference supported a recommendation by Moderator William H. Anderson that the college should bring more teachers and lecturers of an "evangelical persuasion" to the school and that there should be a stronger emphasis on creating a "spiritual atmosphere where faith in Christ can be fostered."[53] General Conference did commend the administration for its handling of the explosive situation on the campus in the aftermath of the Kent State tragedy in 1970 and of the student pressure in 1971 to liberalize the policies regarding dorm visitation and the use of alcohol.[54]

Many in the Brethren Church, however, were dismayed and incensed when, in the 1971–72 academic year, the administration reversed its policy and allowed 3.2% beer on campus. The Board received letters calling for a return to the previous prohibition of alcoholic beverages from the Pennsylvania, Central, Indiana, and Ohio districts of the Brethren Church and from the Marion, Indiana, Brethren Church. When the Board upheld the administration's position on 14 August 1972, General Conference adopted a carefully worded motion on 18 August 1972 that sought a balanced response to the issue:

> . . . we respectfully petition the Board of Trustees of Ashland College, the Executive Committee of the Board, the Administration, the Student Life Policy Council, and other responsible groups to reaffirm the Christian morals and ethics as commonly interpreted by the Brethren Church and to re-establish the practice thereof.
>
> We further recommend that the churches support the College and Seminary through prayer, through College and Seminary enrollment, and through financial resources.[55]

The Board, on its part, had also sought to maintain a conciliatory attitude toward the church in spite of supporting the administration's position. Immediately after the vote to back the administration's policy, the Board adopted the following motion: "It is the desire of this Board of Trustees to continue a good and constructive relationship with the Brethren Church."[56] The Board and administration were caught in a difficult dilemma. Facing student and faculty activism on one side and the conservative values of the church on the other, the Board, following the lead of the administration, opted to seek peace within the campus community and risk the displeasure of the Brethren Church.

Another factor contributing to the concern that the church was losing its influence on the college was changes to the composition of and selection process to the Board. Three times between 1964 and 1981 the Board approved restructuring of its membership. In 1964 the number of at-large members was increased, lowering the percentage of Brethren members from 71% to 63%. The restructuring in 1971 did not change the percentage of Brethren on the Board, though it did increase the number of at-large members (some of the at-large seats on the Board were to be held by Brethren, thereby maintaining the same ratio as before). After a major restructuring and downsizing of the Board in 1981, however, Brethren held only a simple majority on the Board, though in practice some of the at-large seats not specifically set aside for the Brethren have been held by Brethren.[57]

A controversial change to the selection process for Board members was adopted in 1965. Districts of the Brethren Church continued to be able to nominate candidates to serve as trustees, but the Board was now authorized to submit nominees for trustees from each district as well. The district representatives on the Board from Pennsylvania were deeply concerned that this change would seriously jeopardize the influence that the church had on the Board. They brought a motion to the 1965 General Conference asking the conference to memorialize the Board of Trustees to set aside this proposed amendment. Another member of the Board, J. Garber Drushal, spoke in opposition to the motion and moved that it be tabled. In a vote no doubt reflecting the deep concern in the church about the direction of the college, Drushal's motion passed by a slim majority of 100 to 98.[58]

This constitutional change was motivated primarily by certain legalities associated with funding for the college's building projects. The college was more likely to receive federal grants if control of the college was vested in a Board of Trustees that was not legally accountable to any other group, including the church. As noted in an earlier chapter, the Board in 1937 had adopted a controversial change to the selection process of trustees. The change had specified that each district should nominate twice the number of people for each open position on the Board. The Board then elected the member(s) to represent a given district of the Brethren Church from the nominations brought by that district. This change was deemed to give the Board greater freedom to select its members as it chose. But legal counsel in 1965 felt this process was still problematic. The change adopted in 1965 specified that:

> The Conference of Ohio and the various district conferences of the Brethren Church . . . may nominate candidates to serve as trustees from the respective conferences. The Board of Trustees, either by its Nominating Committee or from the floor, may also submit nominees for trustees from each conference. From the nominees thus submitted the members of the Corporation Ashland College shall elect the appropriate number of trustees from the Conference of Ohio and each District Conference.[59]

This amendment clearly changed the amount of direct control that the church had over the college, though the 1937 change had served to limit the church's control as well. The effect of the change for many in the church was to further reinforce the sentiment that the college was slipping away from the control of the church.

A gauge of the relationship between the college and church is reflected in discussions related to the college that occurred at the 1979, 1980, and 1981 General Conferences of the Brethren Church. The 1979 conference was held shortly after Joseph Shultz became interim president of the college. Dale RuLon brought a motion to the floor that:

> We, The Brethren, gathered in the 91st General Conference of the Brethren Church, wholly support Dr. Joseph R. Shultz as Interim President of Ashland College. We support him with our prayers and our finances as he assumes the leadership of the college. We pledge our support to the purpose of Ashland College, that of training men and women in their vocation with a strong foundation of Biblical principles upon which they may mold their lives. We, as The Brethren Church assembled in Ashland, Ohio, on August 15, pledge our support to the administration, faculty, and trustees of Ashland College. May God richly bless Dr. Joseph R. Shultz as he assumes the presidency of Ashland College.[60]

In spite of the potential for change represented by Shultz's coming to the college, other delegates at the conference felt the direction taken by the college in the 1970s did not warrant such a strong affirmation of the college situation, even with the change in leadership. Reflective of this view was Floyd Benshoff, who offered a substitute motion that "this Conference moves to stand in prayer and pledge their prayerful following of the situation as it has confronted Ashland College." Lengthy discussion ensued. A vote to table the matter until the next day was defeated. The substitute motion was then defeated and the original motion carried.[61]

The Board of Trustees was meeting concurrently with the 1979 conference. Pleased by the conference's expression of support for the college in its current crisis, the Board issued the following resolution to the conference:

> The Board of Trustees of Ashland College expresses its deepest appreciation for the Resolution of concern and support of the College at this time in its history. It was moved by [Ohio State] Senator Thomas Van Meter, seconded by Reverend James Black, that the Board of Trustees pledges itself to its best efforts not only to the continuance but also the upbuilding of Ashland College toward the traditions upon which it was founded. The motion carried by a unanimous vote.[62]

Board member Thomas Stoffer moved the conference's reception and adoption of the resolution. Before the vote, which was affirmative, Stoffer stated that the Board itself expressed concern "at some of the campus activities and indicated their willingness to help the administration in the review and modification of the rules that govern student activity." The conference did, however, raise an issue of continuing concern. Immediately following the above vote, Harold Barnett moved that the "Conference go on record as supporting the trustees and administration of Ashland College in any effort to eliminate alcoholic beverages from the campus."[63] The conference passed the motion. Though the conference expressed strong affirmation of Shultz and offered its support to the college, it had ongoing concerns about the direction of the college and some, at least, exhibited a rather critical attitude about even the current state of the institution.

In 1980, after Shultz's first full year in office, Harold Barnett reminded the conference of the 1979 action regarding the elimination of alcoholic beverages from the conference. He questioned whether "any progress had been made in this regard and expressed the desire that this would be a continuing concern."[64] His remarks came across as an accusatory lecture of Shultz and the failure to rid the campus of alcohol. Shultz was very upset by this public reprimand, especially since he was still fighting for the college's very survival.[65]

One of the most contentious episodes in the church-college relationship since the 1930s occurred at the 1981 General Conference. The Pennsylvania District Conference recommended the approval of the following statement and its delivery to the Chairman of the Board of Trustees:

> The 93rd General Conference of the Brethren Church desires to renew and strengthen its protest to the sale of and the permission to use any alcoholic beverages at Ashland College. We believe that God cannot fully bless the college or its supporters as long as this sinful practice continues. Therefore, if you desire the continued support of the Brethren Church, we insist that alcoholic beverages be banned from the Ashland College Campus immediately—before another class of college freshmen is introduced to it.[66]

When discussion of the motion was taken up the next day (it had been introduced late in the business session), J. D. Hamel made a motion to end the statement after the first sentence. Jim Miller then presented the following amendment to Hamel's motion:

> We request from Dr. Joseph Shultz, President of Ashland College, a written report detailing his short and long range plans for transforming Ashland College into a Christ centered college of the Brethren Church; that a task force be appointed to study options and alternatives that the Brethren Church has with regard to our future with Ashland College, including methods by which the voice of the Brethren can be more strongly heard and listened to, or any other recommendations it sees as necessary; that

both of these parties report at this time next year and a course of action be decided at that time.[67]

After considerable debate, Miller's amendment was passed, though a standing vote was necessary after a voice vote was inconclusive. A ballot vote was taken for the amended motion; it passed by a vote of 239 for and 103 against the motion.

There are several noteworthy points about the motion and its aftermath. The motion clearly reflected the church's concern that the college had moved beyond its Brethren roots and the sense that the church had lost significant control over the college. Intriguingly, there is no indication that Shultz ever developed the stipulated report or that a task force was ever convened. The leadership of the church may not have had the heart to pursue a course of action which would lead only to greater animosity between the church and college. Barnett did renew his annual litany of opposition to alcohol in 1982, though with a far more conciliatory tone. His motion to "heartily continue our support of the administration and trustees of Ashland College in their efforts to rid the campus of alcoholic beverages" was approved; however, a motion to rescind this action was offered, but failed after a division of the house.[68] It is also interesting that Shultz gave only one college report at Brethren conferences between 1983 and 1991, preferring to have other college/university personnel perform this function. He may have felt that, for his own emotional welfare, he needed to maintain some distance between himself and the church at these times of accountability.

The 1970s and early 1980s were the low point of college-church relations. The fact that the church was unable to supply the resources necessary to keep the college viable forced the college to turn to other constituencies for students, faculty, and financial support. This reality was also reflected in the changing composition of the Board. All these factors, plus the college's renewed emphasis on the liberal arts, tended to work against the traditional Christian emphasis of the college. The administration and faculty dropped any sense that Ashland was a Christian college by the early 1960s, adopting the language of Ashland being a church-affiliated or church-related school. Some within the college community went further, however, espousing the perspective of the secular college/university with regard to religion. For them, religion was viewed in terms of a sociological and anthropological phenomenon; overt promotion of any faith, including Christian, was to be avoided. Though clearly not all administrators or faculty would have taken this latter stance, the college/university has tended to move in this general direction from the 1970s to the present.

The Coming of Age of Ashland Theological Seminary

The Push for Accreditation (1963–1970)

While the college was facing some of its darkest days during the 1970s, the seminary was emerging into a new era of growth and broader recognition. In 1963, when Joseph Shultz assumed the leadership of the seminary, the school had only 27 students. In 1982, when Frederick Finks came as the new vice president of the seminary, the seminary had grown to 436 students. In this same period of time the faculty and administration had grown from six full-time personnel to thirteen. The budget had grown from about $50,000 in 1963 to over $600,000 in 1982. These remarkable changes were primarily linked to the seminary's achievement of accreditation in 1969.

The push for the accreditation of the seminary by the American Association of Theological Schools that had begun in the late 1950s was the dominant concern of Joseph Shultz when he arrived as dean of the seminary in 1963. The most significant issues that needed to be addressed if accredi-

Faculty, staff, and students in 1963; the faculty and staff in the front row, from left to right, are: Joseph Shultz, Charles Munson, Bruce Stark, Wretha Palone, Nancy Rhoades, and Edwin Boardman

Owen H. Alderfer

tation were to become a reality were the size of the faculty and student body and a significant expansion of the library holdings. In actuality, however, nearly every phase of the seminary's life was affected in the process.

In 1963 the full-time seminary teaching faculty consisted of Flora, who was on sabbatical leave during the 1963–64 academic year, Boardman,

Louis F. Gough with students (left to right) Ralph Fry,
Ed Biggs, Robert Young, Charles Ready, and Steven Cole

Albert T. Ronk

Munson, and Stark. Klingensmith divided his time between the college and seminary. One of the major goals for obtaining Associate membership in the American Association of Theological Schools was to increase the faculty numbers from 4½ to 6. Though only one full-time position was added through 1969, the seminary made greater use of faculty resources at the college, of specialized personnel, and of adjuncts. In 1965 Boardman was given Professor Emeritus status but continued to work in the seminary as a consultant to senior students for their theses. He was replaced in the field of church history by Owen H. Alderfer. Alderfer had earned degrees from Upland College (B.A.), Asbury Theological Seminary (B.D.), and Claremont Graduate School (Ph.D.). Joining the faculty in 1968 as a professor of New Testament and Theology was Louis F. Gough, who was educated at Anderson College (B.S., B.Th.), Duke University (B.D.), and Princeton Theological Seminary (Th.D.). In 1971 Gough had the distinction of being the first member of the seminary faculty to deliver a paper at the Society of Biblical Literature.[69] Albert T. Ronk also joined the faculty in 1968 as the archivist and Brethren Church historian; he died in 1972. In the 1968–69 seminary catalogue three college faculty are listed: Klingensmith (Systematic Theology), George Spink (New Testament), and Andrew Gregersen (Voice). Llewelyn Owen also appears in the catalogue as a professor of Psychology and Counselor, though he would have served in an adjunct role. Though the American Association of Theological Schools would continue to press the seminary to add full-time faculty, these faculty resources proved to be sufficient to obtain accreditation in 1969.

In 1962 the Seminary Committee indicated that an enrollment of 25 students would meet the requirements for Associate membership in the American Association of Theological Schools; full membership would require 50 students. The goal for Associate membership was achieved by the 1963–64 academic year when 27 students were enrolled. Enrollment in the seminary continued to grow steadily throughout the decade. The 1965–66 academic year saw 49 students enrolled in the school with enrollment rising to the required 50 students in the 1968–69 academic year and 55 the following year. Increasingly, the student body was becoming less Brethren. In the 1970–71 academic year, for example, there were 17 Brethren students out of a total enrollment of 70 (24%). Students came from 15 denominations; Brethren did have the most students of any denomination represented in the seminary, however. By the end of the 1960s most of the students were coming from colleges and universities other than Ashland College. In the 1968–69 academic year only 45% of the students came from the college; the student body represented 21 different colleges and universities.[70] This growth was occurring due to more aggressive recruitment outside the Brethren and Ashland College constituencies. The attainment of Associate membership in the American Association of Theological Schools in 1966 also contributed to the growth. The changing composition of the student body is also underscored by the seminary's welcoming of its first of many international students, K. Prasanth Kumar, in the 1965–66 academic year. He would return

K. Prasanth Kumar

David Loi Lee-Hoot

to his native India in 1969 in order to begin missionary work for the Brethren Church in Rajahmundry. In 1970 the second international student arrived at the seminary, David Loi Lee-Hoot. He likewise returned to his homeland in Malaysia in 1974 to begin a Brethren mission work in Penang.

One of the most daunting challenges facing the seminary in order to achieve accreditation was the stipulation that the library should have 25,000 catalogued volumes and a minimum budget for book and periodical acquisition of $8,700.[71] In September 1963 the library had only about 7,300 catalogued volumes. Shultz used several creative methods to significantly increase the library holdings. In 1966 five seminary professors went to Grand Rapids, Michigan, and bought approximately 3000 volumes of used books for the collection. Shultz was authorized to travel to England in the summer of 1966 where he acquired another 12,000 books. He purchased complete private libraries as well as works from the Oxford University Press. The seminary was also the recipient of about 2000 volumes from the Oberlin Graduate School of Theology, which closed in 1966. Catalogued volumes reached 17,990 in June 1967 after the buying spree of 1966 and 30,258 volumes in June 1969.[72] In 1964, when the significant thrust for the upgrading of the library began, the new seminary librarian, Nancy L. Rhoades,

Nancy L. Rhoades

also began reclassifying the existing collection from the Dewey Decimal System to the Union Theological System.

The commitment to this major expansion of the library meant that additional resources needed to be marshaled: personnel, finances, and physical space. Assisting Rhoades in the monumental task were a number of part-time and full-time personnel, most notably Gwen Hershberger, Agnes Ballantyne, Mary Alice Thompson, Lena Golding, and Becky Adams. Significant financial resources above and beyond the seminary budget were necessary to underwrite these major acquisitions. The seminary found a willing partner for the venture in the National Laymen's Organization of the Brethren Church. In 1960 the Laymen adopted the recommendation that "$1,000 be allocated to the Seminary for Library expansion. The [Executive] committee, realizing the existing needs of the Seminary, hopes that this will set a precedent for future years."[73] The precedent indeed was established, for in 1961 the Laymen committed themselves to "raise $30,000 for the Seminary Library in a program not to exceed 10 years as a project."[74] In 1969 the Laymen paid the final installment for this project, receiving appropriate thanks from Shultz for their long-term commitment. Even these funds were insufficient for underwriting the buying spree of 1966, however. In April 1966 the Seminary Committee authorized the expenditure of up to $25,000 for the purchase of books with funds to be borrowed if necessary, which was indeed the case.[75]

The greatest challenge posed by these acquisitions was the need for additional library space. In 1962 Clayton had recommended several modifications of the seminary building to the Board of Trustees. Among the recommendations was an addition of a library wing and provision for classroom space. The Board authorized the renovation of the seminary building at its April 1964 meeting. Other modifications would be made to the front stairway, the hallways, the chapel area, the old kitchen and master bathroom, and would include a student recreation area in the lower level. Many of the smaller projects, including the chapel, were completed in time for the 1964–65 school year. However, financing for the library wing and classroom space became a problem, because the Board did not want to include this project in its own bond issues. With the architect, James Crawfis, having completed his drawings for the addition by November 1964, the Prudential Committee of the Board finally authorized Clayton in January 1965 to borrow up to $200,000 for the renovations. He was able to negotiate a loan of $175,000 with the Goodyear State Bank of Akron, Ohio. The library renovation and construction of classrooms moved ahead quickly and were completed in time for the opening of classes in the fall of 1965.[76] The beautifully renovated library was named in memory of Roger Darling (1875–1965), a Brethren elder from Los

A chapel service in the former chapel above the library

*A side view of the administration building
and library; the renovated library is on the right*

Gatos, California, who had given stock to fund a $25,000 annuity bond, the proceeds of which were used for seminary development.[77]

Another critical issue that the seminary faced in its move toward accreditation was the need for student housing. The increasing number of students, particularly students with families, forced Shultz to address this issue even while the renovations to the seminary building were occurring. A partial remedy for this major need became available in the summer of 1964

Roger Darling

The 80 Samaritan Apartments; now called the Holsinger House

when Edgar Walters offered to sell his apartment building at 80 Samaritan Avenue to the seminary. On 9 September 1964 the Finance Committee of the Board authorized the college administration to purchase the apartment building and an adjoining lot. The building supplied housing for eight married seminary students and was very quickly filled.[78]

Shultz maintained his pressure on the Board for additional housing. But two significant obstacles faced the seminary: acquiring additional land for new construction and raising the funds necessary to underwrite this and other major seminary needs. Shultz addressed the latter obstacle in conjunction with the library and classroom project. In April 1964 he launched a two phase Seminary Development Program that was scheduled to run for three years (it actually ran longer to include fund raising for the second phase). Phase One targeted the library renovation, while Phase Two was to be directed toward student housing. Shultz again looked to the Brethren Church to provide the principal support for these projects. He sought to raise $200,000 in Phase One. In an accounting of giving toward the Development Program in August 1968, Shultz indicated that $276,500 had been given toward the projects. As much as three-fourths of the total was raised within the Brethren Church. With these funds Shultz was able to pay off the 12-year Goodyear State Bank loan for the library renovation in 5 years.[79]

Shultz was well aware that the seminary needed to acquire additional land to allow future expansion of the campus. The Myers Gardens, to the west of the seminary building, were deeded to Ashland College for use by the seminary on 31 December 1963. But this land was not well suited for building construction because of drainage issues.[80] In the summer of 1964 the Seminary Committee began conversation with the Finance Committee of the Board about the acquisition of a house and adjacent lot on High Street from Florence D. Brindle. This property was immediately adjoining the seminary property. On 19 August 1965 the Board, upon the recommendation of the Finance Committee, authorized the purchase of the lots for $18,000. Shultz was able to apply $3000 from funds contributed to the seminary by the Woman's Missionary Society of the Brethren Church and $2000 from a previous gift toward the reduction of the Goodyear loan amount. Though Shultz originally intended the house to be used for preseminary students and one seminary couple, he later proposed that it house two married seminary couples. It would eventually be called the Koinonia House because seminary faculty and students would gather for lunch and fellowship on Wednesday and Friday each week. In January 1967 Shultz and the Seminary Committee went on record as supporting the purchase of five other properties on High Street adjacent to the existing seminary property and the five properties on Center Street between High Street and College Avenue. The Board of Trustees was generally unfavorable about the purchase of additional land for the seminary because of the limited financial resources of the seminary.

The Myers Gardens, west of the Myers home

Students and faculty eating lunch together in the Koinonia House around 1969; seated foreground: Bill Syndram; far left: Ken Sullivan; five in background left to right: Doug Denbow, Jim Geaslen (standing), Eugene Shaver, Fred Finks, and Charles Munson

But the Buildings and Grounds Committee of the Board did agree in April 1967 to purchase the High Street and Center Street properties as they became available. Priority was to be given to the High Street properties, however.[81]

Shultz continued lobbying for student housing throughout 1965 and 1966. In 1966 the Seminary Committee asked the Building and Grounds and Finance Committees to explore possible locations for an apartment building. None of the existing land seemed suitable. In spite of this drawback, James Crawfis, the architect who had worked on the library and classroom addition, was asked in 1967 to prepare preliminary plans for an apartment building on the Myers Gardens site. Crawfis brought his plans to the Seminary Committee in October 1967. The estimated price tag at this time was $400,000. Though the Seminary Committee wanted to move ahead, the Board was reluctant to take action because of the financial situation of the seminary. Shultz's tenaciousness paid off when the Board, at its August 1968 meeting, authorized the construction of the apartment building for the estimated $400,000. But the Finance Committee continued to balk on the financial arrangements for the loan (the estimated cost seemed too high to be able to service a loan of this size through rents).

Several new wrinkles also entered the picture. In the December 1968 minutes of the Building and Grounds Committee, there is a note about the possibility of acquiring the Helen Miller property from T. W. Miller Jr. This property adjoined the seminary property on the south and included a small apartment building, a swimming pool, loggia, tennis court, and several service garages. The land also included a lot on Samaritan Avenue. On 7 November 1969 the Finance Committee authorized the purchase of this desirable piece of land for $49,000. The purchase was made possible by a timely gift from the estate of Wilma Bashor, the only child of Stephen and Samantha Cordelia (Corda) Bashor, of nearly $50,000. This land was far more ideal for the construction of the student apartment building than the proposed Myers Gardens location.[82]

"And now the Rest of the Story"

Just off the sidewalk that leads from the seminary chapel to the student apartments stands a plaque that reads: "In loving memory of Stephen Henry Bashor, Pioneer Evangelist, The Brethren Church, By his Daughter Wilma Bashor." The plaque was originally set in place at the 1971 commencement service of Ashland Theological Seminary. It honors one of the greatest evangelists in the Brethren movement. Bashor (1852–1922) is credited with the conversion of over ten thousand people during his ministry.

To quote Paul Harvey's radio program, "and now the rest of the story." Bashor and his wife, Samantha Cordelia Weller Bashor (1854–1927), had only one child, Wilma, who was born 10 October 1889. She was an accomplished violinist, touring the Midwest in 1909 as the featured soloist with the Scott Prowell Grand Orchestra and Chorus. In 1914 she married Samuel Bruce Galloway, the son of a prominent industrialist in Waterloo, Iowa. They lived for a time in Texas, but the marriage ended in divorce. Wilma legally assumed her maiden name. She moved to Los Angeles, California, in 1926 (her mother died in Los Angeles in 1927). In the 1930 census she is listed as a professional musician. She took sociology, psychology, and anthropology courses at the University of Southern California and eventually ended up in social work. In 1931 she took a temporary position as a social worker with the Motion Picture Relief Fund; she filled in for an employee who was on vacation. Two and a half months after her temporary hire, Wilma's administrative skills had become recognized, and she was named Director of Welfare for the Motion Picture Relief Fund. The organization was founded in 1921 to provide assistance to those in the motion picture industry who had fallen on hard times. Among the founders were such celebrities as Mary Pickford, Charlie Chaplin, Douglas Fairbanks, and D. W. Griffith.

In 1938 Wilma became the executive secretary of the Motion Picture Relief Fund and in 1954 its executive director. She retired from this position in 1962 at the age of 72. In an article that appeared in the *Los Angeles Times* on 22 July 1957, the following was said about Wilma: "She has known all of the Hollywood 'greats' and knows everything, good and bad, about them. Behind her calm, pleasant face is a mind holding more secrets than all of the gossip columnists and so-called 'exposure' magazines together, but she guards her secrets well."

Three or four years before her death on 26 April 1964 she had returned to Waterloo, Iowa, to visit some of her cousins. She had been raised in the First Brethren Church of Waterloo; her parents had moved to Waterloo in 1893. She called the pastor of the church at the time of her visit, Albert T. Ronk, who invited her to his study at the church. During their very pleasant conversation, Ronk asked about her church affiliation. She indicated that she had transferred her membership to her husband's church when they were married. However, after her divorce she was so ashamed that she never asked for a

(continued)

letter of transfer. She had never become a member of a church in the intervening years. Ronk suggested that she find some spiritual anchorage, a church home, and that she should consider being reinstated in the Waterloo church. Since she could no longer get a letter of transfer, Ronk indicated that she could be received by relation if she would write a request accompanied by a recommitment to her church vows. In a few days Ronk received just such a letter and Wilma was received by the congregation by unanimous vote.

When Wilma's will was probated, it was revealed that her estate was to be equally divided between the First Brethren Church of Waterloo and Ashland College. The college administration decided that the most appropriate use of the nearly $50,000 would be to invest it in the campus of the seminary. The funds came at the very time that T. W. Miller Jr. made the Helen Miller property available for the use of the seminary for $49,000. The plaque that stands on this property is a most fitting legacy to the Bashor family. (Stephen Bashor held the first public service in the newly finished Founders Hall of Ashland College in 1879.)

Albert Ronk eulogized Stephen Bashor at the dedication of the plaque during the seminary commencement service on 17 June 1971. Ronk stated:

"If Elder Bashor was cognizant of what we were doing today, taking a pilgrimage into our heritage, he would hold us quite remiss if we considered the heritage he had left to his church, only the title to three or four acres of dirt.

"The heritage of Stephen Bashor, along with the other fathers of the church, lies not in

Wilma Bashor

monetary worth but in spiritual values of faith and life. It was they of the past who blazed the path for us today. It was they who carried the torch of truth in their teaching and example. It was they who anchored the foundations of the Brethren Church and gave to us a basis upon which to build our future. How evident it is, that heritage and destiny are inseparable and we can no more evade the legacy of the past than we can avoid the responsibilities of the future. We may criticize the past and fear the future but life will go on until the architect of life is ready to write *finis* to this present age in His scheme of things."

Albert T. Ronk, "Elder Stephen H. Bashor: Heritage and Destiny," 17 June 1971, TMs [photocopy], Ronk Files, Brethren Church Archives, Brethren Church National Office, Ashland, OH and Cal Sale, Notes on the Stephen Bashor Family, Ronk Files, Brethren Church Archives, Brethren Church National Office, Ashland, OH.

The other wrinkle was the escalating cost of construction of the apartment building. In April 1969 the architect, James Crawfis, was instructed to prepare preliminary drawings for a 23 or 24 apartment facility on the Myers Gardens site, but he cautioned that his original estimate of $400,000 was two years old and that it might have increased 20 to 25%. Indeed, when bids were received in November 1969, the cost of the building had soared to $628,000! Disheartened by this figure, Shultz began to explore other possibilities. He contacted Scholz Homes, Inc., a firm that had gained a reputation for building "low-cost but high quality apartments for campuses, church retirement centers and other groups."[83] The firm presented a very appealing proposal to the Seminary Building Committee[84] for a 24 unit apartment building at a very reasonable cost of $12,000 to $13,500 per unit, roughly half of the amount bid on the Myers Gardens plans. After the presentation the Seminary Building Committee authorized the college administration to secure a firm proposal from Scholz Homes, to investigate zoning and building regulations with the city, and to negotiate a settlement with the architectural firm of Marr, Knapp, and Crawfis, which had already completed the working drawings for the building.

James Crawfis was very understanding of the situation and his firm was willing to settle their interest in the project for a reasonable "out-of-pocket" fee. Though there were some restrictions for construction on Samaritan Avenue, the City Council cleared the way for the building project on the new Miller property (the site was actually set back over 250 feet from Samaritan Avenue). Financing the construction also proved to be a complicated process. Because the structure was to be used for religious purposes, the financing for the project could not be added to the blanket mortgage on the college property. A bank mortgage would need to be secured, but to do this the college bond holders had to agree to the release of the site. A bank loan was eventually negotiated with First National Bank of Ashland, but after the building had already been dedicated. When one considers all the potential dead-ends that could have stymied construction of the seminary apartments, their completion stands as a testimony to the faith and perseverance of Shultz and Clayton.

The actual construction process moved forward very quickly. Scholz Homes completed its drawings in the early spring, and the Board accepted the low bid of C. A. King and Sons, Inc. for $351,383 on 9 April 1970. The beautiful new apartments, eventually called the Hoseck Apartments, were dedicated on Thursday night of the Brethren General Conference on 20 August 1970. Charles F. Pfeiffer, professor of Ancient Literatures at Central Michigan University, gave the dedicatory message. The twenty-four apartments were filled when fall classes began in 1970.[85]

Shultz again found willing partners to finance the housing project in the Brethren Church. At the 1968 General Conference of the Brethren Church, Smith Rose, a member of the Seminary Committee of the Board, had presented a resolution to the conference that stated in part: "That they

*The Hoseck Apartments with seminary graduates Vincent and
Shanti (daughter of Prasanth Kumar) Edwin in the foreground*

[each local Brethren congregation] support more fully the work of the Seminary by prayer, by sacrificial giving for seminary housing, and by regular and increased support to complete the obligations of Phase 1 and of the operational budget of the Seminary."[86] The conference unanimously approved the resolution. In April 1970 Shultz reported that there was already $173,000 available for the construction of the facility; most of this figure was raised among Brethren sources. In an article concerning the dedication ceremony, Shultz singled out the Lanark Brethren Church, the Washington, DC, Brethren Church, the Meyersdale Brethren Church, and the Louisville Brethren Church. He also gave a well deserved thanks to the National Woman's Missionary Society for raising $40,000 by the time of the article and to Ira J. Hoover and Thomas H. and Carrie Diffenderfer for annuities, the proceeds of which were used to help underwrite the project.[87]

It's all about Relationships

Joseph Shultz, in his history of his time at Ashland Theological Seminary and Ashland University, shares a poignant personal interest story.

"After thirty one years one learns that what is called 'fund raising' and 'development' has much more to do with friends and friendship than it has with money. In the early seventies [actually 1968], I received a postcard with writing that was almost illegible. My associate, Virgil Meyer, deciphered the writing and traced the signature. A man, Ira J. Hoover, originally from the Waterloo Brethren Church, was now living

(continued)

in Winter Haven, Florida. I made an appointment and went to visit him. Ira was a tall, stately, handsome man in his nineties. He always wore a dark suit, white starched shirt, and red-striped tie. He was almost blind.

"We would have a great time talking 'about the good old days' in Iowa. His life's profession was forestry with the government, during which time he acquired 4,000 acres in south Georgia. He grew trees for pulp wood and veneer. He then sold his business to St. Regis Paper Company and was deciding whether to make a gift to Ashland or to a college in central Florida.

"On each visit, we would go for lunch at the local drugstore counter. The waitresses were kind and helpful, always serving the same menu: tomato soup, grilled cheese, and a glass of milk. As we walked home slowly, I would listen to his life's story.

"Finally, he decided to make his gift to Ashland. To complete the paperwork we needed to clear a $30,000 note in a bank in Waycross, Georgia. The banker, a five-foot miniature Napoleon, refused to take our word. I drove Mr. Hoover from Florida to Georgia to talk directly with the bank; he still refused. I then called President Clayton to wire me $30,000—he choked but sent the money. The next morning we were standing in front of the bank at nine. Without invitation, we walked directly into the banker's office and laid down the money. The banker still hesitated; I got tough and he finally signed the release of the mortgage. We went outside and Mr. Hoover smiled and said, 'You are a genius, you are a genius.' Of course, we all knew better, but we completed the paperwork and received a gift of $311,000. It just happened that this gift was the means of the college balancing the budget for the year [this occurred in 1976].

"My last meeting with him I felt compelled to ask him about his funeral arrangements. He was alone in the world and I was afraid the city would put him in a potter's field. I, of course, was afraid that he would object to the question. However, he literally pushed me down in a chair and, in fifteen minutes, we had made all the arrangements. He couldn't thank me enough.

"A year later I was traveling with a group of students in the Middle East and received a call that Mr. Hoover had died. By prearrangement, an alumnus in Florida took care of the body and personal belongings. My good friend, Prof. Charles Munson, conducted the funeral in Waterloo, Iowa. Mr. Hoover had been gone so long that the congregation had forgotten him. I then called another friend, Abe Glessner, to be sure that twelve couples, deacons, attend the funeral and sing his favorite hymns. We also placed a nice marker on the grave. I am sure that Mr. Hoover is pleased with the end of his life. I am pleased that I gained a friend and found a way of friendship."

Glenn Clayton reveals further details about the financial side of the story:

"On May 27, 1976, the college received $117,368 from the St. Regis Paper Company for the Seminary. The payment was in full settlement for the residue of the 'Hoover annuity.' In May of 1968, thanks to the work of Dr. Joseph R. Shultz, the college received a gift from Ira J. Hoover in the form of a note for $240,000 used for the purchase of some forest land. The note was payable on an annual basis through 1995, with the proceeds and interest payable to Ashland College for the Seminary, after certain covenants with Mr. Hoover were fulfilled. After Mr. Hoover's death . . . , the property which secured the note was purchased by the St. Regis Paper Company in New York, which continued to make the annual payments to the college for the seminary. Then, after talks with Dr. Shultz and me, St. Regis paid off the note in a lump sum. The money was temporarily used in the summer of 1976 to meet 'cash flow' needs of the college, then was deposited in the seminary accounts."

Joseph R. Shultz, *Ashland: From College to University* ([Ashland, OH]: Landoll, Inc., n.d.), 73–74 and Glenn L. Clayton, "Whispering Pines and Purple Eagles," 1979, TMs [photocopy], p. 337, Ashland University Archives, Ashland University, Ashland, OH.

The Woman's Missionary Society (renamed Women's Missionary Society in 1995) needs special recognition for the ongoing support that they have given the seminary. This women's auxiliary of the Brethren Church contributed $19,000 to the seminary housing project in 1970 and $7,500 the following year. In addition, from 1970 through the early 1980s this organization consistently gave between $6,000 and $6,500 to the Seminary Development Fund, the seminary's endowment fund. The commitment of the Women's Missionary Society to the seminary continues until the present.

Though Shultz seemed to have a gift for raising funds for the needed expansion of the physical plant of the seminary, balancing the operational budget of the seminary continued to be a concern. Shultz and Clayton hoped that completion of the seminary housing facility and the acquisition of accreditation would lead to increased enrollment and, thereby, balanced budgets.[88] Clayton regularly shared concern in the Seminary Committee and Board meetings about the challenges of meeting the operational expenses of the seminary, which had grown to over $100,000 by 1968.[89] Shultz outlined his long-term goal for underwriting the seminary budget in 1967. He sought to obtain one-third of the annual budget from endowments in the Seminary Foundation, one-third from the Brethren Church, and one-third from student fees and special gifts. The immediate challenge facing Shultz was highlighted in a report for the 1970–71 budget year. Student fees that budget year accounted for 20% of the annual budget, while gifts from the Brethren Church accounted for 25% of the budget. Funding the remaining 55% of the budget was the problem.[90]

When Shultz came to the seminary in 1963, there was still no charge for tuition, though there were fees totaling $35.50 per quarter for such items as field trips, lecturers, health services, clinical classes, and funding the library. Tuition of $4.00 per quarter hour was first charged in the 1965–66 academic year and rose to $6.00 per quarter hour in the 1969–70 academic year. Revenues from tuition had risen from $6,639 in 1965–66, to $8,840 in 1968–69, and to $43,000 in 1971–72. The annual budget in 1971–72 was $173,975.[91] The balance needed to be made up from other sources of income.

Shultz took every opportunity to remind the Brethren Church that Ashland Theological Seminary was the sole training ground for Brethren pastors, missionaries, and other Christian workers. For this reason the church needed to carry a significant portion of the funding for the seminary. In 1969 Shultz indicated that he was seeking $50,000 annually from the Brethren Church toward the operating budget. Rarely, however, did annual church giving for the operating budget reach this figure (in 1968–89 $32,865 was received from the church; in 1971–72 $46,000 was received).

The goal of accreditation was a motivating factor in several significant changes to the seminary curriculum during the mid and latter 1960s. Twice curriculum revisions occurred during these years. The first, which was implemented in 1964, the year after Shultz came to the seminary, featured a "core curriculum." This curricular approach provided greater depth in theological and biblical studies and a greater flexibility in electives. Of the 144 quarter hours required for the Bachelor of Divinity degree, 110 hours were cores; the remaining 34 were elective hours.[92]

Shultz and the faculty undertook a lengthy review of the curriculum during the 1966–67 academic year. The rationale for the revised curriculum was to do three tasks more effectively:

(1) To present to students in the seminary a course of study that will effectively broaden horizons, deepen insights, and strengthen abilities in and for Christian ministry.

(2) To expose [students] to experiences in Christian ministries, thereby quickening sensitivity to persons and maturing the student.

(3) To open the door to people presently in Christian ministries that they may be strengthened in their labors for God and man.[93]

The Bachelor of Divinity degree would now have 140 quarter hours in contrast to the previous 144 hours. There would be four courses per quarter, each of which would be four quarter hours. Previously students took six or seven courses per quarter, each being two or three quarter hours. The 140 quarter hours were composed of 96 hours of cores, which were spread across Old and New Testaments, theology, church history, and practical ministry. The remaining 44 hours were elective; 24 hours in a specialized area, including a thesis or project, would lead to a major in that field.

Several unique features were built into the curriculum. The winter term was divided into three segments of about four weeks each. Students would work on only one course in each of the three segments. This structure allowed the seminary to invite guest lecturers and resource people who could provide an enriched learning experience, often interdisciplinary in nature. Each student was also required to have an off-campus experience in some Christian ministry during the winter of their second year or the summer between their second and third years. This experience was designed to help students clarify their calling and motivate them "to pursue the necessary disciplines for an effective ministry." The new curriculum was inaugurated in the 1967–68 academic year.[94]

In another curricular change Ashland followed other seminaries in discontinuing the Bachelor of Divinity degree in favor of the new Master of Divinity (M.Div.) degree. Shultz reveals that discussion of this change was occurring in 1967; in August 1968 the Seminary Committee approved the change of nomenclature for the first professional degree from the B.D. to the M.Div. effective in June 1969. Though the new degree made its debut in the 1969–70 catalogue, the first conferrals of the degree occurred in June 1969. Those who had graduated with a B.D. degree could exchange this degree for the M.Div. with the completion of twelve additional hours.[95]

One of the majors offered with the new M. Div. degree was a special major in Pastoral Psychology and Counseling that was initiated in 1969. Students in this major were required to complete the regular three-year theological program plus clinical training at Cleveland Psychiatric Institute or the Ohio Chaplain's In-service In-Training program. The clinical program involved thirty-two hours of credit taken over two years. It was the first of a number of such counseling programs that have been a significant part of the seminary curriculum.[96]

The seminary sought to enrich the educational experience of its students in several unique ways in the late 1960s. In the summer of 1968 the seminary hosted the first of what became almost annual trips to the Holy Land over the next several decades. In addition by 1969 Ashland had been accepted as an associate member of the American Institute of Holy Land Studies. Students could spend three weeks in the Holy Land, not only studying Biblical languages and literature, geography, and history, but also participating in an archaeological excavation.[97]

In 1968 the seminary began a Continuing Education program in conjunction with its innovative winter term in the revised curriculum. This program brought in special speakers who addressed a variety of practical and integrative topics. Some of the topics addressed in the January through March session were "Christian Education and the Ministry," "Biblical Theology and Christian Missions," and "The Preacher and Contemporary Issues." Not only were seminary students able to take advantage of these lectures for credit, but pastors were invited to attend these educational opportunities for "disciplined renewal." Shultz also believed that this program could help to increase the visibility of the seminary.[98]

In 1970 the Continuing Education program was folded into a new educational experience, the All-Institutional Study. For one week during the winter term the entire seminary community studied the theme: "The Middle East—Ancient and Modern." Shultz brought in high-profile speakers for the study: Charles Pfeiffer of Central Michigan University, Herbert May of

Vanderbilt University, John Trevor of Baldwin-Wallace University, and Douglas Young, the Director of the American Institute of Holy Land Studies. The following year the topic of study focused on church and state issues and featured James E. Wood Jr. of Baylor University. The studies continued through 1972.[99]

The seminary began two ongoing publications in the latter 1960s. A seminary newsletter debuted in 1967 that appeared two or three times a year. In 1980 it was named *Koinonia* and continues with this title to the present. In 1968 the *Ashland Theological Journal* first appeared and continues to be published annually.

In August 1968, as Shultz surveyed all the progress that had been made at the seminary since his arrival five years previous, he felt confident that everything was in place for the accreditation visit by the American Association of Theological Schools (AATS). The actual accreditation process involved four major steps. The first step was the acquisition of Associate membership status, which was achieved in 1966. The second step was an initial visit by AATS executive, David Schuller, in November 1968. This visit went very well and Schuller approved the seminary program without notation. The third step was Shultz's completion of the requisite accreditation schedules, which occurred in May 1969. The final step was the site visit by the Accreditation Commission Team in November 1969. James I. McCord, President of Princeton Theological Seminary, served as the chairman of the team. The team issued a favorable report and at the December 1969 meeting of the full AATS commission Ashland Theological Seminary received an initial provisional accreditation from AATS for two years. At the January Board of Trustee meeting the Board appropriately expressed its appreciation to Clayton, Shultz, and the seminary community for the achievement of full accreditation by AATS.[100] Though Ashland received three notations in 1969, relating to admission standards, field education, and inadequate faculty resources, the long struggle against seemingly insurmountable obstacles had, nonetheless, achieved its goal!

Building upon the Foundations of the 1960s (1970–1982)

Expansion of the Faculty and Administration.   With the prized accreditation now achieved, Shultz was able to turn his attention to building on the foundations that he had already been laying during the 1960s. Again, every phase of the seminary's life was affected. The faculty continued to grow during the 1970s, initially due to pressure from AATS. The Accrediting Commission of AATS had scheduled its two-year revisit to Ashland in October 1971. The Commis-

Bradley E. Weidenhamer   *Joseph N. Kickasola*

sion issued a complimentary report and continued the seminary's accreditation, removing the notations related to admission standards and field education. However, it continued one notation, "The faculty of this school is inadequate for the program of study," and imposed another, "A director of Clinical Education is needed."[101] In spite of a tight budget the seminary sought to address these notations by September 1972 with the hiring of additional personnel. To meet the latter notation the seminary hired Charles G. Ronkos (B.B.A. University of Pittsburgh; B.D. Hamma Divinity School; M.Div. Ashland Theological Seminary; D.Min. Consortium for Higher Education Religion Studies) on a part-time basis in November 1971 as Director of Clinical Pastoral Education. Another personnel change at this time was the hiring of Bradley E. Weidenhamer (B.A. Ashland College; B.D. Ashland Theological Seminary; M.A. The Ohio State University; M.L.S. Case Western Reserve University) in 1970 as head librarian to replace Nancy Rhoades, who had retired.

The seminary had already hired Joseph N. Kickasola (B.A. Houghton College; B.D., Th.M. Westminster Theological Seminary; M.A., Ph.D. Brandeis University) in 1971 in the area of Old Testament to replace Bruce Stark, who had gone to the college to teach in the Philosophy Department in 1970. Shultz added Jerry Flora (B.A. Ashland College; B.D. Ashland Theological Seminary; Th.M. Fuller Theological Seminary; Th.D. Southern Baptist The-

Jerry R. Flora

ological Seminary) to the faculty in 1972 in the field of Christian Theology to specifically address the notation concerning faculty resources (AATS had previously identified the need for faculty in the area of theology). However, AATS continued the notation regarding inadequate faculty resources in December 1972. The need highlighted by AATS was in the area of practical theology, specifically in Christian Education. AATS gave the seminary until September 1974 to respond to this continued notation. Shultz satisfied this

Richard E. Allison

need by hiring Richard E. Allison (A.B. Ashland College; M.R.E. Goshen College; M.Div. Ashland Theological Seminary; D.Min. Consortium for Higher Education Religion Studies) in 1974 in the field of Christian Education. AATS removed this last notation in June 1974; the accreditation process begun in the latter 1960s was now finalized.[102]

The seminary continued to add faculty and staff in the 1970s and early 80s to replace retiring faculty and to meet the increasing curricular needs created by an expanding student enrollment and the opening of extensions. However, in 1978 ATS (the American Association of Theological Schools had changed its name to the Association of Theological Schools in June 1974) issued three notations at the time of the next accreditation review: a notation related to field education, one concerning insufficient training of adjuncts serving in supervisory roles, and the recurring "the faculty was inadequate for one or more degree programs offered." There had been a number of changes in the composition of the faculty between 1972 and 1981. In 1972 Delbert Flora began partial retirement and was named professor emeritus in 1976. In 1977 Louis Gough retired and O. Kenneth Walther (A.B. Wheaton College; M.A.T. Northwestern University; B.D. Northern Baptist Theologi-

O. Kenneth Walther

cal Seminary; Ph.D. University of St. Andrews, Scotland) followed him in the fields of Greek and New Testament. Alderfer left the seminary in 1980 and his church history position was filled by David A. Rausch (A.B. Southeastern College; M.A. Youngstown State University; Ph.D. Kent State University). Douglas E. Chismar (A.B. American University; M.Div. Ashland Theological Seminary; Ph.D. The Ohio State University) also joined the faculty in 1980 in the area of Christian philosophy; he initially was given a "special" contract but received a regular faculty contract the next year. In 1981 John C. Shultz (B.A. Ashland College; M.Div. Ashland Theological Seminary; Ph.D. Purdue University) was hired in the field of Pastoral Counseling. In June 1981 ATS removed its notation regarding insufficient faculty.[103]

Between 1969 and 1981 the seminary faculty grew from 5 full-time positions to12; part-time and adjunct faculty grew from 8 in 1969 to 32 in 1981. These increases reflect the significant growth in student enrollment, in the curriculum, and in the number of extensions. Faculty course load during this period was nine courses (the seminary was on quarters); faculty also taught courses in the summer and September term. In addition, they helped support the expanding extension program. In 1972 the seminary faculty separated from the

Charles G. Ronkos

Arthur M. Climenhaga   *Theron H. Smith*

college's Faculty Forum when the college faculty unionized; and the seminary faculty formed their own group with their own handbook for operations.[104]

The growing complexity of the seminary in the 1970s required an increase in administrative personnel and adjustments in the administrative structure. In 1972 Virgil Meyer came over from the college to serve as the Director of Christian Ministries. His pastoral gifts in working with students were well suited to the seminary setting. In 1972 Clayton and the Board had given Shultz the title of Vice President of the Seminary in the restructuring of the college that Clayton had begun to implement. This title reflected the significant role that Shultz had assumed in the college structure. By the mid-1970s Shultz was feeling the strain of bearing three major administrative responsibilities at the seminary: the chief administrator, the academic dean, and the development officer. He decided it was time to address this problem. In 1977 he moved Charles Ronkos to full-time status; he was to advise D.Min. clinical students, direct the seminary's Cleveland area programs, and teach on the Ashland campus. In 1978 Arthur M. Climenhaga (B.A. Pasadena College; M.A. in Theology, Taylor University; S.T.D. Los Angeles Baptist Theological Seminary) joined the faculty to help with the administrative responsibilities of the seminary and to teach in theology and mission. In 1979 Theron H. Smith (B.A. Asbury College; B.D. Oberlin Graduate School of Theology; M.Div. Vanderbilt University) was hired as Director of Academic Services and to oversee the extension programs. These administrative changes led ATS in June 1981 to remove the other two notations imposed in 1978.

Shultz's move to the presidency of Ashland College in 1979 necessitated the development of an interim administrative structure at the seminary. In

1980 Shultz realigned the seminary's administrative responsibilities. As president of the college and seminary, he retained significant input into the seminary's direction. But Munson became designated Acting Dean; Climenhaga served as Director of Academic Affairs; Meyer became Director of Student Life and Ministry; and Smith served as the Director of Extension Programs. The latter three directors composed a seminary cabinet that ran the internal functions of the seminary.[105] This arrangement was modified somewhat when both Meyer and Climenhaga began semi-retirement in 1981. Shultz began a search for the next vice president of the seminary in earnest in 1980.

Munsonisms

No history of Ashland Theological Seminary would be complete without sharing some of the one-of-a-kind stories about Charles Munson, who now resides in Goshen, Indiana. Munson, who came to the seminary in 1954 in the area of practical theology and retired in 1995, could have made a very good living as a stand-up comedian. He had that unique sense of timing in the delivery of "one-liners" that would keep an audience in a state of uncontrollable laughter. Several of the quips remembered by his colleagues are:

"Life never stops to say please."

"You don't really know what's inside a person until they get bumped."

(A prescription for a happy marriage): "You must be about the business of creating memories."

"In the retirement home, there are two lines in the dining room: Cane and Able."

"A rut is a grave with both ends kicked out."

"Silence is golden; but sometimes it's just yellow."

"Everyone is like the moon. We all have a dark side."

(On the rigors of obtaining a Ph.D.): "I told the Lord that if he would forgive me, I wouldn't do it again."

One of the vintage "Munsonisms" was his slide shows. He would gather all of his "throwaway" slides that were overexposed, underexposed, blurry, nearly all black, etc. He would put these together into a slide show of places he had been, important people he had known, and various unique experiences. He then took his audience on a hilarious journey as he created word pictures that drew his listeners into the very scene he was describing. His powers of imagination and sense of timing made the nonsensical slides come alive for those "along for the ride."

Munson was also the target of many practical jokes. One of his colleagues from 1968 to 1977 was Louis Gough, a professor of New Testament and Greek. Munson had a silicon hand in his office. Each day before he arrived at his office, Gough would move it to another location somewhere in Munson's office. Even when Gough was out of town, he would arrange for a student to move it so that Munson had no clue who the culprit was. Not until Gough retired did he confess to his sleight of hand.

Munson had an unusual depth of spiritual discernment and wisdom. Many went to him for spiritual counsel and direction. Michael Reuschling, now a professor of pastoral counseling at the seminary, remembers the impact that Munson had on him while Reuschling was a student at the seminary. Reuschling was part of a small group led by Munson. He fondly remembers Munson's "warmth, sense of humor, willingness to share of himself, and devotion to the Lord. He was and is an inspiration to me. When I look at him, I see Jesus."

What was probably the last chapel service in which Munson spoke was an especially powerful one. Though I (the author) cannot remember the theme of his message, I can distinctly remember its impact. Munson so drew the seminary community into the Lord's presence that at the conclusion of the service no one moved. We all wanted to linger in the sweet sense of communion with the Lord. Munson had the ability to say things in a simple, yet profound, way that struck to the very heart of the matter and drew one into the very heart of Jesus.

Enrollment and Student Life.   Student enrollment figures during the 1970s reflect the positive impact of accreditation as well as such factors as the opening of new extensions and the creation of new curricular programs. In 1970–71 the seminary had an enrollment of 70 students; in 1975–76 enrollment stood at 185; in 1980–81 enrollment had grown to 378. Significant shifts occurred in the composition of the student body during the 1970s. With the opening of various extension programs in metropolitan areas, the student body included 95 African-Americans in 1980. The first African-American students to graduate from the seminary were Stanley Bagley, Bennie Mosley Jr., and David B. Nickerson in 1973. All of these students graduated in the newly developed M.Div. with a major in Pastoral Psychology and Counseling and transferred credits in from prior degrees at other schools. The first African-American to complete his M.Div. degree fully at Ashland was George W. Primes Jr. in 1975. In the fall of 1971 there were only 3 women out of a total enrollment of 91; in 1980 there were 59 women out of a total of 378 students. Though women had graduated over the years with various degrees from the seminary, Irene C. Stock became the first woman to graduate with the M.Div. degree in 1971. She completed the M.Div. with a major in Pastoral Psychology and Counseling and transferred credits in from a prior M.A. degree. The first woman to complete her entire M.Div. degree at Ashland was Pam Martin in 1974. Notably, from 1964 until 1979, catalogues included in the "Purpose" statement at the front of the catalogue the phrase (with only minor edits over these years): "We invite young men called of God . . ." In the 1980–81 catalogue this statement was changed to: "We invite persons called of God . . ."[106] The faculty were becoming more sensitized to the increasing number of women who were responding to the call of God in their lives.

A strong feeling of community permeated the seminary during the 1960s and 70s. A number of factors contributed to these fellowship ties. Most students lived in or near Ashland; the seminary was essentially a residential campus. Because there generally were not multiple sections of given courses and because the conspectus of courses for the M.Div. degree was strictly adhered to, students usually were in the same classes with one another during their junior, middler, and senior years (this was especially true during the junior and middler years when there were few electives in the conspectus). Students had numerous opportunities to share with one another and with faculty. The seminary community gathered for chapel each day, Tuesday through Friday. Students and faculty met together for lunch and fellowship several times each week in the Koinonia House on High Street through 1976 when it was torn down to make room for much needed park-

Fred Finks and Gerald Barr playing ping-
pong in the lower level of the Myers home

ing. After the remodeling of the seminary building in 1964 students and faculty could play ping pong and, a bit later in the 1960s, even pool in the basement recreational area. The seminary community began each new academic
year with a retreat at Camp Bethany, a camp owned by the Ohio District of
the Brethren Church outside Loudonville. In 1980 the retreat was moved to

The annual junior versus the middler and senior students football
game at Camp Bethany in 1974: identifiable are left to right Terry
Lodico, William (Bill) Hess, Paul Deardurff, and Dale Stoffer

Inspiration Hills, a Church of the Brethren camp near Burbank, Ohio. Part of the tradition of the retreat was a football game between the junior students and the upperclassmen. The juniors were victorious on a number of occasions in these contests.

Several formal organizations were part of the community life of the seminary. A Student Association was elected by the students and planned and administered recreational, social, and special devotional programs. The Seminary Students' Wives, popularly called "Sem Wives," was an organization that met for "fellowship and for developing a better understanding of the role of the wife in the Christian ministries."[107] In the 1980–81 catalogue two new or modified organizations made their initial appearance, reflecting the changing demographics of the seminary. The Sem Wives had been reorganized into Sem Women, reflecting the growing number of women seminary students. Single students in the seminary had organized Sem Singles, a group that offered monthly social events to help singles feel a greater sense of community in their seminary experience.

These formal and informal expressions of community in the life of Ashland Theological Seminary reflect the high priority given to community in the formation of Christian character. As was stated in every catalogue from 1966–67 to 1996–98:

> The Seminary is more than a "school"; it is a "community" of seekers and learners bonded by the common cause of Christ. Both Faculty and Students feel a mutual concern for their fellows. There is a conscious effort made to maintain a free exchange in all areas of academic and personal life.[108]

In 1998 the commitment to community would be highlighted by including it as one of the four core values of the seminary.

Curricular Development and Enrichment.   During the 1970s significant changes occurred to the curriculum of the seminary. A number of new degrees were initiated during this period. There had been discussion about a Master in Religious Education degree in 1967 and 1968, but nothing materialized from these deliberations. The M.Div. remained the only degree offered by the seminary until the approval of the Doctor of Ministry (D.Min.) degree. The earliest discussion of this degree was in August 1970 and was in the context of a proposal to establish a committee of faculty and Board members to review the seminary's degree programs. AATS had approved the D.Min. as a new theological degree at its biennial meeting in June 1970.

Shultz advanced the idea of joining a consortium of other seminaries in Ohio, the Ohio Consortium of Theological Schools, which had been formed in 1971 to, among other purposes, jointly offer the D.Min. degree. In August 1971 the seminary received Board authorization to join the consortium. The D.Min. degree was administered by the academic arm of the consortium, the Consortium for Higher Education Religion Studies (CHERS). The degree program featured the selection of "core faculty," resource people drawn from either inside or outside seminary faculties; a support group composed of laypeople in the participant's own ministry setting; and peer groups of D.Min. students who resided in proximity to each other to provide mutual encouragement and support.

In the 1972–73 academic year Ashland already had four students enrolled in the D.Min. program. Some of the first Ashland graduates from this unique program were Charles Ronkos (1973), Richard Allison (1975), and Donald Rinehart (1975).[109] Directors of the D.Min. program at Ashland have been Owen Alderfer (1971–1978), Arthur Climenhaga (1978–1980), Richard Allison (1980–1994), Eugene Gibbs (1994–1997), Richard Parrott (1997–2003), Elaine Heath (2003–2005), and Leroy Solomon (2005 to the present). In 1977 CHERS divided into two regions, Southern Ohio and North Central Ohio. Ashland joined with two other North Central Ohio seminaries, the Methodist Theological School and Trinity Lutheran Seminary, to offer the D.Min. degree as the Columbus Cluster D.Min. program. Ashland began offering its own independent D.Min. degree in 1991.

The committee alluded to above apparently brought back the recommendation for the initiation of another degree, the two-year Master of Arts (M.A.). In January 1971 Shultz reported that the seminary faculty supported this recommendation and cited several reasons for this proposal: (1) there was a large market for the degree; (2) it could be developed with a minimum of effort; (3) it would require little additional faculty or administrative resources and the library holdings were adequate to support the degree; (4) the North Central Association would accept the evaluation and accreditation of AATS for the degree; and (5) the program could be coordinated with the college Religion Department so that faculty resources at the college could help support the degree.[110] As reflected in this proposal, the seminary was interested in obtaining accreditation through the North Central Association as well as AATS. Discussion about the M.A. degree later in 1971 indicated a desire to offer the degree in such select areas as Pastoral Psychology and Counseling, Christian Education, and Religious Studies.[111]

The seminary did not implement the M.A. in Religion degree until the 1974–75 academic year when twenty students enrolled in the program. ATS "received" Ashland's report concerning the degree in January 1975, indicating that it would send a visiting team when the degree was sufficiently developed. The first description of the degree appeared in the 1976–78 catalogue. As stated in the catalogue, the degree was designed to serve:

> (1) persons desiring to equip themselves for service in professional ministries, Christian Education, Pastoral Counseling, or Associate Pastoral ministries; (2) persons desiring graduate study in Religion; and (3) persons desiring to serve as effective Christian laypersons through an enriched and deepened understanding of the Christian faith.[112]

By 1977 ATS had changed the nomenclature for this degree from the M.A. in Religion degree to simply the Master of Arts degree; this change was reflected in the 1980–81 seminary catalogue. In June 1981 ATS was satisfied with Ashland's development of the M.A. and voted to approve the degree program. The M.A. degree in its various forms has proven to be a very popular degree option at the seminary from its inception.

The seminary's offering of the D.Min. and M.A. degrees spurred the college to seek approval from the Ohio Board of Regents and the North Central Association for granting both master's and doctoral level degrees. The college gained approval from the Ohio Board of Regents for graduate education in 1975 and from the North Central Association in 1977. The North Central Association treated the college and seminary as one entity, a policy that continues to the present. In their decision to grant doctoral rating to the college in 1977, the North Central Association added a notation at the time that limited the doctoral degree to the seminary. Ironically, the seminary received accreditation by the North Central Association for the D.Min. degree before its approval of the M.A. and M.Div. degrees. The North Central Association wanted to consider these latter two degrees later in 1977 in conjunction with the college's master's program. With these actions the seminary had achieved full recognition of its degree programs from ATS, the Ohio Board of Regents, and the North Central Association.[113] Another important recognition of the seminary occurred in 1982 when the University Senate of the United Methodist Church authorized Ashland Theological Seminary as an approved seminary for the training of United Methodist students. This action was significant. By 1982 and continuing to the present, United Methodist students have been the largest denominational group in the student body.[114]

Throughout this period and to the present the seminary has remained on quarters. But the seminary experimented with several scheduling formats during the 1970s and early 80s. Throughout this period the first quarter ended before Christmas break (quarters were ten weeks). The innovative winter term mentioned above was dropped in 1972. In 1972 a September intensive term was added to accommodate the teaching of Greek to those students who had not had Greek in their undergraduate education. At the time it was expected that juniors move directly into Greek exegetical courses; only one quarter of Hebrew was required. The September intensive term was discontinued in the 1980–81 academic year. An interesting "first" for the seminary that appeared in the curriculum in 1980 was the offering of a course entitled "Computers and Christian Ministry."[115]

The philosophy represented by the curriculum during this period continued to reflect the historic Progressive Brethren commitments of fidelity to Scripture, dedication to scholarship, and nurture of spirituality all directed toward practical Christian ministry. Many of the statements expressing the philosophy of the seminary that had been written by Alva McClain forty years prior still appeared in the catalogues. Though their source had long since been forgotten, they continued to capture the spirit and ethos of the seminary.

The seminary sought to enrich its curriculum with several special lectureships each year. The Workman Lecture Series was begun by 1971 and continued through the latter 1970s. Generally held during the winter quarter, it brought such speakers as Lyman Coleman, Win Arn, Ronald Sider, David Burnham, and David Seamonds to the campus. The Continuing Education program that had, in the early 1970s, been combined with the All-Institutional Studies, was reinstituted in 1974. In 1975 it was held in conjunction with the Workman Lecture Series. In 1976 the Continuing Education program was recast into the Alumni Pastors' Conference, which likewise was tied to the Workman Lecture Series. These linked conferences combined several features: continuing education for pastors, a reunion time for alumni, and lectures by outstanding leaders in a variety of practical ministries. The Fall Lecture Series, begun in 1975, invited such outstanding Christian leaders to Ashland during the 1970s and early 80s as James Earl Massey, Timothy L. Smith, Charles H. Kraft, David Breese, and Carl F. H. Henry. Missionary Conferences, often held during the winter quarter, had begun by 1968 and kept the community aware of the missions mandate and the current status of worldwide missions. By 1980 an annual Spring Ministries Conference was instituted. Some of the lecturers in this series through the early 1980s were Carl George, Lyle Schaller, Kenneth O. Gangel, Elizabeth Elliott, and James Earl Massey. The seminary also hosted an annual Seminary Alumni Banquet in conjunction with graduation from 1973 until 1982. Tom Skinner and Kenneth Kantzer were a few of the featured speakers for this occasion. In 1983 the Alumni Banquet was shifted to the Alumni Pastors' Conference.

Shultz felt a great sense of satisfaction in 1975 as he reviewed the progress of the seminary since his arrival in 1963. In two different forums, his August 1975 report to the Board of Trustees and the November 1975 seminary newsletter, he reviewed the substantial strides that the seminary had taken over these years. He noted that the Seminary Committee had established some lofty goals in 1964 (the lists in the two documents are slightly different; they are conflated in this list):

1. "Continue and strengthen the Seminary's heritage of conservative Biblical teaching."
2. "Validate the academic program by accreditation by the Association of Theological Schools" and the North Central Association.
3. "Develop a financially self-sufficient theological seminary upon the principle: one-third income from tuition, one-third income from endowment and auxiliaries, and one-third income from church gifts."
4. "Develop a qualified faculty in every department of theological education" who all possess an earned doctorate.
5. "Recruit a student body of sufficient enrollment for a self-supporting seminary serving the church."
6. "Build a campus with sufficient resources including administrative offices, classrooms, library, chapel, and student housing."
7. Offer a "full complement of [degree] programs including Master of Arts in Religion, Master of Divinity, Doctor of Ministry, and Clinical Education."

Shultz concluded the list in the seminary newsletter with the succinct affirmation, "Goals attained—1974."[116]

Development of Extensions.   Probably the most significant thrust during the 1970s that would change the entire ethos of the seminary was the opening of extensions. The initial impetus for extensions was to provide meaningful contexts for the seminary's pastoral psychology and counseling program. This program, begun in 1969 as a specialized major in the M.Div. degree, was originally housed at the Cleveland Psychiatric Institute. Additional sites were opened in the 1970s: the Northeast Clergy Training Institute of Western Reserve Psychiatric Habilitation Center, which met at Hawthornden State Hospital (1976), EMERGE Counseling Center in Akron (1976), the Toledo Counseling Center (1979), and the Youngstown Family Counseling Center (1980). In addition to the M.Div. major in Pastoral Psychology and Counseling, the seminary also offered a concentration in Pastoral Psychology and Counseling in the new Master of Arts in Religion degree.

Shultz was well ahead of other seminaries in the opening of extensions. He envisioned a "seminary without walls," which took theological education to metropolitan areas without the benefit of such training. Shultz aggressively opened other extensions between 1970 and 1982. A short-lived lay certificate program was offered in Warsaw, Indiana, from 1970 to 1972. In 1974 clergy in the Cleveland area approached Shultz about the possibility of bringing graduate theological education to Cleveland. The largest city in Ohio at the time, Cleveland had no accredited program of Protestant theological education. In August 1974 Shultz reported that the seminary would begin a pilot theological program for the 1974–75 academic year. The classes would be housed at Trinity United Church of Christ Church. During the 1975–76 academic year the Cleveland Center for Theological Education had an enrollment of 22 students (up from 20 the first year) and met in the facilities of the Church of the Covenant. By the fall of 1981 there were 111 students enrolled in the Cleveland Center. In 1977 the Center moved to Cleveland State University where it remained until 1999. From 1999 until 2003 the Cleveland Center met in the facilities of the eastern campus of Cuyahoga Community College, and since 2003 has rented office space jointly with Ashland University in Warrensville Heights, Ohio.[117]

Current location of the Cleveland Center in Warrensville Heights, Ohio

The first director of the Cleveland Center was Charles Ronkos, who served in this role from 1974 to 1979. In 1979 Shultz hired Theron H. Smith to give general oversight to all extension programs. Smith resigned in 1986 in order to pastor a United Methodist congregation in Columbus, Ohio. Since 1986 the Cleveland Center has been directed by Charles Ronkos (1986–87), Douglas Little (1987–89), Mary Ellen Drushal (1989–92), Kenneth Walther (1992–95), Walter Kime (1995–2003), and Mylion Waite (2003 to the present).

The seminary began a number of short-lived extension programs during this period, based upon Shultz's philosophy of taking education to major metropolitan areas.[118] Shultz accordingly began non-degree programs for inner city pastors without access to advanced ministerial training in both Cleveland (1975) and Akron (1979). The Cleveland program was called the Inner-City Ministers' Personal and Professional Development Program and was run in cooperation with Case Western Reserve's Human Resource and Development Program. In 1979 Shultz began offering lay education classes in Wooster at the Church of the Savior.[119] Graduate extension programs opened in Toledo (1980), Youngstown (1980), and Canton (1981), in cooperation with Malone College. Though none of these programs were still active by the mid-1980s (the Toledo and Canton extensions closed in 1984 due to concerns raised by the Association of Theological Schools), they are reflective of the seminary's ongoing commitment to offer theological education to a wider constituency than just those who can reside on or travel to the main campus in Ashland. The extensions likewise add to the diversity and richness of the seminary community and, together with the seminary's international students, mirror the truth that the church is composed of people from every race, nationality, and ethnic group.

Development of the Physical Plant.   One of the goals for upgrading the seminary as far back as 1962 was the building of a freestanding chapel. By 1972 several pressing needs made the construction of the chapel a high priority. The existing chapel was too small for the seminary community; in addition, building a new chapel would free up space for classrooms and the library. In the wake of Albert Ronk's death in October 1972, Shultz proposed calling the facility the Ronk Memorial Chapel, recognizing three brothers who had given substantial leadership and resources to the church, college, and seminary for over sixty years: George, Willis, and Albert. On 15 January 1973 the Board authorized the establishment of a "Ronk Memorial Fund." The motion stated:

> In recognition of the faithful services of Doctors George, Willis, and Albert Ronk to college, church and community, a Ronk Memorial Project be es-

tablished with details to be worked out between the Ronk family, the administration, and the Seminary Committee of the Board of Trustees.[120]

By 12 August 1973 sufficient interest had been generated for a fitting memorial that the Seminary Committee authorized the preparation of plans. Shultz talked with members of the Ronk family and other interested parties and proposed the construction of a freestanding chapel and general meeting facility. He brought plans for the chapel to the 11 August 1974 Board meeting. The plans were based on the recently completed facility of the Jefferson Brethren Church, north of Goshen, Indiana. Because only $45,000 of the estimated cost of $175,000 was on hand, the Board deferred action until more funds were available. On 28 January 1975 Shultz had solicited sufficient funds and pledges for the Board to authorize construction of the chapel. As they had been doing since the 1890s, the women of the Brethren Church again came to the aid of the seminary. The Woman's Missionary Society selected the Ronk Memorial Chapel as their 1974–75 project and gave slightly over $9000 toward the chapel over the next two years.

Construction of the chapel moved ahead quickly. It was put into use 1 January 1976 and immediately relieved the shortage of classroom space by opening the former chapel for a large classroom. The construction cost of the chapel was $167,877, which was more than covered by gifts that totaled $175,323. The excess funds enabled the seminary to tear down two homes

Ronk Memorial Chapel and Wall of Remembrance (dedicated in 2006)

on High Street, one of which was the Koinonia House, in order to meet parking requirements established by the City of Ashland.[121]

In 1977 the seminary had its next accreditation visit by the Association of Theological Schools (ATS). Though the seminary was accredited for another ten years, ATS issued three notations: field education needed more adequate supervision, the faculty was inadequate for one or more degree programs offered, and the library facilities were inadequate. In February 1978 Shultz and the Seminary Committee highlighted seven significant needs of the seminary, many of them occasioned by the ATS visit: (1) the administration needed to develop a strategic plan for the school; (2) new faculty were needed; they were stretched too thin; (3) additional administrators should be hired; (4) students should have more experience in a well-supervised ministry context; (5) the library facilities needed to be expanded; (6) additional funds should be devoted to library acquisitions; and (7) there was a need, especially in Cleveland, to provide ministerial training to pastors who lacked the requisite educational qualifications for formal seminary education.[122]

Shultz and the Seminary Committee gave immediate attention to these points. As noted above, Shultz addressed points 2 and 3 by hiring additional faculty and administrators and he responded to point 7 with non-degree courses for inner city pastors. Shultz was particularly concerned about point 5 and advocated building a new classroom addition to the main building, which could open up space for the library. In March 1978 the Executive Committee asked Shultz to bring more detailed information about the addition. Plans were drawn by the architectural firm that had worked on the original addition to the main building, Marr, Knapp and Crawfis. The initial estimate came in at $150,000 to $200,000. Shultz brought these plans to the Executive Committee in April 1978. The committee gave tentative approval to the project; final approval by the Executive Committee was dependent on having cash on hand. Shultz had launched a $100,000 Capital Funds campaign in 1977 for the purpose of raising the needed funding; he was targeting special friends as well as donors in the Brethren Church.[123]

Apparently, lack of sufficient cash stymied further action for a year. But the financial plight of the college was also having a negative impact on this project and funding for library acquisitions at the seminary. There was reticence on the college campus about any further construction and the seminary library budget had been cut due to the budget problems at the college. The Seminary Committee appealed to the Board at its January 1979 meeting that an addition was critical for maintaining accreditation. The committee presented a motion that the Board approve the retaining of an architect for drawings, the submission of the drawings for bids, and the construction of an addition, the size of which would be determined by available funds. The Board gave its support to the motion.[124] If one reads between the lines in the documentary evidence, the impression is given that insufficient funding forced Shultz to rethink the size of the addition. In April 1979 Shultz proposed a three phase project, with the first two phases being additional classrooms, costing $64,902 and $56,060 respectively, and the third phase being additional internal alterations, costing $3,725. The seminary had $67,035 in cash and pledges, so the Executive Committee gave its support, with the understanding that the pledges would be converted to cash as the project proceeded. Plans for Phase I called for enlarging the west entryway to the seminary and adding a large classroom to the southwest corner of the main seminary facility, opposite the library. Carl E. Kauffman Construction of Ashland presented the low bid for the project and served as the general contractor. Construction occurred over the summer of 1979 and was completed for the fall quarter of 1979. The new classroom allowed the old chapel area to be used for the library and for seminar classes.[125]

When an Association of Theological Schools accreditation team revisited the seminary in May 1981, all three notations issued in 1977 were removed. However, a notation was added about program integration, which continued in force until 1989.[126]

Financial Considerations.   Though the financial difficulties of the college had repercussions upon the seminary in the late 1970s, the fiscal picture of the seminary was actually very positive throughout most of the 1970s. Shultz announced in 1974 that the seminary was self-supporting. Increasing student enrollment and thereby increasing tuition revenue was a key to self-support. Tuition revenue grew from $42,170 in 1971–72, to $205,000 in 1977–78, and $441,300 in 1982–83. As enrollment grew, the seminary became more dependent on tuition revenue as a percentage of the total budget. For example, in 1971–72 seminary enrollment was 91; tuition revenue represented $42,170 of the total budget of $173,975 (24.2%). In 1982–83 seminary enrollment stood at 436; tuition revenue represented $441,300 of the total budget of $630,850 (70%). Because the growth of the seminary made the budget more tuition driven, regular increases in tuition were necessary. In 1971–72 the comprehensive fee was $225 per quarter ($20 per quarter hour). Tuition had increased to $300 per quarter ($25 per quarter hour) in 1976–77 and $625 per quarter ($50 per quarter hour) in 1982–83. In spite of these increases Ashland remained in the lower third of tuition cost among all seminaries.

The seminary continued to support its budget through several other sources of income. The Brethren Church remained a faithful fiscal partner of the seminary. Gifts from the church generally amounted to between $50,000 and $80,000 per year during the 1970s and early 80s. The primary means of funding the seminary through the Brethren Church was through a "fair share" per member apportionment from local Brethren churches. Shultz asked for $4 per member from 1971 until 1975; the amount was increased to $5 per member in 1976 and $7.50 per member in 1980. By this latter year the Brethren Church had agreed on a per member apportionment for all the ministries of the church.[127]

By the mid-1970s the seminary was conducting an annual alumni scholarship telethon that raised funds among the seminary alumni for much needed student scholarships. The telethon has continued to the present. Student scholarships were also funded through the seminary endowment funds. The seminary endowment continued to grow during the 1970s and early 80s, reaching $170,235 in 1982. The endowment also funded faculty chairs, campus buildings, and the Annual Fund. In 1977 the Ashland Theological Seminary Foundation was chartered and received proper tax status. The foundation was established as an entity independent of Ashland College. A major impetus for this action was the grave financial situation of the college; Shultz and others were deeply concerned about the devastating effects upon the seminary if the college were to go into foreclosure. The independent status of the foundation would make it possible to provide the financial resources to purchase the seminary campus if this were to happen. Since its inception the foundation has purchased several properties necessary for the expansion of the seminary; funded building campaigns and endowments, faculty chairs, and student scholarships; underwritten seminary programs; and provided an annual source of interest revenue for the seminary.

Unique Gifts to the Seminary.   The seminary received several special gifts from Leon and Ruth Hoseck of Dallas, Texas, in 1978. The Hosecks created the seminary's first endowed chair, the Louis F. Gough Chair of New Testament Studies, in the interest of scholarly, conservative teaching of the New Testament. The Hosecks were close friends of Gough, who had retired from the seminary in June 1977 but died 15 January 1978. The Hosecks also established an approximately $1 million trust that would, upon their decease, underwrite the expenses of the seminary apartment building, which was appropriately renamed the Leon and Ruth Hoseck Apartments.[128]

The seminary conducted two capital campaigns during the latter 1970s and early 1980s. In 1977 a campaign sought to raise $100,000 for the

Charles F. Pfeiffer

classroom addition and in 1981 the seminary joined the college's $7.7 million "A Time of Opportunity" capital campaign by assuming $1 million of the total amount. It is not clear how much funding either of these campaigns raised.

During the 1960s and 70s the seminary was the recipient of a number of unique gifts. The seminary library received several special collections of books. Besides being given the entire collection of J. Allen Miller's books by the college, the library also received rare Brethren materials from D. C. White (1967 and at other times) and the family of Gerald Bronson (1971). The Albert T. Ronk family donated a collection of books on Mary, Queen of Scots (1970). A significant donation to the library was the nearly 10,000 volume collection of Charles F. Pfeiffer, a retired professor of Ancient Literatures at Central Michigan University. Pfeiffer, who had served as an adjunct professor at the seminary, died in July 1976 and had willed his valuable library, featuring Near Eastern, archaeological, and Old Testament materials, to the seminary. The old chapel was renovated and dedicated as the Charles F. Pfeiffer Room and became the home of the collection in 1977.[129]

In 1969 the seminary was able to acquire an organ for the chapel, thanks to a gift from Thomas H. and Carrie Diffenderfer, in memory of their daughter, Ruth Elaine. In 1970 Gene R. and Rita M. Hollinger presented a reproduction of the Rosetta Stone to the seminary in memory of Gene's great-aunt, Martha Elma Hollinger. The seminary acquired a second reproduction of the

*The Rosetta Stone (left) and the obelisk (right) of the Assyrian
ruler, Shalmaneser III, in the side entryway to the administration building*

Rosetta Stone from Robert Kinsey, a long-time member of the Seminary
Committee and retired pastor of Trinity Lutheran Church in Ashland. One
of the replicas is displayed in the corridor off the main hallway between the library and administrative building and the other is found in the side entrance
to the administrative building. In 1980 Kinsey also donated a reproduction of
the obelisk of the Assyrian ruler, Shalmaneser III, to the seminary. Kinsey had
ordered the replica from the British Museum and had displayed it in his church
office until his retirement. The obelisk was initially placed in the newly constructed seminary entrance area by the library in the addition of 1979, but now
stands in the side entrance area to the administrative offices.

One of the most important acquisitions of the seminary was the archaeological collection of Robert H. Smith. Smith, a professor at the College of Wooster, had acquired the twelve hundred piece collection while at
the American School of Oriental Research in 1958–59 and on subsequent
trips to Jordan and other Mediterranean countries. The seminary purchased
the collection in 1971 for $15,000. Delbert Flora devoted considerable time
during his retirement to cataloguing the collection, which contained objects from the Early Bronze Age through the Byzantine period. Initially,
Flora featured only a few of the items in revolving exhibits. With the completion of the Ronk Memorial Chapel in 1975, the former chapel became

the home for the collection. Flora exhibited a significant portion of the collection in display cases that lined the walls of the former chapel. When the Pfeiffer collection was added to the room in 1977, the combined collections offered a unique combination of resources for the study of ancient Near Eastern cultures. Few seminaries have such resources available as teaching aids for students. By the end of the 1970s the old chapel, for good reason, began to be referred to as the "Arch Room."[130]

The 1970s and early 1980s were exciting times in the life of the seminary. Nearly every year new records were established for students, budgets, and faculty. There was a strong sense of camaraderie among the faculty, administration, students, and staff. A pervasive feeling of optimism and anticipation prevailed throughout these years, in spite of a variety of growing pains. The seminary's growing reputation for a firm commitment to the evangelical faith drew increasing numbers of students to the seminary and requests from churches and pastors to begin extensions throughout northern Ohio.

Concluding Observations

The fortunes of college and seminary went in opposite directions during the 1960s and 70s. The years of seemingly limitless expansion at the college in the 1960s were the same years that the seminary was questioning its very existence, followed by the trials of seeking accreditation, with all that this entailed, with only limited resources. By the 1970s the college was sent reeling by the combined punches of decreasing enrollment, financial crisis, faculty and student unrest, and deepening malaise. At the same time the seminary was beginning a period of unprecedented growth, fueled by its commitment to a biblical, evangelical faith, the opening of new extensions, and the development of new programs and degrees. The amelioration of the fortunes of both institutions was largely due to the irrepressible leadership of Joseph Shultz.

Chapter 7

An Era of Expansion and Consolidation (1982–2006)

Introduction

After living on the brink of financial disaster for nearly a decade, Ashland College emerged in the mid-1980s as an entirely new institution, radically transformed by the very strategies that had enabled its survival. The entrepreneurial expansion under President Joseph Shultz during the 1980s would be followed, however, by a period of consolidation and missional and structural definition under President William Benz. Though the characteristics of expansion and consolidation were not as drastically juxtaposed at the seminary as they were during the presidencies of Shultz and Benz at the college/university, nonetheless, during the entire period that Frederick Finks was at the helm of the seminary, the themes of expansion, consolidation, and institutional definition were interwoven.

The College Becomes a University

The institution that emerged from the financial crises of the latter 1970s and early 1980s was radically different from its predecessor. The very strategies that saved Ashland College transformed it into Ashland University. Much of the credit for this recasting of the college goes to the creative genius and entrepreneurial inventiveness of Joseph Shultz. He intuitively understood what neither of the previous two presidents, Clayton and Schultz, had been able to—that the future of the college depended on new, non-traditional programs that could provide the financial resources to underwrite the undergraduate program.

While the college had begun to address the needs of non-traditional students in the early 1970s, it was Shultz who made non-traditional programs the centerpiece of the college's renewal. With the demographics for traditional, residential undergraduate students continuing to show limited growth and even decline, Shultz sought ways to package education for a new clientele of students. He expanded evening and weekend course offerings for both undergraduate and graduate students and continuing education opportunities in the fields of both business and education. He further developed an existing program of undergraduate education for incarcerated students. He gave prominence to the two master's degree programs initiated in the latter 1970s: the M.Ed. and M.B.A. He took these programs to the people through the establishment of off-campus centers. It was Shultz's goal to establish these centers and to gain approval for them from the Ohio Board of Regents and the North Central Association before other schools began to compete for their share of the market.[1] In 1990 there were nineteen such "satellite centers."[2] An indication of the financial impact that these various programs were having on the institution's budget can be seen in the projected revenue figures for 1991–92. Projected total revenue was $41.9 million; non-traditional programs accounted for $14.4 million or 34% of the total revenue.[3] It is noteworthy that the number of non-residential students (including graduate students) surpassed the number of residential students in the latter 1970s; in 1983 non-traditional students, which included undergraduate part-time students and full-time and part-time graduate students, first outnumbered traditional students; graduate students outnumbered undergraduate students for the first time in 1999.

If Shultz provided the conceptual imagination for these new programs, Lucille Ford should be credited with their formulation and implementation. During Shultz's presidency she served successively as Vice President and Dean of the School of Business Administration, Economics, and Radio/TV (1979–1985), Vice President for Academic Affairs (1985–90), and Provost (1990–92). Shultz and Ford exhibited great mutual respect and shared a synergy of creativity that reshaped the college/university in the 1980s. Writing in 1985, Ford expressed their joint philosophy quite succinctly:

> While many colleges are suffering serious student decline, this is not true at Ashland College. Part of our college's strength is the ability to meet shifting demand for educational service to traditional and non-traditional students. This flexibility is a prime concern of our institution, one recognized and fully supported; in fact, it is a way of life at Ashland College.[4]

These initiatives slowly helped the college to dig itself out of the deep hole of indebtedness, both long-term and accumulated short-term, that

Lucille Ford

made the future of the college so precarious in the latter 1970s and early 1980s. Steady progress was made on reducing the long-term debt during Shultz's tenure. On 1 May 1979 long-term indebtedness stood at $14,437,000; at the end of his presidency in 1992 it had been reduced to $4,183,000. The accumulated deficit was $1,711,789 on 1 May 1979; it was eliminated during the 1986–87 fiscal year. The endowment grew during Shultz's tenure from $2,090,000 to $13,598,282 (as of 31 March 1992).

The financial picture significantly improved through the restructuring of a major portion of the college's long-term debt in 1984 and by two successful capital campaigns during the 1980s, one of which, "A Time of Opportunity," was discussed in the previous chapter. The refinancing of the long-term debt was occasioned by an offer to the college by the Connecticut Mutual and Phoenix Mutual Life Insurance Companies to buy back $3.7 million in first mortgage bonds for a discounted price of $2.6 million. The bonds covered the indebtedness on Kilhefner and Clark Halls, the Arts and Humanities building, and the Physical Education facility. In December 1984 a $5 million "Master Loan" was consummated with three Ashland banks: Bank One of Ashland, First National Bank, and Huntington Bank. This loan not only realized a $947,000 discount that was applied to the 1984–85 operating budget, but it turned short-term debt into long-term debt, effectively eliminating it (though short-term debt continued to be tracked), and it created a $1.3 million open line of credit. Just as important, the loan made it possible for the college to meet the North Central Association requirement that short-term debt be eliminated by 1 July 1985.[5] The Master Loan was paid off in January 1992.

The second capital campaign, "Partnership in Excellence," was chaired by Weldon W. Case and had a $14 million goal. The campaign focused in three major areas: endowment ($7 million), unrestricted giving ($6 million), and campus improvements ($1 million). The campaign ran from 1 November 1985 to 30 June 1990, concluding with a total of $16,636,722. It invested endowment income into faculty chairs, student scholarships, and academic programs. It also helped to eliminate deferred maintenance on the campus.[6]

Throughout her time as Vice President for Academic Affairs and as Provost, Lucille Ford gave attention to faculty development. She increased the number of Deans' Grants for faculty study, conference attendance, and travel to academic events. She recognized faculty who traveled to off-campus locations through a Road Runners luncheon. Through Professional Grants she was able to assist faculty toward completion of their terminal degree. In the 1986–87 academic year she implemented the Mentor Recognition program, in which senior students nominated faculty who had made a significant impact on their academic and personal development. In the 1987–88 academic year she announced the inception of fully funded one semester Senior Faculty Study Leaves. Two leaves were offered each year; John Nethers and Charles Ferroni were the first recipients in 1988. In 1988 she instituted an annual Faculty Recognition for scholarship. In order to enhance all areas of faculty development she advocated the creation of the position of Coordinator of Faculty Development in 1988; Kathleen Flanagan was hired for the position. Other faculty development opportunities initiated by Ford were Journal Writing Grants, which provided assistance with expenses associated with the publication of articles; New Dimension Project Grants, which funded course redesign to improve the learning experience; and Professional Discipline Experience Grants, which allowed faculty to teach half-time and work half-time in the marketplace to keep current with professional methods and needs.[7]

Shultz shared this commitment to faculty enhancement. He initiated annual faculty retreats in 1982. In 1986 he gained final Board approval for the title and position of Regius Professor (renamed Trustees' Professor in 1995), which recognized faculty with the rank of professor who had demonstrated exceptional achievement in teaching, or research and publication, or creative professional achievements. He significantly increased funding for faculty development. During his presidency endowed faculty chairs at the college and seminary grew from one to twelve (not all were fully funded). Shultz invested significant financial resources in increasing the size of the faculty. When he came to the college in 1979 there were 110 faculty; when he left the university in 1992 there were 188 (these numbers include the seminary). Based on an Ashland College Wage Consistency study in 1987, funding was designated in both the 1988–89 and 1989–90 fiscal years to adjust faculty salaries due to the fact that newer faculty were being brought in at higher salaries relative to the salaries of existing faculty.[8]

During Shultz's tenure a number of important changes to the curriculum were implemented. The faculty adopted a new curriculum in the 1983–84 academic year. A key component of the curriculum was a Freshman Studies program that had a fourfold purpose: (1) to create a bond between freshmen students and the college; (2) to aid new students in making the social and academic transition from high school to college life; (3) to improve basic skills of incoming students in communication, reading, writing, speaking, and listening; and (4) to make freshmen aware of such school services as registration procedures, academic counseling, and social and health services. In fall 1987 another significant component was added to the curriculum, the Interdisciplinary Studies Program. This program, developed under the leadership of Douglas Chismar, required all undergraduate students to take four courses in which more than one discipline was represented and which contributed to the integration of learning. In 1987 the Honors Program went through a major revision in order to enhance the educational experience of gifted students. In the 1987–88 academic year the college initiated the Writing Center to assist students with their writing skills; it would be one of many such student support services that would be established over the next two decades at the college/university.[9]

The substantial progress made in all the areas mentioned above fostered an optimistic spirit within the institution in the last half of the 1980s that was in stark contrast to the demoralized perspective that dominated the late 1970s. There was a greater sense of unity and cooperation between the administration and faculty than had existed at any time since the late 1960s and student morale was likewise high. No doubt the appearance of President Ronald Reagan at the college on 9 May 1983 to inaugurate the newly created John M. Ashbrook Center for Public Affairs enhanced the recognition of the school regionally and nationally. Enrollment figures offer tangible proof of the new appeal of the college. In 1979 when Shultz arrived as the interim president of the college, full-time undergraduate enrollment was 1365. It bottomed out in 1982 at 1196 and rose to 1275 in 1985 and to 1630 in the fall of 1991, Shultz's last year. Total enrollment in all programs for these years was 2522 in 1979, 2876 in 1982, 3429 in 1985, and 5144 in 1991. Not only did this progress lead to a more unified sense of direction in

*President Ronald Reagan delivers the inaugural address for the
John M. Ashbrook Center for Public Affairs at Ashland College*

the campus community but it also set the stage for two important developments in the latter 1980s: the next accreditation review of the college by
the North Central Association and the formal recognition of the transition
of the institution from a college to a university.

At the previous accreditation review by the North Central Association in 1978, the college had received notations in the areas of governance,
finances, and long-range planning. The college was required to report yearly
concerning progress in these areas. By 1985 the college had made such a remarkable turn-around that no further report was requested until the scheduled 1988 reaccreditation visit.[10] The advances made by the college over
the previous ten years impressed the accreditation team. One can sense the
exhilaration in Lucille Ford's report to the Board: "The North Central Accreditation Team recommends: Maximum approval time of ten (10) years;
with NO report and NO focus visit required!"[11] Though the North Central
Association identified some areas of concern, Ford indicated that the overall review given the college was exceptional. She summarized:

> the powerful accrediting agencies [the Ohio Board of Regents and the Ohio
> Department of Education also visited the college in 1988] have declared
> Ashland understands its mission, its strengths, its weaknesses [and] is stable

and fully capable of delivering educational quality to fulfill its role in the responsibility of education to the greater society.[12]

The other significant advance made possible by the progress in the 1980s was the recognition that the institution of the 1980s was no longer the same school that it had been for over one hundred years. It was no longer primarily a residential college; it was no longer primarily an undergraduate college; it was no longer primarily a single-campus college. The outreach of Ashland College to non-traditional students, especially through the prison, continuing education, and adult education programs, the extraordinary growth in the M.B.A. and M.Ed. degree programs, and the strategy to develop off-campus educational centers had radically transformed Ashland. Shultz first broached the subject of changing the name of the school to Ashland University in Board discussions in the fall of 1985. Not only did he note the factors listed above, but he reminded the Board that the school had been designated Ashland University in the reorganization of 1888 and that the institution was registered with the Ohio Board of Education as a university. The Board decided to hold off focused discussion of the issue until after the reaccreditation visits in 1988. Conversation about the change began in earnest in the spring of 1988. The subject was thoroughly studied through the hiring of an outside consultant and through input from trustees, faculty, students, and alumni. There was an overwhelmingly positive response for the name change, though the students did raise a concern about how the change would affect the commitment to "AC'cent on the Individual." On 12 May 1989 the Board officially adopted the change of the school's name to Ashland University.[13] Later in 1989 in his annual report to alumni and friends of the university, Shultz declared:

> The Board of Trustees of Ashland College voted May 12 to change the name of the institution to Ashland University. The Board determined that "university" more aptly describes what Ashland has become based on its graduate programs in business and education, its professional schools of theology and nursing, and the growth in the institution's enrollment. In making the name change, the Board re-emphasized Ashland's undergraduate mission as well as its philosophy of "Accent on the Individual."[14]

The exuberant feeling of accomplishment that Shultz rightly expressed in his annual report was fleeting, however. In 1991 a cascade of events began that eventually led to Shultz's resignation from the presidency: the passing on to *The (Cleveland) Plain Dealer* of confidential internal memos about the integrity of the university's basketball program by a person connected with

Walter Waetjen

the university; the publicizing of the content of these memos by the *The Plain Dealer* and a resulting inquiry by the NCAA; the surfacing of concerns about Shultz's leadership style from faculty and students; Board investigation of these concerns and hiring of an outside consultant to prepare a report, the so-called Fisher Report, and to make recommendations about the situation. The allegations, rumors, and general turmoil that were swirling about the campus greatly concerned the Board. A Board committee that investigated the situation concluded in March 1992 that there were serious problem areas within the administration, including issues of communication and input, governance, authority, responsibility, and accountability. In May 1992 Shultz reluctantly resigned.[15] The Board then hired a one-year interim president, Walter Waetjen (B.S. Millersville University of Pennsylvania; M.S. University of Pennsylvania; Ed.D. University of Maryland), to provide time to launch a nationwide search for the next president. Waetjen had served as the president of Cleveland State University from 1973 until 1988.

The fallout from *The Plain Dealer* articles and the NCAA inquiry was not serious for the institution in the long run. The NCAA was pleased with the complete cooperation of the institution. The Committee on Infractions assessed less than the minimum penalties: placement of the men's basketball program under probation for two years; the requirement that Ashland University develop and implement a comprehensive educational plan for coaches and athletic personnel; and the filing of progress reports in 1993 and 1994. It was a tribute to Ashland University that its institutional strength and character served it well in the midst of these storms.[16]

An Era of Consolidation, Institutional Definition, and Further Growth

On 16 December 1992 the Board of Trustees selected G. William Benz (B.A. University of California-Riverside; M.A., M.A.L.D., Ph.D. Tufts University) as the next president of Ashland University; he took office in May 1993. The entrepreneurial growth of the 1980s, though ensuring the survival and, eventually, the thriving of the college/university, also created some challenges. Inadequate attention had been given to working out a viable graduate structure for the university; at times the departments, schools, and other structures of the college/university worked independent of one another; the philosophy of multiplying programs and off-campus centers was not always balanced by an evaluation of the effectiveness of and the ability to resource these programs. Though Shultz and the Board had given some attention to strategic planning through an All-Campus Planning Council established in 1988, there was also need for a broad consensus in the university community for the future direction of the institution.

G. William Benz

Perhaps one of the greatest legacies of Benz was his leadership in developing a strategic planning document that guided many of the significant initiatives of his presidency. Waetjen had set in motion the process with the appointment in December 1992 of a Plan for Planning Committee, chaired by Murray Hudson, to begin work on a mission statement and raise questions that needed to be addressed in a strategic planning process. There was agreement that the mission statement needed to be in place to give direction to the strategic planning process. The mission statement received final approval of administration, Board, and faculty in early 1994 (see below for further discussion). A Strategic Planning Committee composed of faculty, administration, staff, students, alumni, and trustees and co-chaired by Lucille Ford and Provost Ruth Person began working on a comprehensive planning document 29 January 1994. The process eventually enlisted the involvement of twenty-five people on the committee and roughly another one hundred on nine task forces. The document, entitled "Embracing Change," received final Board approval on 19 January 1996 and set forth goals for the next five years.[17]

A second phase of the strategic planning process, led by Provost Mary Ellen Drushal (she served as Interim Provost in the 1995–96 academic year and Provost from 1996 to 2001), was initiated in 1999 but was stymied by differences between the Board and the President. There were a number of positive results of this phase, however. The Board approved three statements that provided clearer institutional definition: one entitled "Institutional Core Values,"[18] approved in October 1999; a "Vision Statement,"[19] approved in May 2000; and a revised "Mission Statement," approved in January 2002. This new mission statement, discussed further below, maintained the essential emphases of the previous statement but was more concise, better organized, and sounder grammatically. It also addressed some minor criticisms raised by the North Central Association accreditation team in 1998.

Benz initiated a final phase of strategic planning in 2004. He desired to have a planning document in place for the next North Central Association accreditation review in 2008 and to give direction to the next president. An initial draft, prepared by Benz, went through significant revisions by the faculty. The document received support of the cabinet and faculty, and, in January 2006, the Board. There was a general feeling, though, that the document needed additional revision, but the various constituencies were willing to view it as a work in process that would continue to be developed and refined.[20]

The first of these strategic planning processes was very successful in accomplishing its goals, due, in large part, to the broad buy-in by all the university constituencies. The university community demonstrated a concerted effort to advance the wide range of recommendations found in the "Embracing Change" document. In January 1997 Benz indicated that significant progress had already been made within the first year of the plan. He observed that the process was bearing fruit in such areas as:

> academic governance, academic program review, facilities planning, core curriculum, intercollegiate athletic program review, student center campaign and construction, renovation of Patterson Hall into an Instructional Technology Center, technology enhancement program implementation, and admission processes and policies review and revision.[21]

He noted that other elements of the strategic planning document would be addressed in the following months: "administrative governance, implementation of student outcomes assessment, deferred maintenance, retention, marketing, and increasing development efforts with respect to foundations and corporations."[22] Several of the items in these lists deserve further elaboration.

A major issue that needed attention during Benz's tenure was working out a governance structure that fit with Ashland's status as a university and that brought better organization to the burgeoning graduate programs. Shultz had taken only tentative steps in this direction. In 1987 a Graduate Advisory Council (eventually called the Graduate Council) was formed under the leadership of Lucille Ford to better coordinate graduate activities and policies and help resource the programs. The Council consisted of the Directors of the M.B.A. and M.Ed. programs, the appropriate deans, and the directors of Continuing Education and Graduate Continuing Education. In 1990 Shultz advocated changing the title of the Vice President of Academic Affairs to Provost, noting that this title was more consistent with university status. Advisory Councils for each of the schools were also formed in 1990, though these councils remained unclear about their membership, accountability, and overall purpose until more definite guidelines were created in 1993.[23]

As part of the strategic planning initiative under Benz, the Academic Review Committee of the Faculty Senate gave leadership to the issues of academic restructuring and governance. In November 1996 the Faculty Senate approved the committee's recommendations to restructure the university into three colleges: Arts and Sciences, Business and Economics, and Education and to create an Office of Graduate Studies and Professional Development. The Board gave its support to the proposal in January 1997. In this restructuring the former Schools of Sciences and of Arts and Humanities were combined into the new College of Arts and Sciences (the School of Nursing had been folded into the School of Sciences as a department earlier in 1996). Each of the colleges was to have its own dean; the deans would report to the Provost. The Office of Provost was also reconfigured in July 1997 to include an Associate Provost who would give oversight to graduate and professional development programs and to the university's off-campus sites. These changes represented a major realignment of the university's academic structure that involved creating new administrative positions, restructuring reporting and communication lines, and providing better coordination of academic services. The implications of this restructuring continue to be worked out, with each of the colleges rethinking its own mission, vision, structure, lines of communication, and policies and procedures related to such issues as curriculum and faculty advancement.[24]

One of the related developments in this realignment process that was spurred by the continued growth of the university's graduate programs was the realization that there needed to be greater coordination of these programs. As noted above, initial steps were taken in this direction with the creation of the Graduate Council in 1987. The Associate Provost position created in 1997 had, as one of its primary responsibilities, oversight of the graduate programs. As part of the structural realignment within colleges, both the College of Education and College of Business and Economics had created by 1998 a department of graduate studies separate from the department overseeing the undergraduate program. This change allowed for focused attention on the academic and curricular needs of these graduate programs. In 1998 a family of recruiting materials was produced specifically for the graduate programs and in the same year a graduate catalogue distinct from the undergraduate catalogue made its debut. Two new graduate degrees have been initiated since 1998: the Doctor of Education degree in 1998 and the Master of Arts in American History and Government in 2005, the first graduate degree in the College of Arts and Sciences. A Master of Fine Arts in Creative Writing degree is also being planned.[25]

As a stipulation for the approval of these new master's degree programs, the Ohio Board of Regents required that the university create a Graduate School. To this end, the university gave John Sikula the dual title of Associate Provost and Dean of the Graduate School in 2004. An Interim Graduate Council was created in 2005 to discuss such issues as mission, governance, and graduate faculty designation. The goal was to have a permanent Graduate Council in place in 2006.[26] It is ironic that at the same time that the colleges were working out the details of their "vertical" structure, that is, developing separate departments for undergraduate and graduate programs **within** their colleges, the Board of Regents gave impetus for the creation of a "horizontal" graduate structure that that **cut across** the colleges. The competing structural concepts will need to be worked out in the coming years.

The 1996 strategic planning document had placed special emphasis on enhancing academic quality. Much credit goes to Provost Mary Ellen Drushal for progress in fulfilling this thrust. Significant budgetary resources were targeted for academic areas: 58% of all new revenue dollars were devoted to academics between the 1998–99 and 2002–03 academic years. A process to review all academic programs on an on-going basis was initiated in 1995–96 with the actual review of programs beginning during spring 1997. Beginning in 1995 the faculty engaged in a review of the B.A. degree requirements for the first time since 1983–84. A major outcome of this process was the creation of a new core curriculum. Launched in fall 2000 and overseen by Core Director, Jeffrey Weidenhamer, the curriculum featured two tiers: the first tier provided a breadth of courses to lay a foundation for the liberal arts and the second tier took a more intensive approach to help students develop critical thinking and reasoning skills. The Classroom Effectiveness Project, begun in 1997, was a multi-year effort to improve classroom facilities.[27]

Drushal also gave considerable attention to faculty development. During her time as Provost the criteria for promotion and tenure were strengthened, a more effective process for the allocation and filling of faculty positions was put in place, and opportunities for faculty development were expanded. The number of senior faculty study leaves was increased, though this was motivated by a North Central Association concern that two study leaves per year were insufficient for a school with university status. Provost Robert Suggs (2002–07) gave renewed emphasis to this commitment, targeting twelve study leaves by 2008. New faculty recognition awards initiated in the latter 1990s were the Taylor Excellence in Teaching Award, given annually to a faculty member for teaching effectiveness inside and outside the classroom; the Merit Grant, designed to recognize faculty members who demonstrated outstanding achievement in teaching, research, and service; and the Maude V. Rutt Award, given annually to a faculty member to assist in furthering graduate study or research. Kathleen Flanagan, the Coordinator of Faculty Development, initiated Faculty Colleges in 1996. Originally held three times a year (now twice a year) when students were not on campus, these week-long sessions allowed faculty to choose from a variety of educational opportunities, though initially the focus was on technology.[28]

The faculty, together with administrators and staff, benefited from a six-phase consistency pay increase that sought to bring all university employees to a pay level "commensurate with comparable employees at similar institutions and geographic locations."[29] The six phases were divided into two phases each for faculty, staff, and administrators spread over the budget years from 1993–94 to 2002–03.

One of the results of the Fisher Report, produced in the turmoil surrounding the NCAA investigation in 1992, was the recommendation of a different form of faculty governance. The Board empowered the faculty to develop a detailed proposal for the May 1993 Board meeting. The resulting "Constitution of the Faculty Senate" gained Board approval at that time. Because the Constitution called for direct conversations between the trustees and faculty, without AAUP mediation, it needed the favorable endorsement of the AAUP before it went into effect. As a gesture of good faith with the faculty, the Board continued the policy of faculty representation on the Board, with two faculty members nominated to the Board each year, though without vote. In addition, two members of the faculty were welcomed to the Executive Committee of the Board and one member of the faculty was invited to serve on each of the committees of the Board. The only exception to faculty participation on the Board and Executive Committee would occur when these groups went into executive session. Though this more collaborative working arrangement between the Board and faculty has had to weather some disagreements, it is more in keeping with the historic collegial model of governance of the institution.[30]

A major thrust of Benz's tenure was upgrading the technology resources of the campus. In 1994 Benz established an Institutional Technology Task Force, which studied the future technological needs of the university.[31] The top priority identified by the task force in its 1995 report was a campus-wide network. In January 1996 the Board approved acquiring a $4 million line of credit with three Ashland banks that would be secured by the endowment. The majority of the loan, $3.375 million, would cover costs related to networking the campus: a fiber-optic network of all facilities, including the seminary, off-campus access, faculty personal computers, computerized classrooms, acquisition of software, upgrade of library technology, support services, and faculty training. An additional $700,000 was earmarked for the renovation of Patterson Hall into the Patterson Instructional Technology Center. The technological advances made possible by this funding were impressive. The campus-wide fiber-optic network, appropriately dubbed EagleNet, was completed in January 1997. Three hundred personal computers were distributed in 1996, bringing the total number of university owned computers at the time to seven hundred. In 1997 the online library catalog was introduced and in 1999 the library joined OhioLINK, the largest online database consortium of academic libraries in Ohio. Numerous computerized classrooms were installed throughout the campus from 1996 on; new student computer labs were made available in the recently completed Student Center and at prison sites in 1996; multi-media stations made their debut in classrooms in late 1997. The renovation of Patterson was completed in 1997 at a cost of $1.9 million.[32]

Other significant technological advances were detailed preparations for the non-event of Y2K; the introduction of WebCT in 2000 as the online course environment, which had been adopted by the State of Ohio; the piloting of online registration in 2001; the introduction of wireless service across the campus in 2003; the implementing of GroupWise email system and the installation of video-conferencing capabilities at the regional centers in 2004; and the unveiling of "Ashland Universe," a three-dimensional, interactive, virtual experience of the campus on a newly designed web site in 2005. In order to keep up with these advances an institutional document was prepared in 2000 that established policies and procedures for developing web-based and web-assisted courses. In addition, in 2001 the university combined the separate units of Academic Technologies and Administrative Computing to form the department of Information Technology and hired an Executive Director of Information Services to oversee all aspects of technology on the campus. An indication of the commitment of the university to the enhancement of technology is the fact that technology expenditures for the ten year period of 1992–93 to 2001–02 totaled $15,843,760.[33]

The above advances in strategic planning, curriculum and faculty development, and technology enhancement, together with other important initiatives, placed the university in good stead for the 1998 reaccreditation visit by the North Central Association (NCA). After the NCA accredited the university once again for the maximum ten years, Drushal, with subdued objectivity, declared:

> The [NCA] team noted the significant and broad-based improvement that has occurred over the last ten years in the quality of virtually every aspect of the university, and [it is] the team's judgment that the emerging strategic planning process will ensure such improvements in quality will continue during the next ten years.[34]

Two of Benz's noted achievements during his presidency were the related developments of building campaigns and capital campaigns. Early in his presidency Benz turned his attention to the construction of the Student Center on "the point" formed by Claremont Avenue and King Road. A "Campus Center" had been proposed on this site as far back as 1969, though

Hawkins-Conard Student Center

it was Shultz who gave impetus to the idea during the latter part of his tenure. Benz moved the project from concept to reality with groundbreaking occurring 21 April 1995 and dedication of the facility taking place on 12 October 1996. Naming gifts for the Student Center were donated by Earl and Betty Hawkins and The John and Pearl Conard Foundation. A new covered footbridge over Claremont, replacing an earlier bridge, was completed in January 1997.[35]

The 1994–96 strategic planning process had given impetus to the question of additional facilities. The Board felt that the institution was in a good fiscal position to consider additional construction; by the end of 1995 all buildings were paid for except the library and Student Center. In October 1996 a Master Facilities Planning Committee was established; the following October it presented to the Board a document entitled "Vision of the Future," which outlined a three phase implementation process. Phase I, which was included in the report, was a list of current needs and future requests for campus facilities; Phase II would be a prioritization of this list; and Phase III would develop the fund raising plan. By fall 1998 four major projects had gained general consensus for inclusion in the building campaign: a new facility for the College of Business and Economics, Kettering Science building renovation and addition, a Sport Sciences and Recreation facility, and a seminary Leadership Center (to be discussed in the seminary section).

In order to provide funds for this ambitious building program, the Master Facility Planning Committee proposed to the Board in January 1998 that a major capital campaign be undertaken to coincide with the 125th anniversary of the university in 2003. On 2 October 1998 the Board once again retained Goettler Associates, Inc. to conduct a feasibility study for the campaign (they had done a similar study for the successful campaign in the early 1980s). The campaign, designated "Building on Strength," kicked off in May 1999 with Lucille Ford serving as the campaign chair. The goal was set for $55 million, with $35 million earmarked for the proposed capital projects and $20 million for continued support of scholarships, endowment, and programs. The highly successful campaign concluded with a victory celebration on 30 September 2004 at which time over $59.4 million had been raised.[36]

The funds raised through the capital campaign enabled the university to move ahead with its building campaign. In the midst of the campaign the Board also authorized two building projects in addition to the four buildings already proposed: three senior apartments and a new facility for the College of Education.[37] The senior apartments were completed prior to fall 2002 and the Richard E. and Sandra J. Dauch College of Business and Economics and Burton D. Morgan Center for Entrepreneurial Studies were dedicated on 14 November 2003 and 21 November 2003 respectively. On 4 May 2006 the university held a double dedication: the Arthur L. and Maxine Sheets Rybolt Sport Sciences Center and adjacent Recreation Center and the Dwight Schar College of Education. On 29 September 2006 the addition to and renovation of the Kettering Science Center was dedicated as part of the Homecoming festivities.

The period of the 1980s through the mid-2000s saw Ashland University become a very complex institution. There has been a multiplication of student organizations as well as student support services. There is an ongoing need to develop an effective graduate structure for the burgeoning graduate programs. In all aspects of the university structure the Board, administrators, and faculty have given detailed attention to defining roles, responsibilities, and accountability, and to improving communication. The recent emphasis by accrediting bodies for comprehensive institutional assessment has resulted in additional layers of data-collection, analysis, and reporting. An indication of the growing complexity of the university is the growth of the administrative and staff personnel relative to faculty. In 1986 there were 48 full-time administrators (15.2% of the total personnel), 124 full-time faculty (39.4% of total personnel), and 143 full-time staff (45.4% of total personnel). In 2006 there were 166 full-time administrators (22.3% of total personnel), 235 full-time faculty (31.6% of total personnel), and 343 full-time staff (46.1% of total personnel). The figures for both years include the seminary.[38]

In addition to the challenges posed by the increasing complexity of the institution, Ashland University shares a number of challenges with higher education in general. In April 2000 Benz identified these challenges:

> the cost of higher education; access [to higher education] (financial aid); improving quality while containing costs; consequences and implications of technology to teaching and learning; and lessening dependency on tuition (increasing enrollment and/or gaining additional revenue from auxiliary services, gifts and grants, and endowment income . . .). For Ashland to continue to be successful, these issues must be addressed forthrightly with the goal of finding innovative and effective strategies for meeting these challenges.[39]

Ashland University also finds itself facing once again a period in which, on one hand, enrollment growth will be more difficult to sustain, especially in its graduate programs,[40] while, on the other, there are increased costs from long-term debt that must be borne by the budget. But this situation is different from that found in the latter 1970s and early 1980s when long-term debt as a percentage of total revenue was as high as 206.4% in 1975. In 2004 when the bonds were issued for the building projects the maximum long-term debt to revenue percentage was 62%.[41] These challenges may call upon Ashland University to do what it has done so often in the past when faced with adversity: enter into a new era of entrepreneurial and visionary creativity.

Because Ashland University continues to be tuition driven, enrollment is critical to its future development. The following enrollment figures reflect the challenges that the university faces because of its dependence on tuition.

Year	Undergraduate Enrollment	Graduate Enrollment	Total Enrollment
1990	2764	2015	4779
1995	3031	2540	5571
2000	2819	3236	6055
2004	2859	4063	6922
2005	2791	3681	6472

The record enrollment at the university occurred in 2004. Though the undergraduate enrollment has shown only a modest decrease since 2000, the graduate enrollment has dropped rather significantly since 2004 (see endnote 40 for reasons). This drop has occurred at the very time that the university has assumed major financial indebtedness for its building projects.

In spite of these challenges the Benz era was marked by significant development in many areas of the university's life. In May 2005 Benz announced his retirement effective 30 June 2006. However, he resigned in May 2006 after having been placed on administrative leave by the Executive Committee of the Board for undisclosed reasons.[42] The Board had entered into a search process for the next president of the university in the fall of 2005. The process concluded in December 2005 with the announcement of Frederick Finks as the 28th president of Ashland University. He took office on 1 June 2006. His achievements as the president of Ashland Theological Seminary, his knowledge of the university, and his strong ties to the Ashland community not only impressed the search committee and Board but also bode well for the future of Ashland University.

The Institutional Philosophy of Ashland University

The years between 1982 and 2006 were a period of unparalleled change in the identity of Ashland College/University. The change of the name of the institution in 1989 underscored the major shifts that had occurred during the Shultz era: from primarily a residential campus to a school with multiple program centers; from an undergraduate college to a university with a burgeoning graduate program; from a school that targeted primarily full-time students to one that developed a host of special programs to meet the needs of non-traditional students.

It is ironic that even though Shultz engineered these radical shifts in the college's identity, essentially to assure the college's survival, he never developed a mission statement for the institution. Generally speaking, this quality is one of the marks of the entrepreneur—leaving the work of definition, clarification, and structuring to others. The statement crafted under Arthur Schultz in 1978 continued to be used through the Shultz years.

Though Shultz produced no official document delineating the uniqueness of the college/university, he did pen several lists of characteristics of the school that indicate that he had a good sense of what made Ashland unique. In 1989, for example, he described Ashland's historical hallmarks as: "liberal arts as the core of any and all professions and careers; Judeo-Christian beliefs; conservative political, economic, social, and religious philosophy; individualized student education; quality dedicated faculty; independent self-governing Board; faith in the future."[43] Note that "Judeo-Christian" first appeared as a "hallmark" under Arthur Schultz and that several of these traits reflect commitments of Shultz as much as Ashland

College, specifically the "conservative" emphasis and "faith in the future." It is true that Ashland would have been historically conservative, but this depiction of the college becomes emphasized under Shultz through the Ashbrook Center, authorized by the Board in 1982 and espousing a conservative Republican viewpoint, the Gill Center for Business and Economic Development, which took a conservative stance on issues of economics and business, and the seminary, with its evangelical commitment. An inherent feature of Shultz's entrepreneurial spirit was his optimism that a visionary, creative perspective will always be able to "find a way."

A significant feature of Benz's legacy was the attention to institutional definition and structure. As noted above, two mission statements appeared during his tenure. Work on the first was initiated by Waetjen; it received Board approval in 1994. The statement, as it appeared in the 1994–95 university catalogue, is as follows:

Mission Statement for Ashland University

Ashland University is a mid-sized regional teaching university, historically related to the Brethren Church. Our mission is to serve the educational needs of all students—undergraduate and graduate, traditional and non-traditional, full and part time—by providing educational programs of high quality in an environment that is both challenging and supportive.

These educational programs emphasize both the importance of the liberal arts and sciences and the need to provide initial and advanced preparation in selected professional areas—including business, education, and theology—which enables our students to lead meaningful and productive lives in the world community.

The educational and social environment is built upon a long-standing commitment to Judeo-Christian values and a tradition that stresses the importance of each individual. In this environment, the members of the Ashland University community continually seek ways to challenge and support each other to develop intellectually, spiritually, socially, culturally and physically.[44]

Besides being more concise than the previous mission statement, this statement explicitly indicated that the university was related to the Brethren Church. It reflected the diverse nature of the student body that had developed during the Shultz years, specified the areas of professional training offered by the university, and included clear reference to emphasis on the individual that had been omitted in the Schultz statement. It retained the language of "Judeo-Christian values" found in the previous statement.

The second mission statement of the Benz era gained Board approval in 2002. This statement affirmed:

Mission Statement for Ashland University

Ashland University is a comprehensive university, historically related to the Brethren Church. The University serves the educational needs of each student by providing programs of high quality that incorporate high expectations of achievement in a challenging and supportive environment. These programs stress both the centrality of the liberal arts and sciences and the importance of professional preparation.

Judeo-Christian values are the foundation of the educational and so-cial environment of the University and shape the character of the institu-tion. Members of the University community focus on intellectual, spiritual, cultural, physical, and social development for the purpose of leading mean-ingful lives in the world community.[45]

While being more succinct and better organized than the 1994 statement, it retained the essential elements of the previous document. One notewor-thy change, however, was the shift from "mid-sized regional teaching uni-versity" to simply "comprehensive university." This change reflects a continuing move of Ashland toward the broader, more complex, character of the typical university and away from the simpler structure, focused on teaching, that is inherent in the collegiate model.

Even though there are clear changes in the identity and character of Ashland College/University represented in these statements, there con-tinue to be elements of continuity with its heritage. Attending to the needs of the individual student, merging of a solid liberal arts education with pro-fessional training, recognizing the value of a strong spiritual foundation for the institution and of its historic ties to the Brethren Church, and develop-ing the whole person are themes that tie the university to its historic roots.

The University's View of the Christian Faith

If the references that are found in the Board minutes to Christian activities on the Ashland campus are any indication, the 1980s were generally not a period marked by a strong Christian ministry on campus. There is almost nothing said in the minutes about Christian faith or activities. Even though there continued to be an Office of Religious Affairs that was headed by James Menninger from 1981 until 1989, no reports from this office appear in the minutes. Indeed, there is no reference to the Religious Affairs Office in the college/university catalogue throughout the 1980s. Intriguingly, there has also been no mention of the successor to this Office, the Department of Religious Life, in catalogues since it was renamed in 1992. This void is quite ironic because of the Christian commitments of Joseph Shultz and his dedication to the seminary and the Brethren Church.

The few statements that do mention Christian activities are found in the latter half of the 1980s. In 1986 Shultz indicated that there was a new emphasis on religious activities on campus. He specifically mentioned three Christian ministries that were active at this time: HOPE Fellowship, the Newman Club, which was the Catholic campus ministry, and the Fellowship of Christian Athletes. In 1988 there is mention of the organization of a Religion Club by the Department of Religion that provided student enrichment programming on religious issues.[46] Note that the trend to subsume Christian faith under the more generic and "modern" label of religion continues throughout this period.

Catalogues from the 1980s reflect this same dearth of references to the Christian faith. The only allusions to Christianity are found in the introductory description of the college and in the objectives of the Religion Department. The statement of mission notes the Judeo-Christian tradition of the college and indicates that the college is church related, though there is no mention of what this church is. The "Ashland Plan" in its revised format also continues to be included with its statement that the college's educational experience is "based on sound Christian ideals and designed to make possible viable Christian experiences." Yet there is no indication of how students are to be exposed to such Christian experiences. There are no regular chapel services mentioned at this time; the Student Affairs section of the catalogue does indicate that there are opportunities for spiritual development, though no Christian organizations are mentioned (indeed, no student organizations are mentioned except for fraternities and sororities). All undergraduate students are expected to take one or two courses in the Religion Department, however. The Religion Department does seek "to furnish a basic Biblical understanding and appreciation of Christian thought for all graduating students" and "to provide courses of study for students who have interests in Christian involvement in community and church."[47]

It is most interesting that increased references to the Christian faith occur in the Board minutes under Waetjen and Benz. Waetjen was responsible for renaming the Office of Religious Affairs the Department of Religious Life. Michael Gleason replaced Menninger in 1989 as the Director of Religious Affairs; his position was renamed Director of Religious Life in 1992. Waetjen included regular reports from Gleason with the other Board reports beginning in October 1992. In fact, for the years 1993–96 Benz placed Gleason's reports immediately after or very close to his own in the packet of reports sent out to the Board members.

Gleason helped to revitalize the Christian ministry on the campus. In addition to the already existing programs of HOPE Fellowship, the Newman Society, and Fellowship of Christian Athletes, in 1989 he began "Meal and More," voluntary chapel services over lunch on the first and third Wednesdays of each month. In 1990 he initiated the International Student Fellowship to provide support and encouragement for Christian international students and to share the Christian faith with those from other faith perspectives. Campus-wide worship convocations were offered at Thanksgiving, Christmas, and Easter. In the 1993–94 academic year he began the Adventure Club, which offered off-campus outdoor activities combined with various forms of Christian enrichment. This same year a grassroots organization of Christian faculty and students, the Ashland University Christian Fellowship, was created in order to pray for the Ashland campus and to discern ways of more effectively communicating their faith in Jesus Christ. In 1995 Don Rinehart, Chair of the Department of Religion, reintroduced the Religion Club, which met over lunch on the second and fourth Wednesdays of each month. In the spring semester of 2000 Gleason started weekly voluntary chapel services every Wednesday over lunch and also introduced a Spiritual Enrichment Week, in which high-profile Christian speakers were brought to campus. In addition to these activities, the Department of Religious Life sponsored Bible studies in the dorms, gospel teams, leadership training, especially through the Joshua Teams which began in 2000–01, and contemporary worship experiences, notably Celebration and then The Well. Participation in Christian campus ministries grew throughout the 1990s; in fact the Fellowship of Christian Athletes was the largest student organization for several years in the late 1990s.[48]

Gleason resigned his position in 2003 and was followed by Dan Lawson as the Dean of Religious Life and Aaron Wardle as the Associate Dean of Religious Life. Lawson and Wardle brought a new perspective to the work of the Department of Religious Life which they described as "a new ministry approach (relationship based), philosophy (discipleship rather than superficial, fun entertainment), and strategy (a host of subculture groups)."[49] As part of this new perspective Lawson and Wardle launched such ministries as HUB, which sought to empower those students involved in the Religious Life program to reach out to other students; the Isaiah Project, which offered short-term service and missions opportunities to students; and the Servant Leadership House, which housed students who were committed to involvement in religious life, community service, and leadership in the former Kappa Sigma fraternity house. Undergraduate students at the university were exhibiting renewed interest in spiritual issues throughout the 1990s and early 2000s. Significantly, Lawson reported in October 2004 that one-third of all students were voluntarily participating in some aspect of religious life (in contrast, Jim Menninger reported in 1984 that over 10% of undergraduate students were involved in the Christian campus ministry). It is noteworthy that this formal and informal expansion of Christian ministry among the students on the Ashland campus has been entirely voluntary.[50]

Another facet of the story of the institution's view of the Christian faith relates to the desire of the Board, first minuted in the October 2003 Executive Session of the Board, to discuss the issue of expectations of prospective faculty relating to matters of faith and life. In 1992 the Board had amended Article III, Section 2 of the Constitution to read: "No person shall be elected a professor in the institution who is not a person of approved Judeo-Christian faith and life." The former reading had been " . . . who is not a person of approved Christian faith and life."[51] Concern was expressed by the Board in 2003 that this policy was not being followed in the university's hiring practices for faculty. The Board gave considerable attention to this and related matters throughout 2004. In October 2004 the Board approved a minor change to the Constitution, dropping the word "approved" from the statement. The minutes clarify the intent of this change. The Board wanted to determine whether a candidate understood the deep commitment the institution had to its mission statement and Judeo-Christian values and whether the candidate was in strong support of those values in both personal faith and life. The minutes reflect that the Board intended that the policy should be applied only to new hires.[52]

When faculty became aware of this change, a significant number of faculty reacted very strongly to the policy. Faculty were deeply concerned about enforcing a portion of the Constitution and Bylaws that had not been previously enforced. Some faculty indicated that they would not have accepted a position at the university if this policy had been in force. Faculty expressed disappointment that they had no input into an issue that directly affected them. Due to this reaction, the Board in January 2005 expressed its "regret that these changes were not received in the manner intended" and voted to rescind its former action. As the faculty, administration, and Board navigated the highly charged situation, there grew a consensus that the best approach to this issue was to make the mission statement of the university the standard for discerning faculty commitment to the institution. In May 2005, therefore, the Board approved the following statement, which had general support in the university community: "All faculty of the University shall support the Mission Statement, including its commitment to Judeo-Christian values; support the policies and act in the best interests of the University."[53]

There is no doubt that better communication among all constituencies of the university would have ameliorated the stormy reaction generated by this situation. But it is also the case that many of these faculty members were hired during the 1980s and early 1990s when, as noted above, there was a noticeable lack of conversation about Christian faith and life. Since this situation would have influenced faculty hiring decisions in the 1990s and early 2000s as well, the reaction of the faculty is understandable, in spite of the fact that the policy had been "on the books" the entire time. The Board may not have fully understood this reality, but as the Trustees of the institution, they felt a responsibility to hold the institution true to its governing documents.

The Relationship of the University to the Brethren Church

After the rocky relationship between the college and the Brethren Church during the 1970s and early 1980s, the mid and later 1980s were marked by an attitude of seeming disengagement by the church about the affairs of the college. The only references to the college in the minutes of the General Conference of the Brethren Church during these years were the requisite annual reports about the college. The sole exception to this pattern was in 1989 when Frederick Finks made the additional announcement to the conference that "Ashland was now 'officially' a dry campus."[54] A threefold explanation could be given for this detachment from the affairs of the college. First, the conference may have felt that they had an ally in Joseph Shultz as the president of the college and that they could trust him to "mind the store." Second, and more probable, though, is that the church had come to realize that the college had grown beyond the control of the church. The small college intimately tied to the church was a distant memory as the college was increasingly being transformed into a complex university under Shultz's leadership. Third, a number of the Brethren members of the Board

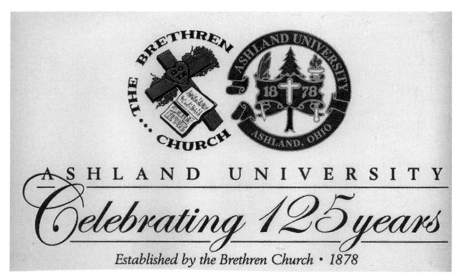

Logo for the 125th Anniversary celebration of Ashland University

of Trustees did not play an active role in their responsibilities as trustees or in bridging the interests of the college and church. For these reasons the Brethren Church has felt much more affinity with the seminary than the college/university ever since the 1980s.

The same irony that was noted above in discussing the strength of the Christian presence on the college/university campus during the Benz years in contrast to the Shultz era applies also to the church's relationship to the college/university. In comparison to the Shultz era, the 1990s and early 2000s have been marked by greater engagement between the church and university. Benz sought to work with the church on issues of mutual interest, symbolized dramatically in the logo for the 125th anniversary of the university (2003), which linked the seals of the university and Brethren Church. This change was also the result of several Brethren trustees working intentionally at building bridges between the church and university, notably Emanuel Sandberg, Christopher White, David Cooksey, and Thomas Stoffer. The hiring of Dan Lawson and Aaron Wardle in the Department of Religious Life has also helped to strengthen the ties between the university and the church.

The Brethren Church has been involved at several important points in the life of the university since the early 1990s. In 1991 the University Church was started as a joint venture of the university, seminary, Park Street Brethren Church, and the Brethren National Office. Ministering to the university campus as well as the Ashland community, this congregation was pastored successively by Ken Cutrer (1991–96), Leroy Solomon (1996–99), and John Allison (1999–2003). This congregation was folded into the ministry of the Five Stones Community Church, which began meeting in the university chapel in 2003.[55] In 1993 the General Conference Executive Council shared concerns about the current draft of the proposed mission statement. In a letter to the Board, the council encouraged the university "to embrace a stronger commitment to its Christian heritage and the values of The Brethren Church and to express that commitment in its mission statement."[56] Note that this statement of concern was raised in the time period following the Shultz era and during the interim presidency of Waetjen. The planning committee for the previously mentioned 125th anniversary of the university was intentionally composed of representatives from the church as well as the university.[57]

Interestingly, the catalogues that cover the Benz years are much more explicit about the relationship of the university with the Brethren Church than those of the 1980s. Whereas the catalogues during Shultz's presidency did not mention with which denomination the college/university was related, the first catalogue from Benz's presidency declared: "The rich heritage of the University includes a strong relationship with the Brethren Church and a commitment to the values of the Judeo-Christian tradition."[58] Both mission statements adopted during Benz's presidency also explicitly state that the university is "historically related to the Brethren Church."

The recent history of the relationship between the university and the Brethren Church has been stronger than during the 1970s and 80s. Undoubtedly there are questions that are raised on both sides of this relationship. The Brethren Church realizes that the university has grown beyond the intimate ties that were possible with the small college prior to the 1960s. The church still retains a simple majority on the Board of Trustees and recent history has shown how important an active, bridge-building Brethren presence is for maintaining healthy university-church relations. The church is concerned, however, about continuing pressure to move the university toward more of a secular, pluralistic perspective. The university, especially the faculty, is at times suspicious of perceived power-plays by the Brethren-controlled Board. There are questions raised about whether it is time for the Brethren to relinquish control of the Board because of the limited Brethren presence in the faculty and student body and the small percentage of funding that comes from the church. These issues and perceptions can be dealt with in a healthy way only by open dialogue and good-faith communication that seek to be guided by common commitment to the university's mission statement.

Ashland Theological Seminary Becomes a "Leading Evangelical Seminary"

A Period of Consolidation and Laying of Foundations for Growth (1982–1992)

Though he had been relying on a leadership team to guide the seminary during his first years as president of the college, Shultz knew that this arrangement could only be temporary. In 1980 he began to look in earnest for the next vice president of the seminary. His choice for this position was the young, successful pastor of the Winding Waters Brethren Church, Frederick Finks, whom Shultz began courting for the position in 1980. Finks was a graduate of Ashland College (B.A. 1969), Ashland Theological Seminary (M.Div. 1972), and Fuller Theological Seminary (D.Min. 1980). At the 13 November 1981 Board meeting Finks was approved as the next vice president of the seminary. He took office 1 July 1982.[59]

The Challenge of Extensions and Accrediting Bodies.   When Finks arrived at the seminary, he was a novice to theological education. He relied heavily upon the mentoring of several men who had been serving administrative roles in the seminary, particularly Arthur Climenhaga and Charles

Frederick J. Finks

Munson. He inherited a seminary that was basically sound in most areas, though there were several issues that were the focus of his attention throughout most of the 1980s, specifically the numerous seminary extensions and the notations given to the seminary by the Association of Theological Schools (ATS) and the University Senate of the United Methodist Church.

The International Flavor of Ashland Theological Seminary

In 1983 the seminary graduation speaker was Bishop David Gitari from Kenya. It was his first trip to the United States. Fred and Holly Finks had planned to host him for a typical American meal in their home on the Friday night before the Saturday graduation ceremony. Unfortunately, Holly became ill, and Fred came to Kenneth (Ken) Walther's office about three o'clock on Friday afternoon and asked whether he and his wife, Linda, would host the bishop. He encouraged the Walthers to invite David Gitari to their home for the meal so he could get a taste of an authentic American meal in an American home. Ken immediately called his wife, who was still at her school (she taught at Ashland High School), and they laid plans for the evening. Because she had no time to prepare anything elaborate, Linda asked Ken to go to Kentucky Fried Chicken and pick up a bucket of Original Recipe chicken to go along with some vegetables and fixings for a salad that they had on hand.

Bishop Gitari arrived around five-thirty. They sat down at the table where Linda had placed the chicken on a platter along with the serving bowls containing vegetables and the salad. She indicated that this was a very typical American meal. Before Ken was able to share grace, however, Bishop Gitari reached out his fork and thrust it into the chicken and said, "Ah, Original Recipe! My family and I, when we go to downtown Nairobi, like to eat at Kentucky Fried Chicken. Original Recipe is our very favorite type of chicken there." Though they had a delightful time with the bishop, Ken and Linda were embarrassed that Bishop Gitari might have been expecting an authentic home-prepared American meal. Little did they know that the bishop was a connoisseur of American chicken, being able to identify the unique blend of herbs and spices in KFC's Original Recipe.

Kenneth Walther, interview by author, 5 June 2006, Ashland, OH.

In 1980 a group of pastors and civic leaders in the Detroit area contacted the seminary about the possibility of offering graduate level theological education in Detroit. At the time, Detroit had no Protestant seminary. Key figures in these initial discussions were Daniel Aldridge, the Assistant to the Mayor of the City of Detroit, and Milton Henry, an influential attorney and civic leader. Soon after Finks arrived in Ashland, he was given the project by Shultz to open a Detroit extension. On 27 July 1982, Finks traveled to Vandalia, Ohio, with Theron Smith, who oversaw the seminary's extensions, to talk with representatives of ATS about what would be needed to begin a new work in Detroit. The message he received was short and to the point: "Tell Joe Shultz he can't go to Detroit until he gets more faculty."

Shultz, in typical fashion, instructed Finks to go ahead with the extension anyway. This action would put Ashland on the "radar screen" of ATS, but not in the manner desired.[60]

The approval of the Detroit Center by the Michigan Department of Education proved to be a drawn-out process, but authorization was finally received in August 1983. Classes began in Detroit on 17 September 1983 in the facilities of Wayne State University. A total of 24 students were registered at the beginning of the quarter; eventually 31 students were enrolled during the quarter, 28 of whom were African-American and 3 of whom were white. The Detroit Center remained at Wayne State until 2000 when it moved into its own rented facilities in an office complex in Southfield, Michigan. The Detroit Center was initially overseen by Theron Smith. From the time of his resignation in 1986, the Detroit Center has been guided by on-site directors: David E. Kornfield (1986–88), Jim Holley (1989–91), and Ronald R. Emptage (1991 to the present). Emptage (A.D. Olivet Nazarene College; M.A., M.Div. Ashland Theological Seminary; Ph.D. Michigan State University) was named Dean of the Detroit Center in 1999.

The aggressive development of extensions under Shultz, coupled with Ashland's moving forward with the Detroit Center, caused ATS in 1983 to put pressure on the seminary to increase faculty resources in order to service

Current facility of the Detroit Center; the center occupies space on the third floor of the building on the right side

its numerous extensions. Shultz and Finks traveled to Vandalia, Ohio, in December 1983 to address this concern directly with Marvin J. Taylor, the Associate Director of ATS. They were made aware of proposed changes to the standards for the M.Div. degree that would require students at extensions to have one year's residency on the main campus. Finks indicated in his January 1984 report to the Board that, as a result of this meeting, the seminary was conducting a voluntary evaluation of all of its extension programs with the goal of consolidating some of them.[61]

Additional pressure came from the University Senate of the United Methodist Church, which was responsible for granting approval to non-Methodist seminaries for training United Methodist students. Ashland had initially received approval from the University Senate to train Methodist students in 1982. At that time and to the present Methodist students have represented the largest denominational group in the seminary. During the first several years of Ashland's association with the University Senate, Ashland faced yearly approvals from the University Senate. In 1982 and again in 1983 Ashland received notations from the University Senate for lack of women and minorities on the faculty (ATS had also recommended the hiring of an African-American faculty member).[62]

In response to the concerns of both of these bodies, the seminary took several actions in 1984. (1) The seminary closed the Malone extension after spring quarter 1984 and planned to offer Saturday classes at the main campus to meet the needs of Malone and other commuter students. (2) The seminary also closed the Toledo extension following spring quarter 1984 and accommodated these students by offering a similar schedule in Detroit. (3) A number of new faculty, both part-time and full-time, were hired to alleviate the excessive use of adjunct professors. Hired in 1984 were the first woman full-time faculty member, Mary Ellen Drushal (Music B. of Ed. Ashland College; M.S. Peabody College; Ph.D. Vanderbilt University) in the fields of Christian Education and Church Administration (she assumed the position of Interim Provost and then Provost of Ashland University in 1995); the first African-American faculty member, William H. Myers (B.B.A., M.B.A. Cleveland State University; M.A., M.Div., D.Min. Ashland Theological Seminary; Ph.D. University of Pittsburgh) in New Testament (he would also develop the Black Church Studies program); and Ben Witherington III (A.B. University of North Carolina; M.Div. Gordon-Conwell Theological Seminary; Ph.D. University of Durham, England) in Biblical and Wesleyan studies (he took a position at Asbury Theological Seminary in 1995). The seminary also added three part-time faculty members: Duane F. Watson, JoAnn Ford Watson, and Dale R. Stoffer.[63]

Mary Ellen Drushal   *William H. Myers*

Both ATS and the University Senate continued their scrutiny of the seminary. Representatives of the University Senate and the East Ohio Conference of the United Methodist Church visited the Ashland campus in 1985 and were pleased with the progress being made. The University Senate approved Ashland for the 1985–86 academic year. In 1985 ATS conducted a focused visit of both the Cleveland and Detroit extensions. Though the reports were generally favorable for both extensions, ATS imposed three notations in January 1986 related to quality of faculty, library holdings, and the inequity between the extension programs and those on the main campus. Specifically, ATS recommended hiring additional minority adjunct faculty and improving the library resources at the extension centers. ATS indicated that the university libraries available to extension students in both Cleveland and Detroit did not have adequate holdings in religion. Ashland would need to make library resources available to extension students through computerizing the catalogue system. The ATS visit also surfaced the critical need to expand the library on the main campus and to strengthen the counseling programs and facilities.[64]

The Ashland College library (the seminary library holdings are part of the college/university library system) aided the seminary in responding to the issue of availability of library resources at its extensions; this issue was also important for the increasing number of college extensions. The college library was implementing a Computer Output Microform catalogue system that would enable students both in Ashland and its extensions to access the library's holdings via microfilm and/or microfiche beginning in the 1986–87 academic year. All off-campus sites were provided with a microfiche reader and microfiche cards of the college library card catalogue. Students at these sites could identify the desired materials, call an 800 number, and have them sent to them through the mail. The seminary likewise had become a member of the Ohio College Library Center, now Online Computer Library Center (OCLC), and was beginning the process of computerizing its library holdings.[65]

Continuing pressure by ATS concerning Ashland's extension programs caused Shultz and Finks to travel once again to meet with ATS personnel on 6 June 1986. Shultz and Finks challenged the two notations relating to faculty qualifications and to the inequality of the extension programs with those on the main campus. As a result of this visit, ATS reversed its decision on these notations, deciding not to impose them. The third notation concerning the seminary library would be removed when a planned expansion of the library was completed. The Board minutes reflect a measure of smugness on Shultz's part when they record his comment that "several rule changes were made by the Association of Theological Schools as a result of the meeting with and challenge to the Association by the Seminary as to the notations charged."[66] Shultz proved to be every bit as tenacious as the ATS personnel.

Early in 1986 the seminary received word from the Michigan Department of Education that it had approved the seminary's request to increase the number of quarter hours that students were allowed to take on site at the Detroit Center from forty-eight to ninety-six. This approval meant that Detroit Center students could take up to two years of the M.Div. degree in Detroit, though the remainder of their studies would need to be at the main campus in Ashland (this arrangement conformed to the residency requirements adopted by ATS that were noted above). The Department of Education also indicated that students could take all but twelve hours of the M.A. degree at the Detroit Center.[67]

The seminary responded to the ATS recommendation to strengthen its counseling programs by closing one program at the end of the 1986–87 academic year, the Toledo Counseling Center, and by hiring Douglas M. Little (B.A. Miami University; M.A., Ph.D. Michigan State University; M.Div. Ashland Theological Seminary) in 1987 to direct the Cleveland Psychiatric Institute Pastoral Counseling Program as well as to oversee the Cleveland Center (he retired in 2003). With the closure of the Toledo program, the seminary had only three counseling programs remaining: the Cleveland Psychiatric Institute, Western Reserve Psychiatric Habilitation Center, and EMERGE Ministries. In 1989 the program at the Cleveland Psychiatric Institute, begun in 1969, was replaced by a new counseling program at Southwest General Hospital in Berea. Little was able to give more focused attention to this program because Mary Ellen Drushal assumed oversight of the Cleveland Center in 1989.[68]

One of the most challenging issues raised by ATS that would dominate Finks' attention in the latter half of the 1980s and early 1990s was the need for additional space at the main campus. ATS had already expressed concern about the cramped library. But the problem was more complex than building a library addition, for there were multiple needs at the Ashland campus, including offices for faculty and administrators, classrooms, and a student lounge. The entire seminary program, except for chapel, was crammed into the John C. Myers home and the additions made to it during the Shultz years. The four classrooms were bulging at the seams; the library was running out of shelf space; the student lounge consisted of a 12 foot by 20 foot space in the basement; even the original bathrooms were being used for office space.

Finks made an initial presentation of the space needs of the seminary, focusing on the library, to the Board on 15 November 1985. The Board approved a fund raising project for an addition, though it deferred action about linking this project to the college's new capital campaign. In working with the architect selected for the project, Richard Van Auken, President and CEO of Jennings and Churella Construction Company, Finks realized that a separate classroom building would need to be constructed first. The plans for the library called for an expansion that would include the existing classrooms. By May 1986 the seminary had become an official part of the college's $14 million "Partnership in Excellence" capital campaign. The seminary assumed $1.5 million of this total, with $500,000 projected for the library expansion, $500,000 for the new classroom building, and $500,000 for faculty endowment.[69] In 1987 the seminary campaign literature indicated that there would be two phases to the building program: Phase I was construction of the classroom building and Phase II involved enlarging and remodeling the existing library.

Plans for the new classroom building were completed by fall 1987. However, though pledges came in steadily, cash-on-hand lagged behind. In the meantime in 1986 and 1987 the Ashland Theological Seminary Foundation purchased two houses on the south side of High Street (27 and 31) that occupied the land for the new facility. The goal was to begin construction in the summer of 1988. However, the Board had stipulated that construction could commence only if the $500,000 construction cost was covered by cash-in-hand. Donations were coming in steadily, but $200,000 in cash was still needed in early spring 1988. Finks and the Seminary Committee were deeply concerned that any delay in the start of construction would drive up the building costs. But Finks received welcome news later in spring 1988 when new Board of Trustees member Kenneth Miller made available a loan to cover the cash shortfall. Other friends of the seminary committed to make the interest payments on the loan so all pledges could be applied directly to the loan principal. With these new developments the Board gave approval on 6 May 1998 for the beginning of construction.[70] Construction was delayed again while awaiting state approval of the building drawings, but ground breaking finally occurred 3 October 1988. The classroom building was dedicated 13 May 1989. As part of the ceremonies, the Delbert and Romayne Flora Holy Land Pottery Collection was dedicated as a permanent part of the seminary's archaeological collection. On 13 February 1990 the faculty of the seminary voted unanimously to recommend to the Board that the classroom building be called the Joseph R. and Doris H. Shultz Academic Center, in honor of their long and faithful service to the seminary. The Seminary Committee and the Board gave their full approval to this recommendation on 11 May 1990. By this time the loan made by Kenneth Miller had been fully repaid. The kitchen was added in the Student Center in the lower level of the classroom building in the winter and spring of 1991. The total cost of the facility was $656,567.44.[71]

Attention now turned to Phase II of the building project, the addition to and renovation of the library. This project moved forward in two stages. The first stage, approved by the Executive Committee of the Board on 3 August 1989, was the remodeling of the existing library space. The remodeling involved moving the circulation desk to the lobby area of the west entrance, turning classroom three into offices for the librarian and assistant librarian, and moving the Biblical Studies section of the library into classroom four. These modifications, completed in early 1990, did not have to be changed when the remainder of the project was completed. During the summer of 1990 a glass-enclosed entryway was added to the library entrance. A bequest from the Dorothy Carpenter estate funded the renovation cost of $71,966.30 as well as a student scholarship in memory of Dorothy and her parents.[72]

The Executive Committee of the Board approved the drafting of drawings for the second stage of the library project on 11 May 1990. Groundbreaking for the addition to the library, which included new restrooms and

Shultz Academic Center

faculty offices, occurred 10 May 1991. Construction proceeded quickly and was essentially completed by September 1991 at an estimated cost of $230,966. Over the Christmas break work on the library and office addition was completed and the hallway between the library and main administration building received a new ceiling and paneling. When classes resumed in January all 75,000 volumes in the library collection had been relocated and rearranged. The addition was dedicated 11 January 1992 and was named in honor of George W. Solomon (1920–85). A 1957 graduate of the seminary, Solomon was a longtime and highly effective pastor in the Brethren Church and served as a mentor to many younger pastors.[73]

The seminary capital campaign, which concluded 30 June 1991 (the seminary portion of the university's "Partnership in Excellence" campaign ran a year longer), was highly successful. The last full accounting of the campaign in the Board minutes indicates that the building campaign had received $1,019,928.79 in pledges toward a goal of $1,225,000 (the goal had been increased from the original $1 million). Notable donors besides the Campaign Committee, the Ashland Theological Seminary Foundation, and unnamed Friends of the Seminary were the Central District of the Brethren Church ($83,183.49), the Woman's Missionary Society ($16,130.82), and Trinity Lutheran Church in Ashland ($40,000). The student scholarship endowment had received $540,547.29 since the beginning of the campaign in July

1985. A total of $671,482.44 had been given toward seminary operations and an additional $109,500 of miscellaneous gifts had been received.[74]

A most significant aspect of the campaign were pledges designated for the establishment of three faculty chairs and one pledge for faculty support totaling $1,383,021.91. Two chairs were fully funded at $500,000. The Charles and Anna Frey Brethren in Christ Chair, established by the Jacob Engle Foundation in 1987, supported Brethren in Christ faculty at Ashland. Initially, Fred Holland and Arthur Climenhaga shared this position. The H. R. Gill Family Chair of Theology was announced in 1988 and completely funded in 1991. Harry Gill, Chairman of National Latex Products Company in Ashland, established the chair in memory of his mother, Tina Phillips Gill, and brother, David Frederick Gill. The chair, designated for a faculty member in the area of theology, has been held by JoAnn Ford Watson. The Kenneth and Lois Miller Chair in Evangelism/Music was announced in 1988. Their love of music and commitment to the seminary led them to establish the chair at Ashland. It was fully funded in 1995 and was held initially by Ronald L. Sprunger. In addition, an endowed fund had been established in the name of Mary Myers Garber for faculty support. The total of all pledges and gifts for the campaign amounted to $3,724,480.43 toward an initial goal of $1.5 million. Though the seminary announced a $6 million follow-up campaign, "Financial Foundations for Our Future," in 1991 in conjunction with the university's new capital campaign, the campaign never materialized because it was disrupted by the change of leadership at the university.

The progress mentioned above, much of it spurred by pressure from both ATS and the University Senate of the United Methodist Church, had a significant effect both on the next accreditation review in 1988 and upon the growth of the seminary in general. The North Central Association and ATS made a concurrent visit on 21–23 March 1988. In the exit interview these accrediting bodies identified the following strengths and weaknesses of the seminary:

Strengths:

1. Financial equilibrium: the seminary has a stable budget and solid resource base for continued growth in scholarships, building, and endowment.
2. The physical facility was commendable; the team applauded the commitment to the classroom and library projects.

3. The faculty are well fitted for their work. There is good will and congeniality among the faculty and they are committed to the school and its leadership.
4. The student body was delightful and appreciative of the opportunity to study at Ashland. They had a strong commitment to professional ministry.
5. The team was very complimentary of Ashland's sense of mission and its service to its extension programs in Cleveland and Detroit.
6. The library is adequate and will be able to continue to build its resources with the new addition.
7. All three degrees are well developed and supported by the curriculum.
8. They commended Ashland's requirements for theses and projects in the master's program.
9. The administration provides sound leadership and has the full support and confidence of the faculty.

Weaknesses:

1. The classroom and library projects must be completed.
2. The faculty load needs to be reduced. The faculty feel overburdened and there are high demands placed on them. They need additional time for research.
3. Students desired greater faculty support in building community.
4. Library resources need to be expanded at the extensions.
5. There needs to be additional faculty resources in homiletics and ethics.[75]

Overall the team was highly complimentary of Ashland and recommended that the seminary be reaccredited for the maximum ten years. Ashland did receive three notations as a result of the visit: excessive expectations of faculty, inadequate development and implementation of evaluation procedures, and inadequate attention to faculty competencies in the D.Min. program. The seminary satisfactorily answered all three, the last one being removed in June 1989. For the first time since January 1978 Ashland had no outstanding notations from ATS.[76] Ashland also received excellent news from the University Senate of the United Methodist Church in spring 1989. The University Senate approved Ashland, without qualification, from 1989 to 1992. Up to this point Ashland had received only yearly approval and always with notation.[77]

Much of the visible progress that Ashland made during the 1980s was spurred by ATS and the University Senate. This observation is especially true in such areas as the addition of faculty, the hiring of women and minority faculty members, and the expansion of the physical plant of the seminary. However, the pressure from ATS to close or consolidate a number of extension works was a major factor in keeping the enrollment numbers basically flat during the 1980s. In 1982, when Finks came to the seminary, the enrollment was 436. In 1989 it was 450. The figures stayed within a narrow range during these years, reaching a high of 464 in 1983 and a low of 412 in 1986. But beginning in 1990, there has been a period of nearly uninterrupted growth until the present. While there has been a variety of reasons for this growth (see below), the primary reason was the development of personnel, physical, and financial resources during the 1980s that made such expansion possible. These critical resources were, to a large measure, cultivated in response to concerns raised by the accrediting bodies.

New and Innovative Ventures.   It would not be appropriate, however, to suggest that all the progress made until 1992 was the result of pressure from external forces. Indeed, the period from 1985 to 1992 was marked by a new creative energy that spurred a number of innovative ventures. Exemplifying this new progressive spirit were such developments as creating the first mission statement, developing new degree programs and concentrations that fit the theological educational "market" well, offering students more options in course scheduling, and serving the needs of constituencies outside the normal focus of graduate theological education.

In the winter and spring of 1985 the faculty developed the first statement specifically identified as a "Mission Statement." It replaced a "Purpose" statement, originally developed by Shultz, that had first appeared in the 1964–65 catalogue. The "Purpose" statement had reinforced the need for trained ministers; Ashland's commitment to a Bible-centered, orthodox faith; the importance of crafting a curriculum that brought the biblical witness to bear on the modern situation; and the call of God to declare God's Word.[78] The new "Mission Statement," though lengthy, captured very well the unique character of the seminary.

> Ashland Theological Seminary is a graduate division of Ashland College, a liberal arts college founded by members of the Brethren Church in 1878. The Brethren, a denomination in the Anabaptist and Pietist traditions, continue to sponsor the Seminary and welcome all who value its program.

Ashland Theological Seminary exists to equip committed Christians for leadership in ministries of the pastorate, missions, education, counseling and community life. This preparation includes the spiritual formation of students together with the academic specialization and practical training necessary for serving God in a pluralistic world. In order to accomplish this, the Seminary brings together a faculty with shared commitment to biblical, evangelical conviction; the pursuit of excellence in teaching; and their personal desire for continuing education and research. This interdenominational team of instructors attempts to create a community of fellowship as well as a climate for learning and academic curiosity.

Ashland Theological Seminary seeks to serve men and women who are preparing to minister in a variety of global contexts. Students are welcomed from around the world and from American minorities to provide a cross-cultural perspective. This climate facilitates the appreciation of persons and ideas from other Christian heritages. Students are affirmed in their own denominational allegiance and are encouraged to deepen that relationship and involvement. At the same time, they are urged to participate in the wider Christian Church in the spirit of ecumenism.

Ashland Theological Seminary intends its graduates to be servant-leaders in the ministries to which they are called. The years of study here initiate a life-long pursuit of competence in the capacity to care for people through ministry and evangelism; administration and church growth; hermeneutics and theology; homiletics and worship; education and counseling. The Seminary community fosters a collegial approach to ministry that incorporates the best of biblical conviction and tolerance while balancing the responsibilities of family, personal development, and vocational service.[79]

This statement captures very well what would become the four core values of the seminary that first appeared in the 1998–2000 catalogue: Scripture, spiritual formation, community, and academic excellence. It also affirms a number of other qualities of the seminary: the interdenominational composition of both faculty and students, the affirmation of women as well as men in ministry, the commitment to serve both the minority and international communities, and the goal of producing graduates who are truly servant-leaders after the model of Christ. Note also how the relationship between the Brethren Church and the seminary is described: the church sponsors the seminary.

One of the expressions of the seminary's Pietist heritage that is highlighted in the statement is the commitment to spiritual formation. Long before spiritual formation became a "buzz word" among seminaries, Ashland was taking seriously the importance of encouraging and modeling a deepening spiritual life with God and an obedient application of God's Word. As far back as the 1937–38 catalogue, the following statement had appeared (it ran through the 2000–01 catalogue, after which it was dropped because of the redundancy with the four core values):

> The main emphases of the Seminary are complete and uncompromising loyalty to the biblical and historical Christian Faith, the inculcation of competent Christian Scholarship, the nurture of a deeper spirituality in the Christian Life—all directed toward the goal of a practical Christian Ministry.[80]

These emphases, including spiritual formation, reflect commitments that had already been ingrained into the seminary's core identity.

In 1984 the seminary began laying plans for the development of spiritual formation groups. Implemented in the 1985–86 academic year, the groups met on Fridays and incorporated prayer, scripture reading, and fellowship (since 1990 the groups have met on Wednesday mornings). Finks wrote in his seminary report in November 1985: "[The Spiritual Formation program] has truly been a highlight of our new year and has drawn tremendous positive response from both faculty and students alike."[81] This program has continued uninterrupted for over twenty years and contributes to the seminary's commitment not only to inform the mind but, much more, transform the heart.

Another expression of Ashland's creative spirit during the latter 1980s and early 1990s was the development of new degree programs and concentrations. From 1980 through the 1987–88 catalogue three degrees were offered, some with specialized tracks: the D.Min., the M.Div., the M.Div. with a special major in Pastoral Psychology and Counseling, the M.A., and the M.A. with a special major in Pastoral Psychology and Counseling. In 1987 Mary Ellen Drushal conducted a review of the curriculum in anticipation of the accreditation visit in 1988 (the process of curricular review had actually started in 1985 with the development of the mission statement). Out of this process came two new programs that were announced in 1988: an M.A. in Church Administration (approved by ATS in 1989) and a Music major (concentration) within the M.A. degree program. The Church Administration degree, for which Mary Ellen Drushal was the lead professor, may have been the only degree of its kind at the time in theological education. A new faculty member hired in 1988, Ronald L. Sprunger (B.S. Bluffton College; M.A. Kent State University; D.M.M. Southern Baptist Theological Seminary), guided the Music program (he retired in 2003). In addition,

ATS approved another new degree in 1989, the M.A. in Christian Education, for which Drushal and Richard Allison gave leadership. In 1990 William Myers developed a truly unique program, the Black Church Studies program, which offered work at the certificate (non-degree), master's, and doctoral (D.Min.) levels. Ashland was the only evangelical school offering such coursework at the time. The program received approval from ATS in 1991. The certificate program was a joint venture between Ashland and the McCreary Center, founded by Carey McCreary. It continues to bear the name, the McCreary Center.[82]

These and other initiatives changed the scope of the M.A. degree during the period from 1988 to 1992. With but few exceptions Ashland had offered three concentrations in the M.A. degree from 1976 until 1988 (it was first called the M.A. in Religion in seminary catalogues, but changed in 1980 to simply the M.A. to reflect new nomenclature adopted by ATS in 1977): Christian Education, Pastoral Psychology and Counseling, and Religious Studies. In the 1988–89 catalogue two new concentrations appeared: Church Administration and Missions. The latter concentration coincided with the hiring in 1987 of Fred Holland (B.R.E. Messiah College; B.A. Greenville College; M.R.E. Eastern Baptist Theological Seminary; M.A. in Missions, D.Miss. Fuller Theological Seminary). In the 1991–93 catalogue the concentrations had more than doubled to eleven with the addition of concentrations in Biblical Studies, Black Church Studies, Church Music, Historical Studies, Philosophical Studies, and Theological Studies. The Religious Studies concentration had been superseded by a new concentration called Interdisciplinary Studies.

Ashland adopted other curricular and program changes between 1988 and 1992. In 1991 the senior writing project or thesis in the M. Div. and M.A. programs was made optional, though it was still encouraged for those students considering further graduate work. In 1990 the seminary decided to seek approval from ATS to offer the D.Min. degree independent of Methodist Theological School and Trinity Lutheran Seminary in Columbus. The degree had been offered in a cooperative program since 1977. Ashland's D.Min. program, which had over fifty students at the time, had grown to the point that the seminary felt it could better serve its students if it were independent. ATS and the North Central Association approved this change in 1991.[83]

In 1991 Ashland opened its first new extension since the inception of the Detroit Center in 1983. In 1987 Ashland entered into an arrangement to offer courses in Columbus cooperatively with a Christian house-church movement initially called the Fish House Fellowship and, since 1982, Xenos Christian Fellowship. This informal cooperation lasted until 1991

The present location of the Columbus Center, shared with Ashland University

when the seminary decided that it wanted to broaden its potential market in Columbus beyond this movement. In 1991 the seminary received approval from ATS and the North Central Association to open an extension in Columbus. The Columbus Center from this time to the present shares a facility with Ashland University on the north side of Columbus. Since the beginning of the center students in all degree programs have had to take at least half of their coursework at the Ashland campus.[84]

Because of the number of nontraditional students, both at the main campus and the extensions, the seminary supported a number of creative schedule modifications to better serve such students. As Finks observed in 1987, "Our academic program is as innovative and relevant as any in the country. We have options for scheduling and extension work that allow a wide variety of students to take advantage of our institution."[85] The offering of classes on Saturday has already been mentioned. Especially from 1986 on Ashland added more summer and evening courses. Three hour block courses that met once a week were added to the Ashland schedule in the mid-1980s; they were mixed with the more traditional one hour courses offered three times a week. In the 1990–91 academic year the one hour courses were eliminated and replaced by one-and-a-half hour classes offered twice a week. Eventually, in 1994–95 the seminary adopted all three hour block courses, though language classes met twice a week, but still in the block format (half of the six hours was for a tutorial session). In the 1990–91 school year weekend colloquia, courses that met three weekends during a quarter on Friday evening and Saturday morning and afternoon, were initiated (the courses that met just on Saturdays were discontinued). These courses were very appealing to extension students for satisfying their residency requirements on the main campus.

Ashland also demonstrated a commitment to serving constituencies that were outside the normal focus of graduate theological education. Several of these programs were aimed at bringing the theological resources of the seminary to pastors and lay people in the Brethren Church. In 1987 the seminary launched "Seminary for a Day," seminars that sought to provide Brethren laity with a firsthand experience of seminary teaching and, as a result, expose more Brethren to the ministry of the seminary. Seminars were held in Columbus, Ohio; Warsaw, Indiana; and Davenport, Iowa, in 1987 and Tucson, Arizona; Davenport, Iowa; and Warsaw, Indiana, in 1988. The Davenport, Iowa, seminars continued for several more years.[86]

In 1988 Mary Ellen Drushal, with the assistance of Jerry Flora and Douglas Little, initiated the CALM (Church Administration for Leadership and Management) project. The project was designed in three phases. Phase I began as a pilot program with eighty-seven Brethren pastors and sought to help pastors in acquiring skills in administration, conflict management, and leading and managing people. Phase II of CALM, implemented in 1989, broadened the project to include alumni and local Ashland pastors, as well as Brethren. The goal of this phase was to educate pastors and their official boards about how a congregation functions. John Shultz and Richard Allison were added to the CALM team for this phase. Phase III was the creation of a Certificate in Christian Ministries program which was designed to equip laypeople for leadership ministries in the church. As originally proposed, the program consisted of six video courses that were to be released between 1991 and 1993: *Theology for Life*, by Jerry Flora; *Knowing the Word's Worth*, by Ben Witherington; *Survey of Church History*, by Luke Keefer; *Culture and Ethics of Bible Times*, by Kenneth Walther; *Christian Ministries in the Local Church*, by Mary Ellen Drushal; and *Tools for Biblical Studies*, by David Baker and J. Michael Drushal. Upon completion of all six courses, a person would receive a non-degree Certificate in Christian Ministries. One could also receive a non-degree Diploma in Theological Studies upon the completion of the six video courses and of one college level course in each of the following fields: English, writing, speech, and computer writing.[87]

The driving force behind CALM and its related video curriculum was Mary Ellen Drushal. As exemplified in these programs, she had a deep commitment to the continuing education of pastors and laypeople. Reflecting this commitment, Drushal accepted the dual position of Associate Dean of Continuing Education and Director of the Cleveland Center in 1989. In this capacity she organized the seminary's first Continuing Education Conference for Hispanics in 1989. Held at the Cleveland extension, the conference focused on church growth and was led by Juan Carlos Miranda. Miranda was a product of the Argentine Brethren Church; he was a 1972 Ashland Seminary graduate and a Brethren church planter in southern California and Mexico City.[88]

Addition of Faculty and Administrators.   With the expanding programs, facilities, and locations, Ashland continued to add faculty and administrative staff during the latter 1980s and early 1990s. New faculty during this period, besides those already mentioned, were David W. Baker in 1986 in the fields of Old Testament and Semitic Languages (B.A. Temple University; M.C.S. Regent College; M.Phil., Ph.D. University of London); Luke L. Keefer Jr. in 1987 in Church History and Theology (B.A., B.Th. Messiah College; M.Div. Asbury Theological Seminary; M.A., Ph.D. Temple University); JoAnn Ford Watson in 1989 in Theology (B.A. DePauw University; M.Div. Princeton Theological Seminary; Ph.D. Northwestern University); and Bill T. Arnold in 1991 in Old Testament and Semitic Languages (B.A. Asbury College; M.Div. Asbury Theological Seminary; Ph.D. Hebrew Union College). Arnold, together with Ben Witherington, took a position at Asbury Theological Seminary in 1995.

Ashland hired its first full-time admissions and recruitment personnel during the latter 1980s and early 1990s. Thomas O. Brohm (1986–1990) and Richard Fischl (1990–1995) both held the title of Director of Admissions. With the seminary being very dependent on tuition revenue, an aggressive recruitment program became very important. Some significant strides were made in faculty development between 1988 and 1992. Until the mid-1980s the faculty had a nine-and-one-half course load. The half course derived from the requirement to teach one course during the summer every other year; Finks dropped this half course requirement during the mid-1980s. As noted above in the 1988 accreditation visit, the exit interview had recommended the reduction of faculty load. The faculty felt overburdened by their responsibilities and desired more time for research and writing. The administration on the very day of the exit interview decided to reduce the course load to eight courses. When Mary Ellen Drushal became dean in 1991, the course load was further reduced to seven courses. This load places Ashland in the lower range for faculty course load among seminaries. In 1991 Ashland received $8000 from the Lilly Foundation for faculty scholarship development. This grant was used to fund four projects: (1) supply five research assistants for faculty with writing contracts; (2) provide funding for a faculty person to initiate a new concentration in spiritual formation; (3) purchase computer hardware and software for faculty research; and (4) host a dialogue with denominational representatives to discuss outcomes expected of congregational leaders and the needs of the church in the twenty-first century.[89]

The Faculty on Retreat

The faculty, as far back as Joseph Shultz's years as dean/vice president, have begun each new academic year with a faculty retreat. There have been many memorable moments during these retreats. Under Shultz, the faculty were in charge of planning the retreat and selecting its location. They were also expected to pay their way for the retreat. When Finks came in 1982, this tradition was followed initially.

Early during his tenure two faculty members, Doug Chismar and David Rausch, selected a camp near Millersburg as the site for the retreat. The entertainment highlight was being able to feed two carp, named Shamoo and Shamee. That was the proverbial straw that broke the camel's back. The following year Finks reserved and paid for rooms at a Holiday Inn in Wooster. This has been the practice ever since. About every three years Finks brought in faculty spouses as well as trustees and their spouses in order to build a stronger sense of community among faculty, trustees, and spouses.

Activities during these retreats have been varied: canoeing, rafting, horseback riding, maneuvering a ropes course, and going on a book-buying spree to Grand Rapids, Michigan. The horseback outing had one unforgettable episode. Finks had the joy of riding a horse named "Drummer," who had a knack for knocking riders off his back. Every time Drummer came to a tree, Finks would have to pull his leg up, because Drummer would try to knock him off by brushing Finks' leg against the tree. Another episode that Richard Allison and Rick Fischl would have preferred to forget was a canoe trip on the Mohican River. No sooner had they climbed into their canoe than it flipped over, dumping them both into the river. Fischl lost his glasses, without which he could hardly see. In 2003 the faculty took on a ropes course at Camp Nuhop near Mohican State Park. Some of the faculty exhibited great nimbleness in traversing the ropes; other took the white-knuckle approach, hanging onto anything that didn't move. John Shultz gave the camp staff a scare when he went up-side down on a zip-line, an act prohibited because of its danger. These retreats have served to enhance the bonds of community by providing occasions for discussing important issues in the life of the seminary; for sharing extended periods of time together in one-on-one and small and large group experiences; and for just having fun together.

Frederick Finks, interview by author, 28 July 2005, Ashland, OH.

There were several other noteworthy developments related to faculty between 1987 and 1992. The *Faculty Handbook* was revised both in 1987 (this was the first revision since the 1970–71 academic year) and in 1992. Along with other changes in the seminary schedule that were made in the

1990–91 academic year, faculty meetings were moved from once a month on Tuesday over an extended lunch period to once a month on Friday afternoon, when no classes were offered in the new course scheduling. Faculty also shared significant input into a long-range planning process that began in 1989 and continued to be updated during the 1990s.[90]

The first ten years of Finks' tenure as head of the seminary were marked initially by responding to notations from ATS and the University Senate. Pressure from these accrediting bodies did spur the seminary to consolidate its extensions, hire additional faculty, especially women and minorities, and construct much needed classroom and library facilities. However, a new wave of creative energy became noticeable at Ashland by the latter half of the 1980s that manifested itself in a clearer sense of mission, new degrees and concentrations, innovative and flexible course scheduling, and a commitment to continuing education. These factors, some prompted by external pressure, others generated by a renewed creative vision, positioned the seminary for a period of unparalleled growth by the 1990s. Finks had already begun to use the statement by 1985 that Ashland was a leading evangelical seminary.[91] Its reputation was growing among its peer institutions and by the end of the 1980s Ashland had left behind its former identity as a regional, relatively unknown seminary, to find a place among evangelical schools of national recognition.

A Period of Dynamic Growth and Unique Programs (1992–2006)

The last fourteen years have witnessed a period of exciting growth at Ashland Theological Seminary and the proliferation of creative programs that continue to place the seminary on the cutting edge of theological education. These developments have not occurred without challenges and tensions, but they have served to enhance Ashland's reputation and recognition in the larger theological community.

Enrollment and Student Life.   The growth in student enrollment is impressive over this period. After basically plateauing during the 1980s, seminary enrollment increased every year except for two between 1990 and 2006. The seminary surpassed an enrollment of 500 students in 1991, 600 students in 1994, 700 students in 1998, and 800 students in 2000. In 2006 the seminary's enrollment was 896 students.

Several changes in the enrollment statistics deserve special comment. African American students continue to be a significant percentage of the student body, due mainly to the extensions in Cleveland and Detroit. Note the following statistics for the period from 1980 to 2005.

Year	Total Enrollment	Total African-Americans	Percentage
1980	378	95	25.1%
1985	424	86	20.3%
1990	494	152	30.8%
1995	645	166	25.7%
2000	801	253	31.6%
2005	879	283	32.2%

Especially noteworthy is the increase in the percentage of women in the student body over the same period.

Year	Total Enrollment	Total Women	Percentage
1980	378	59	15.6%
1985	424	112	26.4%
1990	494	168	34.0%
1995	645	256	39.7%
2000	801	378	47.2%
2005	879	450	51.2%

Major reasons for the increasing number of women in the seminary are greater openness to women in ministry, at least in some denominations, and particularly the large number of women entering the seminary's counseling programs. In the new cohort of counseling students for 2005 in the Midwest program, there were 47 women out of the 58 total students in the program (81%). The 2006 cohort had 39 women out of 61 total students (64%).

There have been other changes in the student body. The number of second career students in the seminary rose dramatically during the 1990s, so much so that the average age of students in the seminary has hovered around forty since the early to mid-1990s. In 1999 a survey revealed that 53% of the seminary students drove over sixty miles. The same year there were 114 students who resided in Ashland; 646 students commuted to Ashland or one of the extension campuses. These statistics reflect the transition of the seminary away from primarily a residential program in the 1970s to a predominantly non-traditional format in the 1990s. There were several casualties in this transition to more of a non-traditional, non-residential student body. The retreats held at the beginning of the academic year were discontinued in the mid-1980s. Likewise, the student government organization, the Student Association, disbanded at the end of the 1985–86 academic year due to the difficulty of recruiting students for leadership positions. Contributing to both of these developments was the increasing average age of students by this time (33 years); non-traditional students, many of whom lived off-campus, already had established social patterns in their lives and found it difficult to be active in campus activities. Interestingly, the seminary still draws the majority of its students from Ohio. In 2004 two-thirds of the new students came from this state. When this statistic is combined with student driving distances, the point is underscored that Ashland is a regional seminary, serving most of northern and central Ohio, as well as southeastern Michigan.[92]

Several student organizations continue to be active at the seminary. Sem Women reverted to Sem Wives in 1991 due to the unique challenges faced by the wives of those serving in ministry. The International Students Association, which first appeared in the 1985–86 catalogue, provided fellowship, sharing, and cultural perspectives among the growing international student population. In 1986 there were 16 international students enrolled in the seminary; in 1996 there were 75 at the height of the Korean D.Min. program; in 2000 there were about 40 enrolled in various seminary programs. Following 11 September 2001, international student enrollment

Fred and Holly Finks hosting international students and their families

dropped significantly as visas became more difficult to obtain. In 2006 Ashland had only 21 international students. In 1987 Ashland began a chapter of Eta Beta Rho, the Hebrew National Honor Society. Membership is open to those who have an interest in Hebrew and at least a 3.5 grade point average in Hebrew. Ashland's chapter is the most active chapter in the United States, with over 350 inductees since 1987.

Expansion of Faculty, Administration, and Staff.   With the accelerated growth of student enrollment since 1990, there has been an ongoing need to add faculty. New faculty hired since 1992 have been:

Dale R. Stoffer in 1992 in Historical Theology (B.A. Ashland College; M.Div. Ashland Theological Seminary; Ph.D. Fuller Theological Seminary)

Ned Adams Jr. in 1993 (stepped down for medical reasons in 2004) in Pastoral Counseling and as Director of the Detroit Counseling Program (B.P.S. Empire State College; B.C.Ed. Faith Baptist College; M.A., M.Div., D.Min. Ashland Theological Seminary)

Grace Holland, who took over the position vacated by her husband, Fred, when he resigned for medical reasons in 1993 (she retired in 1999) in Missions (B.A. Greenville College; M.A. in Missions, Fuller Theological Seminary; D.Miss. Trinity Evangelical Divinity School)

Eugene S. Gibbs in 1994 (retired in 2005) as Director of the D.Min. program and, later, in Christian Education (B.A. Baylor University; M.R.E. Golden Gate Theological Seminary; M.A. San Francisco State University; Ed.D. University of the Pacific)

Judy V. Allison in 1995 (stepped down for medical reasons in 2004) in Pastoral Counseling (B.A. Taylor University; M.A., Ph.D. Ball State University)

David A. deSilva in 1995 in New Testament and Greek (B.A., M.Div. Princeton University; Ph.D. Emory University)

L. Daniel Hawk in 1995 in Old Testament and Hebrew (B.A. Otterbein College; M.Div. Asbury Theological Seminary; Ph.D. Emory University)

Melissa L. Archer in 1996 (moved in 2001) in Greek and New Testament (B.S. Ashland University; M.A. Ashland Theological Seminary)

Marvin A. McMickle in 1996 in Homiletics (B.A., D.D. Aurora College; D.Min. Princeton Theological Seminary; Ph.D. Case Western Reserve University)

Ronald W. Waters in 1996 (took a pastorate in 2001) in Evangelism (B.A. Ashland College; M.A. Wheaton College; M.Div. Ashland Theological Seminary)

Michael F. Reuschling in 1997 in Pastoral Counseling and as Director of the Midwest Counseling Program (B.A. Bowling Green State University; M.A. Ashland Theological Seminary; M.A., Ph.D. University of Akron)

Terry Wardle in 1998 in Church Planting and, later, Spiritual Formation (B.A. Geneva College; M.Div. Pittsburgh Theological Seminary; D.Min. Fuller Theological Seminary)

David Kerner in 1999 (left in 2001) in Missions (B.A. Ashland College; M.Div. Ashland Theological Seminary)

Paul Overland in 1999 in Old Testament and Semitic Languages (B.A. Seattle Pacific University; M.Div. Western Theological Seminary; M.A., Ph.D. Brandeis University)

Brenda B. Colijn in 2000 in Biblical Interpretation and Theology and as Coordinator of the Columbus Program (B.A. Pennsylvania State University; M.A., Ph.D. Cornell University; M.A. Ashland Theological Seminary)

William P. Payne in 2002 in Evangelism and Missions (B.A. Florida Southern College; M.Div. Candler School of Theology, Emory University; Ph.D. Asbury Theological Seminary)

Melissa (Wyndy) W. Corbin Reuschling (she married Michael Reuschling in 2005) in 2002 in Ethics and Theology (B.A. University of Colorado; M.A. Denver Seminary; Ph.D. Drew University)

John Byron in 2003 in New Testament and Greek (Diploma, Elim Bible Institute; M.A. Regent University; Ph.D. University of Durham)

Anthony Donofrio in 2004 in Pastoral Counseling (B.S., Ph.D. University of Akron; M.A.C.P.C. Ashland Theological Seminary)

J. Robert Douglass in 2004 in Worship and Music (B.A. Messiah College; M.Div. Ashland Theological Seminary; Ph.D. candidate Duquesne University)

David P. Mann in 2004 in Pastoral Counseling (B.A. North Central University; M.A. Ashland Theological Seminary; Ph.D. Kent State University)

Lee Wetherbee in 2004 in Pastoral Counseling (B.A. Malone College; M.Ed. Kent State University; Ph.D. University of Akron)

Michael B. Thompson in 2005 in Practical Theology (B.A. Circleville Bible College; M.A.R. Wesley Biblical Seminary; M.A. Ashland Theological Seminary; D.Min. Drew University Theological School)

Mitzi J. Smith in 2006 in New Testament and Early Christianity (B.A. Columbia Union College; M.A. The Ohio State University; M.Div. Howard University School of Divinity; Ph.D. Harvard University)

The faculty in their regalia in a 2003 photo; top row from left to right: Walter Kime, John Shultz, Marvin McMickle, Shawn Oliver, Eugene Gibbs, Michael Reuschling, Vickie Taylor, William Myers, Russell Morton, Sylvia Locher, David Mann, and David Baker; middle row from left to right: Daniel Hawk, William Payne, Kenneth Walther, Melissa (Wyndy) Corbin Reuschling, Paul Overland, Brenda Colijn, Luke Keefer, David deSilva, Mylion Waite, and John Byron; seated from left to right: Terry Wardle, Robert Rosa, Leroy Solomon, Ronald Emptage, Frederick Finks, Dale Stoffer, Elaine Heath, Richard Parrott, and JoAnn Watson

These faculty members hired since 1992 have included three African Americans (Ned Adams, Marvin McMickle, and Mitzi Smith), one Asian-American (David deSilva), and six women (Grace Holland, Judy Allison, Melissa Archer, Brenda Colijn, Melissa Corbin Reuschling, and Mitzi Smith).

Several important developments related to the faculty occurred between 1992 and 2006. Mary Ellen Drushal and the Personal and Professional Development Committee of the faculty engaged in a thorough revision of the faculty promotion, tenure, and post-tenure review process beginning in 1994. In fall 1996 it received faculty support and was approved by both the Seminary Committee of the Board and the full Board on 31 January 1997. These changes to the *Faculty Handbook* retained tenure after seven years, lengthened the period of time at the assistant professor rank from three to four years and at the associate professor rank from four to five years, and required that tenured faculty with full professor rank develop a professional development plan every five years.

During these years the administration and Seminary Committee of the Board enhanced faculty professional development perquisites by increasing support for attendance at professional conferences, by broadening policies related to study leaves, and by granting course reductions or additional pay for serving as department chair, developing courses using technology, and assuming an exceptional responsibility. In 1993 Ashland signed an agreement with Tyndale House, a major center for evangelical biblical research in Cambridge, England, for Ashland faculty to use the unique resources of the center during their study leaves. These opportunities allowed faculty to contribute to the prestige and recognition of the seminary by their numerous publications, their presentations at professional conferences, and their visibility within the scholarly community.

Seminary faculty have had a variety of professional growth opportunities made available in recent years. A number of seminary faculty have taken advantage of the specialized training in technology offered at Ashland University since 1996 through the Faculty College (originally these training opportunities occurred three times a year but now occur only twice a year, before both the fall and spring semesters at the university). Twice the Academic Dean's Office has brought in Lynne Westfield from the Wabash Center; in 2004 she addressed issues related to teaching and learning and in 2006 she shared ideas about interdisciplinary team teaching. In 2005 Jim Meek shared with the faculty about issues related to assessment, specifically as they related to the M.Div. degree. Ashland was also invited to participate in the Lexington Seminar, funded by the Lilly Foundation, between 2004 and 2006. The seminar teamed five different

A Seminary Foundation trip to England in 1996 that included
a visit to Tyndale House; the warden, Bruce Winter (now retired)
is in the center of the photo; his wife, Lyn, is on the far right

seminaries and offered each seminary the opportunity to focus on an insti-tutional issue it was facing. Representatives from each of the five seminar-ies collaboratively brainstormed about how best to address the issue. Ashland chose to focus its study on critical thinking skills for both faculty and students. As part of this process Ashland faculty participated in a re-treat in April 2005 with Stephen Brookfield, a prominent educator in the field of critical thinking. The process meshed well with the faculty's ongo-ing discussions about academic excellence and with two other major ini-tiatives in the seminary, a curriculum review and the preparation for the next accreditation self study.[93]

Faculty at the seminary have been recognized within the larger Ashland University community for their outstanding achievements in teaching and writing on a number of occasions since 1992. The Mentor Award, instituted at Ashland College in 1986–87, was first awarded to a seminary faculty mem-ber, Douglas Little, in 1998; he was also a recipient in 2000. Other faculty and administrators who have been similarly recognized are Karen Becker in 2002 and JoAnn Watson and John Shultz in 2004. In 2005 David deSilva re-ceived the notable honor of being selected as Trustees' Professor, one of only five Ashland University faculty to be so designated since 1986. He was also awarded a prestigious Humboldt Research Fellowship from the Humboldt Foundation to study in Germany during the 2006–07 academic year.

Adjunct faculty have played an important role in the life of the semi-nary over the last twenty-five years. During this period adjuncts have gen-erally taught about thirty percent of the seminary courses, though the greatest use of adjuncts has consistently been within the counseling pro-grams where specialized expertise is often needed. In 2005 the seminary sought to recognize adjuncts who have demonstrated a long-time commit-ment to the seminary and its mission. The faculty created a new designa-tion, Professional Fellows, which recognized adjuncts who had taught for the seminary at least five years and received strong student evaluations with additional perquisites, including pay. The first six adjuncts so recognized were David Abbott, Allan Bevere, Robin Burkhart, Mark Hendricks, Paul Kaufman, and Robert Kerr.

The growth of the seminary since 1990 necessitated not only an in-crease in the number of faculty but also the addition of administrators and staff. Just as the institutional life at Ashland University during this period could be described as one of increasing complexity, the same is true of the seminary. Administrators and staff were hired at a faster pace than faculty because of this reality. Administrators were added because of new programs: Ned Adams to oversee the Detroit Counseling Program in 1993 (he was followed in this role in 2004 by Jerrolynn Johnson); In Du Chae to oversee the Korean D.Min. Program in 1993 (this program was discontinued in 1997); and Keith Marlett to direct the Smetzer Counseling Center in 2004. Administrators were added to enhance and expand the recruitment, admissions, and development functions of the seminary: Mario Guerreiro in recruitment and later admissions in 1994 (he took a position in another seminary in 2003); Robert Rosa in recruitment in 1995 to replace Richard Fischl (in 2003 Rosa was named Dean of Student Development); Leroy Solomon in development in 1995 (in 2005 he became the Dean of the Doctor of Ministry Program); Cara Selan in admissions in 2003; Don Carver in development (he stayed only for 2004); Glenn Black in admissions in 2005; Eric Sandberg in development in 2005; David Cooksey and Mariah Wright in development in 2006; Rodney Caruthers III in admissions for the Detroit Center in 2006; and Martha Smith in recruitment for the D.Min. program in 2006. Administrators were added to oversee the burgeoning programs of the Sandberg Leadership Center, notably the Pastors of Excellence Program and the Institute of Formational Counseling (see below for details about these programs): Lori Byron in 2003; Lynne Lawson, who initially came to the seminary in 2001; Eugene Heacock, who became the Executive Director of the Sandberg Leadership Center in 2004, replacing Richard Parrott, who resigned in 2004; and Michael Catanzarito in 2006.

Administrators were added to support specialized student services: Karen Becker, who became the first full-time Family Life Counselor in 1998, though she and, prior to her, Morven Baker, had provided counseling services for students and their families on a part-time basis; Elaine Bednar, who replaced Becker when she resigned in 2004; and George Johnson who was hired in 2006 as the Coordinator of Student Support Services. Administrators were also added to support the academic program of the seminary: directors of the D.Min. program were Eugene Gibbs (1994–1997), Richard Parrott (1997–2003), Elaine Heath (2003–2005), and Leroy Solomon (2005 to the present; he has the title of dean); Walter Kime was hired to direct the Field Studies program, along with other responsibilities, in 1995; Shawn Oliver assumed responsibility in 2001 for directing the M.Div. program and, later, was named Associate Academic Dean; and Vickie Taylor was employed in 2001 as the Director of Technology Resources. In addition, the library staff was enlarged with the hiring of a Research Librarian, Russell Morton, in 1999. In 2001 Sylvia Locher became the new head librarian following the retirement of Bradley Weidenhamer. Lori Lower, who came to the seminary in 1988, became such an asset in her role as Assistant Registrar that she was promoted to Registrar in 2004.

Indicative of the growth of the administration and staff relative to the faculty are the following comparative figures for 1992 and 2006. In 1992 there were 5 full-time administrators (18.5% of the total personnel), 14 full-time faculty (some had administrative responsibilities; 51.9% of total personnel), and 8 full-time staff (29.6% of total personnel). In 2006 there were 27 full-time administrators (40.9% of total personnel), 22 full-time faculty (33.3% of total personnel), and 17 full-time staff (25.8% of total personnel). These statistics represent trends that are occurring throughout higher education as numerous factors contribute to the complexity of the educational enterprise: competition for students and funding, increased attention to student services, the emphasis on assessment by the accrediting agencies, and greater governmental scrutiny of education.

Balloons and Birthdays

The seminary community has enjoyed its share of pranks and practical jokes throughout the years. One source of several pranks was the balloons made by Ashland Rubber Products in Ashland, Ohio. This company employed a number of seminary students over the years before it closed down: David Cooksey, John Shultz, Dale Stoffer, James Searcy, and Michael Radcliff. At times, balloons would have to be destroyed for various reasons. On one occasion, an icicle fell off a gutter and broke a window. Glass from the window fell into two cartons containing large balloons known as 16 Paddles which, when inflated, were well over a foot across. Cooksey's supervisor, Vernon Gilmore, told Cooksey to get rid of them because of potential legal issues. Cooksey asked whether Gilmore cared what he did with them and Gilmore said, "No."

Cooksey and Fred Finks were living at the time with Gary and Janis Courtright. Janis happened to be Joseph Shultz's secretary and gave Gary, David and Carolyn Cooksey, and Finks access to the administrative building. They brought along the Courtrights' vacuum cleaner, hooked it up backward, and quickly began to blow up the balloons. Their target was Charles Munson, whose office they soon completely filled. They blocked entrance to his office with the balloons and even filled the shower and toilet in the bathroom that adjoined his office. They then slipped out through the only possible exit, the bathroom door. Munson was able to gain entry to his office only through the same bathroom door. Finks himself would later have his own encounter with balloons during his presidency.

As a side note to this story, Cooksey was called into the office of Bruce Bigham, the president of Ashland Rubber Products, when the story of the balloons was publicized in the *Ashland Times-Gazette*. Bigham asked Cooksey whether he knew anything about these balloons. Cooksey replied, "Yes, I do." Bingham then asked whether he had gotten the balloons from the factory. Cooksey admitted that he had and shared the full story. Satisfied with Cooksey's explanation, Bigham said nothing more about the matter.

Birthdays have always been an occasion for celebration at the seminary. In recent years the seminary administrators, faculty, and staff have gathered once every few months for cake and refreshments to honor those who had recent birthdays. Finks would often get himself into trouble by trying to guess the ages of the ladies being so honored.

(continued)

Lennie Reich at her desk

1999. For her final sixteen years she was the Administrative Assistant to the Seminary President, Frederick Finks. On her fiftieth birthday, the seminary administrators, faculty, and staff decided to give her a surprise birthday party. When she arrived for work, she was seated in a wheelchair and given a bouquet of dead flowers. The hallway from the library to the administrative offices was lined with candles and the lights were turned off. As she was wheeled down the hallway, the faculty were appropriately intoning a funeral dirge, "Umm, umm." She was taken to her office which was decorated with a casket in which a mannequin reposed. About the only normal part of this celebration was the singing of *Happy Birthday*. The occasion was suitably concluded with a black cake.

Such occasions have provided a strong sense of camaraderie and fellowship within the seminary. The seminary, especially when it was smaller, was more than just a place of work; it was a family who enjoyed each other and could laugh and play light-hearted jokes on each other.

One birthday observance, however, was especially memorable. Lennie Reich served at the seminary for twenty-three years, retiring in

Frederick Finks, interview by author, 28 July 2005, Ashland, OH; David Cooksey, interview by author, 31 August 2006, Ashland, OH; Ashland Theological Seminary, Ashland, Ohio 3 (April 1971): 2; and "The Gift," Koinonia 31 (January 2001): 1.

Expansion of the Physical Plant. This growth in students, faculty, and staff was again straining the physical resources of the seminary by 1994. In September 1994 the faculty and the Seminary Committee requested Board approval to commence with architectural drawings and fund raising for additional classroom space. The Board granted such approval on 7 October 1994. Finks made it clear that the seminary campaign would not conflict with the fund raising currently occurring for the Student Center at the university. Donors would be sought who were outside those being solicited for the Student Center. In preparation for future expansion, the seminary had been purchasing homes on High Street as they became available. In 1992 the seminary purchased homes at 37, 42, and 48 High Street. The Board gave formal authorization 22 January 1993 to purchase the remaining homes on High Street between Center and Wood Streets as they became available. The seminary acquired 36 High Street in 1994.[94]

Originally the classroom project was planned as an addition to the Shultz Academic Center. By May 1995, however, the decision had been

Gerber Academic Center with the Divine Servant statue; it is the copyrighted and trademarked creation of Christian artist, Max Greiner

made to construct a separate building, though it would be connected to the Shultz Academic Center. Also by May 1995 the architect for the building, James Meier and Associates, had been selected. The facility, as planned, would be approximately 9000 square feet, with an auditorium seating 162, three classrooms, four offices, and a student computer lab. Groundbreaking for the building occurred 10 May 1996 with construction beginning in August. Progress was slowed, however, when, as expected, the contractor ran into poor soil conditions (this concern had led to the relocation of the student apartment project at the seminary in the late 1960s). An additional eight feet of soil had to be excavated and replaced with compacted fill (Finks affectionately referred to this as his $40,000 hole). Pledges for the project had already surpassed the fund raising goal of $1,131,000 by October 1996. Crucial to the financing of the facility were a naming gift of $300,000 given by Harley and Fae Gerber of Dalton, Ohio, and a gift of $100,000 for the auditorium presented by Frances Smetzer in memory of her husband, Ted. On 17 May 1997 the seminary community dedicated the Gerber Academic Center following the commencement ceremony. Two unique fund raising ventures were connected with this facility: donors could purchase their "own" lecture hall chair for the Smetzer Auditorium for $1000 or get their name etched on a brick for the Alumni Walk outside the facility for $100. The mortgage for the building was burned on 1 October 1998.[95]

A visible expression of the seminary's commitment to spiritual formation began to take shape in 1996 with the creation of a Prayer Garden on the south side of the administration building. Louise Waller, a seminary student at the time, used her artistic talents to fashion a number of lifelike animals which were placed along new walking paths. The Prayer Garden, complete with new landscaping and benches, offers a serene setting in which people can spend some quiet moments with the Lord in prayer and meditation.[96]

The last facility built by Finks had been a longstanding vision of his: the development of a "Center for Creative Leadership." As Finks envisioned it, the center would house a wide range of programs that would prepare Christian leaders for ministries around the globe. Finks first formally proposed a Leadership Center to the Seminary Committee in January 1997, though it had been a part of the seminary's strategic plan since 1993. The facility gained Seminary Committee support in May 1998. In fall 1998 the center became one of four buildings included in Phase I of the university's "Building on Strength" capital campaign. Though the building, as originally conceived in May 1998, called for a conference facility, with rooms for overnight housing, this feature was later dropped when other options for housing became available (see below). The center was to have conference rooms and lounge areas and consideration was being given to additional offices and a counseling wing. The counseling center became a reality in the plans in September 1998 when Frances Smetzer again blessed the seminary with a major gift—a $1 million lead gift to support the Ted and Frances Smetzer Christian Counseling Center.[97]

The architect for the project, Collaborative, Inc. of Toledo, Ohio, had prepared initial plans for the Leadership Center by January 1999, with a

Some of the creations of Louise Waller for the Prayer Garden

preliminary cost estimate of $4 million; the cost was later reduced to $3.6 million. Fund raising for the center moved forward with several more major gifts: Emanuel and Ann Sandberg made a naming gift of $1.5 million and Pete and Nancy Peterson and Kenneth and Lois Miller made gifts that totaled another $800,000. On 8 October 1999 the Board authorized the seminary to proceed with drawings for the Leadership Center. At the recommendation of the architect in January 2000 the proposed location of the facility was shifted from the north side of High Street to the west side of the seminary campus on the location of the existing parking lot. Parking would then be relocated to the north side of High Street. A special feature of this redesign was the creation of a central mall area in the middle of the seminary campus. At the May 2000 Board meeting approval was given to begin construction of the Sandberg Leadership Center. Because construction of the center meant the loss of the existing parking lot, completion of the new lot on High Street was given priority over the summer of 2000. A total of eight houses on High and Wood Streets had been purchased over a period of years for the parking lot site.[98]

Sandberg Leadership Center with the Fisher of Men statue in the foreground; it is the copyrighted and trademarked creation of Christian artist, Max Greiner

Groundbreaking for the 16,000 square foot Leadership Center occurred 8 September 2000 with actual construction beginning in October. The Sandberg Leadership Center was dedicated on 5 October 2001. The north end of the facility houses the Smetzer Counseling Center, including offices, counseling labs, and a conference room. The conference center contains a large lobby and lounge area, seminar rooms, conference room, sacred space for reflection and prayer, a kitchen area, restrooms, and offices. In August 2001 pledges for the campaign goal of $4 million for the Sandberg Leadership Center totaled $3,464,907. Final payment on the center occurred in 2005.[99]

Two statues by the sculptor and artist Max Greiner of Texas have graced these last two buildings. *The Divine Servant*, depicting Jesus washing the feet of Peter, is a fitting symbol for the seminary's commitment to servant leadership and its Brethren heritage, which includes the ordinance of feetwashing. Located in front of the Gerber Academic Center, the statue was acquired through the generosity of Lonnie and Carolyn Bennett of the Carson Oaks Community Brethren Church in Stockton, California. Following the completion of the Sandberg Leadership Center, a beautiful memorial mall was laid out, the centerpiece of which is a statue of Jesus, called *Fisher of Men*. Lonnie Bennett had passed away in 2001 and Carolyn, as a memorial to her husband, made a gift of $65,000 to fund the statue and its surrounding fountain.[100]

The continued growth of the student body and the completion of the Sandberg Leadership increased the need for housing both for residential students and for commuter students and conference attendees needing

Miller Leadership Residence Inn

overnight accommodations. During the winter of 2000 the university acquired the Heritage Apartments on College Avenue, just over a block from the seminary. The university made available this twelve unit complex to the seminary for $600,000. The apartments were put into use during the 2001–02 academic year and initially named the Leadership Residence Inn. When, however, Ken and Lois Miller again made a gracious gift to the seminary, this time of $200,000, the complex was renamed the Ken and Lois Miller Leadership Residence Inn. In 2002 Joseph and Doris Shultz made their two apartment buildings adjoining the west property line of the seminary available to the seminary. The two buildings contained a total of eight one-bedroom apartments and three two-bedroom apartments. The seminary was enabled to purchase the apartments through a $200,000 naming gift by Russell and Edith Rodkey and an estate gift that memorialized Lester Schmiedt.

Financial Considerations.   As intimated above, another crucial resource for sustaining the seminary's growth has been financial. With over 80% of its revenues coming from tuition, the seminary has sought to increase its gift income and its endowment. The Brethren Church continues to be the largest single denominational donor to the seminary, but yearly giving from the church has remained fairly consistent between about $75,000 and $100,000 per year since 1982. The seminary has sought to cultivate other sources of gift income, especially outside the Brethren Church, in recent years, through the annual alumni telethon for student scholarships, through individual non-Brethren donors, and through churches that are not aligned denominationally or that have seminary alumni serving as pastors. The annual alumni telethon for student scholarships has grown from approximately $15,000 in pledges in 1982–83 to $36,870 pledged and $29,345 received in 2005–06. The record amount received was $35,020 in 2003–04 while the record amount pledged was $38,357 in 2004–05. Giving from non-Brethren churches has been increasing in recent years. In the 2000–01 fiscal year, donations from non-Brethren churches was $28,131; in 2005–06 this figure had grown to $35,650. Indicative of the seminary's commitment to expanding its financial base, Finks hired three new personnel in development between 2004 and 2006: Eric Sandberg to focus on alumni, Mariah Wright to oversee the seminary's annual fund, designated the Fund for Theological Education, and David Cooksey to work with Brethren churches.

Finks placed special emphasis on raising the scholarship endowment over his tenure. When he came in 1982 the scholarship endowment was $170,235; in 1992 it had grown to $982,668 and on 30 June 2006 it stood at $4,172,433. Besides working with individuals and congregations, especially in the Brethren Church, to fund endowed scholarships (there are presently 114 such scholarships, the vast majority from Brethren sources), Finks sought other means for raising the scholarship endowment during his presidency. One successful program was originally developed at Ashland College by former president Glenn Clayton, the AC 1000 campaign. Conceived in 1982 as part of the college's "A Time for Opportunity" capital campaign, the program sought 1000 alumni who would donate $1000 over a four year period (the program was later renamed the AU 1000 to coincide with the designation of Ashland as a university). The seminary began its own ATS 1000 in 1982 with the goal of 100 donors over a four year period. The seminary reached the halfway point by the summer of 1984 and surpassed its goal in the summer of 1985. In the last accounting of the program in May 1986, ATS 1000 had 142 subscribers; on 30 June 2006 a total of $148,576 was in this endowment fund.[101]

Finks incorporated funds for student endowed scholarships in both of the capital campaigns that Ashland College/University ran during his tenure. In the college's "Partnership in Excellence" campaign that the seminary participated in from 1985 until 1991, the seminary raised $540,547.29 for the student scholarship endowment. The seminary also participated in the university's capital campaign, "Building on Strength," that began with a "silent phase" in 1999 and ended in 2004. The seminary's campaign ran through 2005 and featured the aforementioned $4 million for the Sandberg Leadership Center and also $4 million for endowed scholarships (eventually this latter goal was modified to endowment in general). The seminary faculty, administrators, and staff pledged $156,633 for the scholarships. The campaign realized a total of $2,108,700 for endowed scholarships.[102] The seminary's commitment to student financial aid is underscored by the distribution of $334,171 in institutional financial support to students in the 2005–06 academic year.

The seminary has been able to assist students in receiving significant scholarships from two foundations in recent years. Ashland students began receiving scholarships from the Opal Dancey Memorial Foundation in the 2002–03 academic year. To qualify for the $3000 renewable scholarship students had to meet certain financial criteria and be enrolled in the M.Div. degree, pursuing pulpit ministry, and in their second year. Ashland students have received a total of nineteen such scholarships since 2002. In 2002 Ashland was selected as one of only eight seminaries to be invited to be recipients of grants from The Kern Family Foundation. The grants provided full scholarships for M.Div. students throughout their three years in the degree program. To qualify students had to maintain a 3.25 grade point average and be full-time, committed to pastoral ministry, no older than twenty-seven years of age, and committed to participate in a network conference with students from the other seminaries. It is the vision of the foundation that by keeping ministerial students focused on their calling by removing financial burdens in seminary and by forming peer support networks among the "brightest and the best" pastoral candidates, these students will be better prepared to provide leadership for developing and maintaining vital local congregations. Through 2006 thirty-one Ashland students have received Kern scholarships.[103]

The efforts of Finks to build the seminary endowment bore dramatic results over his twenty-four year presidency. When he came in 1982, the seminary endowment was $170,235; on 30 June 2006, just after the end of his tenure, the endowment stood at $10,360,349. Besides student scholarships, endowment funds have been designated for other purposes as well. In addition to the faculty chairs previously mentioned, several new faculty chairs have been funded or partially funded since 1992. In 1994 Harlan and Wilma Hollewell of Milledgeville, Illinois, contributed $300,000 toward a chair of evangelism. In 1997 Reilly Smith, the Director of Missionary Ministries of the Brethren Church, proposed funding an endowed chair in church planting at the seminary to facilitate the training of church planters for the Brethren Church. The proposal gained the approval of the Executive Board of the Brethren Church that same year. Initiated in April 1997, the J. Ray Klingensmith Chair in Church Planting received funding from the Brethren Church, the Seminary Foundation, and Robert and Thelma Frank of Ashland, Ohio. The Franks also provided funding for two endowments to underwrite the ongoing ministry of the seminary: a building endowment for the Gerber Academic Center and an endowment to support ministry needs of the seminary.[104]

Curricular Development.   Throughout the years since 1992 Ashland has been committed to creating programs of distinction that express its vision of being a leading evangelical seminary. This commitment can continue to be seen in its creation of new degrees and academic programs. Several new concentrations were added to the M.A. degree during the 1990s, reflecting some of the special emphases of the seminary. In 1993 a Spiritual Formation concentration was implemented and in 1996 a concentration in Anabaptism and Pietism was added.

In 1994 several significant changes to the curriculum were approved by the faculty as part of a curriculum review process that began over three years earlier. The highlight of these changes was a new curriculum model (see illustration). As stated in the 1994–96 catalogue:

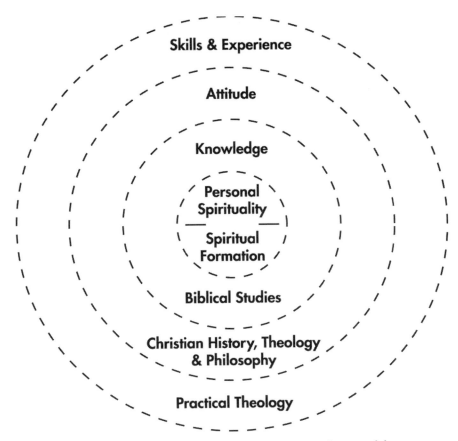

A graphic representation of the 1994 curriculum model

The curriculum model places spiritual formation, or personal spirituality, at the core of the ATS curriculum. Around this core are the traditional departments in classical theological education: Biblical Studies; Christian History, Theology and Philosophy; and Christian Ministries. In courses within these departments students acquire the knowledge, attitudes, skills and experiences necessary to become competent and effective leaders in the local church.

The broken lines comprising the concentric circles within the ATS curriculum model are significant to the structure. The broken lines give evidence that no course is taken in isolation from others, allowing for integration or synthesis of all courses. Each course is impacted by the information and/or ability learned in the entire seminary experience, which in turn influences the development of the whole person for ministry.

The broken line of the outermost circle indicates that the individual cannot sequester all that has been learned and therefore, as a professional church leader, is both impacted by and affects the culture of the society in which he or she lives. Sharing the good news of the Gospel of Jesus Christ becomes the passion of pastors and church leaders. As servant-leaders in local congregations, they empower and equip the laity for effective ministry in a culture with global responsibilities.[105]

This curriculum model is noteworthy for several reasons. It continued the emphasis on spiritual formation that had become explicit since the 1980s, though it had been an implicit part of the identity of the seminary from the beginning. It reinforced the importance of integration of learning across the various disciplines of the curriculum. It emphasized that students must be able to relate their seminary education to the critical issues of culture. It retained the understanding that graduates must be servant-leaders within their congregations (note the emphasis on service to the local church in the statement).

The new model led to several changes in the M.Div. degree in 1994. One spiritual formation course was required of all M.Div. students. The number of hours required in the Christian Ministries area was increased from 40 to 52 (including the two field study courses). However, there was flexibility regarding 24 of these hours, since students could select from a list of ministry courses those courses that best fit their ministry goals. The optional senior writing project was also dropped at this time. The net effect of these changes reduced elective hours to 28 from the previous 36–40 (the senior writing project was either 4 or 8 hours).

The M.Div. degree received another major revamping in 2000. Beginning in 1998, the Christian Ministries Department entered into a process, guided by the dean, David Hartzfeld, to rethink the delivery of the ministry segment of the M.Div. The seminary received a $5000 grant from the Wabash Center to underwrite the process. Out of these deliberations came a redesigned M.Div. that utilized a cohort model similar to the one used in the counseling program. As originally conceived, the M.Div. cohort program was designed for second and third year students. In each of these years students would take paired courses on Monday morning and meet with seasoned area pastors in small groups that afternoon. These small groups not only offered an opportunity to process the lecture material from the morning classes but, even more, took students through a spiritually formative experience of prayer, community, support, and mutual encouragement. Begun in 2000, the second year cohort has been a transformative experience for M.Div. students on the main campus (extension students in Cleveland and Detroit are encouraged, but not required, to participate in this Ashland-based program). The third year cohort was implemented in 2001, but discontinued for both financial and programmatic reasons. The second year cohort shifted to Tuesdays in 2001.[106]

A major curriculum review process guided by the Associate Academic Dean, Shawn Oliver, began in 2003. It will lead to further changes in the M.Div. degree as well as the seminary's other degrees. Most notable is the new curriculum model that will be implemented in the 2007–08 academic year. Central to the new model (see the diagram) is what has been labeled the 4Cs: core identity, character, calling, and competencies. In May 2004 the Curriculum Review team developed the following "Philosophy of Theological Education" that articulates the conceptual philosophy for the new curriculum:

> Ashland Theological Seminary embraces a philosophy of education that develops the whole, spiritual leader through Scripture, community, spiritual formation, and academic excellence. Men and women who are equipped for ministry will be secure in their identity in Christ and devoted

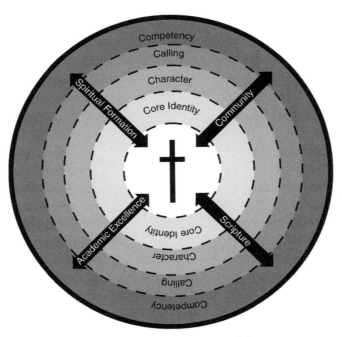

A graphic representation of the
curriculum model to be implemented in 2007

to others. They will allow the Word and Spirit to continually form their character in the image of Christ. Persons equipped for ministry will discern their calling in Christ and will have that calling shaped and confirmed in community. From this foundation of growth, these individuals will be competent to minister the grace and love of Christ to a broken world.

Therefore, Ashland Theological Seminary's curriculum focuses on the development of core identity, the formation of Christlike character, the discernment of calling to ministry, and the development of competencies necessary for effective ministry to the Church and the world.[107]

The full curricular implications of this new emphasis are currently being worked out, but the faculty is committed to an educational process that is not satisfied with the traditional emphasis on competency. Instead, the goal of the curriculum is a transformative process that leads to servant-leaders who are inwardly and outwardly prepared for the challenges of ministry in the twenty-first century. The slogan that appeared on the cover of seminary catalogues in 2004–05 and 2005–06, "More than an excellent education . . . Transformation," succinctly expresses this commitment.

Changes have also taken place in the seminary's M.A. degrees since 1994. That year the seminary restructured the M.A. in Church Administration into the M.A. in Ministry Management and shifted the Biblical Studies concentration from the M.A. degree to a new degree, the M.A. (Biblical Studies), with separate concentrations in Old Testament and New Testament. This latter degree required 96 quarter hours of coursework, in contrast to the 76 quarter hours required for the M.A. degree.

A significant revision of the M.A. degree was occasioned by the realization that Ashland's M.A. degree did not fit the basic guidelines for the M.A. set by the Association of Theological Schools. The M.A. was meant to be a theological or academic degree, not a professional or ministry-related degree. By mixing concentrations that were both academic and ministry-related, Ashland's M.A. was not in conformity with accreditation standards. Therefore, in 1997 the faculty approved several changes to the former M.A. that were implemented in 1998. A new ministry-focused degree, the M.A. in Christian Ministry, was developed that offered students a wide variety of options: Black Church Studies, Christian Education, Church Music/Worship, English Bible, Evangelism/Church Growth, Homiletics, Leadership/Management, Missions and Evangelism, Spiritual Formation, and Sports Ministry (a new field). Courses in these specialized areas could be taken either as a concentration (9 courses, though not all areas offered concentrations) or as a major (6 courses) and minor (3 hours). The hours for this degree were increased to 84 from the 76 hours formerly required in the M.A. The M.A. in Christian Ministry has offered great flexibility in being able to create new specialized offerings and to drop others that had low student enrollment. A challenge, however, is being able to schedule all the courses necessary to support all the options. When the Christian Ministries Department voted to change its name to the Practical Theology Department in 2002, the name of this degree was also changed to the M.A. in Practical Theology.

With the revision of the M.A. degree in 1998, new concentrations were added to the 96 hour academic M.A., specifically Christian Theology, Church History, and, in 2002, Anabaptism and Pietism. Since this time other changes have occurred in the degrees offered at Ashland. In 2002 the faculty voted to discontinue both the M.A. in Ministry Management and the M.A. in Christian Education for three reasons: insufficient faculty resources, low student enrollment, and the ability to offer courses to cover these areas in the new M.A. in Christian Ministry. In 2002 the seminary began consideration of the Master of Theology degree, an advanced research degree. In 2003 the faculty decided not to move forward with this degree due to lack of sufficient resources. There was strong support, however, for another degree, the Master of Arts (Religion), a general biblical and theological degree. A similar course of studies in the former M.A. degree, the M.A. General Studies Concentration, had been dropped in the 1998 revisions and never replaced. This concentration had been quite popular. The faculty gave its support to the new degree in January 2004 and received authorization from ATS to begin offering the degree in fall 2004. These degree options offer Ashland students a wide variety of career opportunities, both professional and academic.[108]

Several important changes have occurred in the counseling programs since 1992. In 1993 the seminary relocated the counseling program at Southwest General Hospital to the main campus, renaming the program the Midwest Center for Pastoral Counseling. The seminary felt that this move would provide greater quality control over such aspects of the program as supervision, recruitment, practicum, and internships. The Midwest Center received approval from the State of Ohio's Counselor and Social Worker Board before the opening of the program in fall 1993. In 1994 Ashland received approval to begin offering courses for the Licensed Professional Clinical Counselor (LPCC) licensure as well as the prior Licensed Professional Counselor (LPC) licensure. An additional thirty hours of credit was required for the LPCC licensure. At the time Ashland was the only Ohio seminary offering LPCC courses with a Christian emphasis. Douglas Little deserves special recognition for his extensive work in developing these programs at the Midwest Center.[109]

In 1996 the seminary received notification that the State of Ohio was increasing the requirements for counseling programs from sixty to ninety quarter hours. This change meant that the previous LPC entry program would now be replaced with a statewide LPCC entry program for counselor training. A major restructuring of the M.A. in Pastoral Counseling (MAPC) degree was necessitated by this new state requirement. The MAPC had been a 96 quarter hour degree, 36 hours of which were the Ashland core classes and the remaining 60 hours the state-required counseling courses. In 1997 the faculty approved a new degree, the M.A. in Clinical Pastoral Counseling (MACPC), which was composed of a streamlined core of 20 hours and the newly required 90 hours of counseling courses. This 110 hour degree gained ATS approval in June 1997 and was launched in fall 1997. In addition, the 144 hour M.Div. (Pastoral Counseling Track) was re-vamped into a 174 hour M.Div. (Clinical Pastoral Counseling Track). The MAPC and M.Div. (Pastoral Counseling Track) were retained, however, for students or pastors not seeking Ohio state licensure and for students in the Detroit Counseling Program, since these counseling degrees still fulfilled Michigan licensure requirements. The quality of Ashland's counseling programs is reinforced by several indicators: (1) by 2004 Ashland had the largest counseling program in Ohio, in spite of the additional seminary core courses, and (2) Ashland has regularly had one of the highest passage rates of any counseling program for the Ohio state licensure exam. Ashland has over two hundred students in its three counseling programs: Midwest, EMERGE, and Detroit. The total number of counseling students increased significantly when both the Detroit program in 1998 and the Midwest program in 2004 went from admitting a new cohort of students every second year to admitting one every year.[110]

Modifications have also occurred in the D.Min. program. In 1992 the seminary began a Korean D.Min. program, initiated as a result of conversations with several Korean denominations. The seminary hired a Korean director for the program, In Du Chae, in 1993 and began to offer some of the D.Min. classes in Korea in 1994. However, serious questions arose in 1997 about maintaining the quality of the program and about its administration. These concerns led the faculty in May 1997 to support the discontinuation of the program. Since 1997 changes have occurred in the structure of the D.Min. degree, particularly in the required core courses and the development of specialized concentrations. The 1998 catalogue listed five concentrations: Leadership, Spiritual Formation, Black Church Studies, Canadian Church Studies (a unique cooperative program with Canterbury College in Windsor, Canada, that began in 1995), and Individualized Study. A unique concentration, Formational Counseling, which combines Christ-centered counseling, spiritual direction, and formational prayer, was added in 2002 and a short-lived Women in Prophetic Leadership concentration was initiated in 2004. The current dean of the D.Min. program, Lee Solomon, has developed a well-structured program that has grown to over two hundred students.[111]

Development of the Extensions.   Under academic deans David Hartzfeld and Dale Stoffer there has been a commitment to upgrade the degree offerings at the extensions. Subsequent to the 1998 accreditation visit by ATS, the following changes occurred in the course and degree offerings at the extensions. Cleveland was approved for offering up to 50% of the M.A. degree and two-thirds of the M.Div. degree. Detroit was approved for offering up to two-thirds of the M.Div. degree and was approved for offering the full M.A. in Pastoral Counseling and M.A. in Christian Ministry degrees (these two degrees were belatedly submitted for approval to the North Central Association in 2004). In 2000 Columbus was approved by ATS for offering up to 49% of the M.A. and M.Div. degrees. In 2004 Cleveland was approved for offering the full M.A. in Practical Theology degree and that same year the full M.A. (Religion) degree was approved for both Cleveland and Detroit.

In 2004 an Extension Task Force was created to develop a strategic plan for each of the seminary's extensions. One of its recommendations was to seek approval for the full M.Div. degree in Detroit as soon as possible. With the hiring of Mitzi Smith in Biblical Studies in 2006 one of the last hurdles for seeking such approval was met. Both ATS and the North Central Association gave their approval for implementing the full degree in Detroit in fall 2006.

Ashland continues to have a strong commitment to its extension programs as evidenced by the following statement developed by the Extension Task Force and adopted by the faculty 3 December 2004:

A Rationale for ATS Extensions

Though the main campus of Ashland Theological Seminary has existed in Ashland, Ohio, since 1906, the seminary has had a long history of responding to the needs of the larger church beyond the Ashland area. The seminary's commitment to extensions as an integral part of its life and mission began with Cleveland in 1974. Critical to the decision to begin work in both Cleveland and Detroit was the invitation by clergy in these locales to offer theological education in major metropolitan areas that had no Protestant seminary. Our expansion to Columbus was again by invitation to offer evangelical theological training in this rapidly growing area.

As a result of these partnerships the main campus and the extension campuses have received mutual blessings in these ventures. The extensions make theological education available within the unique contexts of each location and also contribute a valuable multicultural perspective to the seminary's life. The diversity that these campuses bring to Ashland Theological Seminary is a gift that we must treasure. To be sure, development of extensions has its unique challenges, but these challenges must always be framed within the context of the blessing that the entire seminary community experiences through this partnership. This diverse community, united by our common identity in Jesus Christ and his Word and shaped by the transforming power of the Spirit, is, in small measure, a reflection of the *koinonia* that God himself is in the process of fashioning in and through Christ Jesus for his eternal pleasure.

Out of these experiences has grown a commitment to contextual theological education. In partnership with its extensions, ATS commits itself to assuring theological education of a quality commensurate with the main campus experience, while seeking to affirm and encourage the unique ethos

Detroit students being inducted into Eta Beta Rho, the Hebrew National Honor Society, in 2004; back row left to right: Thang Chu, Bennie Oliphant, Jan Brown, Donna Laird (the Hebrew instructor), Rodney Caruthers (Detroit Recruitment Counselor), Elizabeth Day, Twylla Lucas, Deborah Watt, and Kevin Carpenter; front row left to right: Luann Rourke, Emma Williams, Christina Munson, and Dawn Clark

and opportunities represented within each locale. ATS likewise commits itself to providing sufficient resources—facilities, administrative personnel, faculty, and courses—to support theological education at its extensions.[112]

The seminary also expressed its commitment to its extension work by adding the following statement to the list of guiding principles that were linked to the current mission statement of the seminary: Commitment to theological education through extensions.[113] The following statistics reveal the progress of the extensions since 1985.

	1985	1990	1995	2000	2006
Extension					
Cleveland	78	109	63	90	80
Columbus	–	11*	25	38	57
Detroit	38	81	141	205	128

*This figure is the enrollment in the cooperative venture with Xenos Christian Fellowship.

Accreditation Review (1998).   The commitment to developing quality programs of distinction placed the seminary in good stead for the accreditation review by ATS and the North Central Association on 26–28 January 1998. Ashland decided to write its self-study based on the new standards adopted by ATS at the 1996 biennial in Denver. These standards required the revamping of the M.A. degree described above as well as the design of a rigorous process of institution-wide assessment. The ATS visiting team recommended that Ashland receive a full ten year extension of its accreditation. The seminary was asked, however, to respond to six concerns by December 2000. These concerns were: (1) revision of the library collection development policy and provision for adequate human resources for the library; (2) the development and implementation of outcome assessments for all degree programs, with particular attention to appropriate summative evaluations; (3) the development and implementation of appropriate support for student placement; (4) the monitoring of residency requirements for students pursuing professional master's programs at the extension sites; (5) the monitoring of post-M.Div. ministry experiences of students admitted to the D.Min. degree; and (6) the overall use of evaluative data in the institutional planning process.[114]

The seminary responded to these concerns in a document dated 1 November 2000. (1) A revised collection development policy for the library received faculty approval in November 1999 and on 1 July 1999 the seminary hired Russell Morton as its research librarian. (2) Ashland sought to address the issue of assessment by having each department develop assessment tools that would assist them in determining how effectively they were achieving their departmental goals. It is worth noting that though this approach served to assess the quality of Ashland's degree programs, it did not address the issue of assessing student learning. (3) The Director of Admissions was given the responsibility of devising a suitable student placement process. (4) The Assistant Registrar developed a means of tracking the number of courses that extension students took towards their residency requirements on the Ashland campus. (5) The admissions committee of the D.Min. program would monitor all applicants to the program to be sure they had the requisite three years of ministry experience prior to admission to the program. (6) The Academic Dean would work with the departments and the Academic Committee to create a process to make assessment a part of the institution's culture.[115] In the intervening years since this report, the seminary has faced its greatest challenges in the area of assessment. The pressure being placed on education at all levels by the U.S. Department of Education and the regional accrediting agencies for developing institution-wide assessment processes has meant that schools have had to face a steep learning curve to meet these expectations.

Advances in Technology.   Another development that has had immense impact upon teaching and education in general since the late 1980s is the incorporation of technology in the classroom and office. The days of "low-tech" blackboards, chalk, and easels, though not completely gone, are going the way of record players, pen and paper datebooks, and, very soon, VCRs. Seminary education is no exception. Ashland began its deliberations about the role of technology in the seminary in the 1993–94 academic year when a Technology Task Force was created to research technology needs and draft the first strategic plan for technology. In the 1996–97 academic year the task force was replaced by a faculty committee, the Media and Technology Committee. The role of the committee was to provide opportunities for faculty training in the use of technology, to coordinate the purchase and maintenance of equipment, and to research the possible uses of new forms of technology. Significant outcomes of the work of this committee were the hiring of a Director of Technology Resources, Vickie Taylor, in 2001 at the recommendation of the committee and the completion of a document entitled "Policies and Procedures for Distance Education" in 2005 that developed guidelines for Ashland's distance education efforts. The committee was disbanded in 2005; the sense was that, with established policies in place and a director to oversee the policies, there was no longer a need for the committee.

Ashland began its intentional journey into the rapidly expanding field of technology in January 1995 with the opening of the first computer lab in the library. This journey has been advanced at several crucial junctures by the seminary's connection to the university. Most significantly, the university's major investment in developing a fiber-optic network for the entire campus, including the seminary, opened incredible new vistas for the seminary. This project, completed in January 1997, was coupled with the provision of personal computers for all faculty in the university and seminary. All faculty now had convenient access to email; students and faculty had off-campus access to the resources of the main campus, especially the library; the seminary had its first computerized classrooms with video-projection systems in the spring of 1997. The seminary also has benefited from the resources of the Information Technology department of the university, which provides the seminary with such support services as network personnel, hardware and software technicians, a webmaster, and content developers for online education.[116]

The seminary has made steady progress in the application of technology. The Media and Technology Committee helped to train faculty in the use of technology especially through "Share the Wealth" segments in faculty meetings between 2001 and 2005. In these sessions members of the committee or Vickie Taylor would share different technological concepts or practices with the community. Various faculty have made the commitment to develop and teach online seminary courses. These course offerings have enabled the seminary to meet ATS standards for being able to offer an increasing number of courses in this format. All seminary classrooms are now computerized with full audio-visual capabilities. In recent years the seminary community and especially the extensions have benefited from a growing number of online resources and services: the catalogue, course schedules, syllabi, forms from the registrar's office, registration, unofficial transcripts, and seminary newsletters. Faculty are able to put course notes on personal webpages, use online discussions to enhance course participation, and, in the 2005–06 academic year, submit grades online and download class rosters. In November 2004 the seminary campus became wireless, allowing students and visitors to use wireless technology inside and outside the classroom. In December 2004 three plasma screens were installed in campus buildings to keep the seminary community aware of upcoming events. One classroom in the Gerber Academic Center was outfitted with video conferencing technology in 2005 that opens the possibility for broadcasting to the Columbus and Cleveland Centers. Though there is still much progress that needs to be made in the use of technology, the seminary has positioned itself well for the next steps it wishes to take.[117]

Institutional Definition.   Growth always brings with it special challenges. Among these are managing growth through strategic planning and maintaining a unified sense of identity. Ashland has been in an ongoing process of strategic planning since 1989. Involving many constituencies of the seminary, this process has sought to be responsive to the needs and opportunities that are present in the seminary's life. The strategic planning document continues to be revised on a regular basis, though, as with any ongoing process, there is constant need to refine the process and develop better strategies for revising the document and implementing its proposals. Nevertheless, many of the proposals that have been a part of this document over the years since 1989 have come to fruition.[118]

One outgrowth of the strategic planning process during the early 1990s was concern over the issues of governance and fiscal stability, especially in terms of the university and seminary relationship. In a document drafted in 1992 and entitled "Seminary Committee Report on Reorganization and Vision," the Seminary Committee made three recommendations. (1) "The title of the Vice President for the Seminary [should] be changed to Vice President for Theological Education/President of the Seminary." It was explained that this change would not affect the organizational structure on the university side but would provide the chief executive officer of the seminary with a title consistent with that officer's job description and with the title of the heads of most seminaries in the United States. (2) "The budget process [should] proceed as previously approved by the board of Trustees [in 1960 and 1963] with the responsibility resting with the Seminary to develop its budget, income and expenses. The surplus would again be available for the use of future expansion and development of the Seminary." This fiscal arrangement had been maintained until the 1980s when the college president, because of the college's financial condition, absorbed the surplus of the seminary. This change of policy had not been approved by the Board. (3) "The Chairman of the Seminary Committee of the Board of Trustees shall be a member of the Brethren Church." This statement was included to "insure commitment to the Brethren Church with regards to the Seminary. The Seminary has a strong relationship with the Church and is listed officially [with ATS] as a Brethren Seminary."[119] These recommendations were brought before the Board for action on 23 October 1992. The Board needed additional time to consider the implications of the recommendations and tabled the discussion pending further study.[120]

The Seminary Committee, in the meantime, decided to incorporate these changes into a broader discussion of issues of governance of the seminary and, eventually, the development of by-laws for the seminary. There were few, if any, written guidelines detailing the selection, responsibilities, and composition of the Seminary Committee and, similarly, there was almost nothing written about the qualifications, selection, and duties of the chief executive officer of the seminary. The study of these issues was advanced by the reception of a Lilly Foundation two-stage grant in 1992 that totaled $27,500. The purpose of the grant, part of a Lilly project known as "Boards and the Practice of Trusteeship," was to train trustees for more effective leadership in theological education. An outgrowth of this process was the development of by-laws for the seminary that served to strengthen and formalize the governance of the seminary.[121]

The by-laws were presented to the Board by the Seminary Committee at the 16 October 1993 meeting of the Board. The salient features of the by-laws were: seventy-five percent of the members of the Seminary Committee were to be Brethren and all the members were to be committed to an evangelical faith; there were to be six advisory members on the Seminary Committee, though they would not be considered members of the Board; the chief executive officer (CEO) of the seminary would be appointed by the president of the university with the advice and counsel of the Seminary Committee; representatives of the Seminary Committee would serve on a search committee when a new CEO needed to be selected; the chairperson of the Seminary Committee was to be Brethren; the CEO of the seminary would have the dual title of President of the Seminary and Vice President of the University; the CEO of the seminary was to be the chief administrative and educational officer of the seminary; the CEO was to be a member of the Brethren Church; the faculty should be composed of all full, associate, and assistant professors, instructors, and administrative officers; and, so far as practical, fifty percent of the faculty should be members of the Brethren Church. Both the Executive Committee and the Board approved the by-laws, with but one minor change.[122]

A significant challenge related to the dramatic growth of the seminary since 1990 and the numerous personnel changes over this period has been acquainting the community with the historic emphases of the seminary. This ongoing need, as well as the desire to keep the identity statements about the seminary fresh and current, has led to several refinements of these statements in recent years. In 1996 the seminary engaged in a process of developing a new mission statement, replacing the lengthy one developed in 1985, and of crystallizing the seminary's core values. These statements, together with a section entitled "Operating Philosophy," were adopted by the faculty and then the Board in October 1996 and first appeared in the 1998–2000 seminary catalogue. Because of their importance, they are quoted in full.

Mission Statement

Ashland Theological Seminary exists to equip men and women for ministry as servant leaders in the body of Christ and the world at large through being a community that is committed to Scripture, academic excellence, spiritual formation, and practical training.

Operating Philosophy

In order to equip men and women for ministry, Ashland Theological Seminary brings together a faculty with shared commitment to biblical, evangelical faith; the pursuit of excellence in teaching; and professional development through continuing education and research. This interdenominational team of educators attempts to create both a community of fellowship and a climate for learning.

The Seminary creates a learning environment that emphasizes both biblical conviction and tolerance. This climate facilitates the appreciation of persons and ideas from diverse Christian traditions within a cross-cultural perspective. Students are encouraged to deepen their understanding of and involvement in their own denominational traditions.

Students are challenged to develop a relationship of intimacy with God as they grow to maturity in Christ under the guidance of the Holy Spirit. The curriculum is designed to develop competence in hermeneutics, biblical studies, history, and theology, as well as ministry areas such as preaching, teaching, worship, pastoral care, counseling, spiritual formation, missions, evangelism, and administration. The Seminary models and fosters a commitment to life-long learning which balances ministry and family life.

Core Values

Scripture

Ashland Theological Seminary believes God's saving revelation has been made supremely in Jesus Christ. The Bible is the complete and authentic record of that revelation. We are committed to both the Old and New

Testaments as God's infallible message for the church and the world. The Scriptures are foundational to the education process at Ashland Seminary.

Spiritual Formation

Ashland Theological Seminary believes that Spiritual Formation is at the heart of all we do. Spiritual Formation is the process of nurturing an intimate relationship with God, encompassing heart, soul and mind. Spiritual Formation is obedience to the Word of Christ and an intentional commitment to grow, study, pray and be held accountable for our life and witness, both before God and one another.

Community

Ashland Theological Seminary builds community through shared faith. As students, staff, faculty and administration, we identify ourselves as community. We express community through Chapel, classes, Spiritual Formation groups, social events, conferences, prayer cells and joint ministry experiences as we work and live together. Within this environment of support and challenge, it is possible for us to grow inwardly, in our relationship with God and others, and in our outlook on the world.

Academic Excellence

Ashland Theological Seminary is committed to academic excellence. While seminary education is unique, Ashland creates an atmosphere conducive

The seminary community in worship at a chapel service

to academic studies and sustains high scholastic standards from an internation-
ally recognized faculty. Integrated within our curriculum is the whole framework
of the Seminary's Core Values leading to a goal of lifelong learning expressed
through servant leadership.[123]

The new mission statement is far more concise and focused than its
forerunner. Though the first part of the statement is rather generic, except
for the concept of servant leadership, the last part introduces the core values that are more specific to Ashland. The "Operating Philosophy" retains
much of the language of the 1985 mission statement, but in a better organized presentation. Nothing new is added with the exception of the strong
affirmation of spiritual formation: "Students are challenged to develop a relationship of intimacy with God as they grow to maturity in Christ under
the guidance of the Holy Spirit." The only section of the former mission
statement that is omitted is the opening material about the seminary's relation to Ashland University and to the Brethren Church with its Anabaptist and Pietist roots. This material is covered more appropriately in the
"Statement of Relationship," though there is no mention of Anabaptism in
the statement.

The section on "Core Values" develops in detail what have been essential commitments of the seminary for nearly its entire history. All but
the core value of community were present in a statement called "Emphases
of the Seminary" that had been in seminary catalogues since 1937. Even
community had been a conscious commitment of the seminary since the
mid-1960s, though the fellowship and camaraderie that existed among the
seminary students and faculty from the beginning of the seminary were expressions of this core value. Note that the statement on Scripture draws
heavily upon the section on Scripture in "The Message of the Brethren
Ministry," which last appeared in the 1998–2000 catalogue.

Further refinements of the identity statements of the seminary occurred in the 2001–02 online catalogue and printed catalogues since
2002–04. These changes involved: (1) omitting "The Message of the
Brethren Ministry," due to the feeling that the seminary's "Statement of
Faith"[124] provided sufficient theological definition together with greater detail and breadth than the "Message"; (2) revising the "Statement of Relationship" to set forth more fully and accurately the Anabaptist and Pietist
heritage of the seminary and the history of the Brethren Church and of the
seminary; and (3) eliminating the section entitled, "Emphases of the Seminary," due to the redundancy with the "Core Values" material. A rather
convoluted discussion of the historic Brethren balance between conser-

vatism and progressivism that was found in the "Church Relation" section of prior catalogues appeared in a far more succinct form: "conservative in its commitment to Scripture and to the historic Christian faith and progressive in its commitment to modern methods and contemporary relevance."[125]

Specialized Ministries and Co-Curricular Opportunities.   This commitment to modern methods and relevance has been exemplified not only in the development of distinctive programs in the seminary curriculum, but also in the creation of cutting edge ministries of a co-curricular nature. The completion of the Sandberg Leadership Center (SLC) in 2001 made possible the development of a number of unique continuing education programs. Even before the spades moved the initial dirt at groundbreaking, the seminary had already launched its first two programs in anticipation of the center's completion. Renewing Pastor and People, a program designed by Terry Wardle and Richard Parrott to bring spiritual renewal to pastors and renewed vision to their churches, was initiated in 1999 and ran through 2002. During this time the program impacted the ministry of thirty-five pastors and churches. Terry Wardle initiated another ministry in 1999, the Church Planting Seminars. Held once or twice a year since that time, the seminars combine individual assessment of potential church planters, counsel for self-care and spiritual health, and presentations to prepare participants for the work of church planting. One of the truly unique ministries offered through the SLC is the Institute of Formational Counseling. Launched by Terry Wardle in 2003, the institute equips Christian leaders to minister to broken people by helping them discover new-found freedom in Christ. Several times each year the institute sponsors seminars and conferences dedicated to this purpose.[126]

From the outset the SLC has hosted a series of roundtables on various aspects of leadership in both the church and the marketplace. Some of these roundtables have been: Leadership Character (October 2001), Power and Leadership (March-April 2003), and Leadership Ethics (November 2006). The SLC has also been the site of a variety of other conferences and workshops, including leadership training for State Farm Insurance agents developed by the first executive director of the Center, Richard Parrott. The present executive director of the Center, Eugene Heacock, has developed the following statements for the SLC, which capture quite well its ministry focus:

> **Vision:** SLC serves as a catalyst for generating new models of Christian leadership by bringing together leaders from church and society for dialogue on and response to contemporary issues of character and ethics.

> **Mission:** A transformational learning center, committed to the spiritual development of authentic leaders in the church and society. Leaders today know that change is challenging for people and organizations. The SLC is dedicated to helping leaders and organizations deal with change through a commitment and strategy of transformational leadership.[127]

As an expression of these ideals, Heacock announced in 2005 the creation of the Christian Leaders of Excellence Program. Made possible by a $500,000 endowment by Richard Ferrari, an alumnus of Ashland University and highly successful businessman, the program envisions the development of Christian business leaders through a "transformational learning experience incorporating assessment, small group interaction, seminary-style instruction, a mentor relationship and self-directed learning."[128]

Since its inception the SLC has sought to serve the varied needs of pastors and their churches. One of the most innovative and transformative programs developed through the Center has been the Pastors of Excellence (POE) program. This program was made possible by a nearly $1 million grant received from the Lilly Endowment, Inc., in 2002. The grant proposal, written by Terry Wardle with the assistance of Richard Parrott, Lee Solomon, and Dale Stoffer, was submitted in response to Lilly's offering of $57.9 million to religious organizations to participate in a national program called "Sustaining Pastoral Excellence."

Ashland's program, initiated in 2003, was a three year process involving the development of training materials (year one), the selection and training of twenty (eventually eighteen) pastor-mentors (year two), and the selection and mentoring of ninety pastors (year three). The eighteen pastor-mentors were each responsible for working with five other pastors in the third year of the program. Key elements of the process were not only mentoring in the context of small groups but also seminars that reinforced such critical components as spiritual maturity, personal well-being, healthy relationships, competent ministry skills, and healthy church renewal. Many of the participants also took advantage of a specialized retreat for the renewal of pastoral couples. At the conclusion of the program in 2005 the POE leadership team received numerous testimonies of how this program had transformed both the personal lives of the participants and their marriage, family, and congregational relationships.[129]

The overwhelming desire of many in the POE process was to continue with a second phase. When the Lilly Endowment, Inc., invited Ashland to submit a proposal for the continued funding of POE in 2005, the leadership team presented a request for a $2 million program, funded equally by Ash-

A Pastors of Excellence workshop

land and the Lilly Endowment, Inc. The proposal featured two ministries: (1) the continuation of POE and (2) a series of retreats for POE couples to deal with issues of brokenness through a process of personal, spiritual, and emotional healing in the Lord. With the reception of funds from the Lilly Endowment, Inc., late in 2005, Ashland launched both ministries in 2006. In conjunction with Lilly's Sustaining Pastoral Excellence initiative, Gene Heacock also collaborated with representatives of Duke Divinity School and Green Lake (Wisconsin) Conference Center in 2005 for a $10,000 mini-grant from the Lilly Foundation to study issues of leadership assessment, enhancement, and training.[130]

Ashland has received other grants that have contributed to the improvement of the physical campus and to faculty and curriculum development. As noted earlier, Ashland received $8000 from the Lilly Foundation in 1991 for faculty scholarship development. In 1990 Ashland was one of forty-one seminaries in the United States to receive a $50,000 grant from the Lilly Foundation for deferred maintenance and an energy audit. The outgrowth of this audit was the installation in 1994 of not only a computer system to control heating and cooling in the Shultz Academic Center but also energy efficient lights and ballasts throughout the campus and windows in the library. In 1999 Ashland received a $10,000 grant from a Lilly Foundation grant administered by Gordon-Conwell Theological Seminary for redesigning the D.Min. curriculum. The $5,000 Wabash Center grant received in 1999 for redesigning the M.Div. program has been noted earlier. Paul Overland has received two grants from the Wabash Center for innovative teaching of Hebrew. The first was a $1,375 grant in 2002 that was utilized for developing techniques that would enhance the comprehension and retention of the Hebrew language. The second, awarded in 2005, was a substantial grant of $70,000 that sought to bring together a team of leading scholars "to develop and field-test a new model for teaching Hebrew."[131]

Other expressions of the seminary's commitment to enriching the educational experience of students, alumni, and friends of the seminary are the continuing tradition of hosting international tours. The annual tours of the Holy Land during the 1970s became sporadic during the first part of the 1980s due to decreased student interest. They resumed on a regular basis during the latter 1980s, though the 1986 tour was cancelled due to the threat of terrorism. These tours, which the faculty would take turns leading, again were sporadic during the 1990s and first part of the 2000s, with the tours for 1994, 2001, and 2002 being cancelled due to unrest in the Middle East. Two tours of the Holy Land occurred in 2006 during the seminary's centennial celebration. Luke Keefer sponsored three tours of the British Isles between 1990 and 2000 and he and Dale Stoffer hosted a tour of the Reformation Lands in 2001. The Seminary Foundation has also scheduled yearly trips to a wide variety of destinations since its inception (it was chartered in 1977); these tours are designed especially for development purposes.

Another unique treasure that has contributed to the learning experience of students and the broader Ashland community is the seminary's archaeological collection. Based on the recommendation of Frederick Finks, the Board, on 7 May 1993, approved naming the room housing the collection the Flora Archaeological Center after Delbert B. and Romayne K. Flora. The Center was dedicated on 4 August 1993. Additional items continue to be added to the collection, notably a footwashing vessel in 1993. Kenneth Walther became the curator of the collection in the mid-1980s.[132]

During 1993 the "Arch" Room was remodeled; the platform, baptistery, and closet at the west end of the room were removed. In their place an Archive Room was created in 1994, separated from the archaeological collection by a ten foot glass wall with glass doors. This room has become the home for another unique collection of the seminary. In 1993 an alumnus of the seminary, Douglas Sherman, and his wife, Jean, of Ann Arbor, Michigan, made an initial donation of $50,000 to begin building a collection of early biblical and non-biblical manuscripts and written documents to show

Kenneth Walther in the Flora Archaeological Center

the history of writing and of biblical manuscripts. Items purchased with this initial donation included a sixteenth century Torah scroll on animal skins, a hand written page from the Wycliffe Bible, several pieces of Egyptian papyrus dating as early as the fourth century B.C., and a cuneiform tablet from the time of Abraham. The Shermans have continued their support to provide additional items for the collection: a second edition of the Geneva Bible from 1580 and a 1616 small folio edition of the King James Bible, acquired in 1996, and a 1566 edition of the Great Bible, obtained in 1997.[133]

In 1997 Bud and Jane Frank of Mansfield, Ohio, enabled the seminary to expand its collection of ancient cuneiform texts. Their donation of $30,000 resulted in the acquisition of twenty pieces of cuneiform from the gallery of Bruce Ferrini of Akron, Ohio. Ferrini made his own donation of fourteen fragments of cuneiform tablets to the seminary as well. One of the most recent acquisitions for the manuscript collection occurred in 2004, when the seminary obtained a fragment on leather from the Dead Sea Scrolls through the generosity of two donors. The fragment contains a portion of Psalm 11:2. It complements other parchment and papyrus materials written in Coptic, Syriac, Greek, and Latin. Not only the seminary community but also public and private school students and church and community groups have benefited from these special collections.[134]

Another co-curricular commitment of the seminary has been to develop resources for the study of the Anabaptist, Pietist, and Brethren movements. These movements, upon which the foundations of the seminary were built, continue to inform many aspects of the life of the seminary. Reflective of the continuing commitment to maintain this heritage is a priority given to these movements in the seminary library's collection development policy, the acquisition of rare publications related to these movements, and the development of a concentration in Anabaptism and Pietism in the M.A. degree. In 1994 the seminary hosted the Eleventh Believers' Church Conference, sponsored by churches which practice believer baptism. The theme of the conference was "The Lord's Supper: Believers' Church Perspectives." Another important development has been the creation of an archives for the Brethren Church in 2004 in the basement of the Brethren Church National Offices across College Avenue from the University Memorial Chapel. Made possible by the generous gifts of time and money by Jim Hollinger, the archives serves as a repository of materials connected to the history of the church, including the university and seminary. Due to the inadequacy of the seminary's Brethren archive room, all the Brethren related materials in this room were moved to the new archives. Jim Hollinger and the seminary have also cooperated over the last several years in the acquisition of rare Anabaptist, Pietist, and Brethren publications for the archives, especially works published by the Sauer and Ephrata presses during the colonial period in America.[135]

Since 1994 the seminary has received several gifts to enhance the music ministry on the campus. In 1994 the seminary received an anonymous gift of $50,000 to purchase a new organ for the chapel. A new Rogers Pipe Organ was installed over the summer of 1994 and dedicated in a chapel service on 7 October 1994. In 1998 Frances Smetzer made a gift of a new Boston Grand Piano for the Smetzer Auditorium in the Gerber Academic Center. She had previously made the naming gift for the auditorium in memory of her deceased husband, Ted Smetzer. In 2001 Dan and Ann DeVeny donated a piano in honor of Dan's parents, Richard and Mary Jane DeVeny. The piano provides instrumentation for the various programs that are hosted in the Sandberg Leadership Center.[136]

Service to the Community and the World. Ashland continues to be committed to serving the larger community and world outside its own walls. This commitment has taken a number of shapes in recent years. In 1997 the seminary teamed with the Brethren Church and the Argentine Brethren Church to lay plans for offering theological education in Argentina and, through this location, to other countries in Latin America. This exciting opportunity became a reality with the graduation of Eduardo and Mariela Rodriguez from Ashland Theological Seminary in 1997. They returned to their hometown of Colon, Argentina, in 1997 to open the South American Theological Seminary (STS). The first classes began in March 1998 with 120 students enrolled. In 2001 two women, Marcela Rivero and Monica Santiago, joined STS following their graduation from Ashland Theological Seminary (Marcela Rivero has since left the work to pursue other ministry). Ashland has been vitally involved in the development of STS, providing several professors each year without cost to teach at the school, sending a work team in 2004 to assist with construction of an addition to the STS facility in Colon, donating over a thousand books to its library, funding student scholarships, and offering other financial support. In November 2002 Finks and representatives of the Ashland Theological Seminary Foundation were on hand to celebrate the graduation of the first three students from STS. In February 2006 STS suffered a tragic loss in the death of Mariela Rodriguez, after a long battle with cancer, but the leaders of the school are committed to moving forward with this vital ministry.[137]

Ashland has expressed its commitment to outreach in other ways as well. Part of the vision for the Smetzer Counseling Center was serving the emotional and spiritual needs of the Ashland community by offering free counseling services, though donations have been encouraged. For the twelve month period from October 2005 to September 2006, the center logged 1059 client appointments from the community, an average of 88 per month. In November

Eduardo and Mariela Rodriguez

The facilities of the South American Theological Seminary in Colon, Argentina

2005 twenty students, staff, and their families traveled to Waveland, Mississippi, to aid in the relief efforts following Hurricane Katrina. The seminary has also contributed to the construction of churches in India in support of the ministry of seminary graduate Prasanth Kumar.[138]

Looking to the Future.   As the seminary prepares to enter its next century of existence, it does so with new opportunities, a new vision, and new challenges. As early as 1985 Finks had referred to Ashland as a "leading evangelical seminary" and this vision statement was formally adopted by the seminary in 1989. In 2002 Finks shared with the Seminary Committee that the seminary had achieved this goal and that the faculty had now adopted a new vision statement: "Ashland Theological Seminary shall lead evangelical seminary education as it impacts leaders in both church and society." He cited seven ways in which this statement was already true of the seminary. The seminary had:

1. Developed a leading Field Education program
2. Completed a Leadership Center (one of only six on seminary campuses)
3. Developed a leading program in Church Planting
4. Developed a "Sustaining Pastoral Excellence" program for national church leaders
5. Designed a program for inner healing (only one known on a seminary campus)

6. Designed a program for formational counseling (only one known on a seminary campus)
7. Designed a program for women in prophetic leadership (only one known on an evangelical seminary campus)[139]

There is more recently, however, a desire to move away from the language of a "leading evangelical seminary" or "shall lead evangelical seminary education" because of the inherent comparison of Ashland with other seminaries. Those who share this conviction believe that Ashland needs to be following its own unique calling and that it should not evaluate itself by what other seminaries are doing.

Ashland has positioned itself with its physical and personnel resources to continue to be on the cutting edge of theological education. The curriculum review process, with a new approach to theological education built on the 4Cs of core identity, character, calling, and competency, has the potential to fulfill in a dynamic way the slogan on recent catalogues: "More than an excellent education . . . Transformation." The quality of the seminary faculty is outstanding and the seminary has developed a reputation and name recognition among its peers that could never have been imagined thirty years ago. There is good reason that the seminary has grown from the 25th largest seminary in North America to the 12th during Finks' tenure.

To be sure Ashland still has its challenges. It is still overly dependent on tuition. It is questioning where it fits within an evangelical ethos that is overly politicized and does not always share its concern for a balance between social concern and evangelistic mission. It continues to sort out the proper balance for itself between a commitment to academic excellence and a sense of call to serve the church and world. It faces the need to develop a new consensus of vision and mission that captures the imagination and allegiance of the many new personnel who are Ashland Theological Seminary. Yet these very challenges can invest the seminary community with a constructive energy and creative spirit that will continue the innovative ideas and programs that have come to epitomize the seminary since the late 1960s.

With the transition of Frederick Finks to the presidency of Ashland University after twenty-four years at the helm of the seminary, the seminary launched its own presidential search in January 2006. In April 2006 John Shultz was announced as the eighth president of Ashland Theological Seminary. As with any new beginning, there is always a bit of uncertainty and anxiousness, but the seminary continues to feel that "God truly has his hand on this place" and enters upon this new century of existence with confident trust in the One who has been so faithful over the last one hundred years.

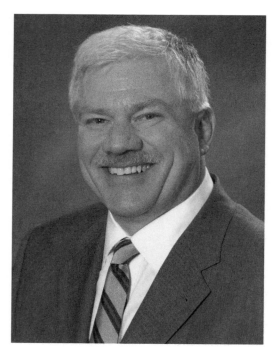

John C. Shultz

"God Has his Hand upon this Place"

During the last decade Fred Finks often shared his conviction that God's hand was upon the seminary in a profound way. This conviction was born of adversity following the departure of two senior level faculty members from the Biblical Studies Department: Bill Arnold and Ben Witherington. They had been offered positions at Asbury Theological Seminary in 1995 after Asbury had been the recipient of a significant endowment by Ralph Waldo Beeson. In the aftermath of their departure Finks began wrestling with God in prayer, asking, "Why would you allow something like this to happen when the seminary was moving ahead so strongly?"

One day after having just such a conversation with God during his day at work, Finks returned home and became aware of the Lord's presence. Finks heard the Lord distinctly telling him: "I can do anything I want to do; I can take anyone away from here whom I want to; I can even remove you if I want to. But, my hand is on this place." At that moment Finks became acutely aware of his arrogance and, falling on his knees, he confessed this before God. He committed himself to trusting the Lord through this season of disappointment. Eventually, the seminary was able to hire two quality United Methodist faculty members: Dan Hawk and David deSilva.

(continued)

Sometime after this experience, Finks' secretary notified him that a new student wanted to talk with him, but the student wouldn't relate the subject of the conversation. Usually Finks sought to obtain the nature of the desired conversation so he could direct the person to the right personnel if necessary. When the student entered Finks' office, the student closed the door behind him. Finks thought to himself, "This student must really be upset about something!" The student began by saying that Finks probably didn't know who he was. Finks had met him at new student orientation and remembered that his name was Steve. The student continued: "Something happened to me last week that I need to share with you. I was in church last Sunday and, while the minister was preaching, suddenly something like a screen was lowered in front of the stage. On the screen were a picture of the seminary and a picture of you. This happened three different times during the service. The Lord said to me, 'You are to go to Fred Finks and tell him that my hand is on this place and that I love him.'"

As the student was sharing this, Finks began to weep. The student remarked, "I don't know what this means." Finks replied, "That is okay, because I do!" This episode was especially powerful because Finks had never shared what the Lord had said to him with anyone else. Now this student was sharing the very words that God had spoken to him at his home: "My hand is upon this place."

Remarkably this was not the end of the story. About a month later an alumnus from Kentucky was visiting the seminary. He came to Finks' office and, after he and Finks had talked about a number of things, he asked whether he could pray for Finks. He prayed a word of blessing on the ministry of the seminary. As he ended, he placed his hand of Finks' shoulder and said, "I just want to tell you that God's hand is on this place."

A third event happened after Finks for the first time shared these stories in chapel. A student stayed after chapel was over. She was sitting in the back of the chapel and Finks noticed that she had been crying. He asked, "Is there anything wrong; can I be of help?" She said, "No, but you were speaking to me today. I was planning to go to another seminary. I was praying to God about going to that seminary, but he said, 'No, you are not to go there. You are to go to Ashland because my hand is upon this place.'"

Finks acknowledged that the message had come through to him loud and clear after the first encounter. But God's repetition of the message sensitized Finks to the powerful and manifold ways that God has worked in and through Ashland Theological Seminary over the course of his years at the seminary.

Frederick Finks, interview by author, 13 March 2006, Ashland, OH.

This transition occurred in the midst of the centennial year celebrations at the seminary. As part of the celebrations on Founders' Day Weekend (classes began on 11 September 1906), the seminary community dedicated a Wall of Remembrance on 10 September 2006.[140] The granite wall features the names of all the faculty and administrators at the seminary during its century of its existence; a separate plaque also lists all the present employees of the seminary. The dedication service offered an exceptional opportunity to look backward with gratitude to the Lord for his grace and to the many who have served so faithfully and so sacrificially; to look at the present with wonder at the personal, physical, and financial resources with which God has blessed the seminary; and to look to the future with renewed dedication to serve the Lord through our mission to "equip men and women for ministry as servant leaders in the body of Christ and the world at large . . ."

Concluding Observations

Both the college and seminary faced significant challenges during the 1980s. At the college the burden of financial indebtedness, both short term and long term, weighed heavily upon the institution. But the entrepreneurial synergy of Joseph Shultz and Lucille Ford developed creative programs, new extensions, and outreach to nontraditional students that dramatically changed the fortunes of the college. These very innovations served to transform Ashland College into Ashland University in 1989. The seminary had its own challenges during this period. The faculty and facilities were insufficient to keep up with the student growth and multiplication of extensions that occurred in the 1970s. The Association of Theological Schools placed pressure on the seminary through much of this period to address these deficiencies. In reality this very pressure forced the seminary to marshal the resources that made possible the rapid growth since 1990.

The sixteen years since 1990 have been marked at both the university and seminary by a period of continued growth and especially by growing complexity. The university worked an ambitious strategic plan that made significant strides in such areas as faculty development, technological advancement, and financial strength. The construction or acquisition of twelve facilities at the university and its off campus locations during these years has provided the physical resources that will meet the university's needs for years to come. The seminary entered into a period of dramatic growth in 1990, more than doubling its student body. Its stature among its peer institutions has grown apace. With new leadership at both institutions, with adequate resources in place, and with a history of creative vision, the university and seminary are well positioned for the future.

Conclusion

The history of Ashland College/University and Ashland Theological Seminary is punctuated by periods of seemingly insurmountable hurdles which have served as catalysts for dynamic innovation and dramatic growth. More often than not, these challenges have been financial, though leadership issues often are just under the surface. Up through the mid-1950s the fortunes of the seminary and college were very much linked. But during the period of the 1960s through the 80s, the college and seminary were frequently moving in opposite directions. Since the 1990s both schools have experienced times of maturing as institutions, with the development and growth of solid programs, adequate financial and physical resources, and capable administrators, faculty, and staff.

There are significant lessons that can be gleaned from this history that can serve as guideposts for future generations of leaders at both institutions. First, as mentioned above, both institutions have been faced at times with great challenges. There were times in the life of both schools when thought was given to closing them forever. Yet in every case the right person has come to the helm of leadership to help steer the institution to promising new horizons. The entrepreneurial spirit has been a gift to the college/university and seminary that should never be forgotten or lost. Second, there have also been cases in which that very leadership has been unable to adapt to the new circumstances that they created. Leadership must be sufficiently discerning to realize that adaptation is necessary as new challenges and opportunities present themselves. Third, the history of the relationship between the college/university and the seminary has not always been a mutually affirming one. At times open controversy has existed between the heads of the two schools and the student bodies have disdained one another. The removal of the seminary to a separate location in 1958 provided sufficient distance to allow both institutions to develop their own identities without the previous friction. Effort must be made to keep the relationship between university and seminary collegial and mutually rewarding. Though the schools have tended, at times, to go their separate ways, there are a number of signs in the last decade that point to a desire on both sides to collaborate and work toward some mutually beneficial goals. This cooperative spirit has been evidenced in the classroom, in administrative circles, and in informal settings.

This tension between the college/university and the seminary is actually inherent in the very identity of the institution. The original charter of the college made no mention of theological education because of the fear of the Annual Meeting of the German Baptist Brethren Church that such a course of study would lead to a professional ministry. But after the ouster of the Progressive Brethren from the German Baptist Brethren Church in 1882, the opportunity for the Progressives to express their desire for an educated ministry presented itself when the college was rechartered in 1888. In the constitution developed at that time, the very first article of the constitution included the declaration: "The training of suitable men for the ministry of the gospel shall always be sacredly regarded as one of the main objects of this institution." This "sacred" calling of the college/university has at times maintained an uneasy tension with the historic commitment to the liberal arts.[1] This tension broke out into open conflict during the mid-1930s under seminary dean Alva J. McClain. Yet, this very tension can be a blessing to both callings of the university. The reminder of the Christian roots of the college can assure that the academic thrust of the university will not be at the expense of the formation of the moral and spiritual character of students, a commitment that has historically been very important to the college/university and is especially necessary today. Intellectual rigor can assist the process of training people for ministry by sharpening their critical thinking skills and by developing a discerning quality that avoids religious fads and fancies, traits that are likewise much needed today. Academia does not need to live in fear of faith, nor should faith be threatened by the academic life. A creative, mutually respectful and energizing synergy ought to be the goal of Ashland's dual allegiance to faith and intellect. People like J. Allen Miller, Leslie Lindower, J. Ray Klingensmith, Delbert and Jerry Flora, and others demonstrate that this is possible.

A major challenge that has faced both the college/university and seminary is the relationship between the institution and the Brethren Church. The college had to face this challenge earlier, particularly in the 1930s and the 1960s and 70s. At the heart of the issue is that the Brethren Church is too small to provide the resources of finances, faculty, and students that are necessary to make the school viable. In the 1930s the college realistically and intentionally began to broaden its faculty, student, financial, and governance (the Board) bases beyond the church. The same issue came to the fore in the 1960s when the college grew at such a pace that the Brethren personal and fiscal presence was dwarfed. In spite of an outcry from the church during the 1970s and early 80s about the direction of the college, especially regarding the spiritual and moral climate on the campus, the church exercised a diminishing influence on the direction of the school. The church felt even more distanced from the college as it grew into the complexity of a university. Interestingly, however, due to the concerted effort of some Brethren trustees, there has been a renewed sense of connection to the university in recent years. It needs to be reinforced, however, that the church has never directly "owned" the university. There were compelling reasons in both 1878 and 1888 that the church and Board did not want to make the church legally responsible for the college's welfare.

One of the fascinating subplots of the history of the college-church relationship is the story of how the Christian faith is perceived at the college. There was a strong Christian presence and identity in the college until the early 1960s as testified by the fact that it was officially referred to as a Christian college until 1961. The rapid growth of the college during the 1960s, the counter-cultural perspective of students and faculty in the 1970s, and a growing openness to a secular perspective in the 1970s and 80s, especially among some faculty, served to lessen the Christian perspective on the campus. The official language of the relationship between the college and church was that the college was church-related or was affiliated with the church, but this relationship tended to be down-played. In 1978 Judeo-Christian, as the faith tradition of the college, also first appeared. Nonetheless, the continued affirmation of the spiritual foundations of the university in all recent identity statements speaks to the ongoing importance of the Christian faith, as well as the Jewish roots from which it sprang, within the character of the university. Ashland University is not a Christian college, but neither is it a secular university. In the coming years the university will need to grapple with how it understands its spiritual heritage and identity as it lives between these two poles. The recent differences between the faculty and the Board need to be placed within the larger context of this very issue.

An intriguing realization that has come from this research is how ingrained certain philosophies have become in the DNA of Ashland College/University. The theme of "Ac'cent on the Individual," though coined in 1964, reflects an educational philosophy that goes back to the 1930s when Charles Anspach developed his personalized and wholistic approach to higher education. In truth, however, this emphasis can be traced back to the earliest days of the college when the goal of the curriculum was to both train the mind and develop a character informed by Christian values. A second theme that can be traced throughout the history of the college/university is the dual commitment to a broad liberal arts education and to practical training for professions and careers. This dual emphasis can be seen in the earliest catalogues as well as recent ones. Integration of the liberal arts with professional training has been a hallmark of Ashland College/University. In 1989 Lucille Ford set forth Ashland's mission as "a fusing of the liberal arts and the professions. Professional education provides critical skills for given work positions while Liberal Arts education provides horizon lifting and vision, broadening experience."[2] There has also been a desire throughout the history of the institution to prepare students for the full range of personal and civic responsibility. This commitment is characteristic of liberal arts education but also is exemplified in Anspach's philosophy of a wholistic educational process that prepared the student socially, spiritually, physically, professionally, and civically.

Like the university, Ashland Theological Seminary has faced the challenge of forging an identity that encompasses constituencies beyond the Brethren Church. Joseph Shultz understood in the 1960s that if the seminary was to have a future, it could not rely exclusively on funding, students, and faculty from the church. The majority of the students were non-Brethren by the early 1970s and the majority of the full-time faculty were non-Brethren by the early 1980s. However, the Brethren Church still provides substantially more funding to the seminary than any other church or denomination. Whereas the Brethren Church emotionally distanced itself from the college during the 1980s, feeling it had lost any significant influence on the college's direction, the church has continued to maintain a strong commitment to the seminary. It is still seen as the preferred training ground for all Brethren ministerial students and its appeals for student scholarships, building campaigns, and special projects continue to receive significant support in the church from individuals and congregations. Nevertheless, the seminary must continue to cultivate broader relationships in the Christian community for the vital resources of students, faculty, and finances.

The identity of the seminary has been forged over the years both by its connection to the college/university and by several influential professors and deans. The legacy of J. Allen Miller to the seminary was a high regard for scholarship, but it was always understood that this scholarship should be in service to the church. This emphasis can be seen in the following statement from the 1937–38 catalogue:

> The main emphases of the Seminary are complete and uncompromising loyalty to the biblical and historical *Christian Faith*, the inculcation of competent *Christian Scholarship*, the nurture of a deeper spirituality in the *Christian Life*—all directed toward the goal of a practical *Christian Ministry*.[3]

Similar language can be found in official statements in seminary catalogues up to the present. It has remained a constant during the tenures of McClain, Flora, Shultz, and Finks. This idea of wedding training of the mind with preparation for professional life mirrors the philosophy of education that has been a tradition at the college/university.

The legacy of Joseph Shultz can be seen in the commitment to the development of extensions and the creation of programming for non-traditional students. He pioneered this concept first at the seminary, expressed in his idea of a "seminary without walls," but he made it the *modus operandi* for helping the college to survive in the early 1980s and to thrive in the latter 1980s. This spirit of innovation has continued to be a part of the seminary's psyche ever since, as seen in the desire to be a leading evangelical seminary during the tenure of Frederick Finks.

To Shultz is owed the original vision of taking theological education to the major urban centers, especially in service to the African-American community. Finks continued this vision, enhancing it with the further development of the work in Cleveland and the establishment and expansion of works in Detroit and Columbus. To Finks is owed the conviction to open the doors of the seminary fully to women, to the point that there are now more women in the seminary than men. Though there had always been a willingness at the seminary to provide theological education to women, there was also a reluctance to open pastoral training to women. To Finks is also owed the change in Article I of the university's constitution from the "training of suitable *men* for the ministry of the gospel shall always be sacredly regarded as one of the main objects of this institution" to the "training of suitable *persons* . . ." (italics mine).

Foundational to the education process of Ashland Theological Seminary have been several emphases that have been given explicit reinforcement in recent years. The core values of Scripture, Spiritual Formation, Community, and Academic Excellence, though first articulated in 1996, have been an essential part of the seminary's identity from the start. Just as important, the seminary's new curriculum model, which highlights the 4Cs of core identity, character, calling, and competence, makes explicit what has been implicit in the seminary's educational process since the inception of the seminary. The formation of the inner spiritual life has been seen from the start as the foundation upon which the rest of the student's training rests.

For the last decade the sense that "God has his hand on this place" has been a powerful reminder of his grace and of the calling that the seminary has to continue to be faithful to the One who is Lord of all, including Ashland Theological Seminary. Since 1993 the seminary's commencement service has concluded with the singing of *Find Us Faithful* by Jon Mohr. This music has stirred the collective soul of the seminary for these many years and has become almost a seminary anthem. It forms a fitting challenge and conclusion to this work.

> We're pilgrims on the journey of the narrow road,
> And those who've gone before us line the way;
> Cheering on the faithful, encouraging the weary,
> Their lives a stirring testament to God's sustaining grace.
> Surrounded by so great a cloud of witnesses,
> Let us run the race not only for the prize;
> But as those who've gone before us,
> Let us leave to those behind us
> The heritage of faithfulness passed on thru godly lives.
>
> Chorus:
>
> O may all who come behind us find us faithful;
> May the fire of our devotion light their way.
> May the footprints that we leave lead them to believe,
> And the lives we live inspire them to obey;
> O may all who come behind us find us faithful.
> After all our hopes and dreams have come and gone,
> And our children sift thru all we've left behind;
> May the clues that they discover and the mem'ries they uncover
> Become the light that leads them to the road we each must find.
>
> Chorus:
>
> O may all who come behind us find us faithful;
> May the fire of our devotion light their way.
> May the footprints that we leave lead them to believe,
> And the lives we live inspire them to obey;
> O may all who come behind us find us faithful.

Used with permission

May indeed we be found faithful in our generation as those entrusted today with the leadership of the seminary. May we pass on a legacy of faithfulness that will inspire dedication in the coming generations to the same vision that guided the founders of Ashland Theological Seminary. The "gleam of shining hope" that motivated J. Allen and Clara Worst Miller to dedicate a lifetime of sacrificial service to the college and seminary beckons us to dream what God can continue to do in both institutions as we remain faithful to him.

Miscellaneous Information About Ashland Theological Seminary

Key Administrators, Outstanding Alumni/Alumnae, and Lecture Series Speakers at Ashland Theological Seminary

Deans, Vice Presidents, and Presidents of Ashland Theological Seminary

J. Allen Miller	Dean	1906–1933
Alva J. McClain	Dean	1933–1937
Willis E. Ronk	Dean	1937–1943
Melvin A. Stuckey	Dean	1943–1951
Delbert B. Flora	Chairman of the Faculty	1951–1953
	Dean	1953–1963
Joseph R. Shultz	Dean	1963–1972
	Vice President	1972–1979
Charles R. Munson	Acting Dean	1980–1981
	Dean	1981–1985
Frederick J. Finks	Vice President	1982–1993
	Vice President of AU and President of ATS	1993–2006
John C. Shultz	Dean	1985–1988
	Vice President of AU and President of ATS	2006–
O. Kenneth Walther	Dean	1988–1991
Mary Ellen Drushal	Academic Dean	1991–1995
David F. Hartzfeld	Academic Dean	1996–2001
Dale R. Stoffer	Interim Dean	2001–2002
	Academic Dean	2002–

Directors, Coordinators, Deans of Extensions

Charles Ronkos	Cleveland Director of Counseling and Extension Programs	1974–1979
Theron H. Smith	Director of Extension Programs	1979–1986
Charles Ronkos	Director of Cleveland Programs	1986–1987
David E. Kornfield	Director of Detroit Program	1986–1988
Douglas M. Little	Director of Cleveland Programs	1987–1989
Jim Holley	Director of Detroit Program	1989–1991
Mary Ellen Drushal	Director of Cleveland Program	1989–1992
Ronald R. Emptage	Director of Detroit Center	1991–1999
	Dean of the Detroit Center	1999–
O. Kenneth Walther	Director of Cleveland Program	1992–1995
Walter J. Kime	Director of Cleveland Center	1995–2003
Brenda B.Colijn	Coordinator of Columbus Program	2000–
Mylion Waite	Associate Director of Cleveland Center	2003–

Outstanding Alumnus/Alumna Recipients

1976	Donald Rowser
1977	Kenneth Hulit
1978	Charles Kraft
1970	E. Phillip Lersch Jr.
1980	K. Prasanth Kumar
1981	George W. Primes Jr.
1982	Juan Carlos Miranda
1983	Alvin S. Shifflett
1984	Delbert B. Flora
1985	Charles R. Munson
1986	George W. Solomon
1987	Virgil E. Meyer
1988	Jerry Durham
1989	William Kerner
1990	Margaret Lowery
1991	Milton R. Henry
1992	John Christopher Thomas
1993	William R. Hoke
1994	No recipient
1995	Richard E. Allison

1996	Ruth C. Shannon
1997	No recipient
1998	David M. King
1999	Edward L. Branch
2000	Jerry R. Flora
2001	Robert L. Keplinger
2002	William H. Myers
2003	Gerald D. Cardwell
2004	Marc Farmer
2005	Maqdalena Winarni Kawotjo
2006	Frederick J. Finks

Fall Lecture Series Speakers

1975	James Earl Massey
1976	Raymond Dillard
1977	Timothy L. Smith
1978	Charles H. Kraft
1979	Albert J. Wollen
1980	Donald F. Durnbaugh, Stephen Olford, and Joseph R. Shultz (Jubilee Week Celebration)
1981	David Breese
1982	Carl F. H. Henry
1983	Richard N. Longenecker
1984	Samuel H. Moffett
1985	Owen H. Alderfer
1986	Dennis F. Kinlaw
1987	Richard Lovelace
1988	Gordon Fee
1989	J. I. Packer
1990	C. K. Barrett and Garth Rosell
1991	Thomas V. Morris
1992	Thomas V. Morris
1993	Christopher Armitage
1994	Gordon Wenham
1995	Bruce Winter
1996	Donald F. and Hedwig (Hedda) Durnbaugh
1997	Willard Swartley
1998	Barbara von der Heydt Elliott

1999	Donald E. Gowan
2000	Steve Harper
2001	Adela Yarbro Collins
2002	Clark Pinnock
2003	M. Daniel Carroll R.
2004	Miroslav Volf
2005	Cain Hope Felder
2006	Randall Balmer

(Spring) Ministry Conference Speakers

1980	Lyle Schaller
1981	Carl George
1982	Kenneth O. Gangel and J. Oswald Hoffmann
1983	Elisabeth Elliott and James Earl Massey
1984	Gene Getz
1985	George G. Hunter III
1986	Henry H. Mitchell
1987	Gary Collins and Gardner C. Taylor
1988	Donald Joy
1989	George G. Hunter III
1990	C. Peter Wagner
1991	William Bontrager
1992	Knute Larson
1993	Fred Craddock
1994	Siang Yan Tang
1995	Leith Anderson, David Augsburger, and Parker Palmer
1996	I. Howard Marshall
1997	Dieter Zander
1998	Martin Sanders
1999	Jerry R. Flora
2000	Gary Moon
2001	Richard Parrott
2002	Knute Larson
2003	Marva Dawn
2004	Marvin A. McMickle
2005	Douglas E. Rosenau
2006	Anthony T. Evans, Bill Hybels, and Knute Larson

Information about Commencement Services of Ashland Theological Seminary

Prior to 1979 seminary degrees were conferred at the commencement service of Ashland College. However, the seminary also held its own Graduate Service the day before the college commencement service at which the graduates of the seminary were honored. This service was held on the seminary grounds throughout the 1960s and 70s. The first time that the seminary had its own commencement service, including the conferral of degrees, was 1979. Following are details of the commencement services of Ashland Theological Seminary.

The 1982 graduation ceremony on the grounds of the seminary

Year	Location	Graduation Speaker	Number of Graduates
1979	Seminary Grounds	Paul L. Morell	61
1980	Seminary Grounds	Raymond Donald Shafer	97
1981	Seminary Grounds	Kenneth S. Kantzer	89
1982	Seminary Grounds	Bruce J. Nicholls	95
1983	Memorial Chapel	David Gitari	87
1984	Memorial Chapel	Richard Halverson	98
1985	Memorial Chapel	Paul E. Toms	85

(continued)

Year	Location	Graduation Speaker	Number of Graduates
1986	Memorial Chapel	Ernest L. Boyer	96
1987	Memorial Chapel	Dennis Campbell	93
1988	Memorial Chapel	Otis Moss Jr.	81
1989	Memorial Chapel	Charles R. Munson	88
1990	Memorial Chapel	Sanford C. Mitchell	93
1991	Memorial Chapel	James Earl Massey	89
1992	Memorial Chapel	Arthur M. Climenhaga	141
1993	Memorial Chapel	Knute Larson	124
1994	Memorial Chapel	Samuel DeWitt Proctor	137
1995	Memorial Chapel	Richard E. Allison	149
1996	Memorial Chapel	Ruth Shannon	144
1997	Memorial Chapel	Riggins R. Earl Jr.	152
1998	Kates Gymnasium	Gardner C. Taylor	158
1999	Convocation Center	Timothy George	132
2000	Convocation Center	Daniel Aleshire	170
2001	Convocation Center	Samuel T. Kamaleson	161
2002	Convocation Center	No speaker; expanded worship	171
2003	Convocation Center	Ned Adams Jr. Douglas M. Little Ronald R. Sprunger	154
2004	Convocation Center	David W. Baker John C. Shultz JoAnn Ford Watson	186
2005	Convocation Center	Ned Adams Jr. Brenda B. Colijn Eugene S. Gibbs	173
2006	Convocation Center	Frederick J. Finks	176

Faculty and Administrators at Ashland Theological Seminary (1906–2006) and in the Theological Department of Ashland College (1894–1906)

Names in the following list appear in the order that these people came to the seminary or to the college in the case of those who were first employed in the college. The dates are the period of their full-time service. The title represents the last faculty title that these people had in the seminary catalogues. If people served also as Dean, Vice President, or President of the seminary, this is also noted. Any significant administrative title change is likewise noted. Titles for current employees are those held at the beginning of the 2006–07 academic year.

Name	Title(s)	Dates of Service
J. Allen Miller	Professor of History and English Literature	1887–88
	Professor of History and Arithmetic	1888–89
	Dean of the Theological Department	1894–96, 1898
	President of Ashland College	1899–1906
	Dean of the Theological Department	1906–13
	Dean of Ashland Theological Seminary	1913–33
	Professor of New Testament and Greek	1906–35
William D. Furry	Professor of Philosophy	1900–04, 1943–57
	President of Ashland College	1911–19
	Dean of Ashland College	1919–33
Charles F. Yoder	Professor of Hermeneutics and Practical Theology	1902–07
John L. Gillin	Professor of Economics and Sociology	1905–11
	President of Ashland College	1907–11
John A. Garber	Professor of Religious Education	1915–27
Alva J. McClain	Professor of Christian Theology and Apologetics	1925–27, 1930–37
	Dean of Ashland Theological Seminary	1933–37
Kenneth M. Monroe	Professor of Old Testament and Hebrew	1927–35
Melvin A. Stuckey	Professor of Homiletics and Practical Theology	1927–51
	Dean of Ashland Theological Seminary	1943–51
Herman A. Hoyt	Professor of New Testament and Greek	1935–37
Willis E. Ronk	Professor of New Testament and Greek	1937–43, 1955–56
	Dean of Ashland Theological Seminary	1937–43
Leslie E. Lindower	Professor of Old Testament and Hebrew	1937–49
	Head of the Education Department of Ashland College	1951–66
	Dean of Ashland College	1952–72
	Director of the Library and Academic Research Center	1972–74
Delbert B. Flora	Professor of New Testament and Archaeology	1946–75
	Chairman of the Faculty	1951–53
	Dean of Ashland Theological Seminary	1953–63
Edwin E. Boardman Jr.	Professor of Church History	1949–68
Henry Bates	Associate Professor of Old Testament and Hebrew	1950–55
Charles Ralph Munson	Professor of Practical Theology	1954–85
	Acting Dean	1980–81
	Dean of Ashland Theological Seminary	1981–85

(continued)

Name	Title(s)	Dates of Service
Conrad Ralph Verno	Instructor of Hebrew and Old Testament	1955–57
J. Ray Klingensmith	Professor of English Bible	1956–77
Virgil E. Meyer	Director of Church Relations at Ashland College	1956–61
	Director of Religious Affairs at Ashland College	1961–72
	Director of Christian Ministries	1972–80
	Director of Student Life and Ministry	1980–81
Richard L. Hash	Instructor of Hebrew and Old Testament	1957–59
Bruce C. Stark	Professor of Hebrew and Old Testament	1959–70
Joseph R. Shultz	Dean of Ashland Theological Seminary	1963–72
	Vice President of Ashland Theological Seminary	1972–79
	Interim President of Ashland College	1979–80
	President of Ashland College	1980–89
	President of Ashland University	1989–92
Nancy Rhoades	Librarian	1964–79
Owen H. Alderfer	Professor of Church History	1965–80
Louis F. Gough	Professor of New Testament	1968–77
Albert T. Ronk	Brethren Church Historian and Archivist	1968–72
Bradley E. Weidenhamer	Librarian	1970–2001
Joseph N. Kickasola	Professor of Old Testament	1971–85
Jerry R. Flora	Professor of New Testament Theology and Spiritual Formation	1972–2002
Richard E. Allison	Professor of Christian Education	1974–97
	Director of Doctoral Studies	1980–94
Charles G. Ronkos	Professor of Pastoral Counseling	1977–87
	Director of Cleveland Center of Counseling and (Cleveland) Extension Programs	1977–79
	Consultant for the Cleveland Programs	1979–81
	Director of the C.P.I. Counseling Program	1981–87
	Director of Cleveland Programs	1986–87
O. Kenneth Walther	Professor of Greek and New Testament	1977–
	Dean	1988–91
	Director of Cleveland Program	1992–95
Arthur M. Climenhaga	Academic Assistant to the Dean	1978–80
	Director of Academic Affairs	1980–82
	Professor of Theology and Mission	1978–82
Theron H. Smith	Director of Extension Programs	1979–86
	Assistant Professor of Practical Theology	1985–86
Douglas E. Chismar	Associate Professor of Christian Thought	1980–84
David A. Rausch	Professor of Church History and Judaic Studies	1980–91
John C. Shultz	Professor of Pastoral Counseling	1981–
	Dean	1985–88
	President of Ashland Theological Seminary	2006–
Frederick J. Finks	President of Ashland Theological Seminary	1982–2006
	President of Ashland University	2006–

Name	Title(s)	Dates of Service
Mary Ellen Drushal	Associate Professor of Christian Education and Church Administration	1984–95
	Associate Dean of Continuing Education	1989–91
	Director of Cleveland Program	1989–92
	Academic Dean	1991–95
William H. Myers	Professor of New Testament and Black Church Studies	1984–
Ben Witherington III	Professor of Biblical and Wesleyan Studies	1984–95
David W. Baker	Professor of Old Testament and Semitic Languages	1986–
Thomas O. Brohm	Director of Recruitment	1986–88
	Director of Admissions	1988–90
David E. Kornfield	Director of Detroit Center for Theological Education	1986–88
Fred Holland	Professor of Missiology	1987–93
Luke L. Keefer Jr.	Professor of Church History and Theology	1987–
Douglas M. Little	Professor of Pastoral Counseling	1987–2003
	Director of Cleveland Center/CPI	1987–89
	Director of Southwest Pastoral Counseling Program	1989–93
	Director of Midwest Pastoral Counseling Program	1993–97
Lori K. Lower	Faculty Secretary	1988–90
	Administrative Assistant	1990–93
	Administrative Assistant and Assistant Registrar	1993–2004
	Registrar	2004–
Ronald L. Sprunger	Professor of Music	1988–2003
Jim Holley	Director of Detroit Program	1989–91
JoAnn Ford Watson	Professor of Christian Theology	1989–
Richard Fischl	Director of Admissions	1990–95
Bill T. Arnold	Professor of Old Testament and Semitic Languages	1991–95
Ronald R. Emptage	Professor of Church History	1991–
	Director of Detroit Program	1991–99
	Dean of Ashland Theological Seminary–Detroit	1999–
Dale R. Stoffer	Professor of Historical Theology	1992–
	Interim Dean	2001–02
	Academic Dean	2002–
Ned Adams Jr.	Director of Detroit Counseling Program	1993–2004
	Professor of Counseling	1993–2004
In Du Chae	Director of Korean Doctoral Program	1993–97
Grace S. Holland	Assistant Professor of Missiology	1993–99
Eugene S. Gibbs	Director of Doctor of Ministry Program	1994–97
	Professor of Christian Education	1997–2005
Mario Guerreiro	Director of Recruitment	1994–95
	Director of Admissions	1995–2003
Judy V. Allison	Professor of Pastoral Counseling	1995–2004
David A. deSilva	Professor of New Testament and Greek	1995–

(continued)

Name	Title(s)	Dates of Service
L. Daniel Hawk	Professor of Old Testament and Hebrew	1995–
Walter J. Kime	Director of Christian Studies	1995–
	Director of Cleveland Center	1995–2003
	Director of Profiles of Ministry and of Field Studies	1995–2002
	Chaplain of the Doctor of Ministry Program	2001–2004
	Associate Professor of Field Education	2002–
S. Robert Rosa	Director of Recruitment	1995–98
	Director of Student Life and Recruitment	1998–2003
	Dean of Student Development	2003–
Leroy A. Solomon	Director of Development	1995–98
	Dean of Institutional Development	1998–2005
	Dean of the Doctor of Ministry Program	2005–
Melissa L. Archer	Instructor in Greek and New Testament	1996–2001
David F. Hartzfeld	Academic Dean	1996–2001
	Professor of Old Testament	1996–2001
Marvin A. McMickle	Professor of Homiletics	1996–
Ronald W. Waters	Assistant Professor of Evangelism	1996–2001
Richard L. Parrott	Director of Doctor of Ministry Program	1997–2003
	Executive Director of the Sandberg Leadership Center	1999–2004
Michael F. Reuschling	Professor of Pastoral Counseling	1997–
	Director of the Midwest Pastoral Counseling Program	1997–
Karen Becker	Counselor and Director of Family Life Services	1998–2004
Terry Wardle	Professor of Church Planting and Spiritual Formation	1998–
David Kerner	Assistant Professor of Missions	1999–2001
Russell Morton	Research Librarian	1999–
Paul Overland	Associate Professor of Old Testament and Semitic Languages	1999–
Brenda B. Colijn	Associate Professor of Biblical Interpretation and Theology	2000–
	Coordinator of the ATS Columbus Program	2000–
Lynne Lawson	Secretary to the Director of Recruitment and Housing	2001–02
	Seminary Phone Receptionist	2001–02
	Administrative Assistant for the Sandberg Leadership Center	2002–03
	Administrative Assistant for The Institute of Formational Counseling	2003–06
	Assistant Director of The Institute of Formational Counseling	2006–
Sylvia Locher	Head Librarian	2001–
Shawn L. Oliver	Director of Curriculum and Academic Support Services	2001–03
	Associate Academic Dean	2003–

Vickie L. Taylor	Director of Technology Resources	2001–
William P. Payne	Associate Professor of Evangelism/Missions	2002–
Melissa W. Corbin Reuschling	Associate Professor of Ethics and Theology	2002–
John Byron	Assistant Professor of New Testament and Greek	2003–
Lori Byron	Administrative Assistant to the Sandberg Leadership Center	2003–2006
	Associate Program Manager for Specialized Small Group Retreats	2006–
Elaine A. Heath	Director of Doctor of Ministry Program	2003–2005
Cara L. Selan	Admissions Counselor	2003–
Mylion Waite	Associate Director of the Cleveland Center	2003–
Dell Elaine Lunt-Bednar	Family Life Counselor	2004–
Don Carver Sr.	Director of Alumni Relations	2004
Anthony Donofrio	Assistant Professor of Pastoral Counseling	2004–
J. Robert Douglass	Instructor of Music and Worship	2004–
Eugene Heacock	Executive Director of the Sandberg Leadership Center	2004–
Jerrolynn D. Johnson	Interim Director of Detroit Counseling Program	2004–2005
	Director of Detroit Counseling Program	2005–
David P. Mann	Associate Professor of Pastoral Counseling	2004–
Keith Marlett	Director of Smetzer Counseling Center	2004–
Lee Wetherbee	Associate Professor of Pastoral Counseling	2004–
Glenn Black	Admissions Counselor	2005–
Eric Sandberg	Director of Alumni Relations	2005–
Michael B. Thompson	Associate Professor of Practical Theology	2005–
Rodney Caruthers III	Admissions Counselor	2006–
Michael L. Catanzarito	Associate Program Manager to Pastors of Excellence Program	2006–
David Cooksey	Director of Church Relations	2006–
George H. Johnson	Coordinator of Student Support Services	2006–
Martha J. Smith	Admissions Counselor	2006–
Mitzi J. Smith	Assistant Professor of New Testament and Early Christianity	2006–
Mariah A. Wright	Director of the Fund for Theological Education	2006–

Endnotes

Chapter 1: Background to the Establishment of Ashland College and Its Early Years (to 1882)

1. Donald F. Durnbaugh, *Fruit of the Vine: A History of the Brethren, 1708–1995* (Elgin, IL: Brethren Press, 1997), 244. Durnbaugh also notes the sarcasm that Sauer aimed at the "follies of educated persons, to whom he referred by spelling their title as *Doc-tor* (a play on words in German, using the word *tor* or fool)."

2. S. Z. Sharp, *The Educational History of The Church of the Brethren* (Elgin, IL: Brethren Publishing House, 1923), 41–43, lists Henry Kurtz, James Quinter, Peter Nead, Isaac Price, John Wise, and Enoch Eby, among others.

3. The General Mission Board, *Minutes of the Annual Meetings of the Church of the Brethren, Containing all Available Minutes from 1778 to 1909* (Elgin, IL: Brethren Publishing House, 1909), 1853, Art. 28, pp. 138–139. See also 1831, Art. 1, p. 54; 1852, Art. 12, p. 130; and 1857, Art. 19, p. 165.

4. For example, see H[enry]. K[urtz]. of M[ahoning]., "On Education, Colleges, &c.," *The Gospel Visitor* 5 (March 1855): 55; Rufus, "On Education," *The Gospel Visitor* 5 (January 1855): 9–12; and Rufus, "The Contemplated School," *The Gospel Visitor* 6 (September 1856): 246–248.

5. [Henry Kurtz, Editorial Comments], *The Gospel Visitor* 4 (December 1854): 155.

6. Dale R. Stoffer, *Background and Development of Brethren Doctrines, 1650–1987* (Philadelphia: Brethren Encyclopedia, Inc., 1989), 135.

7. General Mission Board, *Minutes*, 1858, Art. 51, p. 178.

8. J. L. Forney, *Christian Family Companion* 3 (2 July 1867): 218.

9. H. R. Holsinger, *History of the Tunkers and The Brethren Church* (Oakland, CA: Pacific Press Publishing Co., 1901), 473–474. Elsewhere in this work, Holsinger, reflecting on the poor homiletic skills of Brethren ministers, stated, "Many a time, but not every time, we have heard a long, rambling, illogical,

ungrammatical, confused, vehement discourse, which would scatter any other but a Tunker congregation to the four winds." Holsinger, *History of the Tunkers*, 248.

10. Clara Worst Miller and E. Glenn Mason, *A Short History of Ashland College to 1953* (n.p. [Ashland, OH]: Ashland College Diamond Jubilee Committee, 1953), 10 and S. Z. Sharp, "The Origin and Early History of Ashland College, Ohio," TMs [photocopy], p. 1, Ronk files, Brethren Church Archives, Brethren Church National Office, Ashland, Ohio.

11. Miller and Mason, *Short History*, 16. Myers is the great-great grandfather of JoAnn Ford Watson, a faculty member at the seminary.

12. Sharp, "Early History of Ashland College," 1 claims that at this time only three men in the German Baptist Brethren Church had obtained a college education: Lewis Kimmel, mentioned earlier, O. W. Miller, president of a short-lived Brethren school, Salem College, and himself.

13. Sharp, *Educational History*, 98 and Donald F. Durnbaugh, ed. *The Brethren Encyclopedia* (Philadelphia, PA: The Brethren Encyclopedia, Inc, 1983), s.v. "Sharp, Solomon Zook," by Elgin S. Moyer and Dennis D. Martin.

14. Miller and Mason, *Short History*, 12.

15. Other important leaders in Ashland who played key roles at this point were Joseph E. Stubbs, a Methodist minister who would later serve as acting president of Ashland College, and president of both Baldwin-Wallace College and the University of Nevada; Judge Osborn, father of Belle Osborn, after whom an elementary school in Ashland is named; Jacob Cahn, a clothier who donated the land for Cahn Grove, a park in Ashland; J. O. Jennings, president of the First National Bank; and B. F. Nelson and L. J. Sprengle, the editors of Ashland's two newspapers. Betty Plank, "Dream, Vision Led to Formation of AU," *Ashland Times-Gazette*, 22 February 2003, sec. A, p. 3.

16. H. [I.] D. Parker and E. L. Yoder, "The New College," *The Ashland Press*, 2 August 1877, 3.

17. Miller and Mason, *Short History*, 14–15. The five temporary trustees were Austin Moherman, John Shidler, Richard Arnold, Henry K. Myers, and E. L. Yoder. "Ashland College," *The Ashland Times*, 21 February 1878, 4.

18. S. Z. Sharp, "Ashland College," *The Brethren at Work* 4 (22 May 1879): 7.

19. The Board of Incorporators was composed of Henry K. Myers, Austin Moherman, John Shidler, Richard Arnold, William Sadler, Isaac D. Parker, and Alpheus M. Dickey. See Miller and Mason, *Short History*, 16. Shidler, Sadler, Myers, Dickey and Arnold were members of the Maple Grove church; Moherman and Parker were from the Dickey church (both Myers and Arnold lived in Ashland and became members of the Ashland City church that was started in connection with the college in 1879).

20. Glenn L. Clayton, "Whispering Pines and Purple Eagles," 1979, TMs [photocopy], p. 331, Ashland University Archives, Ashland University, Ashland, OH. Clayton's book by the same name had not yet been published when I began researching and writing this work. Therefore, all references in this work refer to his original manuscript.

21. Sharp, *Educational History*, 98. Sharp wanted to amend this statement to read: "All its officers shall be members of the Dunker Church and loyal to the decisions of the Annual Meeting of said church." The trustees did not feel this change was necessary because all the officers were members of the church and the majority were elders. Had this change been made to the charter, Ashland College probably would have stayed with the German Baptist Brethren.

22. Several who have written histories of the college have commented about this omission. See Clayton, "Whispering Pines and Purple Eagles," 332 and Miller and Mason, *Short History*, 31.

23. Durnbaugh, *Fruit of the Vine*, 251. Ashland College may have been unique among Brethren colleges in that it provided for a Bible department at the outset. Durnbaugh observes that the earliest Brethren schools omitted Bible departments in order "to reassure the church that religious instruction would remain squarely in the hands of the families and congregations at home." Ashland College's inclusion of a Bible department may indicate the more progressive viewpoint present at the college without, however, stepping over the line of the training of ministers. Observations included in an article in *The Gospel Preacher* immediately following the opening of the college shed additional light on this point. The article noted, "The curriculum embraces a full scientific course, Normal and Preparatory departments, and everything usually taught in colleges, but not a full 'University course.' The Brethren here object to having a department of Law, of Theology, or of Medicine, as all schools have which embrace a complete University course." "Opening of Ashland College," *The Gospel Preacher* 1 (24 September 1879): 2. The omission of such departments was due not only to limited faculty resources, but especially, in the case of law and theology, to Brethren objections to training for these professions.

24. General Mission Board, *Minutes*, 1882, Art. 10, p. 407. This was the same Annual Meeting that disfellowshipped Holsinger and his Progressive followers.

25. Clayton, "Whispering Pines and Purple Eagles," 332.

26. *Annual Catalogue of Ashland College, Ohio, for the Academic Year 1879–80* (Ashland, OH: John C. Stubbs & Brother, Printers, 1880), 21–24.

27. See General Mission Board, *Minutes*, 1874, Art. 10, pp. 317–318 and 1881, Art. 26, pp. 400–401. In both these articles Annual Meeting disapproved of the use of the term "Brethren's School." Annual Meeting reasoned that the phrase was not only offensive to some Brethren, but it also gave the impression that the general church supported the institution.

28. S. Z. Sharp, "Ashland College," *The Brethren at Work* 4 (22 May 1879): 7.

29. The original Board of Trustees was elected by those Brethren who had donated fifty dollars or more to the college. In the 1880 election of the Board, both "brethren and sisters" were encouraged to vote, providing they had donated at least fifty dollars. In fact, those donating more than fifty dollars received one vote for every fifty dollars donated. By March 1881 the Board had assumed control of its own elections. See H. K. Myers, "Ashland College Trustees' Election," *The Gospel Preacher* (14 June 1880): 3 and "The Trustees of Ashland College," *The Gospel Preacher—Supplement* (n.d. [March 1881]): 2.

30. There is some discrepancy in the listing of the first Board. A contemporary notice in one of the Brethren periodical names the trustees as: Austin Moherman, John Shidler, Henry K. Myers, Richard Arnold, I. D. Parker, A. M. Dickey, William Sadler, J. N. Roop, William Workman, A. J. Hixson, E. L. Yoder, George Irvin, Jacob Mishler, J. A. Clement, and Josiah Keim. H. K. Myers, "School Notes," *The Primitive Christian and The Pilgrim* 2 (5 March 1878): 142. This list is identical to one that appears in *The Ashland Times* following the selection of the original trustees. "Ashland College," *The Ashland Times*, 28 February 1878, 5. Clara Worst Miller cites a list compiled by one of the original faculty members, David Bailey, that has all the above names with the exception of adding Richard Moherman, P. J. Brown, and Adam Zimmerman and omitting William Workman and J. A. Clement. Miller and Mason, *Short History*, 17. The lists in *The Primitive Christian and The Pilgrim* and *The Ashland Times* obviously take precedence on this matter. The elders and ministers in these three lists were: I. D. Parker, A. M. Dickey, William Sadler, William Workman, A. J. Hixson, E. L. Yoder, George Irvin (Irwin), Jacob Mishler, John A. Clement, Josiah Keim, and P. J. Brown. The Maple Grove church was represented by William Sadler, Alpheus Dickey, Joseph N. Roop, John Shidler (Shidler was a member of the Dickey church earlier in his life), and Richard Arnold; H. K. Myers, who sided with the Progressives, was originally from this church. Austin Moherman, Richard Moherman, Isaac D. Parker, and Adam Zimmerman were members at the Dickey church. William Workman was an elder in the Loudonville congregation; Armanis J. Hixson was an elder in the Highland congregation in Highland County in southern Ohio; Eli L. Yoder and George Irvin (Irwin) were ministers in the Chippewa congregation in Wayne County (Irvin was the presiding elder); P. J. Brown was an elder in the Mohican congregation in Wayne County; Jacob Mishler was a minister in the Springfield church in Summit County; Josiah Keim was a minister in the Canton church; and John A. Clement was an elder in the Sandy congregation in Columbiana County.

31. The actual purchase occurred on 12 April 1878 and consisted of properties that were held by A. H. Myers, W. H. H. Potter, and the Ashland Real Estate Company. The purchase price was $5,500. *The Ashland Press*, 18 April 1878, 3. The Potter property consisted of 14 acres and accounted for $2,900 of the total purchase price. "Dr. Miller Gives Story of College," *Ashland Collegian* 19 (20 February 1931): 4. J. E. Stubbs, the editor of *The Ashland Times*, praised the "peculiar beauty" of the site. The view from the property was "delightful by its rich and picturesque diversity, hills and valleys, woods and fields, offering a series of panoramic, ever-changing pictures to the eye." The elevation of the plot afforded air that was "fresh and pure"; future students would "find health and delight in its cool exhilaration." J. E. Stubbs, "On the Heights," *The Ashland Times* 18 April 1878, 4. The first catalogue confirmed the importance of these elements in the selection of the site. The grounds "were selected on account of their elevation, pure air, freedom from malarial diseases, and extent and beauty of the landscape." *Catalogue of Ashland College for the Academic Year 1879–80*, 27.

32. The Board of Trustees authorized the construction of the boarding hall at its meeting on 10 June 1879. S. Z. S. [Sharp], "Trustee Meeting," *The Gospel Preacher* 1 (18 June 1879): 2.

33. Sharp, "Early History of Ashland College," 4; Miller and Mason, *Short History*, 20–21; *The Ashland Times*, 19 June 1879, 5; *The Ashland Times*, 7 August 1879, 5; and David Bailey, "Annals of an Unsuccessful Life. (An Autobiography)," *The Brethren Evangelist* (hereafter *BE*) 30 (1 July 1908): 3.

34. There are differing numbers given for both the beginning and ending figures. Accounts of the opening day of the college give enrollment at anywhere from 50 (*The Ashland Times*) to 75 (*The Ashland Press*). "Ashland College," *The Ashland Times*, 18 September 1879, 4 and "Ashland College," *The Ashland Press*, 18 September 1879, 3; see also Miller and Mason, *Short History*, 21. Sharp indicates that opening day enrollment was 60, and I have chosen to use this figure. Holsinger, *History of the Tunkers*, 272, gives the opening enrollment as 60 as well. Sharp also gives the end-of-year enrollment as 102, but Clara Worst Miller cites a report by R. H. Miller, the new president of the college, in December 1880 that nearly 200 students were enrolled at the end of the first academic year. The catalogue for 1879–80 helps to reconcile these latter numbers. It indicates that total enrollment, both undergraduate and preparatory, was 187. *Catalogue of Ashland College for the Academic Year 1879–80*, 13. R. H. Miller's statement that the "first year closed with a total enrollment of nearly two hundred" is based on tabulating all the students who attended the college throughout the first year. Clara Worst Miller indicates that the second academic year opened with 108 students enrolled. Miller and Mason, *Short History*, 22.

35. Jacob Keim, "College Items," *The Gospel Preacher* 1 [3] (24 December 1881): 585.

36. Sharp, "Early History of Ashland College," 4. Sharp places the loan for the boarding hall at $15,000, but other sources place the cost of the boarding hall at $20,000 and the indebtedness on the buildings at $20,000. The discrepancy could be accounted for by some indebtedness resulting from the construction of Founders Hall or by an attempt by Sharp to minimize the amount of indebtedness left at the end of his tenure. See also Albert Ronk, "Ashland College," TMs (photocopy), p. 4, Ronk files, Brethren Church Archives, Brethren Church National Office, Ashland, OH and D.[avid] Bailey, "Solomon Z. Sharp and the Ashland City Church," *BE* 9 (21 December 1887): 2.

37. Holsinger, *History of the Tunkers*, 272, reveals that Sharp was forced to resign due to personal disputes with the Trustees. He also indicates that though Sharp "was a popular teacher, he lacked in executive ability as the head of the institution." David Bailey reveals that the Board of Trustees was especially concerned about Sharp's failure to canvass for funds and students. Bailey, "Solomon Z. Sharp and the Ashland City Church," 3.

38. Sharp, "Early History of Ashland College," 6.

39. E. E. Jacobs, "A Brief History of Ashland College," *Ashland College Bulletin* 6 (November 1932): 8.

40. Sharp, "Early History of Ashland College," 5.

41. Ibid., 4–5. See also Miller and Mason, *Short History*, 29–30.

42. General Mission Board, *Minutes*, 1881, Art. 4, p. 394.

43. The Progressive Brethren on the Board were H. K. Myers, Richard Arnold, A. J. Hixson, E. L. Yoder, and Josiah Keim. P. J. Brown, who was cited on the list found in Miller and Mason, *Short History*, 17, was also a Progressive Brethren.

44. H. R. Holsinger and S. H. Bashor, "Another College," *The Progressive Christian* 3 (11 November 1881): 2 and S. Kiser, "Progressive College Wanted," *The Progressive Christian* 3 (18 November 1881): 3.

45. Miller and Mason, *Short History*, 28. See also J. Keim et al., "Explanation of the Faculty of Ashland College," *The Progressive Christian* 4 (31 March 1882): 3.

46. Three trustees had resigned shortly after the Board, at Sharp's urging, had approved borrowing funds to build the boarding hall. Presumably, they were Conservative in persuasion. See Bailey, "Solomon Z. Sharp and the Ashland City Church," 2. At the time that the 1881–82 catalogue was published, presumably in the spring of 1881, the Conservatives still held a sizeable majority; there were 10 Conservatives and 6 Progressives on the Board. In the 24 December 1881 issue of *The Gospel Preacher*, H. M. Lichty observed that at this time "about half of the trustees and the President [who had just resigned] are claimed by the Conservatives, and the remainder of the Trustees and teachers by the Progressives." H. M. Lichty, "Ashland College," *The Gospel Preacher* 1 [3] (24 December 1881): 586.

47. At the November 1881 Board of Trustees meeting, Progressives William Kiefer and C. A. Coler were appointed to the vacancies created by the resignation of the Conservative trustees George Irvin and Austin Moherman. S. A. Walker, another Conservative, had also tendered his resignation, but the Board did not accept his resignation. "Editorial Miscellany." *The Progressive Christian* 4 (15 November 1882): 3.

48. Miller and Mason, *Short History*, 28. In an article in late November 1882, E. L. Yoder sought to set the record straight when the Progressives were charged with "turning them [the Conservative Board members] out of the college." He reinforced that the Progressives did not deprive any Conservatives of their right to representation on the Board. E. L. Yoder, "A Correction," *The Progressive Christian* 4 (29 November 1882): 1.

49. *Proceedings of the General Convention of the Brethren Church Held at Ashland, Ohio, on September 21, 22 and 23, 1887*, by Edward Mason, reporter (Ashland, OH: The Brethren Publishing House, 1887), 42. P. J. Brown does indicate that this resolution was a bridge that "when we got there we passed safely over Jordan, and took Ashland College with us."

50. Yoder, "A Correction," 1.

51. *Catalogue of Ashland College for the Academic Year 1879–80*, 24.

52. *Second Annual Catalogue of Ashland College, Ohio, for the Academic Year 1880–81 [1881–82]* (Ashland, OH: John C. Stubbs & Brother, Printers, 1881), 24.

53. *Catalogue of Ashland College for the Academic Year 1880–81 [1881–82]*, 24.

Chapter 2: Years of Crisis and the Beginning of Theological Education (1882–1898)

1. At the 1887 Convention of The Brethren Church, S. H. Bashor observed that "It has been frequently stated that we cannot hold the College, that we have no right to it, and that the G.[erman] B.[aptist]'s can at any moment

have it from us. " P. J. Brown also claimed that "S. Z. Sharp originated the idea among them [the German Baptists] that when we have the debt paid, they will take the College." *General Convention of 1887*, 41, 43.

2. *Report of Progressive Convention, Held at Ashland, Ohio. Commencing June 29, 1882* (n.p., n.d.), 25.

3. Ibid. John H. Worst had a distinguished career in education and politics. The first student to enroll in Ashland College in 1879 (he was in the Biblical Department), he early served as a minister in the Brethren Church. In 1883 he moved to North Dakota and there became a County Superintendent of Schools. Later he was elected to the North Dakota State Senate and to the office of Lieutenant Governor (1895–96). He was a one-time candidate for the U.S. Senate. He became President of the North Dakota Agricultural College, now North Dakota State University, a position he held from 1895 to 1916. In recognition of his distinguished career, Ashland College awarded him an honorary Doctor of Laws degree. Miller and Mason, *Short History*, 22.

4. See the list of unmistakable signs that the German Baptists were not interested in mending the schism in Stoffer, *Background and Development*, 151.

5. *Proceedings of the Dayton Convention held by the Brethren Church, in Music Hall, Dayton, O. on June 6th and 7th, 1883*, by L. B. Clifton, reporter (Dayton, OH: Daily Journal Job Rooms, 1883), 49.

6. Ronk, "Ashland College," 3.

7. *General Convention of 1887*, 30, 42–43 and *The Brethren Annual for the Year of our Lord 1887* (Ashland, OH: The Brethren Publishing House, [1886]), 29.

8. Miller and Mason, *Short History*, 20.

9. For a review of the financial situation facing the college drawn from *Brethren Evangelist* articles, see Ronk, "Ashland College." See also Jacobs, "A Brief History," 8–11; Holsinger, *History of the Tunkers*, 544; and *Brethren Annual for 1887*, 29–30. In the 1888 *Brethren Annual*, David Bailey reveals that the first-term enrollment in 1885 was 5 students, in 1886 the enrollment was 25 students, and in 1887 it was 35 students. The low enrollment was due to both a diminished Brethren clientele because of the division and the tarnished image of the college in the Ashland community due to the turmoil. See *Brethren Annual for 1887*, 34 and *The Brethren Annual for the Year of our Lord 1888* (Ashland, OH: The Brethren Publishing House, [1887]), 24.

10. These curricular changes occurred after the Progressive trustees had a firm hold on the college. As an attempt to cut costs and to retain a faculty amenable to the new directions of the college, all faculty were asked to resign in 1883. Only those faculty who fit into the new philosophy of the college were rehired. The revised curriculum offered the following courses of study: Preparatory, Business, Teachers' (Normal), Scientific, and Classic. Reporter, "College Notes," *The Progressive Christian* 5 (18 April 1883): 3 and David Bailey, "Ashland College," *The Progressive Christian* 5 (2 May 1883): 4. The solicitors who were in the field at various times in 1882 and 1883 were A. J. Hixson, E. L. Yoder, J. H. Swihart, and R. Z. Replogle.

11. *General Convention of 1887*, 22. Holsinger began his canvass of Brethren churches on 29 July 1884. See *The Brethren's Annual for the Year of Grace 1885* (Ashland, OH: H.R. Holsinger & Co., [1884]), 38.

12. *General Convention of 1887*, 27.

13. Ibid., 26.

14. Ibid., 29–31, 44–45. Holsinger's motion was referred to committee and, after the committee had given its report, S. H. Bashor made the following motion, which was adopted by the convention:

> I move that we earnestly urge each member all through the church of the entire brotherhood to pay one dollar per annum until the debt that now burdens the College be paid off; and that the delegates and pastors present at this convention go home, and do all in their power toward making this motion the unanimous sentiment of the whole Brethren Church, and that the proceeds be sent at once to H. K. Myers, Ashland, Ohio.

> Bashor was a powerful orator and the most effective evangelist in the church. The reporter for the convention commented about Bashor's motion and subsequent speech: "The fire took hold of the speaker and spread through the convention until every one was warmed up. The words seemed to burn as they entered the heart, and every one felt that the decisive moment had come as they had never felt it before." *General Convention of 1887*, 44. Unfortunately, the warmed hearts cooled very quickly after the close of the convention.

15. Henry Holsinger, in a note of prophetic realism, closed the conference with the observation that "he had hoped that something definite would be done for Ashland College, but he had been disappointed; others might feel hopeful, but he had seen so many bursts of enthusiasm, that he could not trust to this." Ibid., 55.

16. "The College and Vicinity," *BE* 10 (2 May 1888): 4; Ronk, "Ashland College," 8; Miller and Mason, *Short History*, 33; I. D. Bowman, "A Statement by One of the Organizers of Ashland College," TMs (photocopy), p. 1, Ashland University Archives, Ashland University, Ashland, OH; and *The Brethren Annual, for the Year of our Lord 1889* (Ashland, OH: The Brethren Publishing House, [1888]), 18.

17. *Minute Book of the Board of Trustees of Ashland College* (hereafter *Minute Book of the Board*), 18 June 1888, 12.

18. Bank Street obtained its name because the land in the area was owned and developed by the Citizen's Bank. When E. E. Jacobs was president of the college, he campaigned to change the name of the street to College Avenue. Betty Plank, "Publications Reveal Histories of Area Schools," *Ashland Times-Gazette*, 4 February 2006, sec. A, p. 3.

19. Jacobs, "Brief History," 10 and Sharp, "Early History of Ashland College," 6. Further details about the purchase appear in a *Brethren Evangelist* article in 1890. Josiah Keim reported that "the entire college property was sold out by a receiver for $23,142.50" and that the "old trustees" paid "the deficiency of $17,857.50 out of their own pockets." Josiah Keim, "Richard Arnold Corrected," *BE* 12 (14 May 1890): 8. Presumably the $23,142.50 purchase price included the $4000 paid by the Conservatives for the eastern portion of the college property, the $18,500 pledged in the form of securities by members of the Brethren Church for the property upon which the college buildings stood,

and the $842 worth of "personal property." There is a discrepancy of $200 between these two purchase totals, however. Handwritten notes by A. L. Garber reinforce the significant contributions of the Conservatives to support Ashland College and liquidate its indebtedness. In a list entitled "Sums of Money Paid by Old Trustees of Ashland College," Garber enters the name of twelve early trustees, six of whom were Conservatives—Cyrus Hoover, Reuben Buckwalter, Austin Moherman, I. D. Parker, John Shidler, and George Irwin—and six of whom were Progressives—Richard Arnold, H. K. Myers, A. L. Garber, Josiah Keim, E. L. Yoder, and H. K. [P. J.] Brown. The Conservative ex-trustees paid $20,000 while the Progressives paid $10,566. Apparently these figures included payments made both at the time of the sale of Ashland College and prior to it. A. L. Garber, "Sketch Book, General Convention of the Brethren Church at Warsaw, Ind., August 23–27, 1892," p. 21, Ashland University Archives, Ashland University, Ashland, OH. I. D. Parker also observed in 1882 that the Conservatives had donated much of the money that had made the college a reality. I. D. Parker, "The Difference Again," *The Progressive Christian* 4 (5 July 1882): 2.

20. *Minute Book of the Board*, 8 August 1888, 13. The purchasers failed to meet the conditions of the sale and in December 1888 a second private sale occurred under the supervision of the receiver, Cloyd Mansfield. It is presumed that at this second sale the college property was deeded to Silas E. Shook. See D. C. Christner and the Board of Trustees, *The Legal and Historical Records and Official Report of Ashland University* (Ashland, OH: Johnson Bros., Print, n.d. [1892]), 8–9.

21. J. A. Miller, "Ashland College," *BE* 25 (21 January 1903): 1.

22. The presidents or heads of Ashland College from 1879 until 1898 were:

1879–1880	Solomon Z. Sharp (a Conservative who remained with the German Baptist Brethren)
1880–1881	Robert H. Miller (a Conservative who remained with the German Baptist Brethren)
1882	Joseph E. Stubbs (vice president and acting president; a Methodist minister)
1882–1883	Elijah Burgess (vice president and acting president; presumably non-Brethren)
1883–1885	Hiram Frank Hixson (a professor who served as president; son of trustee, A. J. Hixson, and a member of the first graduating class in 1881; an original faculty member)
1885	A. E. Winters (never assumed office; non-Brethren, though with Brethren background)
1885–1887	W. C. Perry (a former teacher who served as principal; an 1885 graduate)
1887–1888	William W. Felger (an Ashland attorney who served as principal; non-Brethren; an 1885 graduate)
1888–1891	J. M. Tombaugh
1891–1892	D. C. Christner

1892–1893	C. W. Mykrantz (an Ashland teacher; non-Brethren; he taught at the college in 1883; the college apparently was not officially in session under him; the Board minutes indicate that he leased the college facilities from the Board)
1893–1894	S. S. Garst (failed to secure a faculty for fall 1894, German Baptist Brethren)
1894–1895	J. M. Tombaugh (nominal)
1895–1896	J. Allen Miller
1897–1899	J. C. Mackey (nominal, non-resident)

For more details about these presidents and principals of the college, see "Editorial Miscellany," *The Gospel Preacher* 4 (7 March 1882): 2, 3; "Ashland College," *The Progressive Christian* 4 (16 August 1882): 3; "College Notes," *The Progressive Christian* 5 (27 June 1883): 2; Miller and Mason, *Short History*, 23, 27, 29, 38, 97–98; Jacobs, "Brief History," 8–9, 13–14, 19–20; Holsinger, *History of the Tunkers*, 272; *Minute Book of the Ashland City Church* [Park Street Brethren Church], 25 December 1885, 38–43, Brethren Church Archives, Brethren Church National Office, Ashland, OH; D. Ray Heisey, *Healing Body and Soul: The Life and Times of Dr. W. O. Baker* (Grantham, PA: The Brethren in Christ Historical Society, 2004), 311–332; Christner and the Board of Trustees, *Legal and Historical Records and Official Report of Ashland University*; Garber, "Sketch Book," 11; A. L. Garber, "A Brief Review of 'The Legal and Historical Records and Official Report of Ashland University,'" *Supplement to The Prophetic Age* (September 1892): 3–4, 6–8; *Brethren Annual for 1887*, 34; and *Brethren Annual for 1888*, 24.

23. An especially low point in the history of the college occurred in 1891–92. Serious rifts took place between the Brethren denomination and the college, between the college and the Ashland City Church, and between the college and H.R. Holsinger, the editor of *The Brethren Evangelist*. There was also an awkward relationship between Holsinger and the General Conference of the Brethren Church. This discord surrounded an acrimonious relationship that developed between Silas E. Shook, on one side, and the Board of Trustees and, eventually, D. C. Christner, the college president from 1891 to 1892, on the other side. Shook had accepted title to the college property in 1888 on behalf of the Board and the Brethren Church. He was a faculty member and manager of the boarding hall; he also assumed the roles of secretary and financial manager of the college. Serious questions arose about his handling of the college's finances, and the Board found it necessary to dismiss him in December 1891. Shook did not go quietly and was able to gain the support of both A. L. Garber, who was the pastor of the Ashland City Church (1891–94), which met in the college chapel, and Henry Holsinger. Holsinger refused to print the official record of the college for the academic year 1891–92 in *The Brethren Evangelist*; the constitution of the college required that the official report be published in the "official church organ." The college independently printed the report as a pamphlet and distributed it to the Brethren Church.

The rift between the college and Holsinger is further evidenced in the minutes of the Board of Trustees that indicate that Holsinger, David Bailey, and H. K. Myers, who had all served as solicitors for the college, refused to give an accounting of the pledges, notes, and monies they had received.

The conflict also spilled over into the relationship between the college and the Ashland City Church. A. L. Garber, the pastor of the church, sided with Shook and became very critical of the way Christner and the Board managed the college. The minutes of the Board of Trustees briefly note that Garber had "spoken disrespectfully of the present management" of the college. The Board of Trustees, on its part, refused to allow the church to use the college for services unless the church was willing to work in harmony with the college. These troubles were compounded when the threat of foreclosure faced the college in early 1892. Christner was forced to find new loans to cover the loans that were being called in. Shook continued his assault on the college by opening a short-lived opposition school in Ashland, by attempting to take over the pulpit during a college chapel service to publicize his cause (he was arrested), and by distributing handbills in the city of Ashland declaring that "President Christner will be shaken by Shook." Christner eventually resigned after the 1891–92 academic year, no doubt due to the stress created by this situation.

This highly contentious episode, in which both sides showed less than Christian grace, may help to explain several developments, both personal and corporate, in the church. A. L. Garber began to pull away from the college and church and eventually distanced himself from the institutions that had meant so much to him. He obliquely stated in 1904 that he "still regards himself as an honorary member of the Brethren Church . . . and was a party in the management of its College here in Ashland for several years. But the close denominational methods of churches became distasteful to him." [A. L. Garber], "Susan Leedy-Garber-Dyer and her Family," *The Leedy Chronicle* 5 (April 1904): 5, microfiche 4:405. Holsinger's refusal to print the Ashland College report may have spurred the 1892 General Conference to complete the task authorized by the 1887 Convention of purchasing *The Brethren Evangelist* and thereby placing it under church control. *Report of the National Convention of the Brethren Churches, Held at Warsaw, Indiana, August 23rd, 24th, 25th, 26th, and 27th, 1892* (Waterloo, IA: Brethren Publishing Co., 1893), 3–5. Indeed, Holsinger had stated in *The Brethren Evangelist* in 1890 that "This organization [the Waterloo Brethren Publishing Company that published *The Brethren Evangelist*] will not place its control under the direct management of the Church at large." Quoted in Christner and the Board of Trustees, *Legal and Historical Records and Official Report of Ashland University*, 11. The Shook affair exemplified the problematic nature of the private ownership of *The Brethren Evangelist*. For details about this entire episode, see Christner and the Board of Trustees, *Legal and Historical Records and Official Report of Ashland University*; Garber, "A Brief Review"; *Minute Book of the Board*, 17 June 1892, 69–70, 74–76; and *Minute Book of the Ashland City Church*, 54–57.

Relations between the college and the Brethren Publishing Company improved with the change of leadership at the college, with the purchase of the publishing interests of the church by the denomination, and with the return of the Brethren Publishing Company to Ashland in 1893. In October 1893 the college offered free space to the Brethren Publishing Company and to its new editor, S. J. Harrison, and his family in the Boarding Hall for the next five years. The rift between the college and the college church was smoothed when A. L. Garber resigned in 1894 and S. J. Harrison accepted the call to be the pastor of the church. *Minute Book of the Board*, 13 October 1893, 80 and *Minute Book of the Ashland City Church*, 18 February 1894, 59.

24. At the 1893 General Conference of the Brethren Church the Ashland University Finance Committee could find no leading Brethren to canvass on behalf of the college, both because of the lack of confidence in the prior leadership of the college and because there was no assurance that a solicitor could even be paid. *The Brethren Annual for the Year of Grace, 1894* (Ashland, OH: The Brethren Publishing House, n.d. [1893]), 15–16.

   An article that appeared in 1902 in *The Ashland Times* contains an interesting comment on this period of time. The article observes that the subject of Ashland College "at one time was denied a hearing in their [the Brethren Church's] conferences . . ." "At the Hundred Mark. Ashland College Enters upon a New Era of Prosperity," *The Ashland Times*, 15 January 1902, 1.

25. *National Convention of the Brethren Churches, 1892*, 46. This restriction was lifted at the 1894 General Conference after the Board of Trustees promised "to conduct the institution on the most economical and business principles." *The Brethren Annual for the Year of Grace, 1895* (Ashland, OH: The Brethren Publishing House, [1894]), 28. The conference did, however, insist that J. M. Tombaugh, who again was planning to be a non-resident president, move to Ashland. This requirement forced the trustees to seek another head for the college; eventually, J. Allen Miller, who was pastoring at Elkhart, Indiana, was prevailed upon to open the school in 1894.

26. Miller, "Ashland College," 1.

27. Ronk, "Ashland College," 9.

28. Annie S. Arnold, Parsons, Kansas, to Louis S. Bauman, Long Beach, California, 19 May 1929, L. S. Bauman Papers, Grace College Library, Grace College, Winona Lake, IN, microfiche, 329:14, p. 2. For other, though less dramatic, expressions, see A. L. Garber, "Editorial Notes," *The Leedy Chronicle* 4 (January 1903): 15, microfiche 3:325; A. L. G. [Garber], "Parents of Mrs. A. L. Garber," *The Leedy Chronicle* 6 (January 1905): 14, microfiche 4:470; A. D. Gnagey, "Two Friends of the College," *BE* 24 (9 April 1902): 1–2; and [L. L. Garber] to members of the Ashland College Board of Trustees, n.d., L. S. Bauman Papers, Grace College Library, Grace College, Winona Lake, IN, microfiche, 319:54–55.

29. Garber, "A Brief Review," 5.

30. Histories of Ashland College do not specify what these "legal requirements" were. A clue about this name change is found in the 1892–93 catalogue. On the cover the name of the school appears as Ashland Normal University. The

catalogue states, "The ASHLAND NORMAL UNIVERSITY is modeled after the plan of the Ohio Normal Universities and guarantees to its students every advantage that can be secured in any Normal University." The use of the designation "university" may be derived from a practice in Ohio of calling Normal (teacher training) schools "Normal Universities." Because the training of teachers provided a significant portion of Ashland's student body and tuition, the name change may reflect a philosophical commitment to teacher training. Note that 1892–93 is the academic year that C. W. Mykrantz leased the school from the Board of Trustees. *Ashland Normal University. Announcements for 1892–3* (n.p., n.d. [1892]), inside cover.

31. Clayton, "Whispering Pines and Purple Eagles," 336. Clayton gives background about the differing views between the Dayton and Ashland trustees. Further evidence of this conflict is revealed in Garber, "Sketch Book," 7, 10. Garber attributes to Vernon E. Wampler and especially Edward Mason the "scheme" to purchase the college from the receiver in 1888, sell it, and then start a new college in Dayton. There is a hint of this plan in Vernon Wampler's article in *The Brethren Evangelist* dated 6 June 1888. The article, which primarily was devoted to an impassioned plea to raise the funds to save the college, also contains the following statement: " . . . when we once get it [the college] we can decide as to the feasibility of selling it in the future and removing our College farther west." In the very next sentence Wampler makes the equivocating declaration, "I say this, not because I think that we will want to move it, for I think we will be able and strong enough to have a Brethren College in the east and one in the west before many years." V. E. Wampler, "The Decisive Moment Is Here," *BE* 10 (6 June 1888): 5. See also Garber, "A Brief Review," 5.

32. *National Convention of the Brethren Churches, 1892,* 46; "Report of the National Conference of the Brethren Churches," *BE* 16 (5 September 1894): 547 (4); and *The Brethren Annual or Church Year Book, for the Year of Our Lord, 1899* (Ashland, OH: Brethren Publishing Board, n.d. [1898]), [11–12].

33. "College Department," *BE* 10 (15 August 1888): 8.

34. Ibid.

35. Ibid.

36. Miller and Mason, *Short History,* 31. See also *Ninth Annual Catalogue of the Officers and Students of Ashland University, Normal School and Business Institute, for the Collegiate Year of 1887–8. with Announcements for 1888–9* (Ashland, OH: Brethren Publishing House, 1888), 18.

37. *Tenth Annual Catalogue of the Officers and Students of Ashland University, Normal School and Business Institute, for the Collegiate Year of 1888–9. with Announcements for 1889–90* (Ashland, OH: Brethren Publishing House, 1889), 14. Within the next three years the first women were ordained and served as pastors in the Brethren Church. For details about the first women pastors and ordained elders, see Jerry R. Flora, "Ninety Years of Brethren Women in Ministry," *Ashland Theological Journal* 17 (Fall 1984): 4–21 and idem, "Ordination of Women in The Brethren Church: A Case Study from the Anabaptist-Pietist Tradition," *Journal of the Evangelical Theological Society* 30 (December1987): 427–440.

38. *National Convention of the Brethren Churches, 1892*, 46. The request was part of a recommendation for the University Committee to appoint a "pastor of the University" to preach at the college chapel and conduct the Theological Department. This arrangement, whereby the dean of the Theological Department also served as the pastor of the College Church, continued into the second decade of the twentieth century.

39. *Minute Book of the Board*, 24 August 1893, 79. The actual motion at the 1893 General Conference omitted the name of A. D. Gnagey. *Brethren Annual for 1894*, 25.

40. *Minute Book of the Board*, 29 August 1894, 82.

41. *Ashland University, Ashland, Ohio. Announcement for the Year of 1894–5* (n.p., n.d. [1894]), 32–36.

42. *Minute Book of the Board*, 26 March 1891, 32; *Brethren Annual for 1895*, 27; and *Minute Book of the Board*, 29 August 1894, 85. A motion at the 1895 General Conference that would have made the SSCE responsible for raising the full $600 for the Theological chair was defeated. In its place a motion was passed that the church "put forth every possible effort to sustain the Theological chair and concentrate our energies in that direction as much as possible." "The National Conference," *BE* 17 (11 September 1895): 3.

43. *Catalogue of Ashland University for the Year 1895–96* (Ashland, OH: Optimist Publishing Co., [1895]), 22.

44. "Minutes of the National Conference of The Brethren Church, Assembled at Winona Lake, Indiana, August 28th-September 2nd, 1907," *BE* 29 (11 September 1907): 5.

45. See, for example, Clayton, "Whispering Pines and Purple Eagles," 339.

46. *Catalogue of Ashland University for the Year 1895–96*, 24.

47. *Sixth Annual Catalogue of the Officers and Students of Ashland College, and Normal and Business Institute, Ashland, Ohio, for the Collegiate Year 1884–'85* (Ashland, OH: Brethren Publishing House, 1885), 5. There are several notable variations from this form of the statement. In the first catalogue, when the college was still conforming to the "order of the Brethren," there appears the declaration that the college "inculcates the spirit of plainness and economy in dress and manner of living and aims to adorn the mind rather than the body." In the Progressive catalogue of 1884–85 the statement excises reference to plainness of dress in favor of the more general principle that the college "aims to adorn the mind rather than the body." For a few years beginning with the 1889–90 catalogue, the last statement is edited to read: "It aims to develop the student into true, noble manhood *or womanhood* [italics mine]." Though there are sufficient indications in early catalogues to realize that "manhood" needs to be understood generically, it is significant that this edit occurs at the very time when the first women are being ordained and called as pastors in the Brethren Church.

48. Ibid., 4.

49. *Eleventh Annual Catalogue of the Officers and Students of Ashland University, Normal School, and Business College for the Collegiate Year of 1889–90, with Announcements for 1890–91* (Ashland, OH: Sun Job Print, 1890), 6.

50. *Catalogue of Ashland College for the Collegiate Year 1884–'85*, 4.

51. *Eighth Annual Catalogue of Ashland College and Normal, Ashland, Ohio, for the Collegiate Year 1886–'87* (Ashland, OH: Brethren Publishing House, 1887), 13.

52. J. Allen Miller, "Doctrinal and Practical," BE 32 (11 May 1910): 7.

53. *Twelfth Annual Catalogue of the Officers and Students of Ashland University, Normal School, and Business College, for the Collegiate Year of 1890–91, with Announcements for 1891–92* (Ashland, OH: Brethren Publishing House, n.d.), 5.

Chapter 3: The Stabilization and Growth of Ashland College and the Beginning and Early Years of Ashland Theological Seminary (1898–1919)

1. Jacobs, "Brief History," 15.

2. Miller and Mason, *Short History*, 39.

3. Clayton, "Whispering Pines and Purple Eagles," 338.

4. *Minute Book of the Board*, 24 August 1893, 79.

5. *Brethren Annual for 1895*, 28 and *The Brethren Almanac for the Year of Our Lord 1896* (Ashland, OH: Brethren Book and Tract Committee, n.d. [1895]), [17].

6. This quality frustrated those Brethren with more of a Fundamentalist perspective. Louis Bauman, a leading spokesman of the Fundamentalist position within the Brethren Church, described as Miller's "outstanding weakness" his hesitation to disagree with those Brethren who held an opinion contrary to his own. As Bauman stated, " . . . when there is a question at issue between men who are his friends, he 'beats around the bush' or fails to take any definite stand himself." Louis S. Bauman to Joseph Johnston, Los Angeles, California, 12 October 1929, L. S. Bauman Papers, Grace College Library, Grace College, Winona Lake, IN, microfiche, 320:15.

7. "J. Allen Miller, A.M., D.D.," *Purple and Gold* 11 (January 1911): 7.

8. A. H. Lichty, "An Opportunity Afforded only by Ashland College," *Purple and Gold* 8 (May 1908): 2.

9. W. H. Beachler, "An Early Student's Estimate of Dr. Miller as a Teacher," BE 57 (27 April 1935): 8–9.

10. Charles A. Bame, "Dr. Miller as a Bible Teacher," BE 57 (27 April 1935): 5.

11. J. Allen Miller, "Travel Journal, Spring 1926," handwritten manuscript (photocopy), p. 104, privately held by John Allen Miller III, Avon Lake, OH.

12. For additional resources on J. Allen Miller, see *Brethren Encyclopedia*, s.v. "Miller, John Allen," by Dale R. Stoffer; Stoffer, *Background and Development*, 195–214; *A Faithful Christian's Journey: To the Memory of J. Allen Miller*, *Ashland College Bulletin* 8 (May 1935); and "In Memoriam—Dr. J. Allen Miller," BE 57 (27 April 1935): 5–11, 13. As the turmoil increased in the latter 1930s between the Ashland and Grace groups in the Brethren Church, there were many Brethren who felt that the escalating dissension would not have taken place had Miller still been alive. Note the sentiments of George P. Gongwer, an attorney who supported the Ashland Brethren cause.

It appears that Ashland College has suffered very keenly from the death of the late John Allen Miller. John Allen Miller was a devout Christian, a keen scholar and above all a gentleman. No man with whom I have come in contact do I revere and admire as I did him. His was the ability to see through the petty jealousies of a decided minority of the Brethren Clergy and to advise and counsel so that their intentions might not prevail. Unfortunately at his death no leader was present to take his place. He was admired and loved by every loyal friend of the College and all were willing to listen to his sage advice. Had not death taken him from us, today Ashland College would stand in complete harmony with the Brethren Church.

George P. Gongwer, *Who Owns and Controls Ashland College?* (Ashland, OH: Ashland College, n.d. [1937]), 2.

13. *Brethren Annual for 1899*, [11]. There are very few references to this sale of college property. The 1899 *Brethren Annual* indicates that this sale involved

a tier of lots abutting the street running north and south along the west side of the college property [called King's Street at the time], 13 in number, 55 feet wide and 170 feet deep exclusive of an alley for every three lots, twenty feet in width; also a second tier of lots immediately east of the above tier, beginning at the south line of the college ground, running on a parallel to the above named tier, five in number, fifty-five feet wide and 170 deep, exclusive of an alley twenty feet wide.

A note about these lots appears in a report of the 12 June 1906 meeting of the Board of Trustees in *The Brethren Evangelist*. The article indicated that the trustees desired to buy back the tract of land that had belonged to the original college campus but had been given in the 1898 settlement to the old mortgagees of the college. "Meeting of College Trustees," *BE* 28 (20 June 1906): 12. The actual motion in the Trustee minutes seems to be at odds, however, with what appears in *The Brethren Evangelist*: "The following resolution was unanimously passed: That the Board of Trustees instruct the Prudential Committee to carry out the former contract which requires placing on sale of certain lots, west of the college buildings, and paying the proceeds to the ex-mortgagees or their representative." Apparently, the ex-mortgagees held claim to these lots based on the 1898 settlement. The college was to sell the lots and give the proceeds to these creditors to settle their claims against the college. The sale of the lots does not seem to have been consummated, thus explaining the action in the minutes. But the above article in *The Brethren Evangelist* suggests that it was the intent of the Trustees to redeem the lots from the ex-mortgagees. This supposition is reinforced by an additional reference to the lots in a statement in the Trustees' *Minute Book* from 1907 that indicated that $2700 of the $11,452 indebtedness at that time derived from a claim of ex-mortgagees to eighteen lots on the west side of the college campus. *Minute Book of the Board,* 12 June 1906, 142 and 20 March 1907, 150. Apparently, the trustees pursued their desire to reacquire these lots and added the cost of the buy-back to the existing indebtedness of the college.

Presumably, Gillin's liquidation of the college indebtedness in 1908 returned these lots to the college campus. A photo of the Ashland College campus from the first decades of the twentieth century does show two structures upon this land, though it is not known how the buildings had been or were being used. These lots occupied the ground where the football field would be built in 1923 and the second gymnasium in 1926. Presently, Kilhefner Hall and a parking lot occupy this site.

14. "At the Hundred Mark. Ashland College Enters upon a New Era of Prosperity," *The Ashland Times*, 15 January 1902, 1.

15. Ibid. For information about the life of Josiah Keim and the sacrifices he made on behalf of the college, see A. D. Gnagey, "Two Friends of the College," *BE* 24 (9 April 1902): 1–2. Gnagey pays tribute to Keim with these words:

> . . . to write a correct and impartial history of the institution [Ashland College] aside from his name would be an impossibility. He was its treasurer and financial agent for a number of years, traveling throughout the brotherhood, often at his own expense and without salary, soliciting funds for the maintenance of this our only educational institution and to liquidate the debt which was rapidly growing into alarming proportions. Brother Keim has been a warm friend of the institution; the cause of Ashland College from its beginning has kept very close to his heart and he has spared neither money, time nor labor in the saving of the institution to the Brethren church. To him as much as to any other man belongs the honor of rescuing it from what was regarded as a hopeless condition. During the most trying and critical periods of its history, when its very friends seemed to forsake the institution, Brother Keim remained its friend, stood nobly by it and persistently refused to acknowledge failure.

16. *Minute Book of the Board*, 20 March 1907, 150; 15 June 1908, 161, 162; and 7 September 1908, 163. J. L. Clark's gift of $1500 in 1907 to aid the liquidation of the debt at the college was a tangible reflection of a growing commitment to the school in the city of Ashland. "Minutes of the National Conference of The Brethren Church, August 28th-September 2nd, 1907," 5.

17. Gillin reveals that he served as president of the college without pay in order to help retire the debt. J. L. Gillin, "My Apologia," *BE* 41 (4 June 1919): 5.

18. For additional background on Gillin and his role in the liberal controversy in the Brethren Church, see *Brethren Encyclopedia*, s.v. "Gillin, John Lewis," by Richard E. Allison and Stoffer, *Background and Development*, 151–52, 182, 187–93.

19. *Minute Book of the Board*, 14 June 1904, 137; "Personals and Locals," *Purple and Gold* 12 (27 April 1912): 11; and Miller and Mason, *Short History*, 60. The Board minutes indicate that a phone was installed in the "college building" (Founders Hall) in 1904. Allen Hall had a phone at least a year earlier. *The Ashland Times* mentioned people from downtown telephoning the dormitory in April 1903. "College Notes," *The Ashland Times*, 15 April 1903, 1.

20. Miller and Mason, *Short History*, 60, 63.

21. *Ashland College Quarterly: Announcements for the Academic Year beginning September 16, 1913* 6 (1 June 1913): 16, 18, 26–28, 38–72 and *Ashland College Quarterly: The Catalogue 1915–1916* (Ashland, OH: Ashland College, n.d. [1915]), 25.

22. *Minute Book of the Board,* 5 June 1916, 205a.

23. The 1915–16 catalogue indicates that over the history of the college "hundreds of successful teachers" had gone into the teaching profession from Ashland. Further, an estimated "sixty per centum of the teachers in Ashland County have received their training in whole or in part in Ashland College." *The Catalogue 1915–1916,* 66. The following statistics, published in 1921 in the *Purple and Gold,* reinforce the importance of teacher training at Ashland: 99 graduates of the college were teachers, 79 were pastors and church workers, 7 were missionaries, 14 were YMCA and YWCA workers, others were in law, medicine, journalism, dentistry, nursing, and government. The college also had "provided normal training for hundreds of students of the county." "Ashland College," *Purple and Gold* 21 (June 1921): 20.

24. *Ashland College Quarterly: The Catalogue 1915–1916,* 65, 71. The Morris Act took precedence over an Ohio law passed in 1910 that provided that graduates of Normal Colleges would receive a provisional certificate that was valid for four years. This certificate could be made permanent when the teacher had attained at least twenty-four months of successful teaching experience and subsequently passed a limited professional examination from the State Board of School Examiners. Ibid., 65.

25. L. L. Garber to members of the Ashland College Board of Trustees, n.d., L. S. Bauman Papers, Grace College Library, Grace College, Winona Lake, IN, microfiche, 319:55.

26. The Student Volunteer Band of the Student Volunteer Movement, an organization dedicated to the work of foreign missions, was organized by William D. Furry on 31 October 1900; the Christian Endeavor Society was organized by 1901; a chapter of the Young Men's Christian Association was organized 5 December 1901; a chapter of the Young Women's Christian Association was organized through the efforts of Clara Worst Miller on 2 October 1902; and a chapter of the Young Women's Christian Temperance Union was organized 19 January 1909.

27. Alma Leslie, "The Y.W.C.A," *Purple and Gold* 3 (November 1902): 3.

28. W. D. Furry, "The End of Creation," *BE* 23 (15 August 1901): 6.

29. Albert T. Ronk, *A Search for Truth* (Ashland, OH: Brethren Publishing Company, 1973), 83. During the Fundamentalist controversy in the Brethren Church in the late 1930s, A. L. DeLozier, "More inside History," *BE* 61 (12 August 1939): 15 revealed the authors of some of the books that Gillin used in his classes: Marcus Dods, John W. Chadwick, Samuel Henry Kellogg, (?) Watson, William R. Harper, William Garden Blaikie, and Frederick W. Farrar.

30. Premillennialism and postmillennialism are both views of the end times or eschatology. Premillennialism is the belief that Jesus Christ will return to earth (the second coming) and reign for a thousand years (he comes prior to the millennium). This view is usually accompanied by the conviction that a time

of apostasy and tribulation will precede Christ's return; it is generally pessimistic about the future of human society. Postmillennialism is the belief that through the spread of the gospel and the advance of Christian society Christ will return to a predominantly Christianized world (he comes after the millennium). In its liberal form postmillennialism was convinced that human ability and concerted social reform could construct a new world dominated by peace and social, scientific, and medical advancement; it is very optimistic about the future of human culture.

31. Dispensational premillennialism was a view of the end times (eschatology) that originated in the 1830s with the Plymouth Brethren leader, John Nelson Darby. He posited that all of human history from creation to consummation can be divided into seven periods or dispensations. These periods generally coincide with successive covenants between God and humanity; each dispensation is unique in relation to the terms of the covenant, the people with whom the covenant is made, and the blessings of the covenant. For example, the fifth dispensation, the covenant of law, was established with the Jews, who were given the law, with its regulations for sacrifice and temple worship, as well as a promised land, the land of Israel. Dispensationalism made a strict distinction between this dispensation and the dispensation of grace, the church age, in which God offers salvation and deliverance from judgment to any who acknowledge Jesus Christ as Savior.

   Classic dispensationalism believes that the seventh dispensation, the millennium, is primarily for the Jews. Relying on a literal interpretation of Daniel and Revelation especially, dispensationalism holds that many of the prophecies of Scripture have already been fulfilled. There is no further prophecy that needs fulfilled prior to the rapture, when Christ comes secretly to remove the church from earth and renews his work of drawing Israel to himself. This "any moment" rapture triggers the final end time events: the seven-year great tribulation during which many Jews will come to Christ and be martyred for their faith, Christ's visible coming with his saints to establish the millennial kingdom on earth with its capital in Jerusalem, and finally the last judgment and the consummation.

32. For more information on all of these figures in the liberal/fundamentalist controversy, see Stoffer, *Background and Development*, 182–185 and the pertinent articles in *The Brethren Encyclopedia*.

33. For a detailed discussion of the course of the liberal/fundamentalist controversy in the Brethren Church, see Stoffer, *Background and Development*, 186–194.

34. The resolution stated:

> Resolved, that it is the faith of the Brethren church that the holy scriptures as originally written were altogether a record from God, inspired of the Holy Ghost, who so moved the writers thereof as to keep a record absolutely free from error. Therefore, the Bible as we now possess it, when made free from any error or mistake that translators, copyists, or printers possibly may have made, is the infallible Word of the living God, the one, and only authoritative message of God to men.

Minutes of the Twenty-eighth General Conference of The Brethren Church . . . (Ashland, OH: The Brethren Publishing Company, n.d.), 36.

35. Ibid., 56. McClain, one of the members of the committee that drafted the resolution, included the following qualification with his signature: "To me the Resolution is indefinite and evasive." No doubt he would have preferred the inclusion of the terms "verbal inspiration" and "inerrancy" in the statement.

36. At the outset of America's involvement in the war, Furry went to Cleveland to hear Mott speak about America's place in the war. William D. Furry to L. S. Bauman, 1 May 1917, L. S. Bauman Papers, Grace College Library, Grace College, Winona Lake, IN, microfiche, 17:49 (bottom), p. 1.

37. "Doctor Furry Honored," *Purple and Gold* 18 (May 1918): 1 and Miller and Mason, *Short History*, 95.

38. L. S. Bauman to Edwin E. Jacobs, 2 April 1920, L. S. Bauman Papers, Grace College Library, Grace College, Winona Lake, IN, microfiche, 61:6, p. 1.

39. C. L. Keep, Acting Special Agent in Charge, United States Department of Justice, Bureau of Investigation, to Louis S. Bauman, Long Beach, CA, 21 May 1918, L. S. Bauman Papers, Grace College Library, Grace College, Winona Lake, IN, microfiche, 49:6.

40. H. L. Goughnour, "Another Protest," *BE* (15 December 1915): 5.

41. Bauman's first recorded complaint to the college occurred in 1909, even before he had gone to Long Beach. He sent a communication to the Board of Trustees registering concern about alleged affiliation of some faculty in secret societies. *Minute Book of the Board,* 15 June 1909, 171.

42. *Minutes of the Thirtieth General Conference of the Brethren Church . . .* (n.p., n.d.), 6–7. There is no indication whether Bauman's statements met with an "Amen" from the trustees and faculty.

43. "Resolutions Adopted by the First Brethren Church of Long Beach, July 30th, 1919," L. S. Bauman Papers, Grace College Library, Grace College, Winona Lake, IN, microfiche, 49:1–2.

44. The full text of the doctrinal statement is as follows:

> The Trustees of Ashland College, accepting the statement that "The Holy Scriptures of the Old and New Testaments, as originally given of God, are the infallible record of the perfect, final, and authoritative revelation of God's will, altogether sufficient in themselves as a rule of faith and practice" set forth the following statement as the basis of the teaching of the Seminary of the College:
>
> 1. The deity and virgin birth of Jesus Christ the Son of God;
> 2. The fall of man, his consequent depravity, and the necessity of his new birth;
> 3. The vicarious atonement of Jesus Christ through the shedding of his blood;
> 4. The resurrection of the body of Jesus Christ from the dead, the earnest of our own resurrection;

5. Justification by faith in our Lord Jesus Christ, of which obedience to the will of God and works of righteousness are the evidence and result;

6. The personality of the Holy Spirit as the Comforter and Guide of the members of the body of Christ;

7. The personal return of Jesus Christ, King of kings, to this earth;

8. The Gospel principles of non-conformity, non-resistance and non-swearing;

9. The ordinances of the Gospel,—the baptism of believers by triune immersion; confirmation; the washing of the Saint's feet; the Lord's supper, the communion of the bread and wine.

45. L. S. Bauman, Long Beach, CA, to E. E. Jacobs, Ashland, OH, 10 April 1920, L. S. Bauman Papers, Grace College Library, Grace College, Winona Lake, IN, microfiche, 61:14, p. 2. Bauman reveals that it was Gnagey who pushed for this change.

46. L. S. Bauman, "The Problem of the Christian College," *BE* 38 (1 October 1919): 10. The complete text of the article can be found in Bauman, "Problem," *BE* 38 (24 September 1919): 8–9 and (1 October 1919): 9–10.

47. Though Bauman had been in Philadelphia as late as 14 April 1919 (he was staying with McClain), he intended to be back to Long Beach by the middle of May. He was certainly in Long Beach by 28 May 1919. Bauman gives no indication in his papers that he attended the conference, but he was well aware of its work from McClain and other sources. See Bilhorn Brothers, Chicago, IL, to L. S. Bauman, Philadelphia, PA, 5 April 1919 and 18 April 1919, L. S. Bauman Papers, Grace College Library, Grace College, Winona Lake, IN, microfiche, 30:54, 56; L. S. Bauman, Philadelphia, PA, to The First Brethren Church, Long Beach, CA, 10 April 1919, L. S. Bauman Papers, Grace College Library, Grace College, Winona Lake, IN, microfiche, 61:10–11; and Ellen (Bauman's sister), Morrill, KS, to L. S. Bauman, Long Beach, CA, 28 May 1919, L. S. Bauman Papers, Grace College Library, Grace College, Winona Lake, IN, microfiche, 46:42, p. 1. For McClain's attendance, see Alva J. McClain to L. S. Bauman, Long Beach, CA, 19 January 1920, L. S. Bauman Papers, Grace College Library, Grace College, Winona Lake, IN, microfiche, 64:26, p. 4.

48. Bible Conference Committee, *God Hath Spoken* (Philadelphia: Bible Conference Committee, 1919), 19.

49. Gillin, "My Apologia," 6.

50. Stoffer, *Background and Development*, 191–192.

51. The full text of "The Message of the Brethren Ministry" follows:

The Message which Brethren Ministers accept as a Divine Entrustment to be heralded to a lost world, finds its sole source and authority in the Bible. This message is one of Hope for a lost world and speaks with finality and authority. Fidelity to the apostolic injunction to preach the Word demands our utmost endeavor of mind and heart. We, the members of the National Ministerial Association of the Brethren church, hold that the essential and constituent elements of our message shall continue to be the following declarations:

1. **Our Motto:** The Bible, the whole Bible and nothing but the Bible.
2. **The Authority and Integrity of the Holy Scriptures.** The Ministry of the Brethren church, desires to bear testimony to the belief that God's supreme revelation has been made through Jesus Christ, a complete and authentic record of which revelation is the New Testament; and, to the belief that the Holy Scriptures of the Old and New Testaments, as originally given, are the infallible record of the perfect, final and authoritative revelations of God's will, altogether sufficient in themselves as a rule of faith and practice.
3. **We understand the Basic Content of our Doctrinal Preaching and teaching to be:**
   (1) The Pre-existence, Deity, and Incarnation by Virgin Birth of Jesus Christ, the Son of God;
   (2) The Fall of Man, his consequent spiritual death and utter sinfulness, and the necessity of his New Birth;
   (3) The Vicarious Atonement of the Lord Jesus Christ through the shedding of His own blood;
   (4) The resurrection of the Lord Jesus Christ in the body in which He suffered and died and His subsequent glorification at the right hand of God;
   (5) The justification by personal faith in the Lord Jesus Christ, of which obedience to the will of God and works of righteousness are the evidence and result; the resurrection of the dead, the judgment of the world, and the life everlasting of the just;
   (6) The personality and Deity of the Holy Spirit who indwells the Christian and is his Comforter and Guide;
   (7) The personal and visible return of our Lord Jesus Christ from heaven as King of Kings and Lord of Lords; the glorious goal for which we are taught to watch, wait, and pray;
   (8) The Christian should "be not conformed to this world, but be transformed by the renewing of the mind," should not engage in carnal strife and should "swear not at all;"
   (9) The Christian should observe, as his duty and privilege, the ordinances of our Lord Jesus Christ, among which are (a) baptism of believers by Triune Immersion; (b) confirmation; (c) the Lord's Supper; (d) the Communion of the Bread and Wine; (e) the washing of the saints' feet; and (f) the anointing of the sick with oil.

Minutes of the Thirty-Third General Conference of the Brethren Church . . . 1921 (n.p., n.d.), 16.

52. Alva J. McClain, "Prof. McClain Speaks of 'The Faith of Dr. Miller,'" *Ashland College Bulletin* 8 (May 1935): 12.

53. Albert T. Ronk, *History of The Brethren Church* (Ashland, OH: Brethren Publishing Company, 1968), 15, 368 and Delbert Flora, interview by author, 2 April 1979, Ashland, OH, tape recording, Ashland University Archives, Ashland University, Ashland, OH.

54. Ronk, *History of The Brethren Church*, 446.

55. *Ashland College Quarterly: Catalogue Number* 6 [7] (1 June 1914): 42. Women were not generally encouraged to go into pastoral ministry by this time, though occasionally women were still being ordained. Most women in professional church work in the Brethren Church served as missionaries or as pastor-missionaries in new church development. See the case of Mary Pence, who was ordained by E. M. Cobb and served a Brethren congregation in Limestone, Tennessee. E. M. Cobb, Dayton, OH, to L. S. Bauman, Long Beach, CA, 15 July 1919, 24 June 1919, and 25 March 1919, L. S. Bauman Papers, Grace College Library, Grace College, Winona Lake, IN, microfiche, 39:10–11, 20, 56. Interestingly, Cobb would have considered himself a Fundamentalist, but Fundamentalists generally opposed the practice of ordaining women.

56. *Ashland College Quarterly* n.s. 1 (June 1907): 38 and *Ashland College Quarterly: Catalogue Number* 6 (1 June 1913): 41, 42.

57. *Ashland College Quarterly: The Catalogue 1915–1916*, 61–63.

58. *Minute Book of the Board*, 14 June 1906, 129.

59. E. D. Burnworth, "The Demand for Leadership and its Supply," *Purple and Gold* 8 (May 1908): 3.

60. *Minute Book of the Board*, 14 June 1906, 128–29.

61. *Ashland College Quarterly: Announcements for the Academic Year 1913*, 38.

62. Ibid., 8, 38–39.

63. See, for example, *The Ashland Theological Seminary of The Brethren Church: Catalogue and Announcements, 1931–32* (n.p., n.d.), 9.

64. See *Ashland College Bulletin: The Ashland Theological Seminary, Announcements for 1943–1944* (n.p., n.d.), 5.

65. *Ashland College Quarterly: Annual Catalogue 1926–27* (Ashland, OH: Ashland College, [1926], 52 and *Ashland Theological Seminary Catalogue 1955–56* (Ashland, OH: Ashland College, n.d.), 9. This latter catalogue celebrates "Fifty Faithful Years: 1906 to 1956." There is some rationale given in the Board of Trustee minutes from 1955 for choosing 1906 as the start of the seminary in anticipation of the fiftieth anniversary celebration. Delbert Flora, in his dean's report to the Board, indicated that they were relying upon the history of the college recently written by Clara Worst Miller and E. Glenn Mason for this date. The two reasons cited in his comments were that "a separate department of Theology was established in the College in 1906" and the department "was even then frequently called 'the seminary.'" The first of these reasons is clearly erroneous and the second, though true informally, was not true of the formal designation of the department. "Report of the Dean of the Seminary," *Minute Book of the Board*, 14 April 1955, 20.

66. In the 1905–06 catalogue there are no faculty who are wholly dedicated to teaching in the theological department. There were only fifteen courses listed in the catalogue in the curricular area entitled "Exegesis, Doctrinal and Practical

Theology." Another twenty-six courses that related to theological education could be found in the curricular areas of languages, history, and philosophy. Four students are identified as seniors in either the English or Classical Divinity Courses. By 1913 there was one full-time faculty member in the seminary (Miller) and several others supplemented the teaching in the seminary. All courses related to theological education were gathered into the section describing the seminary. The fifty-four courses listed in the seminary curriculum were divided into Old Testament History and Literature, New Testament History and Literature, Biblical Languages, Doctrinal and Practical Theology, Introduction to the Holy Scriptures, Hermeneutics, Church History, and Philosophy of Religion and Christian Ethics. A total of twelve students graduated from the English and Classical Divinity Courses.

67. "Meeting of College Trustees," *BE* 28 (20 June 1906): 12.

68. See examples of these assertions in *Ashland Theological Seminary, 1990–91 Catalog* (Ashland, OH: n.p.), 7; Ronk, *Search for Truth,* 76; and Clayton, "Whispering Pines and Purple Eagles," 340.

69. See "The Brethren Church," *BE* 27 (3 May 1905): 1.

70. "Minutes of the National Conference of The Brethren Church, August 28th-September 2nd, 1907," 4–5 and J. Allen Miller, "A Greater Theological Department," *Purple and Gold* 10 (February 1910): 3.

71. "Work of the Theological Department," *Purple and Gold* 8 (May 1908): 8.

72. "Editorial," *Purple and Gold* 9 (March 1909): 8. See also [Editorial], *Purple and Gold* 7 (March 1907): 9.

73. Miller, "A Greater Theological Department," 3 and "Minutes of the National Conference of The Brethren Church, August 28th-September 2nd, 1907," 4.

74. "The Theological Association," *Purple and Gold* 13 (October 1912): 8; *Ashland College Quarterly: The Catalogue 1915–16* (Ashland, OH: Ashland College, [1915]), 113; and "Theological Association," *Purple and Gold* 16 (May 1916): 32.

75. *Ashland College Quarterly: Annual Catalogue Number* 4 (May 1910): 8; *Ashland College Quarterly: Announcements for the Academic Year 1913,* 13; "Editorial," *Purple and Gold* 16 (January-February 1916): 16; and *Minute Book of the Board,* 5 May 1919, 218.

76. *The Brethren Annual or Church Year Book for the Year of Our Lord 1906* (Ashland, OH: Brethren Publication Board, [1905]), [9, 21].

77. *Minute Book of the Board,* 15 June 1908, 161. See also *Ashland College Quarterly* n.s. 1 (June 1907): 38. Could Albert Ronk's experience (see sidebar) have been behind this protest?

78. *Ashland College Quarterly: The Catalogue 1915–16,* 53.

79. *Ashland College Quarterly: Annual Catalogue Number* 4 (May 1910): 6.

80. *Ashland College Quarterly: Announcements for the Academic Year 1913,* 8.

81. *Ashland College Quarterly: The Catalogue 1915–16,* 118.

82. "Ashland College," *Purple and Gold* 6 (February 1906): 16.

83. J. Allen Miller, "An Educational Ideal," *Purple and Gold* 6 (October 1905): 4.

84. J. Allen Miller, "What Shall I Do during the Winter?," *Purple and Gold* 5 (December 1904): 13. Miller's use of inclusive language is unique for this time period.

85. N. Lois Frazier, "Opportunity for Spiritual Growth and Activity in Ashland College," *Purple and Gold* 15 (September 1914): 2.

86. *Minute Book of the Board*, 8 August 1888, 16–17.

87. Ibid., 12 June 1917, 206 and *Ashland College Quarterly: The Catalogue 1915–16*, 71–72.

88. *Ashland College Quarterly: Announcements for the Academic Year 1913*, 12.

89. Ibid., 13.

90. "Editorial," *Purple and Gold* 16 (January-February 1916): 16.

Chapter 4: Years of Challenge: College Accreditation, Graduate Theological Education, Depression, and Division (1919–1939)

1. Jacobs, "A Brief History," 16–17.

2. Edwin E. Jacobs, "Standardizing Colleges," *BE* 41 (16 July 1919): 5–6 and "What Ashland Needs," *BE* 41 (6 August 1919): 4.

3. Miller and Mason, *Short History*, 76, 80.

4. "The Brethren Bicentenary Movement Page," *BE* 42 (15 July 1920): 4.

5. Miller and Mason, *Short History*, 76, 78.

6. Jacobs, "A Brief History," 17 and Miller and Mason, *Short History*, 77, 81.

7. "Ashland College: A Record of Fifty Years of Service to the Brethren Church," *Ashland College Bulletin* 10 (July 1937): 5.

8. Miller and Mason, *Short History*, 69–71. Mason indicates other factors in the growth of the college: (1) lack of jobs for youth under twenty-one led to a greater demand for high school training and (2) as the number of high school graduates grew between 1918 and 1930, there was a corresponding increase in college attendance and expansion of course offerings.

9. *Ashland College Quarterly: Annual Catalogue 1922–23* (Ashland, OH: Ashland College, [1922]), 14, 17, 31.

10. *Ashland College Quarterly: Summer School Number* (Ashland, OH: Ashland College, 1928), 11 and *Ashland College Bulletin: Annual Catalogue 1930–31* (Ashland, OH: Ashland College, [1930]), 28.

    ...er and Mason, *Short History*, 72, 83.

    ...d Glenn Mason, "Inside Survey of Ashland College, Ashland, Ohio,"
    ...esis, The Ohio State University, 1926), 89. One of the purposes of
    ...sis was to supply the data and analysis necessary to move the ac-
    ...cess forward.

    Short History, 72–74. Mason indicates that membership in
    Association was regained in 1936. However, the "Affiliation
    ...e North Central Association for Ashland College/Uni-
    ...te of reinstatement as 1938. It is probably the case that
    ...th Central Association recommended reinstate-
    ...probable though than 1936) and the recommen-
    ...Central Association in 1938.

14. Report of Special Committee, A. V. Kimmell, Chairman, to Brethren Churches of Southern California, 24 July 1920, L. S. Bauman Papers, Grace College Library, Grace College, Winona Lake, IN, microfiche, 69:31–34, p. 2.

15. Edwin E. Jacobs, Ashland, OH, to Milton Puterbaugh, 20 July 1922, Brethren Church Archives, Brethren Church National Office, Ashland, OH. Jacobs had already had a very pointed exchange of letters with Bauman in 1920 concerning the alleged support of postmillennialism at the college. Jacobs viewed the doctrines of premillennialism and postmillennialism as non-essentials to the faith (Bauman considered premillennialism an essential of the Christian faith). He also rejected the notion that anyone at the college was a "bald" postmillennialist. Other issues raised in this correspondence were Bauman's concerns about militarism in the college under Furry and the college's support of the IWM and Jacobs' complaint that Long Beach gave significant support to missions but virtually nothing to education. Bauman insisted that he was not against education, but it had to be education of the right sort. He declared: "Ashland College can never win our loyal support until she wins our faith." For the exchange see Louis S. Bauman, Long Beach, CA, to Edwin E. Jacobs, Ashland, OH, 5 March 1920, L. S. Bauman Papers, Grace College Library, Grace College, Winona Lake, IN, microfiche, 61:19–22; Louis S. Bauman, Long Beach, CA, to Edwin E. Jacobs, Ashland, OH, 2 April 1920, L. S. Bauman Papers, Grace College Library, Grace College, Winona Lake, IN, microfiche, 61:6–7; Edwin E. Jacobs, Ashland, OH, to L. S. Bauman, Long Beach, CA, 5 April 1920, L. S. Bauman Papers, Grace College Library, Grace College, Winona Lake, IN, microfiche, 61:8–10; and L. S. Bauman, Long Beach, CA, to Edwin E. Jacobs, Ashland, OH, 10 April 1920, L. S. Bauman Papers, Grace College Library, Grace College, Winona Lake, IN, microfiche, 61:13–18.

16. J. L. Gillin, "Gifts to Colleges with Conditions Attached," BE 45 (7 February 1923): 6; E. G. Mason, "From a Layman's View Point," BE 45 (4 April 1923): 6–7; G. T. Ronk, "Conditional Gifts to Colleges,—Query," BE 45 (28 February 1923): 7; and Louis S. Bauman, "A Preacher's View Point of 'A Layman's View Point,'" BE 45 (6 June 1923): 5–6.

17. Alva J. McClain, Ashland, OH, to Louis S. Bauman, Long Beach, CA, 14 December 1925, L. S. Bauman Papers, Grace College Library, Grace College, Winona Lake, IN, microfiche, 208:54–55 (below), p. 2. McClain was reserving judgment until he had been at the college for at least one full year, though he did harbor some unspecified concerns at this time.

18. Edwin E. Jacobs, "News of the College," BE 49 (25 June 1927): 14 and McClain "Santa Monica, California," BE 49 (1 October 1927): 12. In sonal correspondence McClain had revealed to Bauman that he was lusioned by financial and interpersonal issues—McClain felt alone battle in Ashland. See Louis S. Bauman, Long Beach, CA, to Alv Clain, Ashland, OH, 29 April 1926, L. S. Bauman Papers, Grace brary, Grace College, Winona Lake, IN, microfiche, 227:33–40,

19. Alva J. McClain, "The Background and Origin of Grace Theolo nary," in Charis, ed. John Whitcomb (n.p., 1951), 12.

20. *Ashland College Bulletin: The Seminary* 2 (June 1929): [2]. The curricular revisions in the Arts Course may have been those that occurred in the 1922–23 academic year.

21. *Ashland College Quarterly: Annual Catalogue 1925–26* (Ashland, OH: Ashland College, [1925], 47–49; *Ashland College Quarterly: Annual Catalogue 1926–27* (Ashland, OH: Ashland College, [1926], 52–53; and *Ashland College Bulletin: The Seminary* (1929), 4–10.

22. Miller and Mason, *Short History*, 77.

23. Alva J. McClain, Ashland, OH, to Louis S. Bauman, Long Beach, CA, 13 February 1926, L. S. Bauman Papers, Grace College Library, Grace College, Winona Lake, IN, microfiche, 227:43–46, p. 2 and *Minute Book of the Board*, 16 March 1926, 272. The boarding house was eventually closed in 1935. *Minute Book of the Board*, 30 April 1935, 42.

24. *Ashland College Quarterly: Annual Catalogue 1926–27*, 53.

25. *Ashland College Quarterly: The Catalogue 1915–16*, 118.

26. *Ashland College Quarterly: Annual Catalogue 1922–23*, 35.

27. Ibid., 36.

28. Ibid., 37.

29. While the number of Brethren students at the college stayed relatively constant between 1922 and 1930, the percentage of Brethren students enrolled in the college generally decreased. The rapid growth during this period was primarily due to increased numbers of non-Brethren drawn from Ashland and surrounding counties (in the 1934–35 academic year 36.6% of the student body was from Ashland and Ashland County; in the 1936–37 academic year 76% of the student body was from Ohio). Interestingly, the percentage of Brethren students rose gradually during the depression years. The numbers of Brethren students, though down, was not as adversely affected as the enrollment of non-Brethren students. This trend may reflect loyalty among Brethren to their denominational school, in spite of financial hardship, and the affects of the loss of accreditation in 1933. Note the statistics below for students in the four-year collegiate program:

Academic Years	Number of Brethren students	Percentage of the student body
1922–23	80	51%
1925–26	110	37%
1930–31	78	23%
1933–34	52	20%
1936–37	88	33%

See Mason, "Inside Survey of Ashland College," 68 and "Minutes of the Board of Trustees of Ashland College," file for 1937, pp. 47–48, Ashland University Archives, Ashland University, Ashland, OH.

30. Alva J. McClain, "Christian Education," in *Minutes of the Thirty Seventh General Conference of the Brethren Church . . . 1925* (n.p., n.d. [1925]), 61–62.

31. Stoffer, *Background and Development*, 218. See further discussions about the differences between the two on p. 219.

32. Ibid., 219 and Louis S. Bauman, Long Beach, CA, to Joseph Johnston, Los Angeles, CA, 12 October 1929, L. S. Bauman Papers, Grace College Library, Grace College, Winona Lake, IN, microfiche, 320:15.

33. Louis S. Bauman, Long Beach, CA, to C. W. Mayes, Whittier, CA, 19 June 1929, L. S. Bauman Papers, Grace College Library, Grace College, Winona Lake, IN, microfiche, 323:50.

34. Statements that appear in Jacobs' historical sketch of the college in 1932 suggest the weight of importance that he gave to the liberal arts program in comparison to theological education. He wrote:

> It should also be noted . . . that, the words "training of the ministry" or "theological department or training," or "seminary" or any other like expression as relating to the purposes and aims of the school, are not found in any of the earlier statements of the College, and it was not until the presidency of Dr. J. L. Gillin, when the constitution of 1888 was radically revised, that a department was established which could be called a seminary. . . .

> If the constitution of 1888 and the incorporation papers of that date are compared with those of the original founders of the institution, 1878, it will become clear that Ashland College was founded as a college of liberal arts and so continued up till after its control had passed into the hands of the Brethren Church, when it was decided that it should also serve as a place for the training of Christian ministers.

> Jacobs, "A Brief History," 12. Jacobs clearly is arguing for the priority of the liberal arts program over theological education in these statements. It is intriguing to note that just over twenty years later Clara Worst Miller, who often copies Jacobs' statements word-for-word in her historical account of the college (without documentation!), reproduces the second paragraph above with only minor revisions (she omits the first paragraph). But she then adds the sentence: "And this has since been regarded as one of Ashland College's major functions." With this edit, Miller, the wife of J. Allen Miller, entirely shifts the focus of Jacobs' comments to the importance of theological education. See Miller and Mason, *Short History*, 34.

35. McClain, "Origin of Grace Theological Seminary," 14.

36. Charles W. Mayes, Whittier, CA, to Louis S. Bauman, Long Beach, CA, 18 June 1929, L. S. Bauman Papers, Grace College Library, Grace College, Winona Lake, IN, microfiche, 323:52–53 and Louis S. Bauman, Long Beach, CA, to C. W. Mayes, Whittier, CA, 19 June 1929, L. S. Bauman Papers, Grace College Library, Grace College, Winona Lake, IN, microfiche, 323:51.

37. Alva J. McClain, Ashland, OH, to Brethren pastors, 20 May 1930, L. S. Bauman Papers, Grace College Library, Grace College, Winona Lake, IN, microfiche, 342:51 (below).

38. See Henry V. Hall, Long Beach, CA, to L. S. Bauman, 10 February 1919, L. S. Bauman Papers, Grace College Library, Grace College, Winona Lake, IN, microfiche, 48:12–13, p. 1 and Herbert Tay, Xenia, OH, [1920], L. S. Bauman Papers, Grace College Library, Grace College, Winona Lake, IN, microfiche, 68:43 (below).

39. *Minute Book of the Board,* 24 April 1930, 305.

40. The specification of four faculty members for the seminary not only provided the seminary with the breadth of teaching needed for a graduate seminary but also ensured the retention of Monroe and Stuckey, together with Miller. Both Monroe and Stuckey had disagreements with Jacobs about policies on the college campus. See the phone interview with Kenneth Monroe, Santa Barbara, CA, 22 October 1979.

41. McClain, "Origin of Grace Theological Seminary," 17. Note that these three concessions, which were, no doubt, controversial at the time, have been critical in the success of the seminary over the last forty years.

42. *Minute Book of the Board,* 24 April 1930, 306. The president of the college following Jacobs, Charles Anspach, committed himself to build "a memorial chapel and seminary building" as well. "Minutes of the Board of Trustees of Ashland College," file for 1935 (second set), 30 April 1935, p. 41, Ashland University Archives, Ashland University, Ashland, OH.

43. *The Ashland Theological Seminary of The Brethren Church, Catalogue and Announcements 1931–32* (Ashland, OH: n.p., n.d. [1931]), 12.

44. Ibid, 14.

45. Ibid., 18–19.

46. *The Ashland Theological Seminary of The Brethren Church, Catalogue and Announcements 1937–38* (Ashland, OH: n.p., n.d. [1937]), 7.

47. McClain, "Origin of Grace Theological Seminary," 20.

48. Ibid., 10. The 1931–32 college catalogue places the issue of governance at the beginning of the catalogue in a section denoted "Historical." It indicates that the Brethren Church has "conducted" the college ever since it purchased the institution at the time of the division in the 1880s. The catalogue goes on to state that the college "is thus, by its history, frankly Christian but its control is not purely sectarian." *Ashland College Bulletin: Annual Catalogue 1931–32* (Ashland, OH: Ashland College, [1931], 17.

49. *Ashland Theological Seminary Catalogue 1931–32,* 10.

50. Ibid., 10.

51. Ibid., 12.

52. *Ashland Theological Seminary Catalogue 1937–38,* 9.

53. *Ashland Theological Seminary Catalogue 1931–32,* 10.

54. McClain, "Origin of Grace Theological Seminary," 20.

55. See *Minute Book of the Board,* 12 April 1932, 321; *Minute Book of the Board,* 25 April 1933, 330; "Minutes of the Board of Trustees of Ashland College," file for 1935, 30 April 1935, p. 29 and 29 August 1935, pp. 64–65, Ashland University Archives, Ashland University, Ashland, OH; "Minutes of the Board of Trustees of Ashland College," file for 1936, 27 August 1936, p. 48, Ashland University Archives, Ashland University, Ashland, OH; and "Minutes of the

Board of Trustees of Ashland College," file for 1937, 1 June 1937, p. 47, Ashland University Archives, Ashland University, Ashland, OH.

56. Milton Puterbaugh, interview by author, 28 May 1979, Ashland, OH.

57. For more details about this situation, see Ronk, *History of The Brethren Church*, 401–06; Stoffer, *Background and Development*, 219–20; and Conference Secretary, ed., *The Brethren Annual 1933* (n.p., n.d. [1932]), 39–45.

58. Conference Secretary, ed., *The Brethren Annual 1934* (n.p., n.d. [1933]), 40–41.

59. Ronk, *History of The Brethren Church*, 406.

60. Edwin E. Jacobs, "The Teaching of Evolution in Ashland College," *BE* 55 (25 February 1933): 6. See also Dennis Martin, "Law and Grace" (Independent Study, Wheaton College, 1973), 111–12. In a letter to L. S. Bauman written the very same month that the above article appeared in *The Brethren Evangelist*, Jacobs indicates that the source of the accusations about evolution was a certain "Wagner." See Edwin E. Jacobs, Ashland, OH, to Louis S. Bauman, Long Beach, CA, 8 February 1933, L. S. Bauman Papers, Grace College Library, Grace College, Winona Lake, IN, microfiche, 455:22–23, p. 1.

61. Conference Secretary, ed., *The Brethren Annual 1933* (n.p., n.d. [1932]), 42; *Minute Book of the Board*, 25 April 1933, 330; and Conference Secretary, ed., *The Brethren Annual 1934* (n.p., n.d. [1933]), 42–43.

62. Delbert Flora, interview by author, 2 April 1979, Ashland, OH, tape recording, Ashland University Archives, Ashland University, Ashland, OH.

63. McClain, "Origin of Grace Theological Seminary," 21.

64. *Minute Book of the Board*, 25 April 1933, 332.

65. The full text of the statement of faith is as follows:

> Acknowledging the absolute supremacy and Lordship of Jesus Christ, and believing that His Word and Will must be final in all matters to those who claim to be Christian, on His authority we affirm the following truths as the basic faith and teaching of this institution:
>
> 1. The Holy Scriptures of the Old and New Testaments, as originally given of God, are the infallible record of the perfect, final and authoritative revelation of His work and will, altogether sufficient in themselves as the rule of faith and practice.
> 2. The One True God, perfect and infinite in His being, holiness, love, wisdom and power; transcendent above the world as its Creator, yet immanent in the world as the Preserver of all things; self-existent and self-revealing in three divine Persons, the Father, the Son, and the Holy Spirit, who are equal in power and glory.
> 3. Jesus Christ the Eternal Son, Revealer of the invisible God, Who became incarnate by virgin birth, lived the perfect human life upon earth, gave Himself in death upon the Cross as the Lamb of God bearing sin and its penalty in our stead, was raised and glorified in the body in which He suffered and died, ascended as our only Saviour and Lord into Heaven, from whence He will come again personally and visibly to raise and translate His waiting Church, establish His Kingdom fully over all the nations, and at last be the Raiser and Judge of the dead.

4. The Holy Spirit, third person of the Godhead, the divine Life-giver and Artist in creation, history and redemption; Who indwells, seals, empowers, guides, teaches and perfects all them who become children of God through Christ.

5. That Man was the direct creation of God, made in the divine image, not in any sense the offspring of an animal ancestry; and that by transgression man became a fallen creature, alienated from the life of God, universally sinful by nature and practice, and having within himself no means of recovery.

6. That salvation is the free gift of God's grace, received through personal faith in the Lord Jesus Christ, in Whom all those who believe have eternal life, a perfect righteousness, sonship in the family of God, and every spiritual blessing needed for life and godliness; but those who reject the gift of grace in Christ shall be forever under the abiding wrath of God.

7. That Christian Character and Conduct are the outgrowth and evidence of salvation in Christ; and therefore the Christian is bound to honor His Word, to walk as He walked, to keep His commandments and ordinances, and thus bear the fruit of the Spirit which is love, joy, peace, long-suffering, kindness, goodness, faithfulness, meekness, and self-control, against which there is no law; and that the teachings of the Bible on such matters as marriage, divorce and the family are of permanent value and obligation to the Church and society.

66. McClain, "Origin of Grace Theological Seminary," 21. For Bauman's view at the time see Louis S. Bauman, Ashland, OH, to Franklin G. Huling, Buena Park, CA, 29 April 1933, L. S. Bauman Papers, Grace College Library, Grace College, Winona Lake, IN, microfiche, 454:47–48, p. 2.

67. Alva McClain to Dean [McClain respectfully addressed Bauman as Dean in many of his letters], n.d. [1920], L. S. Bauman Papers, Grace College Library, Grace College, Winona Lake, IN, microfiche, 53:30 and Alva McClain to Dean, 23 March 1920, L. S. Bauman Papers, Grace College Library, Grace College, Winona Lake, IN, microfiche, 64:12–16, p. 1.

68. I. D. Bowman, "A Defensive Plea," BE 61 (8 April 1939), 13. See also Bauman's sharp criticism of the administration at the Bible Institute of Los Angeles for its requirement that faculty sign a very slanted statement of faith. Louis S. Bauman, Long Beach, CA, to Alan S. Pearce, Los Angeles, CA, 6 April 1929, L. S. Bauman Papers, Grace College Library, Grace College, Winona Lake, IN, microfiche, 338:32.

69. See the following statement from the 1941–42 Grace Theological Seminary catalogue. This statement continued to appear for a number of years in the catalogues of Grace Theological Seminary.

> The conception of Grace Theological Seminary arose out of an informal and unpremeditated gathering held early in June of the year 1937. Deeply concerned regarding the inroads of modern unbelief in the general field of higher education, and especially about the recent victory of a

coalition of "liberal," worldly and legalistic forces over an institution
which they had been supporting, a number of Brethren pastors and laymen had come together in a private home for earnest prayer and Christian counsel. At this and succeeding meetings which attracted a fast
growing number of interested persons, definitely conscious of the guidance and gracious provision of God, plans were laid for the founding of
an institution of higher theological education where positive Biblical
standards of Christian faith and life could be established and maintained
without the hindrance from destructive modernistic elements, and also
where it might be possible to make effective certain educational ideals
which the founders were firmly convinced would greatly increase the
practical and spiritual values of ministerial training.

. . . Included in the new institution were all the teachers save
one, and all the students except two, from the school which had been
lost to liberal forces. . . .

Grace Theological Seminary Catalogue 1941–1942 (Winona Lake, IN: n.p.,
[1941], 9.

70.   Delbert Flora, interview by author, 2 April 1979, Ashland, OH, tape recording, Ashland University Archives, Ashland University, Ashland, OH.

71.   In the minutes of the Board of Trustees the following tribute was approved at
the time of his resignation. Its final sentence was a portend of future events at
the college.

We recognize our brother has given the best of the prime of his life to
the furthering and progress of our common cause; that he has given
himself and his talent without stint or measure and that the institution
as it stands today, looking forward with hope to the future, is in a large
sense of his building, and the product of his ideals. The realities of today
are a monument to the toil of yesterday and a prophecy of the friction
of the morrow '.

"Minutes of the Board of Trustees of Ashland College," file for 1935 (second
set), 30 April 1935, p. 25, Ashland University Archives, Ashland University,
Ashland, OH.

72.   McClain, "Origin of Grace Theological Seminary," 22; Louis S. Bauman,
"Ashland College—Her Vision and Her Purpose," BE 57 (1 June 1935), 2, 18;
and Louis S. Bauman, Long Beach, CA, to Charles Anspach, Ashland OH, 1
July 1935, L. S. Bauman Papers, Grace College Library, Grace College,
Winona Lake, IN, microfiche, 551:43–44.

73.   Durnbaugh, ed. The Brethren Encyclopedia, s.v. "Anspach, Charles Leroy, " by
Leslie E. Lindower and Alva McClain, Ashland, OH, to Dean, 13 February
1926, L. S. Bauman Papers, Grace College Library, Grace College, Winona
Lake, IN, microfiche, 227:43–46, p. 3.

74.   McClain, "Origin of Grace Theological Seminary," 22. Martin, "Law and
Grace," 115–16 observes that neither McClain nor Anspach may have been

acquainted with the current direction of Wheaton College under President J. Oliver Buswell. (For example, Bauman was well acquainted with Buswell's predecessor, Charles Blanchard.) They may have held, in good faith, visions of Wheaton that did not match the reality.

75. C. L. Anspach, "A Statement of Policy," *BE* 57 (1 June 1935): 6.

76. Fundamentalism had developed a stringent ethical standard defined by separation from the perceived evils of modern life. At the 1935 Board meeting at which Anspach was called to the presidency, McClain had sharply criticized the college's toleration of worldliness among both faculty and students, specifically citing fraternities, smoking, card playing, movie attendance, dancing, and drinking. McClain, "Origin of Grace Theological Seminary," 23.

77. Ibid., 24.

78. Bauman reveals in correspondence with Fred V. Kinzie in 1930 that during his first year on the Board of Trustees (1923–24) he challenged the existing procedure for selecting trustees. The Illiokota District, comprising churches from Illinois, Iowa, and the Dakotas, had sent in the names of two nominees. Bauman indicated that the "Board was about to reject both of them and re-elect J. L. Gillin. Instantly, I was on my feet, and when I got through talking I served notice that that sort of policy had to be changed. As a result, it has changed, although it took considerable 'red tape' to do it legally." Interestingly, this is the last year that Gillin was a member of the Board of Trustees. Louis S. Bauman to Fred V. Kinzie, Harrah, WA, 16 August 1930, L. S. Bauman Papers, Grace College Library, Grace College, Winona Lake, IN, microfiche, 348:9.

79. Bauman, who understood the implications of the change, was irate when the Board adopted the amendment in 1937. See Louis S. Bauman, "Who Owns and Controls Ashland College?," *BE* 59 (19 June 1937): 12–14. Martin, "Law and Grace," 119, n. 1 summarizes the legal technicality that created the situation:

> On 10 July 1888 the college was . . . reincorporated, with the result that election of trustees, indeed all functions of the college, were vested in the Board of Trustees itself by default, since the charter made no mention of qualifications for membership in the non-profit corporation, the Brethren Church was not mentioned, and, under Ohio law, "where the charter and regulations do not expressly provide for membership in a corporation not for profit, the Board of Trustees shall from time to time constitute the membership."

Further light on the thinking of the Board about the change is found in a Board statement in 1938 when controversy was escalating in the church:

> The trustees voted to return to the original method of election from nominees by the District Conferences because that was the evident intent of the trust at the time of its foundation, for an added protection to the trust itself against factionalism. Also, the law holds the Trustee responsible not only for the preservation of the assets of the trust, but also for the wise selection of his successors; the method of

election by the Board from nominees furnished by the districts provides for the exercise of this responsibility.

Cited in Ronk, *History of The Brethren Church*, 422.

80. One other change to the college constitution that stirred some controversy was the statement that "No more than one third of the members of the corporation shall be actively engaged in any single profession from which they derive their main source of income or livelihood." This change was clearly aimed at restricting the number of ministers on the Board. George Ronk, on behalf of the Board, responded to this and other points of controversy in the aftermath of the 1937 Board meeting. He gave the following rationale for the change: "The reason for this [change] is due to the fact that the College Accrediting Association rates an institution down if more than one-third of its members come from any one profession." Bear in mind that the college was seeking to regain its lost accreditation with the North Central Association at this time. Ronk tries to deflect criticism, though probably not successfully, by observing that the change "does not mean that only one-third of the members could be ministers. 80 or 90% of the Board members could be ministers, but they can not be making their sole living from this profession." George T. Ronk, *Ashland College: Pertinent Facts from your College and Seminary in Ashland, Ohio* [n.p., n.d.], [8].

81. C. L. Anspach, "A Statement Relative to Ashland College," *BE* 58 (27 June 1936): 14.

82. Homer Kent Sr., in his history of the Brethren Church, engages in some historical revisionism when he cites this quotation as "not even numbered among the *fundamental* [italics mine] forces outside our church." See Homer A. Kent., Sr., *Conquering Frontiers: A History of the Brethren Church* (Winona Lake, IN: BMH Books, 1958; rev. ed. 1972), 144. There is a significant difference in connotation between the use of "fundamental" and "Fundamentalist." Brethrenist leaders would have felt comfortable describing themselves as fundamental but would have rejected any association with the Fundamentalist movement. Kent's change in wording heightens the perceived unorthodoxy of the college and also reflects a period of time in the development of the Grace Brethren when they were becoming less comfortable with describing themselves as Fundamentalist.

There is great irony surrounding this charge. The implication is clearly that the changes in Board composition and in selection of denominational trustees were catering to people with liberal perspectives. The Fundamentalist Brethren felt the self-perpetuating nature of the Board undermined church control of the college and opened the door to liberal influence. In 1910 the Board of Trustees revised the college's constitution. One of the significant changes was the manner of election of the trustees. The Board adopted the self-perpetuating model that was reinstated in 1937. The 1913–14 Ashland College catalogue has this commentary on the change:

The Board of Trustees of Ashland College is a self-perpetuating body and has the power under the laws of Ohio of electing the members of the Board. . . . *This method of constituting the Board will guarantee fidelity to the spirit and ideals of the Church and provide an institution in which the youth of the Church may be safeguarded against the liberalizing and un-Christian influences of the age* [italics mine].

Ashland College Quarterly: Catalogue Number 6 (1 June 1913): 7–8.

83. Anspach's poor handling of the replacement for Monroe upset McClain. Anspach had authorized McClain to hire Homer A. Kent, pastor of the First Brethren Church of Washington, DC, to fill the vacancy. However, after Kent had accepted the position, Anspach reversed himself, probably for financial reasons. McClain on various occasions had cited the standard of the American Association of Theological Schools, the accrediting association for seminaries, that accredited seminaries needed a minimum of four faculty. See McClain, "Origin of Grace Theological Seminary," 24–25 and "Minutes of the Board of Trustees of Ashland College," file for 1937, 1 June 1937, p. 58, Ashland University Archives, Ashland University, Ashland, OH. Ironically, McClain, who was not at all sympathetic to the standards of the North Central Association relating to the Arts College, because of North Central's perceived anti-religion perspective, used the standards of the American Association of Theological Schools to his advantage. There is no indication, however, that the seminary was seeking membership in the American Association of Theological Schools at this time.

84. Stoffer, *Background and Development*, 221. Anspach later became a close friend and mentor of Glenn L. Clayton, president of Ashland College from 1948 to 1977. In one of their conversations Anspach commented about the events of this period and noted that he had been accused of stealing the college from the church during the controversy. With light-hearted wit, Anspach quipped, "I did not steal the college, but I did fix it so no one else could steal it either." Clayton, "Whispering Pines and Purple Eagles," 58.

    This charge is most interesting given the history of ownership of the college. Bear in mind that when Ashland College was founded the Annual Meeting of the German Baptist Brethren had no interest in building and owning institutions of higher education. Individual members of the church had the freedom to establish such schools, but the denomination did not want to be entangled with what many viewed as a worldly innovation. In 1888 when the school was reincorporated as Ashland University, there were some, like Holsinger, who wanted the church to own the school. But fear of liability for the college's indebtedness caused the deed to be held neither by the church, nor by the Board of Trustees, but by an individual (Silas E. Shook, followed by I. D. Bowman).

85. Ronk, *History of The Brethren Church*, 419. Anspach had proposed a similar conference at the 1936 Board meeting.

86. *The Brethren Evangelist: The Brethren Annual Number 1937, Conference Minutes of the Forty-eighth General Conference of the Brethren Church . . . August 24–30, 1936* 58 (31 October 1936): 9–10.

87. Besides McClain, Hoyt, and Stuckey, only L. L. Garber and Allen Scholl supported the motion. McClain, "Origin of Grace Theological Seminary," 26.

88. Ronk, *History of The Brethren Church*, 422 and Louis S. Bauman, "Our White Gift Offering to Grace Theological Seminary: An Explanation," in church bulletin for The First Brethren Church of Long Beach, California, 26 December 1937, [4].

89. "Minutes of the Board of Trustees of Ashland College," file for 1937, 1 June 1937, pp. 50, 56–59, Ashland University Archives, Ashland University, Ashland, OH.

90. McClain, "Origin of Grace Theological Seminary," 28.

91. "Minutes of the Board of Trustees of Ashland College," file for 1937, 1 June 1937, p. 44, Ashland University Archives, Ashland University, Ashland, OH.

92. *Brethren Encyclopedia*, s.v. "Ronk, Willis E.," by Virgil E. Meyer.

93. *Brethren Encyclopedia*, s.v. "Stuckey, Melvin Atwood," by Bradley E. Weidenhamer.

94. *Brethren Encyclopedia*, s.v. "Lindower, Leslie E.," by Ronald W. Waters.

95. "Minutes of the Board of Trustees of Ashland College," file for 1935, 30 April 1935, p. 45, Ashland University Archives, Ashland University, Ashland, OH.

96. McClain, "Origin of Grace Theological Seminary," 28.

97. *Ashland College Bulletin: Catalogue Number 1938–39* (Ashland, OH: Ashland College, 1939), 16. See also the previously cited statements from the 1941–42 Grace Theological Seminary catalogue.

98. McClain reports that Stuckey attended the initial organizational meeting of the new seminary, but was the only person present not to sign a paper indicating support for the creation of the new school. McClain leveled a harsh commentary against Stuckey for his perceived duplicity: "Although he had been the most vociferous (and heartily disliked by the college) critic of the 'liberalism' in the college during his 7 years as a seminary teacher, and also during his earlier student days, nevertheless he managed to make his peace with the administration, but at a cost which shocked his former colleagues and students." Stuckey also allegedly played a key role in the distribution of the "Open Letter" in 1936. "Origin of Grace Theological Seminary," 30.

99. Stoffer, *Background and Development*, 222.

100. Ibid.

101. For this story, see the author's *Background and Development*.

102. Ibid., 223.

103. *Souvenir Program: Ashland College Golden Jubilee* (n.p., 24 August 1928), [7].

104. *Ashland College Bulletin: Catalogue Number 1934–35* (Ashland, OH: Ashland College, 1934), 12.

105. *Ashland College Bulletin: Catalogue Number 1936–37* (Ashland, OH: Ashland College, 1936), 16–17.

106. Ibid., 14. The only changes made to these objectives prior to 1975 occurred in the 1951–52 catalogue. None of these changes altered the basic thrust of the objectives. In 1975 a major revision of the objectives occurred that reduced the list to four objectives. Anspach's third objective, relating to preparation of people for service to the church, especially the Brethren Church, was dropped. Following are the revised objectives in the 1975–77 catalogue:

> To provide its students with an academic environment that emphasizes scholarship, character and cultural attainments under influences that are based on sound Christian ideals and designed to make possible viable Christian experiences.
>
> To encourage students to organize and unify their experiences into a workable and satisfying philosophy of life.
>
> To provide a broad liberal education for future specialization, with a sufficient amount of the technical to acquaint the student with the practical pursuits of life.
>
> To help the individual student to develop his whole personality by coordinating and integrating the instructional process with campus community activities.

Ashland College Bulletin: Catalogue Number 1975–77 (Ashland, OH: Ashland College, 1975), 9.

107. *Ashland College Bulletin: Catalogue Number 1936–37*, 14.

108. "Minutes of the Board of Trustees of Ashland College," file for 1937, 1 June 1937, p. 53, Ashland University Archives, Ashland University, Ashland, OH.

109 See, for example, *Ashland College Quarterly: Annual Catalogue 1926–27*, 14; *Ashland College Bulletin: Catalogue Number 1929–30* (Ashland, OH: Ashland College, 1929), 17; and *Ashland College Bulletin: Catalogue Number 1936–37*, 12, 13, 14, 24.

110. *Ashland College Quarterly: Annual Catalogue 1922–23*, 19.

111. *Ashland College Quarterly: The Catalogue 1915–1916*, 118.

112. *Ashland College Bulletin: Catalogue Number 1929–30*, 7, 17, 23, 36, 67.

113. In a document from 1925 found in the *Minute Book of the Board of Trustees* and entitled "Expansion Program for Ashland College," the affirmation is made that the Board considered itself "Trustees of a Christian College." Yet the Board also sought to "establish and maintain a STANDARD COLLEGE, meaning thereby a College eligible to membership in the recognized College Associations of Standard Colleges." *Minute Book of the Board*, 28 April 1925, 265a.

114. Miller, "A Greater Theological Department," 3.

115. Jacobs, "A Brief History," 12.

116. Miller and Mason, *Short History*, 34.

117. Louis S. Bauman, Beaver City, NE, to H. V. Wall, 28 September 1928, L. S. Bauman Papers, Grace College Library, Grace College, Winona Lake, IN, microfiche, 315:51.

Chapter 5: Rising from the Ashes: Renewed Vision for the Future (1940–1963)

1. Ronk, *History of The Brethren Church*, 450.

2. In an effort to attract women students, an entire *Ashland College Bulletin* was dedicated to the college years of a typical coed, Mary, from matriculation to

graduation. See "A Typical Coed Attends Ashland College," *Ashland College Bulletin* (Ashland, OH: Ashland College, 1943). The Prudential Committee of the Board of Trustees had encouraged such publicity at its December 1942 meeting: "An increase of women students should be sought and the College offerings made as attractive to women as possible." "Report of the Prudential Committee," *Minute Book of the Board*, 12 December 1942, 66.

3. Betty Plank, *Historic Ashland County II* (Ashland, OH: The Board of the Ashland County Historical Society Museum, 1995), 119–121.

4. *Minute Book of the Board*, 12 December 1942, 66. Interestingly, the Board also gave lengthy deliberation to the establishment of an Air Force ROTC unit on the campus during the Korean War. This time the Board approved the Prudential Committee recommendation, with but one dissenting vote. *Minute Book of the Board*, 4 April 1951, 191, 194.

5. Miller and Mason, *Short History*, 84; *Ashland College Bulletin: Annual Catalog (Abridged) 1942–43* (Ashland, OH: Ashland College, 1942), 2; and *Ashland College Bulletin: Annual Catalog 1958–1959* (Ashland, OH: Ashland College, 1958), 15.

6. Miller and Mason, *Short History*, 91 and *Ashland College Bulletin: Annual Catalog 1948–1949* (Ashland, OH: Ashland College, 1948), 109.

7. *Minute Book of the Board*, 1 June 1943, 56, 98. By the latter 1950s Clayton had appointed a Dean of Special Studies to oversee the expanding extension work which, in 1958, included sites in Mount Gilead, Elyria, Millersburg, Greenwich, New London, Loudonville, Shelby, and Mansfield. The extension classes tended to be teacher training classes but also serviced business and industry with appropriate classes. In 1958, 217 students were enrolled in evening extension courses. [Glenn L. Clayton], "A Time for Action: A Report from the President to the Board of Trustees of Ashland College, August 21, 1958" (Ashland, OH: n.p., 1958), 29–30.

8. *Ashland College Bulletin: Annual Catalog 1947–1948* (Ashland, OH: Ashland College, 1947), 143.

9. Though Clayton claimed in his 1951 report to the Board that men outnumbered women four to one in the 1949–50 academic year, this claim is not accurate. Statistics drawn from the 1950 report to the Board indicate that there were 556 full-time students, of whom 150 to 160 were women. See [Glenn L. Clayton], "Facing the Fifties: A Report from the President to the Board of Trustees of Ashland College" (Ashland, OH: n.p., 1950), 16, 19 and [Glenn L. Clayton], "'. . . *for such a time as this* . . .': A Report from the President to the Board of Trustees of Ashland College" (Ashland, OH: n.p., 1951), 19.

10. Miller and Mason, *Short History*, 85 and *Brethren Encyclopedia*, s.v. "Clayton, Glenn Lowell," by Ida Oliver Lindower.

11. Clayton, "Whispering Pines and Purple Eagles," 13.

12. The demographics of the student body for the 1949–50 academic year are reflective of the fact that the college was, to a significant degree, drawing students primarily from the Brethren Church and from Ashland and surrounding counties. Of the 556 regular students enrolled in the college, 312 students came from the city or county of Ashland and Richland County. The Brethren

Church accounted for 84 students (some of these would be counted in the Ashland figures). [Clayton], "Facing the Fifties: A Report from the President to the Board of Trustees of Ashland College" (Ashland, OH: n.p., 1950), 16. The composition of the student body had changed little during the decade of the 1940s. Enrollment figures for 1941–42 paint a very similar picture. Of the 532 students enrolled, 494 came from Ohio, of whom 206 were from the city of Ashland, 75 were from Mansfield, 62 were from Richland County, 38 came from Ashland County, 32 were from Wayne County, and 81 came from other Ohio counties. Only two other states, Indiana (10) and Pennsylvania (17), had at least 10 students enrolled at the college. By contrast in 1972–73, when fall enrollment in the day college program stood at 2379, the college was drawing significant numbers of students from the major metropolitan areas of central and northeast Ohio as well as from states in the northeast United States. The Ohio county with the largest representation in the student body was Cuyahoga (371), followed by Ashland (241), Stark (90), Richland (85), Wayne (83), Lorain (77), Franklin (62), and Summit (48). The states with the largest representation were Ohio (1629), New York (292), Pennsylvania (232), and New Jersey (117). In all 738 students came from states other than Ohio, while another 12 students came from foreign countries. [Glenn L. Clayton], "Dynamic Perspectives and Old Horizons: President's Report to the Trustees, 1972–73" (Ashland, OH: n.p., 1973), 24.

13. This ultimatum had been issued in the wake of a fatal dormitory fire at Kenyon College on 27 February 1949 that resulted in the inspection of all college buildings in Ohio. The State Fire Marshall condemned both Founders and Allen Halls as fire hazards because of their open stairways. Clayton, "Whispering Pines and Purple Eagles," 21.

14. Ibid., 14–44.

15. The idea of a college chapel goes back to 1925 when the campus YWCA launched a fundraising drive for it. The burning of the original gymnasium in 1926 put a hold on the plans, however. Over a decade later the Woman's Missionary Society resurrected the project and began a serious fund drive for the chapel. When the Korean War erupted and there was a threat of building material shortages, the Board of Trustees and the Board of the Woman's Missionary Society in joint session in 1950 adopted a proposal to the Brethren General Conference to endorse the immediate launch of a building program. The conference gave its hearty support to the plan. *Memorial Chapel of Ashland College Dedication Program, Friday, August 22, 1952, 7:30 P. M.* (n.p., [1952], 3. When the Brethren General Conference gathered in August 1952, there was still an outstanding indebtedness of $52,840 for the chapel; the total cost was $170,631. At the conference the Woman's Missionary Society brought in $15,572.65 and the Friday evening offering at the dedication service raised the total gifts and pledges received at the conference to $40,875.25. A deficit of only $11,965 remained. *The Brethren Evangelist: The 1952–53 Brethren Annual Number Containing the 1952 Conference Minutes of the Sixty-fourth General Conference of The Brethren Church . . . August 18–24, 1952* 74 (9 November 1952): 14.

16. Clayton, "Whispering Pines and Purple Eagles," 70.
17. Ibid.
18. Ibid., 70–71.
19. Ibid., 28–29.
20. Ibid., 129.
21. Ibid., 18.
22. Ibid., 96.
23. Ibid., 158–163.
24. *Minute Book of the Board,* 12 April 1950, 158; 10 June 1953, 141; 21 August 1958, 5; and 18 August 1961, 21.
25. [Glenn L. Clayton], " ' . . . threads of gold': A Report from the President to the Board of Trustees of Ashland College, April 17, 1952" (Ashland, OH: n.p., 1952), 2.
26. [Glenn L. Clayton], "Retrospect and Prospect: A Report from the President to the Board of Trustees of Ashland College, April 8, 1954" (Ashland, OH: n.p., 1954), 351.
27. [Glenn L. Clayton], "Building Together for Quality: A Report from the President to the Board of Trustees of Ashland College, August 17, 1961" (Ashland, OH: n.p., 1961), 24.
28. [Glenn L. Clayton], "The Role of the College: President's Report to the Trustees, 1961–62" (Ashland, OH: Ashland College, 1962), 3.
29. *Minute Book of the Board,* 8 April 1954, 384.
30. *Minute Book of the Board,* 17 August 1961, [3–5].
31. [Glenn L. Clayton], "Dimensions for Quality: President's Report to the Trustees, 1962–63," (Ashland, OH: Ashland College, 1963), 3.
32. [Clayton], "Building Together for Quality, August 17, 1961," 39.
33. [Glenn L. Clayton], "They Share in Excellence: A Report from the President to the Board of Trustees of Ashland College, August 18, 1960" (Ashland, OH: n.p., 1960), 52.
34. Ibid, 26.
35. See, for example, [Clayton] "The Role of the College, 1961–62," 6.
36. [Glenn L. Clayton], " ' . . . unto the hills . . .': A Report from the President to the Board of Trustees of Ashland College, April 14, 1955" (Ashland, OH: n.p., 1955), 37.
37. In 1947 the number of Board members from the Alumni Association was increased from 1 to 3 and in 1949 the Board approved the addition of 6 more at-large members to the Board, 4 of whom were to be Brethren. In 1959 further restructuring occurred with the composition at that time being 10 from the Ohio District of the Brethren Church, 4 each from the Indiana and Pennsylvania Districts, 3 each from the other districts, 6 from Ashland County, 3 from northern Ohio, 3 from the Alumni, and 6 at large, of whom 4 were to be Brethren. *Minute Book of the Board,* 21 August 1947, 39; 5 April 1949, 104; "Prudential Committee," 2 April 1959, [1]; and 20 August 1959, [7]. In 1959 the Board also voted to delete the restriction that no more than one-third of the Board could come from any single profession.
38. *Minute Book of the Board,* 18 August 1961, 21.

39. *Ashland College Bulletin: Catalog Number for the Eighty-Third Year 1961–62* (Ashland, OH: Ashland College, 1961), 15; *Ashland College Bulletin: Catalog Number for the Eighty-Fourth Year 1962–63* (Ashland, OH: Ashland College, 1962), 15; and *Minute Book of the Board*, 4 April 1951, 195.

40. *Ashland College Bulletin: Catalogue Number 1938–39* (Ashland, OH: Ashland College, 1938), 11.

41. Clayton, "Whispering Pines and Purple Eagles," 149–150.

42. Reading between the lines in the reports of Ronk and Mason in the Board minutes leads to the conclusion that there was disagreement between Ronk and Mason on such issues as seminary faculty course load, the hiring of additional faculty (Stuckey was planning to be on leave to do graduate work at Western Reserve Graduate School during the 1943–44 academic year), and scholarships for preseminary students. Ronk and Lindower were already carrying a course load of 46 to 51 hours (these were semester hours spread over two semesters) and were looking at adding 16 to 18 more hours to cover Stuckey's courses. Ronk was rankled by the unfairness of this teaching load, but Mason could not justify the hiring of another professor given the tight financial situation of the college during the war. Ronk also wanted some financial support for preseminary students. The Selective Service System was requiring all pre-professional college men to attend school twelve months a year in order to retain their occupational deferment. Not being able to work during the summers placed a financial burden on these students. Mason again was forced to oppose this request because of the fiscal difficulties the college was facing at this time. See *Minute Book of the Board*, 1 June 1943, 82–83, 96–97, Ashland University Archives, Ashland University, Ashland, OH. Mason may reflect fallout from this tension in remarks he made at the June 1944 Board meeting when he challenged the Brethren Church not to harbor rumors and false reports that were destructive to the college and seminary. *Minute Book of the Board*, 6 June 1944, 161–162, Ashland University Archives, Ashland University, Ashland, OH.

43. *Brethren Encyclopedia*, s.v. "Flora, Delbert Benjamin," by Robert B. Clough.

44. See, for example, *Minute Book of the Board*, 10 June 1941, 245 and 1 June 1943, 82.

45. *Brethren Encyclopedia*, s.v. "Boardman, Edwin E., Jr.," by Muriel B. Aurand.

46. *Minute Book of the Board*, 6 June 1945, 205.

47. *Ashland College Bulletin: Catalog Number 1940–41* (Ashland, OH: Ashland College, 1940), 55–56.

48. In the 1975–77 catalogue Greek was dropped from the preseminary course of study as a result of the discontinuation of the teaching of classical languages at the college. Preseminary students were still urged to take fourteen semester hours of a foreign language, however. *Ashland College Bulletin: Catalogue Number 1975–77* (Ashland, OH: Ashland College, 1975), 51. In the 1980–81 catalogue preseminary students were given more latitude in designing their program of studies, though they were urged to complete a major in religion, as had been the counsel since the 1969–70 catalogue. This approach continues to be reflected in current Ashland University catalogues.

49. *Ashland College Bulletin: Catalog Number 1943–44* (Ashland, OH: Ashland College, 1943), 68, 134.

50. *Ashland College Bulletin: Catalog Number 1941–42* (Ashland, OH: Ashland College, 1941), 102.

51. *Minute Book of the Board,* 10 June 1941, 234.

52. *Ashland College Bulletin: Catalogue Number 1947–48* (Ashland, OH: Ashland College, 1947), 141.

53. *Minute Book of the Board,* 5 June 1945, 207 and *Ashland College Bulletin: The Ashland Theological Seminary Graduate School of Ashland College, Ashland, Ohio Announces the Reorganization of Curricula 1952–1953* (Ashland, OH: Ashland College, 1952), 7.

54. "Annual Report of the Dean of the Ashland Theological Seminary to the President," *Minute Book of the Board,* 6 June 1944, 146 and *The Ashland Theological Seminary of The Brethren Church Catalogue and Announcements for 1949–1950* (Ashland, OH: Ashland College, 1949), 52.

55. "Annual Report of the Dean of the Ashland Theological Seminary to the President," *Minute Book of the Board,* 2 April 1948, 75.

56. Clayton, "Whispering Pines and Purple Eagles," 348.

57. Ibid., 348–349 and *Minute Book of the Board,* 23 August 1951, 13. All of the Brethren members on the Board supported the motion calling for Stuckey's resignation. Stuckey refused to resign and was then dismissed.

58. Clayton, "Whispering Pines and Purple Eagles," 39–40, 349.

59. *Minute Book of the Board,* 17 April 1952, 33–35 and *Ashland Theological Seminary Graduate School of Ashland College Announces the Reorganization of Curricula 1952–1953,* 6–7.

60. See, for example, "Report of the Dean of the Seminary," *Minute Book of the Board,* 8 April 1954, 377.

61. For details about this tour, see the travelogue, written by Freeman Ankrum, that appeared in *The Brethren Evangelist* between 2 January 1960 and 14 May 1960.

62. "Annual Report of the Dean of the Ashland Theological Seminary to the President," *Minute Book of the Board,* 2 April 1948, 74; 5 April 1949, 116; 4 April 1951, 214 and "'Sem Wives,'" *Ashland Seminary Voice* 1 (December 1952): 7. In the 1953–54 academic year, 7 of the 36 Brethren in the preseminary and seminary program were serving Brethren churches. "Report of the Dean of the Seminary," *Minute Book of the Board,* 8 April 1954, 375.

63. *Ashland College Bulletin: The Ashland Theological Seminary, A Graduate School—Ashland College, Ashland, Ohio of The Brethren Church, Announcements for 1944–45* (Ashland, OH: Ashland College, 1944), 8 and *Minute Book of the Board,* 6 June 1944, 171 and 20 August 1947, 37.

64. *Minute Book of the Board,* 14 April 1951, 214.

65. *Minute Book of the Board,* 10 June 1941, 245.

66. See *Minute Book of the Board,* 6 June 1944, 148, 170 and 12 April 1950, 157.

67. *Minute Book of the Board,* 14 April 1951, 215. See also *Minute Book of the Board,* 24 August 1950, 193.

68. *Minute Book of the Board*, 10 June 1953, 202.

69. *Minute Book of the Board*, 11 June 1940, 214; 5 June 1945, 208; and 12 April 1950, 145.

70. For further information about John C. Myers, his home, and his art collection, see Betty Plank, *Historic Ashland County* (Ashland, OH: Endowment Committee of the Ashland County Historical Society, 1987), 154–155.

71. "Prudential Committee of the Board of Trustees of Ashland College," *Minute Book of the Board*, 29 December 1955, [2].

72. *Minute Book of the Board*, 11 April 1957, [4]. See also *Minute Book of the Board*, 4 April 1956, [5] and 16 August 1956, [2].

73. *Minute Book of the Board*, 22 August 1957, [4]. The Myers Building Committee was composed of Robert Ingmand, J. Garber Drushal, A. E. Schwab, Harland Clapper, and Glenn L. Clayton.

74. [Clayton], "A Time for Action, August 21, 1958," 33.

75. "Prudential Committee of the Board of Trustees of Ashland College," *Minute Book of the Board*, 27 January 1958, [2] and 20 August 1958, [1]. [Clayton], "A Time for Action," 17.

76. *Minute Book of the Board*, 20 August 1959, [4–5].

77. "The Seminary Committee of the Board of Trustees of Ashland College, Ashland, Ohio," *Minute Book of the Board*, 15 August 1960, [1].

78. Ibid., [2].

79. [Clayton], "They Share in Excellence, August 18, 1960," 30. There were already seven men in the Orientation Program in 1960. "The Seminary Committee of the Board of Trustees of Ashland College, Ashland, Ohio," *Minute Book of the Board*, 15 August 1960, [1]. See also *Ashland Theological Seminary of The Brethren Church: Catalogue Revised to June, 1960* (Ashland, OH: Ashland College, 1960), 13.

80. "Seminary Development Committee," *Minute Book of the Board,* April 1961, [1–2].

81. [Delbert Flora], "Report of the Dean of the Seminary," in [Clayton], "Building Together for Quality, August 17, 1961," 24.

82. "Seminary Committee," *Minute Book of the Board*, 3 April 1962, [1].

83. "Prudential Committee Meeting," *Minute Book of the Board*, 2 April 1959, [2]; [Delbert Flora], "Report of the Dean of the Seminary," in [Clayton], "Building Together for Quality, August 17, 1961," 24; and "The Role of the College, 1961–62," 10.

84. "Seminary Committee," *Minute Book of the Board*, 3 April 1962, [2] and [Delbert Flora], "Report of the Dean of the Seminary," in [Clayton] "The Role of the College, 1961–62," 9.

85. Clayton, "Whispering Pines and Purple Eagles," 354.

86. *Minute Book of the Board,* 16 August 1962, [2].

87. "Seminary Committee," *Minute Book of the Board,* 24 June 1963, [1–2].

88. *The Brethren Evangelist: The 1963–64 Brethren Annual Number, Containing The 1963 Conference Minutes . . .* 85 (30 November 1963): 20, 57–65.

89. Ibid., 18.

Chapter 6: A Time of Crisis and Opportunity (1963–1982)

1. Clayton, "Whispering Pines and Purple Eagles," 260–262.
2. [Glenn L. Clayton], "A Story of Hope: President's Report to the Trustees, 1967–1968," (Ashland, OH: Ashland College, 1968), 70.
3. Ibid., 93.
4. "Report of the Vice President for Business Affairs," in [Glenn L. Clayton], "Positive Solutions to Current Problems: President's Report to the Trustees, 1974–1975" (Ashland, OH: Ashland College, 1975), 55.
5. Clayton, "Whispering Pines and Purple Eagles," 313–315. Every year through the 1984–85 fiscal year the Board was forced to approve two resolutions. One was the use of unrestricted endowment funds as collateral for bank loans and the other was borrowing beyond the 6% limit of budgeted revenue for a given fiscal year.
6. Even before this round of faculty cuts, the number of teaching faculty had dropped from a high of 200 in 1970–71 to 127 in 1976. See "Report of the Dean of the College," in [Glenn L. Clayton], "A Time for Commitment: President's Report to the Trustees, 1970–1971," (Ashland, OH: Ashland College, 1971), 10 and [Glenn L. Clayton], "The Idea of Ashland College: President's Report to the Trustees, 1975–1976," (Ashland, OH: Ashland College, 1976), 55.
7. Clayton, "Whispering Pines and Purple Eagles," 270–271, 274–282; Joseph R. Shultz, *Ashland: From College to University* ([Ashland, OH]: Landoll, Inc., n.d.), 61–62; and "Meeting of the Board of Trustees, Ashland College, May 14, 1982" ([Ashland, OH]: n.p., 1982), 16. The Yeshiva Principle bears its name because the decision was handed down by the U. S. Supreme Court in 1980 in the case of National Labor Relations Board vs. Yeshiva University.
8. Clayton, "Whispering Pines and Purple Eagles," 279–280.
9. Ibid., 272–274 and *Minute Book of the Board,* 8 August 1972, [3].
10. "Executive Committee," *Minute Book of the Board,* 15 April 1971, [1].
11. *Minute Book of the Board,* 14 August 1972, [4]. Wayne Swihart tendered his resignation on the spot and walked out of the meeting after the vote.
12. "Report of the Director of Student Affairs," in [Clayton], "The Idea of Ashland College, 1975–1976," 38.
13. Though there was an ongoing desire of many in the administration and on the Board by the late 1970s and throughout the 1980s to remove alcohol from the campus, this desire was hampered by the realities of student recruitment and retention and the overwhelming support by the student government for the availability of alcohol on campus. Later, in the 1980s, the Board hoped that the federal and state governments would mandate a resolution of the issue. It was indeed governmental legislation that provided the impetus for Ashland to become a dry campus, though the process was quite complex.

   This process began when President Ronald Reagan signed a bill establishing twenty-one as the legal drinking age in the United States on 17 July 1984. The bill authorized the withholding of a portion of the federal funds available to a state for highway construction and repair if that state failed to raise the legal drinking age to twenty-one. Ohio, whose citizens had voted to keep the drinking age at nineteen, joined South Dakota and other states in appealing the constitutionality of the 1984 law before the U. S. Supreme Court. The case was scheduled to be heard in 1987.

In the meantime, on 9 May 1986, the Executive Committee presented the motion that, as of the fall semester of 1986, the college would no longer serve as a host, vendor, or seller of alcoholic beverages to students. Two amendments were passed which effectively held off final implementation of the policy until appropriate administrative policies were in place for such action and input had been received in the fall from students through the Vice President for Student Affairs. At the November 1986 Board meeting, the Vice President of Student Affairs and the Student Senate President presented a transitional alcohol policy developed by the students and the Student Affairs staff. The goal of eliminating Ashland College as a vendor or seller of alcohol was achieved. However, selective permission was given "to various private organizations on campus, under controlled circumstances, to allow beer to be present at special events."

In 1987 the Ohio legislature passed legislation to raise the legal drinking age to twenty-one, presumably after the Supreme Court had upheld the 1984 law. Student Affairs and Student Senate revised the alcohol policy for fall 1987 to comply with the new state law. Students who were twenty-one years of age could consume beer only in the privacy of their own room. Private event permits were no longer available. On 21 May 1989 the Board recommended that "Ashland University become a dry campus after appropriate consultation with student leadership . . ." On 3 August 1989 the Executive Committee received a "Statement on Alcohol" prepared by ten students and representatives of the administration. The document declared, in part, "In recognition of our leadership role as an institution of higher education and in consideration of the present drinking age law, liability concerns, difficulties in supervision, and the need for appropriate standards, Ashland University does not permit consumption or possession of alcohol by students on Ashland University property." The Executive Committee of the Board accepted with commendation the alcohol policy drafted by the student leaders and further adopted by common consent the policy that "no alcohol will be served at any Ashland University organization meetings such as division, administrative, or faculty meetings, or any other functions which are the responsibility of the university." *Minute Book of the Board*, 9 May 1986, 1849; 7 November 1986, 1942; 12 May 1989, 89–45 and 89–44 (for a period of years Board minutes are paginated by "year–page number"); Murray Hudson, "Student Affairs," *Minute Book of the Board*, 21 April 1987, 57 and 1 September 1987, 19; and "Executive Committee," *Minute Book of the Board*, 3 August 1989, 89–64.

14. "Property and Insurance Committee," *Minute Book of the Board*, 17 August 1977, [1].

15. Goettler Associates, Inc., *Study Conducted for Ashland College, Ashland, Ohio* (Columbus, OH: n.p., 1980), part III, 42.

16. Shultz, *Ashland: From College to University*, 18; "President's Report," in "Meeting of the Board of Trustees, Ashland College, May 15, 1981" (Ashland, OH:

Ashland College, 1981), 24; and "Student Affairs," in "Meeting of the Board of Trustees, Ashland College, May 15, 1981," 49–51.

17. Clayton, "Whispering Pines and Purple Eagles," 321–323 and "Properties and Insurance Committee," *Minute Book of the Board*, 26 January 1977, 2160.

18. "Executive Committee," *Minute Book of the Board*, 6 August 1979, 2389–2387 (the pages are numbered in reverse order).

19. Shultz, *Ashland: From College to University*, 17.

20. Ibid., 17–19.

21. Clayton, "Whispering Pines and Purple Eagles," 301–302. Because the seminary was already offering a doctoral degree at this time, the Doctor of Ministry degree, and the North Central Association wanted to deal with the college and seminary together, the college needed to receive authorization to offer the doctoral degree as well as the master's degree. The North Central Association added a notation in its authorization that indicated that the seminary was specifically approved for doctoral work.

22. Shultz, *Ashland: From College to University*, 44.

23. Clayton, "Whispering Pines and Purple Eagles," 283–284; "Executive Committee," *Minute Book of the Board*, 13 August 1972, [3]; [Clayton], "Dynamic Perspectives and Old Horizons, 1972–1973," 3–4; and [Clayton], "Positive Solutions to Current Problems, 1974–1975," 3.

24. Clayton, "Whispering Pines and Purple Eagles," 229.

25. At the September 1979 Executive Committee meeting, Shultz presented three options to deal with the organization of the academic side of the institution. He indicated the resulting economic impact of each option. (1) The college could severely reduce its academic programs, funding only those which were financially productive. But this approach would ruin the strong liberal arts program at the college and make recruiting very difficult in the future. (2) The college could retain the status quo and keep slicing away at its academic programs each year in order to maintain a balanced budget. This option would destroy programs, leading to a demoralized faculty and student body and, in turn, to increasing attrition and decreasing enrollment. (3) The college could bring a creative approach to the current academic programs by redesigning them with the following goals: (a) keep all programs, though possibly cut some majors; (b) re-tool the faculty to teach across department lines; (c) redesign the curriculum in each department or division with the goal of combining necessary courses and thereby increasing class sizes and opening up more faculty time for teaching in off-campus programs; and (d) build up existing programs that had the potential of producing more students and income. "Executive Committee," *Minute Book of the Board*, 20 September 1979, 2434–2433.

26. "Bush Visit Evidence of School's Financial Rebound," *Mansfield News Journal*, 29 April 1984, Sec. A, p. 11.

27. *Minute Book of the Board*, 15 November 1979, 2450 and Shultz, *Ashland: From College to University*, 22.

28. This new attitude of optimism among the faculty was mirrored in two events from the early 1980s. On 14 November 1980 Betty Brodbeck, who, as the

Faculty Senate president, was present at Board meetings, was instructed by the faculty to inform the Board that the faculty were pleased with the management of the college. In a budget shortfall crisis in the 1981–82 academic year, the faculty joined the administration in raising over $25,000 in pledges and gifts to help offset the shortfall. *Minute Book of the Board*, 14 November 1980, 2637 and "Development Committee," *Minute Book of the Board*, 14 May 1982, 2764.

29. Shultz, *Ashland: From College to University*, 22, 27–28.
30. "Executive Committee," *Minute Book of the Board*, 6 August 1979, 2387 and 14 December 1979, 2484; [William H. Etling], "Report to the Executive Committee from the Vice President for Development," *Minute Book of the Board*, 29 April 1985, 22; and Shultz, *Ashland: From College to University*, 65.
31. [Clayton], "The Idea of Ashland College, 1975–1976," 1–2.
32. *Minute Book of the Board*, 17 August 1978, [5] and 2316.
33. Goettler Associates, Inc., *Study Conducted for Ashland College*, part I, 10–11.
34. Clayton, "Whispering Pines and Purple Eagles," 150.
35. [Glenn L. Clayton], "A Personal Challenge: President's Report to the Trustees, 1964–1965," (Ashland, OH: Ashland College, 1965), 50; see also 3, 6.
36. [Glenn L. Clayton], "The Essence of College Education: President's Report to the Trustees, 1968–1969," (Ashland, OH: Ashland College, 1969), 94. See also [Clayton], "A Story of Hope, 1967–1968," 11. These modifications reveal that the Ac'cent Program was flexible, reflecting shifts in emphasis of Clayton and the college.
37. *Ashland College Bulletin: Catalogue Number 1968–69* (Ashland, OH: Ashland College, 1968), 57.
38. *Ashland College Bulletin: Catalogue Number 1969–70* (Ashland, OH: Ashland College, 1969), 126.
39. Note the list of the departmental objectives, which also first appeared in the 1969–70.

> (1) To furnish a basic Biblical understanding and appreciation of Christian thought for all graduating students.
> (2) To provide preliminary studies for students wishing to do graduate studies in religion.
> (3) To prepare students to enter seminary training, religious vocations, and related social professions.
> (4) To provide courses of study for students who wish to teach religion in primary and secondary schools.
> (5) To provide courses of study for students who have interests in Christian involvement in community and church.

Ibid., 126–127. These objectives have continued to appear in Ashland University catalogues to the present. The purpose statement for the department was dropped in the 1990–91 catalogue and replaced by a new mission statement in the 2001–02 catalogue. This statement is as follows:

> The Department of Religion furnishes a basic Biblical understanding and appreciation of Christian thought for all graduating students. It

seeks to help students become aware of how religious commitments and values continue to shape our world views and affect our ethics. It also seeks to be a learning environment for intensive and advanced work in religious explorations as a means of preparing students for graduate study and professional careers in churches and ministry.

Ashland University 2001–2002 Catalog (Ashland, OH: Ashland University, 2001, 135. It is noteworthy that this mission statement returns to a focus on Scripture, Christian thought, and preparation for service to the church as well as the more general training in the subject of religion.

40. Clayton, "Whispering Pines and Purple Eagles," 150; [Clayton], "A Time for Commitment, 1970–1971," 17; and John D. Baker, "Annual Report: Academic Affairs, June 1977," ([Ashland, OH]: [Ashland College], 1977), 5.

41. [Clayton], "Positive Solutions to Current Problems, 1974–1975," 4.

42. [Clayton], "Dynamic Perspectives and Old Horizons, 1972–1973," 108; [Glenn L. Clayton], "Ashland—The Student-Centered College: President's Report to the Trustees, 1973–1974," (Ashland, OH: Ashland College, 1974), 4, 9; and [Clayton], "The Idea of Ashland College, 1975–1976," 4.

43. *1977 General Conference Annual* (Ashland, OH: Brethren National Office, 1977), 71.

44. *The Brethren Evangelist: Annual Number, Minutes and Reports of 85th General Conference of the Brethren Church, August 14–20, 1972* 95 (13 October 1973): 53; *The Brethren Evangelist: Annual Number, Minutes and Reports of 87th General Conference of the Brethren Church, August 11–17, 1975* 97 (25 October 1975): 46, 60–61; *1977 General Conference Annual*, 70–71; *1978 General Conference Annual* (Ashland, OH: Brethren National Office, 1978), 54; and *1979 General Conference Annual* (Ashland, OH: Brethren National Office, 1979), 50–51. The 1975 action was occasioned by the feeling that the existing Christian Campus Ministry had not been working sufficiently in harmony with the college. It was also spurred by rumors that the Grace Brethren were considering a ministry on the Ashland College campus.

45. *Ashland College Bulletin: Catalogue Number 1963–64* (Ashland, OH: Ashland College, 1963), 10.

46. *Ashland College Bulletin: Catalogue Number 1966–67* (Ashland, OH: Ashland College, 1966), 10.

47. *Ashland College Bulletin: Catalogue Number 1963–64*, 19.

48. *Ashland College Courses of Study 1972/73* (Ashland, OH: Ashland College, 1972), 8. See also *Ashland College Bulletin: Catalogue Number 1963–64*, 20.

49. *Ashland College Bulletin: Catalogue Number 1975–77* (Ashland, OH: Ashland College, 1975), 9.

50. See, for example, ibid., 8.

51. [Glenn L. Clayton], "Toward Quality in Personalized Education: President's Report to the Trustees, 1965–1966," (Ashland, OH: Ashland College, 1966), 35; [Glenn L. Clayton], "Continuity and Crisis: President's Report to the Trustees, 1971–1972," (Ashland, OH: Ashland College, 1972), 37; [Clayton], "Ashland—The Student-Centered College, 1973–1974, 50; and [Clayton], "The Idea of Ashland College, 1975–1976," 68.

52. "The Constitution, Rules, and Regulations of the Members of the Corporation of Ashland College," revised August 1976, art. 3, sec. 1.

53. *The Brethren Evangelist: The 1965–66 Brethren Annual Number, Containing The 1965 Conference Minutes . . .* 87 (30 October 1965): 16.

54. *Conference Annual 1970, Minutes of the Eighty-Second General Conference . . . August 17–23, 1970* (October 1970): 25 and *Conference Annual 1971, Minutes of the Eighty-Third General Conference . . . August 16–22, 1971* (October 1971): 26.

55. *The Brethren Evangelist: Annual Number, Minutes and Reports of 84ᵗʰ General Conference of the Brethren Church* 95 (17 February 1973): 42.

56. *Minute Book of the Board,* 14 August 1972, [4].

57. The composition of the Board that was approved in 1964 was as follows:

> 10 from the Ohio Conference
> 4 each from the Pennsylvania and Indiana districts
> 3 each from the other districts (there were four others at the time)
> 6 from Ashland County
> 15 at-large, at least 4 of whom were to be from the Brethren Church
> 3 from the alumni

The composition of the Board approved in 1972 was:

> 10 from the Ohio Conference
> 4 each from Pennsylvania and Indiana districts
> 3 from Southeast district
> 1 each from the other districts (there were four others at the time)
> 6 from Ashland County
> 20 at-large, at least 9 of whom were to be from the Brethren Church
> 3 from the alumni

The composition of the Board approved in 1981 was:

> 1 from each of the districts of the Brethren Church (there were nine)
> 9 at-large members from the Brethren Church
> 14 at-large members
> 3 from the alumni

Minute Book of the Board, 30 April 1964, [4–5]; 18 August 1971, [3]; and 15 May 1981, 23. The 1981 change reduced the number of Board members from 54 to 35.

58. *1965–66 Brethren Annual,* 25.

59. "The Constitution, Rules, and Regulations of the Members of the Corporation of Ashland College," revised August 1976, art. 7, sec. 3a.

60. *1979 General Conference Annual* (Ashland, OH: Brethren National Office, 1979), 13.

61. Ibid.
62. Ibid., 23.
63. Ibid., 24.
64. *1980 General Conference Annual* (Ashland, OH: Brethren National Office, 1980), 16.
65. David Cooksey, interview by author, 3 August 2006, Ashland, OH.
66. *1981 General Conference Annual* (Ashland, OH: Brethren National Office, 1981), 13–14.
67. Ibid., 16.
68. *1982 General Conference Annual* (Ashland, OH: Brethren National Office, 1982), 13–14.
69. "Report to Seminary Committee Board of Trustees and Advisors by Dean Joseph R. Shultz," *Minute Book of the Board*, 2 January 1971, [1].
70. "Enrollment Increase," *Ashland Theological Seminary*, Ashland, Ohio 1 (November 1968): 4; "Seminary Enrollment," *Ashland Theological Seminary*, Ashland, Ohio 2 (November 1970): 2; and Shultz, *Ashland: From College to University*, 49.
71. Various times in the sources, especially from the early and mid-1960s, the required number of catalogued volumes to achieve accreditation was stated to be 30,000. But the number that Shultz used as the visits for full accreditation drew closer and that he cited in his memoirs (though Shultz's memory was notoriously not always accurate) was 25,000. See, for example, "Seminary Committee," *Minute Book of the Board*, 29 January 1965, [2]; "Report of the Dean of the Seminary," in [Clayton], "A Story of Hope, 1967–1968," 64; and Shultz, *Ashland: From College to University*, 49.
72. "Seminary Committee," *Minute Book of the Board*, 29 January 1965, [2]; "Report of the Dean of the Seminary," in [Clayton], "The Essence of College Education, 1968–1969," 77, 79; Shultz, *Ashland: From College to University*, 49; and "Seminary Committee," *Minute Book of the Board*, 29 January 1967, [2]. The closure of the Oberlin Graduate School of Theology and its merging with the Divinity School of Vanderbilt University in 1966 meant that Ashland Theological Seminary was the only graduate theological school in northern Ohio.
73. *The Brethren Evangelist: The 1960–61 Brethren Annual Number, Containing The 1960 Conference Minutes...*82 (26 November 1960): 55.
74. *The Brethren Evangelist: The 1961–62 Brethren Annual Number, Containing The 1961 Conference Minutes...*83 (25 November 1961): 56.
75. "Seminary Committee," *Minute Book of the Board*, 27 April 1966, [1] and "Projects," *Ashland Theological Seminary*, Ashland, Ohio 1 (March 1967): [3].
76. *Minute Book of the Board*, 16 August 1962, [2] and 30 April 1964, [4]; "Seminary Committee," *Minute Book of the Board*, 28 April 1964, [1–2] and 29 January 1965, [2]; and "Prudential Committee," *Minute Book of the Board*, 18 January 1965, [2]. The Board did not want to combine the funding for the renovation of the seminary building with the financing of the major building projects at the college to avoid jeopardizing the bank credit of the college. Shultz expressed frustration over the double standard shown by the Board for financing seminary projects: "the seminary was required to have cash for its projects while at the same time the college borrowed everything, even using

the seminary property as collateral. However, this proved to be a blessing in the end." Shultz, *Ashland: From College to University*, 48. Though the Board did, with some hesitation, authorize the loan for the library and classroom project, it generally did expect cash-on-hand for other seminary projects. Ironically, Shultz inherited the financial burden of having to deal with the significant indebtedness of the college when he became the college president in 1979.

77. "Finance Committee," *Minute Book of the Board*, 18 March 1965, [1] and "Report of the Dean of the Seminary," in [Clayton], "A Personal Challenge, 1964–1965," 54.

78. "Finance Committee," *Minute Book of the Board*, 1 July 1964, [3] and 9 September 1964, [1–2]. The Finance Committee at first concluded that it was not advisable to purchase the building and tabled the offer. Shultz and the Seminary Committee persevered in their advocacy for the building at committee meetings associated with the Board meetings in August 1964 before the final decision in September. The purchase agreement that was negotiated was a purchase price of $52,000 with a $6,000 down payment and the balance amortized at 5% interest. Shultz indicated that he had two individuals who were willing to loan the down payment on 5 year notes at 5% interest.

79. Shultz, Virgil Meyer, and Charles Munson canvassed Brethren churches during 1964 for this campaign. As was typical of Shultz the details about this campaign program vary as to its name, amount to be raised, and length. "Seminary Committee," *Minute Book of the Board*, 28 April 1964, [1]; "Report of the Dean of the Seminary," in [Clayton], "A Personal Challenge, 1964–1965," 54; "Report of the Dean of the Seminary," in [Clayton], "A Story of Hope, 1967–1968," 64; "Report of the Dean of the Seminary," in [Clayton], "The Essence of College Education, 1968–1969," 75; and Shultz, *Ashland: From College to University*, 49.

80. Clayton, "Whispering Pines and Purple Eagles," 156, 197.

81. "Seminary Committee," *Minute Book of the Board*, 19 August 1964, [2]; "Finance Committee," *Minute Book of the Board*, 24 June 1965, [1–2] and 6 October 1965, [2]; *Minute Book of the Board*, 19 August 1965, [3–4]; "Koinonia Effective," *Ashland Theological Seminary*, Ashland, Ohio 1 (November 1967): [4]; and "Building and Grounds Committee," *Minute Book of the Board*, 25 April 1967, [2]. Though two of the identified properties came available in July 1967, the Finance Committee did not approve their purchase because of their inflated prices. "Finance Committee," *Minute Book of the Board*, 5 July 1967, [1].

82. "Building and Grounds Committee," *Minute Book of the Board*, 19 December 1968, [2]; "Finance Committee," *Minute Book of the Board*, 7 November 1969, [1] and 12 January 1970 [1]; Clayton, "Whispering Pines and Purple Eagles," 242; Shultz, *Ashland: From College to University*, 49; and "Miller Property Expands Ashland Seminary Campus," *Ashland Theological Seminary*, Ashland, Ohio 1 (November 1969): 1–2.

83. Clayton, "Whispering Pines and Purple Eagles," 242.

84. The Seminary Building Committee was formed in order to guide the process for the construction of the seminary apartments. It was composed of Smith

Rose, Thomas Stoffer, Herbert Ganyard, Clarence King, R. Wellington Klin-gel, C. Rex Martin, Elton Whitted, and Glenn Clayton. Shultz was also present at the meetings. "Seminary Building Committee," *Minute Book of the Board*, 15 May 1969, [1].

85. Clayton, "Whispering Pines and Purple Eagles," 242–244 and "Dedication of Campus and Apartment Complex," *Ashland Theological Seminary, Ashland, Ohio* 2 (November 1970): 1.

86. *The Brethren Evangelist: The 1968–69 Brethren Annual Number, Containing The 1968 Conference Minutes...*(January 1969): 32. The full recommendation stated:

> The Seminary Committee of the Ashland College Board of Trustees is happy to report the action of yesterday's College Board meeting in relation to Seminary expansion. They approved unanimously authorization for the building of the first Seminary Housing project for approximately $400,000. Our committee is very thankful for both the attitude and co-operation of the College Board in the growth and in the development of Ashland Theological Seminary and also in its service to the Church and to the world. Our committee would like to introduce the following resolution to the 80th General Conference of the Brethren Church:

> **Resolved:**

> That each local Brethren congregation give themselves to prayer for the sending forth of laborers into God's harvest fields;
> That they earnestly endeavor to guide their young people into the areas of Christian service, especially the ministry and missionary endeavor; and
> That they support more fully the work of the Seminary by prayer, by sacrificial giving for seminary housing, and by regular and increased support to complete the obligations of Phase I and of the operational budget of the Seminary.

> ### Seminary Committee:
> Helen Jordan
> J. Garber Drushal
> Paul Bird
> Tom Stoffer
> Smith F. Rose, Chairman

> ### Advisory Committee:
> W. Clayton Berkshire
> John Porte
> Charles Higgins
> Wade Johnson
> L. M. Johns
> Dr. R. S. Kinsey
> Harlan Jennings

87. "Finance Committee," *Minute Book of the Board,* 10 April 1970, [1] and "Dedication of Campus and Apartment Complex," 1.

88. "Report of the Dean of the Seminary," in [Clayton], "Toward Quality in Personalized Education, 1965–1966," 55 and [Clayton], "A Story of Hope, 1967–1968," 61.

89. "Seminary Committee," *Minute Book of the Board,* 27 April 1966, [1] and [Clayton], "A Story of Hope, 1967–1968," 61.

90. "Seminary Development," *Ashland Theological Seminary, Ashland, Ohio* 1 (1 June 1967): 3 and "Financing a Seminary," *Ashland Theological Seminary, Ashland, Ohio* 3 (April 1971): 4.

91. *Minutes and Reports of 85ᵗʰ General Conference of the Brethren Church, August 14–20, 1972,* 59–60.

92. "Report of the Dean of the Seminary," in [Glenn L. Clayton], "The Personal Equation: President's Report to the Trustees, 1963–1964," (Ashland, OH: Ashland College, 1964), 39 and *The Ashland Theological Seminary Catalogue 1964–65* (Ashland, OH: Ashland College Theological Seminary, 1964), 26.

93. "A New Curriculum and Teaching Concept at Ashland Theological Seminary," *Ashland Theological Seminary, Ashland, Ohio* 1 (November 1967): [1]. The statement introducing the Bachelor of Divinity degree in the catalogue gives this further description of the new model:

> The curriculum at Ashland Theological Seminary is designed to lead a man or woman into a program of basic preparation for the Christian ministries. The Seminary recognizes the fact that today the Christian ministry takes many forms including pastoral, Christian Education, social work, and institutional chaplaincy. The multidimensionality is relative not simply to the historical context which demands a qualified ministry, but to the essence of Christian mission. The faculty believes that Christianity embraces every dimension of life and speaks to all men.

Ashland Theological Seminary Catalogue 1967–68 (Ashland, OH: Ashland College Theological Seminary, 1967), 34.

94. "A New Curriculum and Teaching Concept at Ashland Theological Seminary," [1] and *Ashland Theological Seminary Catalogue 1967–68,* 30, 33–34.

95. "Report of the Dean of the Seminary," in [Glenn L. Clayton], "ac'cent on Personal Dynamics: President's Report to the Trustees, 1966–1967," (Ashland, OH: Ashland College, 1967), 59; "Seminary Committee," *Minute Book of the Board,* 13 August 1968, [2] and 4 January 1969, [2]; and "Report of the Dean of the Seminary," in [Clayton], "The Essence of College Education, 1968–1969," 74.

96. "Report of the Dean of the Seminary," in [Clayton], "The Essence of College Education, 1968–1969," 75 and *Ashland Theological Seminary* [Catalogue 1970–71] (Ashland, OH: Ashland College Theological Seminary, 1970), 33. This more formal program of clinical training was preceded by two programs that ran for twelve weeks each during the summer of 1968, one at Hawthornden State Hospital, Northfield, Ohio, and the other at Mansfield State Reformatory, Mansfield, Ohio.

"Clinical Pastoral Education," *Ashland Theological Seminary, Ashland, Ohio* 1 (March 1969): 1–2.

97.   "Report of the Dean of the Seminary," in [Clayton], "The Essence of College Education, 1968–1969," 74 and *Ashland Theological Seminary Catalogue 1969–70* (Ashland, OH: Ashland College Theological Seminary, 1969), 58.

98.   "Continuing Education," *Ashland Theological Seminary, Ashland, Ohio* 1 (November 1967): [1]; "Continuing Education," *Ashland Theological Seminary, Ashland, Ohio* 1 (March 1968): [3]; and "Report of the Dean of the Seminary," in [Clayton], "A Story of Hope, 1967–1968," 62.

99.   "Continuing Education, February 23–27," *Ashland Theological Seminary, Ashland, Ohio* 1 (November 1969): [4] and "All-Institute Study and Continuing Education," *Ashland Theological Seminary, Ashland, Ohio* 3 (April 1971): [1].

100.   "Seminary Committee," *Minute Book of the Board*, 4 January 1969, [2]; "Report of the Dean of the Seminary," in [Clayton], "The Essence of College Education, 1968–1969," 74; "Joint Meeting of Seminary Committee of Board of Trustees and Seminary Advisory Committee," *Minute Book of the Board*, 21 November 1969, [2]; and *Minute Book of the Board*, 5 January 1970, [4].

101.   "Report of the Dean of the Seminary," in [Clayton], "Continuity and Crisis, 1971–1972," 16.

102.   "Report of the Dean of the Seminary," in [Clayton], "A Time for Commitment, 1970–1971," 72; "Report of the Dean of the Seminary," in [Clayton], "Continuity and Crisis, 1971–1972," 16; "Report of the Dean of the Seminary," in [Clayton], "Dynamic Perspectives and Old Horizons, 1972–1973," 91; and "Report of the Dean of the Seminary," in [Clayton], "Ashland—The Student-Centered College, 1973–1974," 39.

103.   Joseph R. Shultz, "Ashland Theological Seminary Annual Report, 1978," (n.p., 1978, photocopied), [2] and "Seminary Committee," *Minute Book of the Board*, 12 November 1981, 2710.

104.   "Seminary Committee," *Minute Book of the Board*, 23 October 1992, 92–93.

105.   "Executive Committee," *Minute Book of the Board*, 27 June 1980, 2621.

106.   *The Ashland Theological Seminary [Catalogue]* (Ashland, OH: Ashland College Theological Seminary, 1978), 5 and *The Ashland Theological Seminary [Catalogue]* (Ashland, OH: Ashland College Theological Seminary, 1980), 5.

107.   *The Ashland Theological Seminary Catalogue 1966–67* (Ashland, OH: Ashland College Theological Seminary, 1966), 16.

108.   *The Ashland Theological Seminary* (Ashland, OH: Ashland College Theological Seminary, 1974), 25.

109.   "Seminary Building Committee," *Minute Book of the Board*, 19 August 1970, [3]; "Seminary Committee," *Minute Book of the Board*, 8 August 1971, [2]; "Report of the Dean of the Seminary," in [Clayton], "A Time for Commitment, 1970–1971," 71; "Report of the Dean of the Seminary," in [Clayton], "Dynamic Perspectives and Old Horizons, 1972–1973," 91; and "Doctor of Ministry Degrees to Be Awarded to Donald Rinehart and Richard Allison," *Ashland Theological Seminary, Ashland, Ohio* 8 (April 1975): 1.

110.   "Dean's Report to Seminary Committee of Board of Trustees," *Minute Book of the Board*, 2 January 1971, [2–3].

111.   "Report of the Dean of the Seminary," in [Clayton], "A Time for Commitment, 1970–1971," 72.

112. *The Ashland Theological Seminary [Catalogue]* (Ashland, OH: Ashland College Theological Seminary, 1976), 34.

113. Clayton, "Whispering Pines and Purple Eagles," 301–302, 359 and Joseph R. Shultz, "Annual Report of The Seminary, June, 1977," (n.p., 1977, photocopied), 1–2.

114. "Report of Ashland Theological Seminary," *Meeting of the Board of Trustees, Ashland College, May 14, 1982* (n.p., 1982), 71.

115. "Ashland Seminary Offers 'Computer and Christian Ministry' Course," *Ashland Theological Seminary, Ashland, Ohio* 12 (November 1979): 4.

116. "Ashland Seminary and Church Growth," *Ashland Theological Seminary, Ashland, Ohio* 8 (November 1975): 1 and "Report of the Vice President of the Seminary," in [Clayton], "Positive Solutions to Current Problems, 1974–1975," 51.

117. "Report of the Dean of the Seminary," in [Clayton], "Ashland—The Student-Centered College, 1973–1974, 41; "Cleveland Center for Theological Education," *Ashland Theological Seminary, Ashland, Ohio* 8 (November 1975): [3]; and *The Ashland Theological Seminary [Catalogue]* (Ashland, OH: Ashland College Theological Seminary, 1978), 60.

118. "Enrollment Sets Record," *Koinonia* 13 (December 1980): 4.

119. "ATS in Extension Work in Four Cities," *Ashland Theological Seminary, Ashland, Ohio* 12 (November 1979): 4.

120. Clayton, "Whispering Pines and Purple Eagles," 287–288.

121. Ibid., 299–300, 356–357 and "National W.M.S. Brethren Church Selects Ronk Memorial Chapel 1974–75 Project," *Ashland Theological Seminary, Ashland, Ohio* 7 (September 1974): 3.

122. "Seminary Committee," *Minute Book of the Board*, 16 February 1978, [1].

123. *Minute Book of the Board*, 18 August 1977, 2231–2230 and "Executive Committee," *Minute Book of the Board*, 17 March 1978, [3] and 19 April 1978, [2].

124. "Executive Committee," *Minute Book of the Board*, 24 January 1979, [4]. At their January 1979 meeting the Board refused to restore the budget cuts that had been made to the seminary budget. As a result several Board members made personal contributions to the seminary library fund totaling $3,025. *Minute Book of the Board*, 25 January 1979, [8] and "Executive Committee," *Minute Book of the Board*, 18 April 1979, [6].

125. "Executive Committee," *Minute Book of the Board*, 18 April 1979, [4]; Shultz, "Ashland Theological Seminary Annual Report, 1978," [2]; Joseph R. Shultz, "Ashland Theological Seminary Annual Report, 1979," (n.p., 1979, photocopied), [3]; and "A Great New Year at Ashland," *Ashland Theological Seminary, Ashland, Ohio* 12 (November 1979): 1.

126. "Seminary Committee," *Minute Book of the Board*, 12 November 1981, 2710.

127. The discussion of "fair share" giving and a unified budget has had a long and interesting history in the Brethren Church. At the 1940 General Conference, the President of Ashland College at the time, E. Glenn Mason, proposed that a committee be created to develop a proposal to bring the missionary, educational, publishing, and benevolent interests of the church into one general budget. The resulting committee was not able to finish its work at the 1940 General Conference, so conference authorized that the proposal continue to be studied and that a plan be brought to the 1941 General Conference. The

proposal that was brought to the 1941 conference recommended that the financing of the primary ministries of the church be pooled into an annual Church Budget that would be administered by a General Board of Finances. But the various denominational ministries feared that such a unified budget would decrease the funds that each would receive. After considerable discussion the proposal was tabled. Miller and Mason, *Short History*, 76–77; *The Brethren Evangelist: The Brethren Annual Number 1941, Conference Minutes of the Fifty-second General Conference of the Brethren Church . . . August 26–September 1, 1940* 62 (9 November 1940): 13, 22; and *The Brethren Evangelist: The Brethren Annual Number 1942, Conference Minutes of the Fifty-third General Conference of the Brethren Church . . . August 25 to 31, 1941* 63 (29 November 1941): 10–12, 23.

The church continued to discuss the concept of a unified budget for the next twenty years without any action. At the 1962 General Conference Moderator M. Virgil Ingraham recommended "that the Central Planning and Coordinating Committee and the Stewardship Committee jointly make a study of plans for a Unified Budget to finance the program of the Brethren Church through General Conference and its auxiliaries . . ." *The Brethren Evangelist: The 1962–63 Brethren Annual Number, Containing The 1962 Conference Minutes . . .* 84 (24 November 1962): 5; see also 16. After four years of study Central Council, the successor of the Central Planning and Coordinating Committee, decided that a unified budget was "not advisable at this time." *The Brethren Evangelist: The 1966–67 Brethren Annual Number, Containing The 1966 Conference Minutes . . .* 88 (October 1966): 22. At the 1970 General Conference Moderator Robert Keplinger again raised a call for "a Unified Budget for the denomination in order that each board may be able to meet their needs and have worthy goals for the future." *Conference Annual 1970*, 18. The recommendation was again sent to Central Council for study. It seems to have been lost sight of or avoided in the midst of a number of other significant issues facing the denomination in the 1970s, however.

A modified approach to budgeting for the various ministries of the church was phased in during the later 1970s. In 1975 General Conference supported a Central Council recommendation to fund the General Conference Budget through a "fair share" scale that based apportionments requested of local congregations on their membership. In 1978 a new scale was developed for local church support of the General Conference Budget called the Church Growth Index (CGI). This index was the sum of a church's membership, average Sunday School attendance, and average worship attendance divided by three. There was also a graduated scale of giving per CGI based on the resulting figure (larger churches paid more per CGI). By 1980 there was agreement on a per member apportionment for all the other ministries of the church, though only the General Conference Budget was based on the CGI. *Minutes and Reports of 87th General Conference of the Brethren Church, August 11–17, 1975*, 20; *1978 General Conference Annual* (Ashland, OH: Brethren National Office, 1978), 11, 85; and *1980 General Conference Annual* (Ashland, OH: Brethren Church National Office, 1980), 15. In 1989 the CGI began to be applied to all denominational ministries. The CGI was multiplied by the agreed upon support amount for each of the boards and ministries of the church to determine the "fair share" that each congregation should be contributing toward denominational ministries.

A truly unified budget resulted from the consolidation of the various boards of the denomination within the structure of General Conference in 1988. An Executive Council gave oversight to the work of the denomination. Only the Missionary Board remained as a cooperating Board of General Conference, but this Board was also subsumed within the structure of General Conference in 1996. By virtue of this significant restructuring of the denomination, the budget for the denomination is fully unified and administered by an Executive Board and ultimately General Conference.

128. *The Ashland Theological Seminary [Catalogue]* 1978, 22, 24 and Shultz, "Ashland Theological Seminary Annual Report, 1978," [3].

129. "In Memory of Charles F. Pfeiffer," *Ashland Theological Seminary, Ashland, Ohio* 9 (November 1976): [1].

130. "Report to Seminary Committee Board of Trustees and Advisors by Dean Joseph R. Shultz," *Minute Book of the Board*, 2 January 1971, [2]; "Smith Archaeological Collection Acquired," *Ashland Theological Seminary, Ashland, Ohio* 3 (April 1971): [3]; and "Smith Archaeological Collection on Display," *Ashland Theological Seminary, Ashland, Ohio* 10 (November 1977): [3].

Chapter 7: An Era of Expansion and Consolidation (1982–2006)

1. In 1983 the Ohio Board of Regents reviewed all off-campus programs conducted by all private colleges in Ohio. Of the 40 private college extension programs, the Board approved only 20. Of these 20 approved programs, Ashland had 10. All of Ashland's extension programs were approved by the Board. Lucille G. Ford, "Vice President," *Minute Book of the Board*, 12 January 1984, 34.

A most revealing statement of Shultz's strategy is found in a document entitled "Ashland University All-Campus Planning Council," dated 22 September 1989. Shultz declared:

The concept of extensions emerged in 1980 when the School of Business and School of Education were given the green light to establish extension centers. It should be clearly understood these centers were established out of concept and plan [Shultz had already made development of extensions a part of his plan for growth at the seminary], even though the particular sites were established according to opportunities. All of this was done to extend the limited base of Ashland, Ashland County, and the church.

It was also clearly understood that we needed to "get there first" as a protection of turf. These bases were established as quickly as possible not only for enrollment, but also to get there before the Board of Regents would clamp down. This is a most significant point which, of course, was not made obvious to the public through written policy.

[Joseph R. Shultz], "Report to the Board of Trustees of Ashland College by the President," *Minute Book of the Board,* 29 September 1989, 4.

2. Joseph R. Shultz, "Report to the Board of Trustees of Ashland University by the President," *Minute Book of the Board,* 16 August 1990, 15 and Joseph R. Shultz, "Report to the Board of Trustees of Ashland University by the President," *Minute Book of the Board,* 8 November 1990, 5.

3. Lucille G. Ford, "Report of the Provost," *Minute Book of the Board,* 21 April 1992, 40.

4. Lucille G. Ford, "Vice President," *Minute Book of the Board,* 17 May 1985, 23.

5. "Executive Committee," *Minute Book of the Board,* 8 November 1984, 1526; *Minute Book of the Board,* 9 November 1984, 1536; and Joseph R. Shultz, "October Report to the Executive Committee, Board of Trustees," *Minute Book of the Board,* 8 November 1984, 13–14.

6. [William H. Etling], "Report to the Ashland College Board of Trustees from the Vice President for Institutional Advancement," *Minute Book of the Board,* 28 October 1985, 17; James D. Harvey, "Report to the Ashland University Board of Trustees from the Vice President for Institutional Advancement," *Minute Book of the Board,* 1 August 1990, 69; and Shultz, *Ashland: From College to University,* 67. A third capital campaign was launched on the heels of the "Partnership in Excellence" campaign. Announced in fall 1990 and called "Financial Foundations for Our Future," the campaign set the ambitious goal of raising $100 million by the turn of the century. The campaign failed to materialize due to the change in leadership at the university. See [Joseph R. Shultz], "Report to the Ashland University Board of Trustees," *Minute Book of the Board,* 20 April 1992, 8.

7. Lucille G. Ford, "Vice President for Academic Affairs," *Minute Book of the Board,* 29 August 1986, 28; 15 April 1987, 22; and 24 October 1988, 43–44 and Lucille G. Ford, "Report of the Provost," *Minute Book of the Board,* 1 November 1990, 27.

8. *Minute Book of the Board,* 15 November 1985, 1726; "Executive Committee," *Minute Book of the Board,* 31 January 1986, 1760–1759; Shultz, *Ashland: From College to University,* 65; and [Joseph R. Shultz], "Report to the Board of Trustees of Ashland College by the President," *Minute Book of the Board,* 8 October 1987, [1].

9. "Executive Committee," *Minute Book of the Board,* 4 April 1986, 1783; 6 November 1986, 1925; and 20 March 1987, 5. In 1990 the Freshman Studies program was folded into the Interdisciplinary Studies Program. "Academic Affairs Committee of the Board of Trustees," *Minute Book of the Board,* 11 May 1990, 90–17. Other student services initiated since 1987 are the Learning Disabled Student Program (begun in 1990 by Karen Little), the Community Service Office, Internships, Minority Student Services, Safety Services, and the Study Abroad Office. Several of these services have come under the

umbrella of Academic Support Services, which includes Academic Advising, the Office of Disability Services, Study Strategies, Peer Tutoring, and the Writing Center.

10. *Minute Book of the Board*, 15 November 1985, 1727.

11. Lucille G. Ford, "Vice President for Academic Affairs," *Minute Book of the Board*, 15 April 1988, 25.

12. Lucille G. Ford, "Vice President for Academic Affairs," *Minute Book of the Board*, 1 September 1988, 5.

13. [Joseph R. Shultz], "Report to the Board of Trustees of Ashland College by the President," *Minute Book of the Board*, 30 October 1985, 7; 20 April 1988, 5–6; and 6 September 1988, 2; "Executive Committee," *Minute Book of the Board*, 16 September 1988, 88–50; and *Minute Book of the Board*, 5 March 1989, 89–49 and 89–48.

14. Joseph R. Shultz, *Report of the President 1988–89* (Ashland, OH: n.p., 1989), inset.

15. "Executive Session of the Executive Committee of the Board of Trustees," *Minute Book of the Board*, 21 January 1992, A-G; 7 May 1992, [2]; and 8 May 1992, [2–4]; "Executive Committee," *Minute Book of the Board*, 7 February 1992, 92–14, 92–13, and 92–12 and 18 March 1982, 92–22 and 92–21; and [Joseph R. Shultz], "Report to the Board of Trustees of Ashland University by the President," *Minute Book of the Board*, 20 April 1992, 7.

16. *Minute Book of the Board*, 22 January 1993, 93–34 and "Executive Committee," *Minute Book of the Board*, 22 February 1993, 1.

17. [Walter Waetjen], "Report to the Board of Trustees of Ashland University by the President," *Minute Book of the Board*, 6 January 1993, 6; *Minute Book of the Board*, 28 January 1994, 94–32; [William Benz], "Report to the Board of Trustees of Ashland University by the President," *Minute Book of the Board*, 18 January 1994, 4; and *Minute Book of the Board*, 19 January 1996, 96–36.

18. Following is this document:

INSTITUTIONAL CORE VALUES
Core Values and Belief Statements

The Importance of Judeo-Christian Values. A strong belief in the importance of value-centered education and, at Ashland University, that these values should reflect those that are basic to the Judeo-Christian tradition.

- Recognizing God as the supreme being
- Behave ethically with moral integrity
- Respect and value each individual
- Know the reason/purpose of one's existence
- Sense one's responsibility to serve others

Distinctive Academic Programs. A commitment to educational programs that include both the liberal arts disciplines and preparation for selected professions (which meant, particularly in the early years, primarily preparation for the ministry).

- Undergraduate and graduate programs
- A continuing education/professional development orientation

- High quality academic culture/environment
- Selected academic programs are accessible at off-campus sites

Comprehensive Student Development. The emphasis has always been on the student at Ashland University and on the importance of promoting the growth of the whole person. An integration of curricula with co-curricular activities requires that student affairs and academic affairs work closely together. The concept of "Accent on the Individual" has been a hallmark of the college since its inception.

- Intellectual growth
- Spiritual/character formation
- Cultural appreciation
- Social experiences
- Physical wellness

Educational Outcomes and Competencies. Ashland University has always been an institution where quality teaching has been emphasized and rewarded. The faculty has historically been comprised of dedicated men and women who are committed to the University's mission and to ensuring that all graduates have the knowledge, competencies, and values which will enable them to live useful and productive lives.

- Develop information literacy
- Read and listen carefully
- Speak and write clearly
- Solve problems logically and creatively
- Act with character and ethically

19. This statement is as follows:

VISION STATEMENT

Ashland University is a distinctive learning community that places an "Accent on the Individual" in an intellectually challenging and supportive environment. Graduates will reflect a strong academic tradition grounded in Judeo-Christian faith and respect, and will be distinguished by their character formation, the quality of their leadership, and service to their communities.

20. *Minute Book of the Board,* 29 January 1999, 99–10; "Academic Affairs Committee of the Board of Trustees," *Minute Book of the Board,* 8 October 1999, 99–80; 12 May 2000, 00–46; 11 October 2002, 10; 1 October 2004, 7; 7 October 2005, 9; and 20 January 2006, 8.
21. G. William Benz, "Report to the Board of Trustees," *Minute Book of the Board,* 21 January 1997, 1.
22. Ibid.
23. Lucille G. Ford, "Vice President for Academic Affairs," *Minute Book of the Board,* 2 November 1987, 34 and *Minute Book of the Board,* 11 May 1990, 90–35; 9 November 1990, 90–72; 22 January 1993, 93–33; and 7 May 1993.

24. "Academic Affairs Committee of the Board of Trustees," *Minute Book of the Board*, 10 May 1996, 96–89; Mary Ellen Drushal, "Report to the Ashland University Board of Trustees," *Minute Book of the Board*, 31 January 1997, 4; *Minute Book of the Board*, 31 January 1997, 97–8; Mary Ellen Drushal, "Board of Trustees Report, Academic Affairs," *Minute Book of the Board*, October 1998, 9–10; and G. William Benz, "Report to the Board of Trustees," *Minute Book of the Board*, 30 April 1999, 6.

25. "Board of Trustees Academic Affairs Committee," *Minute Book of the Board*, 8 May 1998, 98–61 and William H. Etling, "Report to the Board of Trustees," *Minute Book of the Board*, 8 May 1998, 29.

26. *Minute Book of the Board*, 1 October 2004, 2 and 7 October 2005, 2.

27. "Academic Affairs Committee of the Board of Trustees," *Minute Book of the Board*, 31 January 1997, 97–37; *Minute Book of the Board*, 29 January 1999, 99–14; Mary Ellen Drushal, "Academic Affairs," *Minute Book of the Board*, January 2000, 7; and "Academic Affairs Committee of the Board of Trustees," *Minute Book of the Board*, 13 October 2000, 8.

28. G. William Benz, "Report to the Board of Trustees," *Minute Book of the Board*, 30 April 1999, 6; "Academic Affairs Committee of the Board of Trustees," *Minute Book of the Board*, 29 January 1999, 99–13; *Minute Book of the Board*, 31 January 2003, 2; and Mary Ellen Drushal, "Report to the Board of Trustees," *Minute Book of the Board*, 28 December 1995, 13.

29. James A. Barnes, "Report to the Ashland University Board of Trustees from the V. P. for Business Affairs," *Minute Book of the Board*, [January 2000], 25.

30. "Executive Committee Meeting of the Ashland University Board of Trustees," *Minute Book of the Board*, 4 April 1993, 93–45, 93–44, and 93–43 and *Minute Book of the Board*, 7 May 1993, 93–92.

31. The story of how the university arrived at this point deserves some further elaboration. Ashland College had obtained its first administrative computer in 1974. During his presidency Shultz had made a number of advances in technology on the campus. A major kick-start for technology was a new initiative begun in 1987 by the Classroom of the Future. Since 1981 Ashland College through its School of Education had been a partner school in Ohio in this program that was funded by the Knight Foundation and that sought to develop creative approaches to teaching and learning. In 1987 the Classroom of the Future provided funding to the college's School of Education to create new methods of instructional delivery via technology. Shortly thereafter the School of Business, recognizing the critical need for networked personal computers, developed the first campus computer network. The pace of further developments began to quicken. Computer labs began to appear in the late 1980s; Jerry Ulrich taught the first distance-learning "telecourse" in summer 1990, using videotaped teaching sessions and study guides; in the early 1990s the computer labs and administrative computers began to be networked; in 1990 Michael Drushal was given a one course reduction per semester to coordinate academic computing for the campus; by 1992 the library had computerized the catalogue and had made a number of databases available through CD-Rom readers and remote dial-up access. All of these efforts were

occurring, however, without overall coordination of efforts and without a strategic plan for addressing major institutional needs.

In 1992 Waetjen recognized the need for an institutional technology initiative and recommended the formation of a new faculty committee, the Academic Computing Committee. The committee, chaired by William Weiss and Douglas Chismar, retained a consultant in 1993 to gather campus-wide input and prepare a report. As a result of the consultant's findings, the position of Director of Academic Computing was established in 1993 as well as a Department of Academic Computing. Most importantly, impetus grew for a campus-wide network. See especially James A. Barnes, "Report from the V. P. for Business Affairs," *Minute Book of the Board,* [January 1996], 21.

32. Ibid., 21, 24–26; Mary Ellen Drushal, "Report to the Board of Trustees," *Minute Book of the Board,* 10 May 1996, 15, 18; October 1996, 14–15; and 9 May 1997, 14, 17; Mary Ellen Drushal, "Report to the Ashland University Board of Trustees," *Minute Book of the Board,* 31 January 1997, 8–9; "Academic Affairs Committee of the Board of Trustees of Ashland University," *Minute Book of the Board,* 23 January 1998, 98–19; and G. William Benz, "Report to the Board of Trustees," *Minute Book of the Board,* 9 September 1997, 6.

33. Office of the Provost, "Board of Trustees Report," *Minute Book of the Board,* Spring 2001, 13; "Academic Affairs Committee of the Board of Trustees of Ashland University," *Minute Book of the Board,* 8 October 1999, 99–87; 13 October 2000, 10; and 26 January 2001, 13; *Minute Book of the Board,* 3 October 2003, 7; 7 May 2004, 6; and 1 October 2004, 2; "Report to the Board of Trustees by the Student Life Committee," *Minute Book of the Board,* 6 May 2005, 38; and William H. Etling, "Report to the Board of Trustees," *Minute Book of the Board,* 25 January 2002, 29.

34. "Board of Trustees Academic Affairs Committee," *Minute Book of the Board,* 8 May 1998, 98–59.

35. *Minute Book of the Board,* 20 August 1969, [2] and James A. Barnes, "Report from the V. P. for Business Affairs," *Minute Book of the Board,* [January 1997], 13.

36. *Minute Book of the Board,* 23 January 1998, 98–10; 2 October 1998, 98–88; 14 May 1999, 99–46 and 99–49; and 1 October 2004, 3 and G. William Benz, "Report to the Board of Trustees," *Minute Book of the Board,* 27 September 1999, 6.

37. The rationale for construction of the senior apartments was to keep seniors on campus, to generate additional income, and to reduce community complaints about off-campus students. The funding for both projects was independent of the capital campaign; the Board sought to take advantage of low interest bonds that were currently available. See *Minute Book of the Board,* 5 October 2001, 6 and 3 October 2003, 6.

38. "Meeting of the Finance and Facilities Committee of the Board of Trustees," *Minute Book of the Board,* 10 May 1996, 96–77.

39. G. William Benz, "Report to the Board of Trustees," *Minute Book of the Board,* 25 April 2000, 5. The university budget continues to be tuition-driven; tuition and fees averaged 76% of the total budget between 1991 and 2004. In

order to make college education affordable, Ashland University, like other educational institutions, invested significant funds into financial aid. The university provided $123,420,930 in financial aid between 1996–97 and 2005–06. In the ten years from 1994–95 to 2004–05, total financial aid had more than doubled from $7,998,887 to $16,001,393. In the 2005–06 academic year, 4,025 undergraduate and graduate students received approximately $50.5 million in total financial aid from all sources. Ashland University contributed about $16.4 million of this total to 2,135 students; the total budgeted expenses for 2005–06 were $102,627,064. The endowment grew significantly during Benz's presidency; on 30 June 1993 the endowment was $17.15 million and it stood at $44.6 million as of 31 December 2005. See "Meeting of the Finance and Facilities Committee," *Minute Book of the Board*, 23 January 2004, 26; 20 January 2005, 5; and 20 January 2006, 22, 29; Student Life Committee, "Report to the Board of Trustees," *Minute Book of the Board*, 20 January 2006, 44; James A. Barnes, "Report to the Ashland University Board of Trustees," *Minute Book of the Board*, [October 1993], 72; and *Minute Book of the Board*, 20 January 2006, 3.

40. After attaining a record total enrollment of 6922 students in fall 2004, enrollment figures for fall 2005 dropped to 6472. The largest drop was in the graduate programs. Some reasons for the drop in the graduate education program are: (1) the crisis in the funding of public education in the state of Ohio that has led to significant cutbacks in many school districts and (2) the increasing competition for graduate education students as other Ohio schools develop graduate education programs. The M.B.A. program also registered a decline for the second straight year in 2005–06. This decline was attributed to: (1) companies were reducing corporate reimbursement for education; (2) companies were downsizing and flattening their organizational structure; (3) fewer international students were applying for and obtaining visas; (4) there was greater competition from for-profit and not-for-profit schools; and (5) there was increasing competition from alternative delivery modes for M.B.A. programs, especially online degree offerings. In addition, the increasing popularity of community colleges has meant more competition for undergraduate students. See "Academic Affairs Committee," *Minute Book of the Board*, 7 October 2005, 11.

41. James A. Barnes, "Report from the V.P. for Business Affairs," *Minute Book of the Board*, 11 May 2003, 20 and "Meeting of the Finance and Facilities Committee," *Minute Book of the Board*, 3 October 2003, 19.

42. "Dr. Benz Presidency Ends," *Accent Ashland University Magazine*, Fall 2006, 16.

43. [Joseph R. Shultz], "Report to the Board of Trustees of Ashland College by the President," *Minute Book of the Board*, 1 March 1989, 1.

44. *Ashland University 1994–95 Catalog* (Ashland, OH: Ashland University, [1994]), 5.

45. *Ashland University 2002–03 Catalog* (Ashland, OH: Ashland University, [2002]), 5.

46. [Joseph R. Shultz], "Report to the Board of Trustees of Ashland College by the President," *Minute Book of the Board*, 22 April 1986, 23 and Donald R. Rinehart, "School of Arts & Humanities," *Minute Book of the Board*, 6 May 1988, 35.

47. *Ashland College 1982–83 Catalog* (Ashland, OH: Ashland College, [1982], 7, 11, 37–38, 93.

48. Michael Gleason, "Religious Life Department Report," *Minute Book of the Board*, [October 1992], 20; [January 1994], 12; [May 1994], 8–9; 6 October 1995, 7; September 1999, 52; January 2000, 52; April 2000, 55; October 2000, 54; and May 2002, 72.

49. Student Life Committee, "Report to the Board of Trustees," *Minute Book of the Board*, 23 January 2004, 50.

50. Ibid., 31 January 2003, 47; 23 January 2004, 50; and 1 October 2004, 5; *Minute Book of the Board*, 7 May 2004, 7; and *1984 General Conference Annual* (Ashland, OH: Brethren Church National Office, [1984]), 16.

51. *Minute Book of the Board*, 23 October 1992, 92–145 and 92–144.

52. Executive Session, *Minute Book of the Board*, 1 October 2004, 2–4.

53. *Minute Book of the Board*, 20 January 2005, 2; 21 January 2005, 8–9; and 6 May 2005, 9.

54. *1989 General Conference Annual* (Ashland, OH: Brethren Church National Office, [1989]), 16.

55. Five Stones Community Church was a church planting venture of Park Street Brethren Church. It was pastored by Don Belsterling from 2003 to 2006 and is currently in pastoral transition.

56. "Meeting of the Executive Committee of the Board of Trustees of Ashland University," *Minute Book of the Board*, 4 April 1993, 93–43.

57. The composition of the committee was as follows. From the Brethren Church were Emanuel Sandberg, Thomas Stoffer, Arden Gilmer, Dan Lawson, Jamie Gillespie, and Bruce Wilkinson; from the university were Jim Barnes, Steve Hannan, John Nethers, Don Rinehart, Margaret Pomfret, and Sue Heimann; and serving *ex officio* were William Benz, Joseph Shultz, and Glenn Clayton. *Minute Book of the Board*, 25 January 2002, 9.

58. *Ashland University 1993–94 Catalog* (Ashland, OH: Ashland University, [1993]), 4.

59. *Minute Book of the Board*, 13 November 1981, 2724.

60. Frederick Finks, interview by author, 28 July 2005, Ashland, OH and "Report of the Detroit Center for Theological Education" (Ashland, OH: Ashland Theological Seminary, 1985, photocopied), 1–2.

61. "Seminary Committee," *Minute Book of the Board*, 2 November 1983, 1434 and Frederick J. Finks, "Ashland Theological Seminary," *Minute Book of the Board*, 12 January 1984, 36.

62. "Seminary Committee," *Minute Book of the Board*, 2 November 1983, 1435 and *Minute Book of the Board*, 2 November 1983, 1454.

63. "Seminary Committee," *Minute Book of the Board*, 11 May 1984, 1488–1487 and Frederick J. Finks, "Ashland Theological Seminary," *Minute Book of the Board*, 11 May 1984, 17.

64. Frederick J. Finks, "Vice President's Report," *Minute Book of the Board*, 9 September 1985, [1] and Frederick J. Finks, "Ashland Theological Seminary," *Minute Book of the Board*, 15 November 1985, 38 and 9 May 1986, 83.

65. Duncan R. Jamieson and Gene Telego, "Academic Affairs," *Minute Book of the Board*, 15 January 1986, 22; Lucille G. Ford, "Vice President for Academic Affairs," *Minute Book of the Board*, 26 August 1986, 27; Frederick J. Rafeld, "School of Business Administration, Economics and Radio/TV," *Minute Book of the Board*, 20 October 1986, 48; and Frederick J. Finks, "Ashland Theological Seminary," *Minute Book of the Board*, 31 January 1986, 34.

66. "Executive Committee," *Minute Book of the Board*, 20 June 1986, 1855.

67. Frederick J. Finks, "Ashland Theological Seminary," *Minute Book of the Board*, 17 March 1986, 31 and "Executive Committee," *Minute Book of the Board*, 4 April 1986, 1782.

68. "Seminary Committee," *Minute Book of the Board*, 10 November 1989, 89–85 and 89–84.

69. "Seminary Committee," *Minute Book of the Board*, 15 November 1985, 1653–1651; *Minute Book of the Board*, 15 November 1985, 1720; and "Seminary to Launch New Campaign," *Koinonia* 19 (August 1986): [2].

70. *Minute Book of the Board*, 6 May 1988, 88–41.

71. "Seminary Dedicates New Classroom Building," *Koinonia* 13 (August 1989): [1] and Frederick J. Finks, "Ashland Theological Seminary," *Minute Book of the Board*, 21 October 1991, 81–82.

72. [Frederick J. Finks], "Ashland Theological Seminary," *Minute Book of the Board*, 14 July 1989, 13–15; "Executive Committee," *Minute Book of the Board*, 3 August 1989, 89–63 and 89–62; and Frederick J. Finks, "Ashland Theological Seminary," *Minute Book of the Board*, 21 October 1991, 81, 83.

73. "Executive Committee," *Minute Book of the Board*, 11 May 1990, 90–40; Frederick J. Finks, "Ashland Theological Seminary," *Minute Book of the Board*, 21 October 1991, 81; and "Seminary Library Addition Dedicated to Rev. George Solomon," *Koinonia* 24 (February 1992): 1, 4.

74. Frederick J. Finks, "Ashland Theological Seminary," *Minute Book of the Board*, 21 October 1991, 82–84.

75. "Seminary Committee," *Minute Book of the Board*, 6 May 1988, 88–19 and 88–18.

76. [Frederick J. Finks], "Ashland Theological Seminary," *Minute Book of the Board*, 14 July 1989, 13.

77. Frederick J. Finks, "Ashland Theological Seminary," *Minute Book of the Board*, 19 April 1989, 95.

78. The statement in full, as found in the 1980–81 catalogue, is:

> The Christian ministry is based upon a divine calling to serve in a demanding world. The complex world demands ministers who can preach and teach the Word of God with ability, conviction, and spiritual power. At the present time there are insufficient trained ministers to supply the minimum needs of the church. If there is to be a spiritual revolution in our century, a great stream of capable Christian leadership must pour from our Seminary. The need is both quantitative and qualitative.
>
> Ashland Theological Seminary is committed to the Holy Scriptures as inspired by God, and to the orthodox faith of the Church. The

total curriculum is in harmony with this basic commitment and the belief that the Spirit effects the teaching of the Word of God. The program of training for Christian ministries combines the Biblical truth with adequate ministerial skills. While our roots are solidly planted in the Holy Scriptures of God we extend ourselves in greater capacities to minister to contemporary man. The curriculum is designed to prepare Christian ministers to address modern man with a vital Faith.

We invite persons called of God to seriously consider the question put by the apostle Paul in his letter to the Romans: "But how are they to call upon him in whom they have not believed? And how are they to believe in him of whom they have never heard? And how are they to hear without a preacher?"

The Ashland Theological Seminary [Catalogue] (Ashland, OH: Ashland College Theological Seminary, 1980), 5.

79. *The Ashland Theological Seminary [Catalogue]* (Ashland, OH: Ashland College Theological Seminary, 1985), 5.

80. *Ashland Theological Seminary Catalogue 1968–69* (Ashland, OH: Ashland College Theological Seminary, 1968), 19.

81. Frederick J. Finks, "Ashland Theological Seminary," *Minute Book of the Board*, 15 November 1985, 37.

82. "Seminary Committee," *Minute Book of the Board*, 11 November 1988, 88–62; "Seminary Introduces new Program in Church Music," *Koinonia* 21 (December 1988): [3]; "Ashland Seminary Stays on the Cutting Edge," *Koinonia* 22 (August 1990): [1]; and "1996 Seminary Graduation," *Koinonia* 28 (July 1996): [2].

83. "Ashland Seminary Stays on the Cutting Edge," [1] and "Seminary Committee," *Minute Book of the Board*, 10 May 1991, 91–12 and 8 November 1991, 91–48.

84. "Seminary Committee," *Minute Book of the Board*, 10 May 1991, 91–12 and 8 November 1991, 91–48 and Frederick Finks, interview by author, 28 July 2005, Ashland, OH.

85. "Seminary Committee," *Minute Book of the Board*, 8 May 1987, 1991.

86. Frederick J. Finks, "Ashland Theological Seminary," *Minute Book of the Board*, 20 April 1987, 58.

87. "Seminary Launches 'CALM' Project," *Koinonia* 21 (December 1988): [2]; "Seminary Committee," *Minute Book of the Board*, 12 May 1989, 89–25 and 89–24 and 11 May 1990, 90–20; and "Seminary Introduces Video Curriculum," *Koinonia* 23 (January 1991): [4].

88. Frederick J. Finks, "Ashland Theological Seminary," *Minute Book of the Board*, 29 September 1989, 43.

89. "Seminary Committee," *Minute Book of the Board*, 8 November 1991, 91–48.

90. The minutes of the meeting of the Seminary Committee for 8 November 1991 record lists of the strengths and weaknesses of the seminary generated by both the Trustees and the faculty. As strengths the Trustees listed "fundamentally sound, campus friendly, evangelical, continuity of purpose, strong and dedicated

faculty, reliable teaching, heart for local church, relevant for today's society, be-coming strong in music/worship, nice facility, financially sound, and ministry to pastors." To this list the faculty added: "a strong and dedicated board, extension beyond Ashland, trans-denominational, willingness to be innovative, interna-tional outreach and breadth of the student body." The Trustees then listed the following weaknesses: "evangelistic thrust, need more endowments, more hous-ing, video teaching, shared learning with the local church, bulletin inserts and better communication." Selected faculty then addressed various suggestions for the long-range plan of the seminary: endowed chairs; faculty positions in homiletics, evangelism/discipleship, spiritual formation, and Brethren history and thought; shared doctoral programs in Old Testament with Ashland Univer-sity and Ohio State University; professional development of faculty; continuing education opportunities for pastors and church leaders; and renew and complete the curriculum review begun in 1985. Ibid., 91–50 and 91–49.

91. [Frederick J. Finks], "Ashland Theological Seminary," *Minute Book of the Board*, [15 November 1985], 1653.

92. "Seminary Committee," *Minute Book of the Board*, 29 January 1999, 99–39 and 21 January 2005, 48 and *Ashland Theological Seminary Self-Study Presented to the Association of Theological Schools and North Central Association of Colleges and Schools and Ohio Board of Regents, January, 1988* ([Ashland, OH: Ashland Theological Seminary], 1988), 103–104.

93. "ATS Participates in Lexington Seminar," *Koinonia* 37 (July 2005): 8.

94. Frederick J. Finks, "Ashland Theological Seminary," *Minute Book of the Board*, 23 September 1994, 62 and *Minute Book of the Board*, 7 October 1994, 94–122 and 22 January 1993, 93–29 and 93–28.

95. Frederick J. Finks, "Ashland Theological Seminary," *Minute Book of the Board*, [May 1995], 36; *Minute Book of the Board*, 12 May 1995, 95–71 and 11 October 1996, 96–143 and 96–142; "Gerber Academic Center Dedicated," *Koinonia* 29 (August 1997): 3–4; and "Seminary Committee," *Minute Book of the Board*, 2 October 1998, 98–118.

96. "Seminary Prayer Garden Helps Contribute to Spiritual Formation," *Koinonia* 29 (January 1997): 4.

97. "Seminary Committee," *Minute Book of the Board*, 31 January 1997, 97–50; 8 May 1998, 98–80 and 98–81; "Meeting of the Development Committee of the Board of Trustees of Ashland University," *Minute Book of the Board*, 8 May 1998, 98–71; and Frederick J. Finks, "Ashland Theological Seminary," *Minute Book of the Board*, 15 September 1998, 45.

98. *Minute Book of the Board*, 29 January 1999, 99–5; 14 May 1999, 99–47; 8 Oc-tober 1999, 99–79; 28 January 2000, 00–10; and 12 May 2000, 00–50; Freder-ick J. Finks, "Ashland Theological Seminary," *Minute Book of the Board*, 20 September 1999, 45; and "Seminary Committee," *Minute Book of the Board*, 8 October 1999, 99–112.

99. "Groundbreaking Services at ATS," *Koinonia* 31 (January 2001): 2; "Leadership Center Construction Underway," *Koinonia* 31 (January 2001): 3; and "Sandberg Leadership Center nears Completion," *Koinonia* 33 (August 2001): 6.

100. "Dedication of Sandberg Leadership Center," *Koinonia* 34 (January 2002): 2.

101. "Executive Committee," *Minute Book of the Board*, 24 September 1982, 7; "ATS 1000 Joins AC 1000 Campaign," *Koinonia* 15 (December 1982): [3]; and "Seminary Committee," *Minute Book of the Board*, 9 May 1986, 1804.

102. "ATS Announces $8 Million 5-Year Capital Campaign," *Koinonia* 31 (January 2001): 4.

103. "The Kern Family Foundation" and "The Opal Dancey Memorial Foundation," *Koinonia* 35 (January 2003): 7.

104. Frederick J. Finks, "Ashland Theological Seminary," *Minute Book of the Board*, 6 January 1995, 52 and "Proclaiming the Word of God . . . Robert & Thelma Frank" and "Dr. J. Ray Klingensmith Chair in Church Planting Founded," *Koinonia* 31 (January 1999): 2, 4.

105. *Ashland Theological Seminary 1994–96 Catalog* (Ashland, OH: Ashland Theological Seminary, 1994), 11.

106. "Seminary Committee," *Minute Book of the Board*, 14 May 1999, 99–73 and 8 October 1999, 99–110 and "Master of Divinity Degree Redesigned," *Koinonia* 31 (January 2001): 4.

107. "Philosophy of Theological Education, Ashland Theological Seminary," D (photocopy) 3 May 2004, Ashland Theological Seminary, Ashland, OH. See also "Seminary Committee," *Minute Book of the Board*, 7 May 2004, 53.

108. "Seminary Committee," *Minute Book of the Board*, 10 May 2002, 54 and 23 January 2004, 54–55 and *Minute Book of the Board*, 11 October 2002, 7.

109. Frederick J. Finks, "Ashland Theological Seminary," *Minute Book of the Board*, 14 April 1993, 79; 11 March 1994, 18; and 29 April 1994, 79.

110. Frederick J. Finks, "Ashland Theological Seminary," *Minute Book of the Board*, 13 January 1997, 50; 22 April 1997, 61; and 21 April 1998, 51; "Seminary Committee," *Minute Book of the Board*, 23 January 1998, 98–43; and *Minute Book of the Board*, 23 January 2004, 7.

111. Frederick J. Finks, "Ashland Theological Seminary," *Minute Book of the Board*, 20 April 1992, 109; "Seminary Committee," *Minute Book of the Board*, 9 May 1997, 97–75; *Ashland Theological Seminary 1998–2000 Catalog* (Ashland, OH: Ashland Theological Seminary, 1998), 61.

112. Extension Task Force, "A Rationale for ATS Extensions" (Ashland, OH: Ashland Theological Seminary, 2004, photocopied).

113. The other guiding principles that were a part of the strategic planning document prepared in 2003 were: (1) commitment to a theologically evangelical position; (2) commitment to the building of a faith community with Christ-centered diversity; (3) commitment to a mission of church and world; (4) commitment to transformational education; (5) commitment to serving students in culturally relevant ways; and (6) commitment to remaining financially stable. See "Ashland Theological Seminary Strategic Vision Document, 2003–2008," D (photocopy), p. 1, Ashland Theological Seminary, Ashland, OH.

114. "Seminary Committee," *Minute Book of the Board*, 10 October 1997, 97–114 and Frederick J. Finks, "Ashland Theological Seminary," *Minute Book of the Board*, 21 April 1998, 52.

115. "Report to The Commission on Accrediting, The Association of Theological Schools in the United States and Canada" (Ashland, OH: Ashland Theological Seminary, 2000), [1–5].

116. Mary Ellen Drushal, "Report to the Board of Trustees," *Minute Book of the Board*, 9 May 1997, 17.

117. "Technology Advancements," *Koinonia* 37 (January 2005): 6. For a discussion of the seminary's journey related to technology, see Vickie Taylor, "Technology Development at Ashland Theological Seminary" (Ashland, OH: Ashland Theological Seminary, 2006, photocopied).

118. Frederick J. Finks, "Ashland Theological Seminary," *Minute Book of the Board*, 23 September 1994, 63.

119. "Seminary Committee," *Minute Book of the Board*, 23 October 1992, 92–93 and 92–92.

120. *Minute Book of the Board*, 23 October 1992, 92–133 and 92–132.

121. Frederick J. Finks, "Ashland Theological Seminary," *Minute Book of the Board*, 5 October 1992, 80–81.

122. Frederick J. Finks, "Ashland Theological Seminary," *Minute Book of the Board*, 23 October 1993, 105–110 and *Minute Book of the Board*, 16 October 1993, 93–136.

123. *Ashland Theological Seminary 1998–2000 Catalog* (Ashland, OH: Ashland Theological Seminary, 1998), 3–4.

124. Minor revisions have been made over the years to the "Statement of Faith" in the seminary catalogue (the statement was originally adopted by the college in 1933). In the 1965–66 catalogue the phrase "not in any sense the offspring of an animal ancestry" was dropped in point five. This change should not be viewed as a concession to evolution, but as a desire to remove an argumentative element from the statement. In the 1970–71 catalogue, the word "Jesus" was dropped from the phrase in point 6: "personal faith in the Lord Jesus Christ." This change may have been an editing error; "Jesus" was returned to the phrase in the 2001–02 online catalogue. Inclusive language was added to point 5 in the 1991–93 catalogue: "That man and woman were the . . . , and that by transgression became a fallen creature, . . . and having within themselves no means of recovery." A number of minor revisions were made in the 2001–02 online catalogue. In point E (letters replaced numbers for the main points in the 1998–2000 catalogue) "became a fallen creature" was changed to "became fallen creatures." In point F "sonship in the family of God" became "adoption in the family of God"; "membership in the body of Christ" was added following the statement on adoption; and "those who reject the gift of grace in Christ shall be forever under the abiding wrath of God" was changed to " . . . shall be forever separated from the presence of God." In point G "That Christian character and conduct are the outgrowth and evidence of salvation in Christ; and therefore the Christian is bound to honor His Word . . ." is changed to "That Christian character and conduct are the expression of one's relationship with Christ and one's life in the community of Christ; and therefore Christians are bound to honor Christ's word . . ." In point G "to the Church and society" is omitted from the statement "that the teachings of the Bible on such matters as marriage, divorce and the family are of permanent value and obligation to the Church and society."

125. *Ashland Theological Seminary 2002–2004 Catalog* (Ashland, OH: Ashland Theological Seminary, 2002), 7.

126. "Renewing Pastor and People" and "Church Planting Seminar," *Koinonia* 31 (January 2000): 3, 6; "Renewing Pastor and People," *Koinonia* 33 (August 2001): 5; and "The Institute of Formational Counseling," *Koinonia* 36 (January 2004): 4.

127. "Sandberg Leadership Center," *Koinonia* 38 (July 2006): 7.

128. "Christian Leaders of Excellence Program (CLE)," *Koinonia* 38 (July 2006): 7.

129. "Seminary Receives Three Grants," *Koinonia* 35 (January 2003): 1, 7 and "Pastors of Excellence (POE)," *Koinonia* 37 (July 2005): 5.

130. "Pastors of Excellence," 5 and "Sandberg Leadership Center: Pastors of Excellence Program" and "SLC Development News," *Koinonia* 38 (July 2006): 5, 7.

131. "Seminary Committee," *Minute Book of the Board*, 9 November 1990, 90–53; *Minute Book of the Board*, 28 January 1994, 94–27; Frederick J. Finks, "Ashland Theological Seminary," *Minute Book of the Board*, 29 April 1994, 80; "Seminary Completes Energy Management System," *Koinonia* 26 (August 1994): [3]; "Seminary Leadership Grant," *Koinonia* 31 (August 1999): 6; "Studying Old Languages in New Ways" and "The Wabash Center," *Koinonia* 35 (January 2003): 3, 7; and "Wabash Center Grant Paves the Way for Innovation in Hebrew," *Koinonia* 37 (July 2005): 7.

132. *Minute Book of the Board*, 7 May 1993, 93–85 and Frederick J. Finks, "Ashland Theological Seminary," *Minute Book of the Board*, 13 January 1994, 79.

133. "Alumnus Contributes $50,000 for Archive Collection," *Koinonia* 26 (January 1994): [2]; "Archive Room Completed," *Koinonia* 26 (August 1994): [2]; "Archeological Center Shows New Acquisitions," *Koinonia* 38 (July 1996): [3]; and "Ashland Seminary Secures a 1566 Edition of the Great Bible," *Koinonia* 30 (January 1998): 2.

134. "The Frank Collection of Ancient Cuneiform Texts," *Koinonia* 31 (January 1999): 4 and "ATS Acquires Artifacts," *Koinonia* 37 (January 2005): 4.

135. "Believers' Church Conference Scheduled," *Koinonia* 26 (January 1994): [4]; "Seminary Acquires Rare Edition of a Swiss Brethren (Anabaptist) Hymnal," *Koinonia* 37 (January 2005): 4; "Recent Acquisition of the Seminary Archives," *Koinonia* 37 (July 2005): 9; and "New Acquisitions for the Brethren Archives," *Koinonia* 38 (January 2006): 2.

136. Frederick J. Finks, "Ashland Theological Seminary," *Minute Book of the Board*, 13 January 1994, 79 and 23 September 1994, 63; "Grand Piano Given for Smetzer Auditorium," *Koinonia* 26 (August 1998): 2; and "Piano Donated by DeVenys," *Koinonia* 34 (January 2002): 5.

137. "Seminary Committee," *Minute Book of the Board*, 21 April 1998, 52; "Seminary Sends Books to Argentina," *Koinonia* 31 (January 2000): 4; "South American Theological Seminary Welcomes Two New Faculty Members," *Koinonia* 34 (January 2002): 4; "STS Celebrates Historic Graduation," *Koinonia* 35 (January 2003): 4; and "Mission Trip to Argentina," *Koinonia* 37 (January 2005): 1, 3.

138. "Seminary Committee," *Minute Book of the Board*, 23 January 2004, 55 and "ATS Hurricane Katrina Relief Missions Trip," *Koinonia* 38 (January 2006): 7.

139. "Seminary Committee," *Minute Book of the Board*, 7 May 2004, 54.

140. Other festivities during the centennial year of 2006 were: the Centennial Dinner on 20 January; Great Commission Week, 6–10 February, featuring Prasanth Kumar and Radu Tirle; two trips to Israel in March; the Spring Ministries Conference, 3–5 April, with Tony Evans, Bill Hybels, and Knute Larson as the special speakers; the commencement service on 3 June at which Frederick Finks spoke; a concert by New Song on 19 July during the week of the Brethren General Conference; and the Fall Lecture Series with Randall Balmer as the special speaker. Two other features of the centennial year were the publication of an *Ashland Theological Seminary Centennial Cookbook* and the preparation of this history.

Conclusion

1. A very recent expression of this tension from the academic side is found in a document entitled "Academic Excellence and the Ashland University President," dated 5 July 2005. Note the following declaration: "These areas (athletic, financial, political, religious) are extremely important to any university and we are blessed that these areas happen to be excellent at Ashland and filled with great people. But strictly speaking, they are not essential to it being a university." This statement would be absolutely true if Ashland were a strictly secular university. But its constitution, heritage, and current Mission, Vision, and Institutional Core Values Statements all reinforce that spiritual values and faith are inherent within the educational process at Ashland. See Departmental Chairs of Ashland University, "Academic Excellence and the Ashland University President," 5 July 2005, D (photocopied), p. 1.
2. Lucille G. Ford, "Vice President for Academic Affairs," *Minute Book of the Board*, 17 April 1989, 7.
3. *Ashland Theological Seminary Catalogue 1937–38*, 9.

Index of Names

Index of Places and Institutions

Index of Subjects